Genetic Criticism

Material Texts

Series Editors: Roger Chartier, Joan DeJean, Anthony Grafton, Joseph Farrell, Janice Radway, Peter Stallybrass

A complete list of books in the series is available from the publisher.

Genetic Criticism

Texts and Avant-textes

Edited by
Jed Deppman, Daniel Ferrer, and
Michael Groden

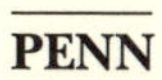

University of Pennsylvania Press

Philadelphia

Printed in the United Sates of America on acid-free paper

10 9 8 7 6 5 4 3 2 1

Published by
University of Pennsylvania Press
Philadelphia, Pennsylvania 19104-4011

Library of Congress Cataloging-in-Publication Data

Genetic criticism : texts and avant-textes / edited by Jed Deppman, Daniel Ferrer, and Michael Groden.
p. cm. (Material texts)
ISBN: 0-8122-3777-3 (alk. paper)
Includes bibliographical references and index.
"The eleven essays in this volume were originally written in French. They appear in English here for the first time"—Editors' note.
1. Criticism, Textual. 2. French literature—Criticism, Textual. I. Deppman, Jed. II. Ferrer, Daniel. III. Groden, Michael. IV. Series
PN81 .G463 2004
801′.959—dc22 2003064531

Contents

Editors' Note vii

1. Introduction: A Genesis of French Genetic Criticism 1

2. Genetic Criticism: Origins and Perspectives 17
Louis Hay

3. Psychoanalytic Reading and the Avant-texte 28
Jean Bellemin-Noël

4. Toward a Science of Literature: Manuscript Analysis and the Genesis of the Work 36
Pierre-Marc de Biasi

5. Flaubert's "A Simple Heart," or How to Make an Ending: A Study of the Manuscripts 69
Raymonde Debray Genette

6. With a Live Hand: Three Versions of Textual Transmission (Chateaubriand, Montaigne, Stendhal) 96
Jacques Neefs

7. Genetic Criticism and Cultural History: Zola's *Rougon-Macquart* Dossiers 116
Henri Mitterand

8. Paragraphs in Expansion (James Joyce) 132
Daniel Ferrer and Jean-Michel Rabaté

9. **Still** *Lost Time*: **Already** the Text of the *Recherche* 152
Almuth Grésillon

10. Proust's "Confession of a Young Girl": Truth or Fiction? 171
Catherine Viollet

11. Auto-Genesis: Genetic Studies of Autobiographical Texts 193
Philippe Lejeune

12. Hypertexts—Memories—Writing 218
Jean-Louis Lebrave

Notes 239

Index 253

Acknowledgments 259

Editors' Note

The eleven essays collected in this volume were originally written in French. They appear in English here for the first time.

This book was a collaborative project in which all three editors participated substantially at every stage. The editors did, however, have specific assignments. Daniel Ferrer and Michael Groden chose the volume's essays and filled in and updated the bibliographies. Jed Deppman, as the book's designated translator, produced the main drafts of the translations and annotations to the essays. Ferrer and Groden drafted the general introduction to the volume, and Deppman wrote the introductions to the individual essays.

Chapter 1
Introduction: A Genesis of French Genetic Criticism

> Nothing is more beautiful than a beautiful manuscript draft. . . . A complete poem would be the poem *of* a Poem starting from its fertilized embryo — and its successive states, unexpected interpolations, and approximations. That's real Genesis.
>
> —Paul Valéry (*Cahiers* 15: 480–81; *Cahiers/Notebooks*, "Poetry" 2: 219)

> Manuscripts have something new to tell us: it is high time we learned to make them speak.
>
> —Louis Hay, "History or Genesis?" (*Drafts* 207)

The eleven essays in this book represent a French literary critical movement called *critique génétique*, or "genetic criticism." As the volume's editors, we faced an embarrassment of riches when we made our selections, for thirty years of activity had produced a wealth of essays and a variety of strains in the movement. To indicate its diversity, we chose general, theoretical analyses as well as studies of individual authors, and because we also wished to emphasize the movement's foundations rather than its latest developments, we included many essays that belong to its early years. Even with these essays, however, we aimed to represent a range of issues that French genetic critics currently tend to deal with, the problems they see, the approaches and models they apply, and the observations and conclusions they make when they look at and listen to manuscripts. None of the essays have previously been translated, yet some have already become classics in France. Since interest in the materiality of texts is now strong in the English-speaking world, we think that this collection has the potential to open up new perspectives and broaden the audience for genetic criticism.

This introduction outlines the development of French genetic criticism in relation to its intellectual and institutional contexts. It also presents some of genetic criticism's main approaches and theoretical terms and describes the important role played by the Institut des Textes et Manuscrits Modernes (ITEM) in its development.

In 1977, Louis Hay considered French genetic criticism to be a "new field of research" and wrote that among the "fairy godmothers" present at its birth the most powerful was "the spirit of paradox" ("La Critique génétique" 227; see page 18 below). A quarter of a century later, genetic criticism remains paradoxical. It aims to restore a temporal dimension to the study of literature, but it cannot be identified with or derived from traditional literary history or New Historicism. It includes features of reception criticism but is mainly concerned with how texts are produced. Unlike Pierre Bourdieu's sociological dismissals of literary phenomena or psychocriticism's reductively psychoanalytic accounts of them, it remains deeply aware of the text's aesthetic dimensions, and yet it is ever ready to accommodate the agency of sociological forces or psychoanalytic drives into its accounts. It grows out of a structuralist and post-structuralist notion of "text" as an infinite play of signs, but it accepts a teleological model of textuality and constantly confronts the question of authorship. Like old-fashioned philology or textual criticism, it examines tangible documents such as writers' notes, drafts, and proof corrections, but its real object is something much more abstract— not the existing documents but the movement of writing that must be inferred from them. Then, too, it remains concrete, for it never posits an ideal text beyond those documents but rather strives to reconstruct, from all available evidence, the chain of events in a writing process.

As a literary theory and practice, genetic criticism is a true child of the French structuralist movement that bloomed in the 1960s and 1970s, and yet it has not only survived Roland Barthes's death, Tzvetan Todorov's retreat into ethics, and Gérard Genette's passage from narratology to general aesthetics, it is only now reaching maturity. It cooperates closely with many different forms of literary study—narratology, linguistic analysis, psychoanalytic approaches of various kinds, sociocriticism, deconstruction, gender theory, and so on—but at the same time refuses to see itself as what René Wellek and Austin Warren once called the "preliminary labours" of criticism and scholarship (57). It is a form of criticism of its own.

Even Hay's claim that it is "high time" to make manuscripts speak is paradoxical, for critics have known for a long time that manuscripts are worth looking at. Joseph Spence speculated in 1730 that it would be useful "for a poet, to compare in those parts what was written first, with the successive alterations; to learn his turns and arts in versification; and to consider the reasons why such and such an alteration was made" (quoted in Gibson vii), and Samuel Johnson remarked in 1779 that "it is pleasant to see great works in their seminal state, pregnant with latent possibilities of excellence; nor could there be any more delightful entertainment than to trace their gradual growth and expansion, and to observe how they are sometimes suddenly advanced by accidental hints, and sometimes slowly improved by steady meditation" (*Selected Poetry and Prose* 407). In the nineteenth century, the genetic outlook grew more complex, as we see in Madame de Staël's 1800 claim that, since "each correction supposes a mass of ideas which decide the mind often without our knowing it . . . one could compose a treatise on style based on the manuscripts of great writers" or in Friedrich Schlegel's 1804 assertion that "one can only claim to have real understanding of a work, or of a thought, when one can reconstitute its becoming and its composition. This intimate comprehension . . . constitutes the very object and essence of criticism" (see p. 18 below).

Surely the best known of all pre-twentieth-century pronouncements of this kind comes from Edgar Allan Poe's 1846 "The Philosophy of Composition," which Charles Baudelaire translated a decade later as "Genèse d'un poème" and which stands as one of the foundational texts of French genetic criticism.[1] Poe calls for an author "who would—that is to say, who could—detail, step by step, the processes by which any one of his compositions attained its ultimate point of completion" (743) and then methodically fulfills his own request for a reconstruction of the poetic process by analyzing "The Raven." Working from the premise that an artist's first task is always to choose the desired effect, he explains how he settled on such elements as the poem's length, its tone of sadness, the central detail of the raven, the versification, the setting, and the word "nevermore" in the refrain. Crucially, Poe counters the assumption that poets "compose by a species of fine frenzy—an ecstatic intuition" (743) by describing his own writing process as mechanical and devoid of problems or complications. In contrast to the inspirational and organic conceptions of literary creation that were popular with the Romantics, Poe's account is a pure example of what Almuth Grésillon later called "constructivism" (108), that is, the view that poets are like craftsmen or skilled workers who learn rules and know when and how to break them.

By the middle of the twentieth century, critics often shared Donald A. Stauffer's opinion that manuscripts are valuable only in relation to the finished work: "What light . . . does the composition of a poem throw upon its meaning and its beauty? What difficulties in a finished poem may be explained, what pointless ambiguities dispelled, what purposeful ambiguities sharpened, by references found in its earlier states?" (*Poets at Work* 43–44). Very few, thought most mid-century critics, for they agreed with T. S. Eliot that "a knowledge of the springs which released a poem is not necessarily a help toward understanding the poem: too much information about the origins of the poem may even break [one's] contact with it" (112). And they also concurred with Wellek and Warren's view that "drafts, rejections, exclusions, and cuts" are "not, finally, necessary to an understanding of the finished work or to a judgement upon it. Their interest is that of any alternative, i.e., they may set into relief the qualities of the final text" (91).[2]

Such a critical paradigm was not conducive to manuscript studies, but some were carried out nonetheless. A few 1950s precursors of modern French genetic criticism can be named: Pierre Clarac, Marie-Jeanne Durry, Alain Ferré, Claudine Gothot-Mersch, Bernard Guyon, René Journet, Gabrielle Leleu, Jean Levaillant, Octave Nadal, Jean Pommier, Robert Ricatte, Guy Robert, and André Vial.[3] For the most part, though—perhaps because they focused unquestioningly on what they took to be the author's conscious intentions, perhaps because they assumed too straight a teleological drive towards the published work—their theoretical and methodological influence on later genetic criticism proved to be negligible,[4] much smaller than that of the subsequent structuralist and poststructuralist movements.

Paralleling French manuscript studies from the 1950s were those from English-speaking scholars. In 1948 a book called *Poets at Work* featured original essays by Rudolf Arnheim, W. H. Auden, Karl Shapiro, and Stauffer based on manuscripts in the University of Buffalo's collection.[5] The volume inaugurated the university's Poetry Collection and its new and then-unique gathering of poets' "worksheets" (as the collection's librarian, Charles D. Abbott, called them). In the 1963 collection *Poems in the Making,* Walker Gibson published statements about the writing process from poets and critics ranging from Spence, Pope, Coleridge, Keats, and Poe to Eliot, I. A. Richards, Shapiro, Stephen Spender, and Kenneth Burke. Manuscript-based studies of individual writers also began to appear in the 1950s and 1960s, and some of them became quite prominent in the scholarship of those authors. Some examples are Mary Visick, *The Genesis of "Wuthering Heights"* (1958); John Paterson, *The Making of "The Return of the Native"* (1960); A. Walton Litz, *The Art of James Joyce: Method and Design in "Ulysses" and "Finnegans Wake"* (1961); David Hayman, *A First-Draft Version of "Finnegans Wake"* (1963); Jon Stallworthy, *Between the Lines: Yeats's Poetry in the Making* (1963); Curtis Bradford, *Yeats at Work* (1965); Michael Groden, *"Ulysses" in Progress* (1977); Helen Gardner, *The Composition of "Four Quartets"* (1978); and Ralph W. Franklin, *The Manuscript Books of Emily Dickinson* (1981). Like their French counterparts, these detailed English-language studies were more of a historical backdrop to the French genetic movement of the 1970s than an active source for it. They tended to be pragmatic and not theoretically self-conscious, to consider textuality and intention as unproblematic, and to see the manuscripts exclusively in relation to the subsequent published work.[6] In Italy the "critica delle varianti" (criticism of variants) of Gianfranco Contini and his followers was more theoretically nuanced, but it too failed to influence French genetic criticism directly.[7]

The decisive fertilizing influence (and necessary foil) was the complex conception of text introduced by structuralism and poststructuralism in the 1960s and 1970s. Emphasizing the textile etymology of *textus* over and against associations with the sacred or profane authority of the immutable written word, theorists such as Roland Barthes and Jacques Derrida saw texts as mobile, multistranded, and overflowing with referential codes. Barthes suggestively described a text as "held in language," a "methodological field," a "weave" of signifiers, a "network," a "force of subversion," "plural," and "caught up in a discourse" in contrast to the literary "work" as "held in the hand," a "fragment of substance," and an "object of a science of the letter, of philology" ("From Work to Text" 57–61). Genetic criticism took up the notion of writing's mobility but observed that a text conceived as methodologically separate from its origins and from its material incarnation can lead to a paradoxical sacralization and idealization of it as *The Text.* According to Hay, what we are actually confronted with is "not *The Text,* but texts" ("Does 'Text' Exist?" 73).[8]

The idea that many texts exist within any text is clearly reminiscent of the postructuralist idea that all texts are fields of free-playing signifiers. Hay and most other geneticists do not unqualifiedly endorse that view, however, for they privilege historical development and context in contrast to a conception of a synchronous or timelessly present text. Like New Historicism, French genetic criticism attempts to restore a temporal dimension to texts; it does so not only by looking for the influence of external social, economic, and cultural circumstances on the text, but also by reading the text's own history, a history that takes into account those external forces and the way they interact—differently in every case—with the text's development.

Thus, for geneticists, instead of a fixed, finished object in relation to which all previous states are considered, a given text becomes—or texts become—the contingent manifestations of a *diachronous* play of signifiers. "The writing," as Hay has put it, "is not simply consummated in the written work. Perhaps we should consider the text as a *necessary possibility,* as one manifestation of a process which is always virtually present in the background, a kind of third dimension of the written work" ("Does 'Text' Exist?" 75). Similarly, in their introduction to *Drafts*—an issue of *Yale French Studies* devoted to genetic criticism—Michel Contat, Denis Hollier, and Jacques Neefs have written that "the work now stands out against a background, and a series, of potentialities. Genetic criticism is contemporaneous with an esthetic of the possible" (2).

This idea of genesis as an open-ended aesthetic, or logic, of possibilities is itself a current critical state in an ongoing historical process. As we have suggested, literary history is peppered with authors whose statements and writing practices have explicitly invited critics to relate their finished texts to genetic processes. Again, Poe's "Philosophy of Composition" seems to call for and exemplify a kind of genetic criticism, but it is important to note that his methodical reconstruction of "The Raven" is utterly unlike such criticism in its modern form, for it describes genesis as purely mental and dismisses preliminary drafts as the ugly locus of "cautious selections and rejections" and "painful erasures and interpolations" (743). Genetic criticism owes debts of many kinds to Poe, but it exploits precisely the resources that he abjured: the foul papers covered with additions, replacements, and erasures.

Stéphane Mallarmé (1842–98) and Paul Valéry (1871–1945), who considered themselves to be disciples of Poe, are more direct ancestors. For Mallarmé the literary work was essentially open; it depended more on the structural indeterminacy of language than on the univocality of a speaking or reading subject. Engineering the disappearance of the subject and recalibrating traditional relationships of texts to time and space, Mallarmé made heavy use of musical, rhythmic, ideographic, and other multivalent aspects of language. The result was a complex poetics that was less wedded to Poe's concepts of mimesis, authorial or readerly control, and emotional response than to the suggestive and symbolic powers of language. As Mallarmé's writings were relayed through modernism and postmodernism, they created the conditions of possibility for books that celebrate the many signifying states and auras of texts—one example is Francis Ponge's 1971 *La Fabrique du "Pré"*, a work that reproduced in facsimile all the drafts of a single poem.

Valéry, for his part, helped shift aesthetic interest from product to production. "Creating a poem is itself a poem," he wrote, and at times he explicitly subordinated the product to the process: "*The making*, as the main thing, and whatever product is constructed as *accessory*, that's my idea." Valéry found fascinating technical and intellectual complexity in the creative process. "Composition itself," he wrote, can be considered "as a dance, as fencing, as the construction of acts and expectations" (1922; *Cahiers* 8: 578; *Cahiers/Notebooks*, "Ego Scriptor" 2: 475). His interest in process rather than product provides a theoretical backdrop for genetic criticism's focus on interpreting composition and the creative process.

One might well ask what ultimately brought the Mallarméan and Valéryan conceptions of text and genesis to the fore in the late 1960s.

How, in other words, did "manuscript studies" become "genetic criticism"? A combination of historical circumstances can help explain it. One factor has already been mentioned—at the time, a new conception of textuality was developing in France. Another is that a renewed drive to collect and preserve manuscripts was then spreading across Europe. Such collections had begun to accumulate in the nineteenth century, and authors' archives had been important cultural institutions since at least 1885, when the Goethe- und Schiller-Archiv was established in Weimar, Germany. That was also the year that Victor Hugo died and bequeathed all his manuscripts to the Bibliothèque Nationale. A decisive turning point in the history of genetic criticism, however, was the Bibliothèque Nationale's acquisition of an important collection of Heinrich Heine manuscripts in 1966. This purchase could have been just one more addition to the rich holdings of the Département des Manuscrits if it had not occurred in the climate of political turmoil, intellectual excitement, and critical renewal that characterized the late 1960s. On the occasion of this purchase, Louis Hay, who would soon be appointed head of a small team of young scholars charged with studying the archive, published in the national press a short article—"Des manuscrits, pour quoi faire?" (Manuscripts: So what?)—that was both defensive and programmatic. He wasted no time with traditional scholarly justifications but instead took a position relative to structuralism and the *nouvelle critique*.[9] He argued that studying the final text is not the only legitimate approach and should be complemented by genetic analysis. For instance, a word can be compared to a text's other words but also to alternate words that the author tried in the same position. After this allusion to the paradigmatic and the syntagmatic axes, so prominent in the thought of the time, Hay introduced the idea of a work's "genetic structure" and then affirmed that the creative process is itself a worthwhile object for literary studies. With great foresight, he concluded that the manuscript work about to begin would open up new perspectives not only on Heine but also on scholarly and critical methods themselves.[10]

Because it is a thorough methodological and theoretical reflection as well as a self-contained case study, Jean Bellemin-Noël's 1972 book *Le Texte et l'avant-texte: Les Brouillons d'un poème de Milosz* can be considered the true beginning of modern French genetic criticism. This book appeared the year after Francis Ponge's *La Fabrique du "Pré"*, and it is significant that both books—one by a poet, the other by a critic—proceed from a new attention to manuscripts and to the writing process. For poets as well as critics, manuscripts were becoming more than objects to be collected on the dusty shelves of an archive or sources for footnoted variants; more and more, they were documents to be exhibited, read, enjoyed, and investigated critically.

By 1972 the intellectual background in France had become decidedly poststructuralist, and while Bellemin-Noël acknowledged the scholars who had worked on manuscripts in the 1950s and 1960s, he politely dismissed their efforts as misguided: they were concerned too much with the conscious intentions of the author and not enough with the dynamics of writing. The key theoretical problem, he suggested, lay in their conceptions of the subject, the sign, and the text. (Although Barthes, Derrida, and Lacan were not named in the essay as models for new conceptions, their presence was palpable.) He argued that draft material should be studied in entirely new ways:

> The point is to show to what extent *poems write themselves* despite, or even against, authors who believe they are implementing their writerly craft; to find any uncontrolled (perhaps uncontrollable) forces that were mobilized without the author's knowledge and resulted in a *structure*; to reconstruct the operations by which, in order to form itself, *something transformed itself*, all the while forming that locus of transformation of meaning that we call a text. (12)

Such an ambitious program required a new critical vocabulary. It seemed especially important to do away with the philological notion of "variant," which implies *one* text with alternative formulations.[11] To make a clean break, Bellemin-Noël used the neologism "avant-texte" to designate all the documents that come before a work when it is considered as a *text* and when those documents and the text are considered as part of a system. This proposal has been generally and enthusiastically accepted: the term "avant-texte" has become the hallmark of the new approach and is used by geneticists of all persuasions.[12] They use the term in somewhat different ways, some more precisely than others, but "avant-texte" always carries with it the assumption that the material of textual genetics is not a given but rather a critical construction elaborated in relation to a postulated terminal—so-called definitive—state of the work.[13]

Armed with theoretical foundations and the first lineaments of a method, genetic criticism seemed poised for a promising career. But it might never have caught on had it not found the right kind of institutional support. As the original Heine unit became the Centre d'Analyse des Manuscrits (CAM), and CAM evolved into ITEM, a structure emerged that made collaborative research possible. The Heine team, led by Louis Hay, joined forces with groups working on Proust, Zola, and Flaubert. Bellemin-Noël's affinities with psychoanalysis were complemented by Claude Duchet's and Henri Mitterand's sociocritical point of view and Raymonde Debray Genette's narratological approach.[14] Professors and young academics from various universities started cooperating with ITEM's few full-time researchers and research assistants as the CNRS

(Centre Nationale de la Recherche Scientifique) became a kind of neutral ground for a common intellectual enterprise. Other teams were added, devoted to new authors (Valéry, Joyce, Sartre) or to "transversal" subjects, such as the linguistic study of manuscripts, the genetic study of autobiographies, and hypertextual genetic editions.[15]

In 1994, when geneticists and theorists and practitioners of textual criticism gathered for a conference at Columbia University, the question was asked whether genetic criticism had any existence independent from ITEM or was simply a Parisian fad kept alive by the support of a state agency (Compagnon 395).[16] Those favorable to genetic criticism met this skeptical query with the observation that over a period of three decades a true fad would have gone out of fashion, whatever its institutional support; genetic criticism would not have risen to prominence had it not possessed its own theoretical and practical strengths and possibilities, and it could easily have faded away even with the backing of ITEM.

On the other hand, it would be naive to think that institutions have no influence on ideas. Over three decades the CNRS structure has provided the stability necessary to unite scholars working on different authors, using diverging critical approaches, and having little in common but an interest in the writing process. Beyond the uncertainties of university appointments, individual careers, and personal choices, researchers from very different circumstances (and different countries) have been able to look up from the absorbing tasks involved in deciphering manuscripts, reflect upon them, and contribute to a methodology and a theory in progress.[17]

From the start, geneticists envisioned a project that would go beyond individual projects and toward, if not a generalized, at least a comparative study of writing practices. All along they sought ways to account for historical and generic parameters as well as authorial idiosyncrasies (Bellemin-Noël 13). Moreover, because the nature of manuscript study makes it very difficult for individual scholars to be conversant with different archives, several kinds of collective study were developed to allow them to compare and synthesize their findings. The different ITEM teams periodically convene in a general seminar, usually for a year or two, in order to study a problem of general interest such as unfinished manuscripts, beginnings, writers' notes, or the semiotics of drafts. Many of these seminars have resulted in published collections of essays.

The fact that ITEM is part of the CNRS, the French national center for *scientific* research, has had other consequences as well. It encouraged an early interest in computer-assisted genetic editions and hypertexts, and it also helped facilitate studies of the material aspects of manuscripts, such as papers and watermarks, and authors' "hands." The result has been a happy counterbalance to Bellemin-Noël's indispensable inaugural gesture of positing the avant-texte as a critical construction abstracted from the amorphous mass of actual documents. It has kept genetic criticism in touch with the materiality of the manuscript and the wealth of nontextual information it contains and at the same time has prevented it from falling into naïve positivism. Whatever it may do, however sophisticated the instruments it may employ,[18] genetic criticism can never be a Galilean empirical science. Rather, it will always belong to what Carlo Ginzburg has called the "indexical paradigm"[19]—a model that bases itself on the interpretation of clues rather than the deduction of universal laws and on qualitative rather than quantitative assessment.

Today genetic criticism is sometimes assimilated to a form of textual criticism or automatically assumed to be a branch of it, but genetic criticism clearly suggests that manuscripts can be used for purposes other than those of textual criticism—that is, for reasons other than establishing an accurate text of a work. Enough overlap exists that the similarities and differences between the two activities should be briefly discussed. Their relationships remain complex. One reason is that the German-, English-, and French-language traditions of textual criticism and editing have been dominated by different models.[20] In Germany the primary model and test case has been Goethe, who published his works in different versions and preserved many manuscripts; there genetic editing dominates and produces scholarly editions establishing texts' prepublication stages. In England and the United States, the model and test case has been Shakespeare, who left no manuscripts at all and only problematical texts published during his lifetime. There an eclectic model has developed in which the editor chooses one state of the text as the copytext and then emends the copytext on the basis of other authoritative states. (According to W. W. Greg's "The Rationale of Copy-Text," editors choose copytext-states mainly in order to have systems of authors' accidentals such as spelling and punctuation.) In France, where the problems and issues have centered on Old French texts, what is known as "best text" editing has dominated: the editor applies scholarly tools to determine which existing text is most accurate and then reprints that text as the edition. There is almost no connection between the "best text" model in French editing and genetic criticism, although both resist conflating different states into a new eclectic text. Anglo-American copytext editing is only somewhat more congenial to genetic criticism, for its overarching goal of establishing a single conflated text tends to subsume all variation into an accuracy-versus-error dichotomy. German genetic editing, since it retains the temporal dynamics of the writing process and often does not attempt to produce a single edited text, is most compatible, and genetic critics have turned to it more than to any other form of textual criticism.[21]

Nonetheless, even the connection with German genetic editing is tenuous because the final goal of French genetic criticism is not to produce a printable text but rather, as the essays in this volume do in very different and intriguing ways, to seize and describe a movement, a process of writing that can only be approximately inferred from the existing documents. Genetic criticism comes closest to textual criticism when it presents—edits—a manuscript or part of a document for presentation in print, but this presentation is only part of a broader goal of reconstructing and analyzing a chain of writing events.

While textual criticism is concerned with repetition (it studies the ways in which one stage in the writing process develops, with varying degrees of accuracy, into the next one), genetic criticism could be defined as the study of textual invention, and thus it is concerned precisely with what is not repetition.[22] Such a statement must be immediately qualified: there can be no such thing as pure invention (if there were, it would lie outside the scope of any science or criticism), so genetic criticism actually confronts a dialectic of invention and repetition.[23] To put it simply, a textual critic will tend to see a difference between two states of a work in terms of accuracy and error or corruption, whereas a genetic critic will see meaningful variation. Although both scholarly activities deal with manuscripts and textual versions, their aims are quite different. Rather than trying to establish texts, genetic criticism actually destabilizes the notion of "text" and shakes the exclusive hold of the textual model. One could even say that genetic criticism is not concerned with texts at all but only with the writing processes that engender them. From this point of view, texts could be compared provocatively to the ashes remaining when a fire is consumed or to the footprints on the ground after a dance is over. But there is nothing mystical in the activities of genetic criticism, which pursues an immaterial object (a process) through the concrete analysis of the material traces left by that process.

In the 35 years since Louis Hay argued in *Le Monde* that the creative process is worth studying, genetic critics have heeded his call to learn to make manuscripts "speak." In that time, not surprisingly, the "real Genesis" celebrated by Valéry has assumed many different forms and the manuscripts have started to speak in different voices. Indeed, genetic criticism has already passed through a number of stages, and some of its current interests and trends could not have been predicted when the earliest essays in this collection were written. For instance, whereas early genetic criticism focused almost exclusively on canonical authors, recent work—as in that devoted to autobiographies—has included noncanonical and anonymous authors (see Philippe Lejeune's essay in this volume). Also, as Jean-Louis Lebrave indicates in his essay, genetic critics have become intrigued by hypertext and the ways in which linked electronic presentation can enhance the representation of complex manuscript archives. Occasionally, the archive itself has grown and spurred new research; for example, the huge new collection of Joyce manuscripts acquired by the National Library of Ireland in May 2002 has significantly changed the avant-texte for *Ulysses* and promises to affect Joyce studies in ways that no material documents have been able to do for almost half a century.[24] In other cases, long available documents are being looked at anew. Genetic critics have been studying certain authors' notebooks for decades (see Pierre-Marc de Biasi's edition of Flaubert's *Carnets de travail* or the ongoing "Finnegans Wake" Notebooks at Buffalo project), but such studies are now becoming part of a more systematic and comparative investigation of the interaction between authors' readings and their writings, an investigation that rests at the interface between genetic work and reception studies.[25]

According to Jean-Michel Rabaté, a new kind of reader has started to emerge in this multifaceted genetic activity: an "ideal genetic reader" or "genreader."[26] This reader is not merely a decoder of textual signals, a detached consciousness, or an emotional being, but rather a kind of "textual agent" who reads texts "in the context of an expanding archive" (196) in order to see both how they are written and how they are read. The eleven essays in *Genetic Criticism* have already done much to create such readers. Perhaps these translations imply that, with them, we are all (ideally) becoming genetic critics now.

The collection begins with Louis Hay's overview of genetic criticism and continues with Jean Bellemin-Noël's essay on the value of a psychoanalytic approach to genetic study. Pierre-Marc de Biasi's encyclopedia article, which spells out the principles and procedures of genetic study, closes the opening trio of general studies.

Next come six essays on the texts and avant-textes of specific authors. Raymonde Debray Genette studies the manuscripts of Flaubert's "A Simple Heart" to see how he crafted its ending; Jacques Neefs compares and contrasts the ideas Chateaubriand, Montaigne, and Stendhal had about the posthumous fate of their writings; Henri Mitterand inscribes Zola's Rougon-Macquart writings into their author's personal circumstances as well as broader cultural contexts; Daniel Ferrer and Jean-Michel Rabaté study the way Joyce manipulated and modernized the structure of the literary paragraph; closing this middle section, Almuth Grésillon and Catherine Viollet use concepts from linguistics to analyze Proust's manuscripts, Grésillon taking up issues of temporality and Viollet concentrating on gender and sexuality.

The volume ends with essays on topics of recent interest to geneticists. Philippe Lejeune addresses the paradox of reading autobiographies for their avant-textes, and Jean-Louis Lebrave argues that the theory of hypertexts has now reached the point where it can provide new and more accurate models for genetic studies, even of centuries-old manuscripts.

Jed Deppman has written separate introductions that outline each author's career and discuss each essay's specific purposes, methods, and arguments.

Works Cited and Other Studies of Genetic Criticism

Aragon, Louis. "D'un grand art nouveau: La Recherche." In *Essais de critique génétique,* ed. Louis Hay. Paris: Flammarion, 1979. 5–20.

Arnheim, Rudolf, W. H. Auden, Karl Shapiro, and Donald A. Stauffer, with an introduction by Charles D. Abbott. *Poets at Work: Essays Based on the Modern Poetry Collection at the Lockwood Memorial Library, University of Buffalo.* New York: Harcourt, Brace, 1948.

Barthes, Roland. "From Work to Text." In *The Rustle of Language.* Trans. Richard Howard. New York: Hill and Wang, 1986. 56–64. Originally "De l'œuvre au texte." *Revue d'Esthétique* 24 (1971): 225–32, and *Le Bruissement de la langue: Essais critiques 4.* Paris: Seuil, 1984. 69–77.

Bellemin-Noël, Jean. "Avant-texte et lecture psychanalytique." In *Avant-texte, texte, après-texte,* ed. Louis Hay and Péter Nagy. Paris: CNRS; Budapest: Akadémiai Kiadó, 1982. 162–65. Translated in the present volume.

———. "Reproduire le manuscrit, présenter les brouillons, établir un avant-texte." *Littérature* 28 (1977): 3–18.

———. *Le Texte et l'avant-texte: Les Brouillons d'un poème de Milosz.* Paris: Larousse, 1972.

Blevins-Le Bigot, Jane. "Valéry, Poe and the Question of Genetic Criticism in America." In *Devenir de la critique génétique / Genetic Criticism,* ed. Robert Pickering. Special issue of *L'Esprit Créateur* 41 (Summer 2001): 68–78.

Bowman, Frank Paul. "Genetic Criticism." *Poetics Today* 11 (1990): 627–46.

Bustarret, Claire, ed. *Genetic Criticism.* Special issue of *Word and Image* 13, 2 (April–June 1997).

Cerquiglini, Bernard. "En écho à Cesare Segre: Réflexions d'un cisalpin." *Genesis* 7 (1995): 47–48.

———. *In Praise of the Variant: A Critical History of Philology.* Trans. Betsy Wing. Baltimore: Johns Hopkins University Press, 1999. Originally *Éloge de la variante: Histoire critique de la philologie.* Paris: Seuil, 1989.

Cherchi, Paolo. "Italian Literature." Greetham, *Scholarly Editing.* 438–56.

Compagnon, Antoine. "Introduction." *Romanic Review* 86 (1995): 393–401.

Contat, Michel, Denis Hollier, and Jacques Neefs, eds. *Drafts.* Special issue of *Yale French Studies* 89 (1996).

———. "Editors' Preface." Trans. Alyson Waters. *Drafts.* 1–5.

de Biasi, Pierre-Marc. "Vers une science de la littérature: L'Analyse des manuscrits et la genèse de l'oeuvre." In *Encyclopedia Universalis Symposium.* Paris: Encyclopedia Universalis France, 1989. 466–76. Translated in the present volume.

Derrida, Jacques. "Psyche: Invention of the Other." Trans. Catherine Porter. In *Acts of Literature*, ed. Derek Attridge. New York: Routledge, 1992. 310–43. Originally published as "Psyché: Invention de l'autre." In *Psyche: Inventions de l'autre.* Paris: Galilée. 1987. 11–61.

D'Iorio, Paolo, and Daniel Ferrer, eds. *Bibliothèques d'écrivains.* Paris: CNRS, 2001.

Eliot, T. S. "The Frontiers of Criticism." In *On Poetry and Poets.* London: Faber and Faber, 1957. 103–18.

Falconer, Graham. "Genetic Criticism." *Comparative Literature* 45 (1993): 1–21.

———. "Genetic Criticism." In *Encyclopedia of Contemporary Literary Theory: Approaches, Scholars, Terms*, ed. Irena R. Makaryk. Toronto: University of Toronto Press, 1993. 70–72.

Ferrer, Daniel. "La Critique génétique: 'Philosophy of Composition' ou 'Gold Bug'?" *Études Anglaises* 53, 3 (July–September 2000): 284–93.

———. "Le Matériel et le virtuel: Du paradigme indiciaire à la logique des mondes possibles." In *Pourquoi la critique génétique? Méthodes, théories*, ed. Michel Contat and Daniel Ferrer. Paris: CNRS, 1998. 11–30.

———. "Production, Invention, and Reproduction: Genetic vs. Textual Criticism." In *Reimagining Textuality: Textual Studies in the Late Age of Print*, ed. Elizabeth Bergmann Loizeaux and Neil Fraistat. Madison: University of Wisconsin Press, 2002. 48–59.

Flaubert, Gustave. *Carnets de travail.* Critical and genetic edition by Pierre-Marc de Biasi. Paris: Balland, 1988.

Franklin, Ralph W. *The Manuscript Books of Emily Dickinson.* 2 vols. Cambridge, Mass.: Harvard University Press, 1981.

Gabler, Hans Walter. "Unsought Encounters." In *Devils and Angels: Textual Editing and Literary Theory*, ed. Philip Cohen. Charlottesville: University Press of Virginia, 1991. 152–66.

Gabler, Hans Walter, George Bornstein, and Gillian Borland Pierce, eds. and trans. *Contemporary German Editorial Theory.* Ann Arbor: University of Michigan Press, 1995.

Gaudon, Jean. "One of Victor Hugo's Discarded Drafts." In *Drafts*, ed. Contat, Hollier, and Neefs. 130–48.

Genesis: Manuscrits, Recherche, Invention. Ed. Jean-Louis Lebrave, Almuth Grésillon, and Daniel Ferrer. 1 (1992)–present.

Giaveri, Maria Teresa. "La Critique génétique en Italie: Contini, Croce et 'l'étude des paperasses.'" *Genesis* 3 (1993): 9–29.

Gibson, Walker, ed. *Poems in the Making.* Boston: Houghton Mifflin, 1963.

Ginzburg, Carlo. "Spie: Radici di un paradigma indiziario." In *Miti, emblemi, spie: Morfologia e storia.* Torino: Einaudi, 1986. "Clues: Roots of an Evidential Paradigm." In *Clues, Myths, and the Historical Method.* Trans. John and Anne C. Tedeschi. Baltimore: Johns Hopkins University Press, 1989. 96–125.

Gothot-Mersch, Claudine. "Les Études de genèse en France de 1950 à 1960." *Genesis* 5 (1994): 175–87.

Greetham, D. C., ed. *Scholarly Editing: A Guide to Research.* New York: Modern Language Association, 1995.

———. "Textual Scholarship." In *Introduction to Scholarship in Modern Languages and Literatures*, 2nd ed., ed. Joseph Gibaldi. New York: Modern Language Association, 1992. 103–37.

Greg, W. W. "The Rationale of Copy-Text." *Studies in Bibliography* 3 (1950–51): 19–36.

Grésillon, Almuth. "Slow: Work in Progress." Trans. Stephen A. Noble and Vincent Vichit-Vadakan. In *Genetic Criticism*, ed. Bustarret 106–23. Originally "Ralentir: Travaux." *Genesis* 1 (1992): 9–31.

Groden, Michael. "The National Library of Ireland's New Joyce Manuscripts: A Statement and Document Descriptions." *James Joyce Quarterly* 39 (2001): 29–51.

———. *"Ulysses" in Progress.* Princeton, N.J.: Princeton University Press, 1977.

Hay, Louis. "La Critique génétique: Origines et perspectives." In *Essais de critique génétique*, ed. Louis Hay. Paris: Flammarion, 1979. 227–36. Translated in the present volume.

———. "Des Manuscrits, pour quoi faire?" *Le Monde* (February 8, 1967), "Le Monde des Livres" Supplement, p. 6.

———. "Does 'Text' Exist?" Trans. Matthew Jocelyn and Hans Walter Gabler. *Studies in Bibliography* 41 (1988): 64–76. Originally "Le Texte n'existe pas: Réflexions sur la critique génétique." *Poétique* 62 (1985): 147–58.

———. "History or Genesis?" Trans. Ingrid Wassenaar. In *Drafts*, ed. Contat, Hollier, and Neefs. 191–207. Originally "Histoire ou genèse?" In *Les Leçons du manuscrit.* Special issue of *Études Françaises* 28, 1 (1992): 11–27.

———. *La Littérature des écrivains: Questions de critique génétique.* Paris: José Corti, 2002.

Hayman, David, and Sam Slote, eds. *Probes: Genetic Studies in Joyce.* Special issue of *European Joyce Studies* 5 (1995).

Johnson, Samuel. *Selected Poetry and Prose.* Ed. Frank Brady and W. K. Wimsatt. Berkeley: University of California Press, 1977.

Joyce, James. *The "Finnegans Wake" Notebooks at Buffalo.* Ed. Vincent Deane, Daniel Ferrer, and Geert Lernout. 9 vols. to date. Turnhout: Brepols, 2001– .

Kasinec, Edward, and Robert Whittaker. "Russian Literature." In Greetham, *Scholarly Editing* 530–45.

Lernout, Geert. "La Critique textuelle anglo-américaine: Une Étude de cas." *Genesis* 9 (1996): 45–65.

Peytard, Jean. "*Les Chants de Maldoror* et l'univers mythique de Lautréamont." *La Nouvelle Critique* 37 (October 1970): 43–55.

Pickering, Robert, ed. *Devenir de la critique génétique / Genetic Criticism.* Special issue of *L'Esprit Créateur* 41 (Summer 2001).

Poe, Edgar Allan. "The Philosophy of Composition" (1846). In *The Norton Anthology of Theory and Criticism*, ed. Vincent B. Leitch et al. New York: Norton, 2001. 739–50.

Ponge, Francis. *La Fabrique du "Pré".* Geneva: Albert Skira, 1971. *The Making of the Pré.* Trans. Lee Fahnestock. Columbia: University of Missouri Press, 1979.

Rabaté, Jean-Michel. "Back to Beria! Genetic Joyce and Eco's 'Ideal Readers.'" In Hayman and Slote, *Probes.* 65–83.

———. *James Joyce and the Politics of Egoism.* Cambridge: Cambridge University Press, 2001.

———. "Pound, Joyce and Eco: Modernism and the 'Ideal Genetic Reader.'" *Romanic Review* 86, 3 (1995): 485–500.

Romanic Review 86, 3 (May 1995). Special issue featuring papers from the International Symposium on Genetic Criticism held at Columbia University in April 1994, organized by Antoine Compagnon, Almuth Grésillon, and Henri Mitterand.

Segre, Cesare. "Critique des variantes et critique génétique." *Genesis* 7 (1995): 29–45.

Speer, Mary B. "Old French Literature." In Greetham, *Scholarly Editing.* 382–416.

Tanselle, G. Thomas. "Textual Scholarship." In *Introduction to Scholarship in Modern Languages and Literatures,* ed. Joseph Gibaldi. New York: Modern Language Association, 1981. 29–52.

Valéry, Paul. *Cahiers.* Facsimile ed. 29 vols. Paris: CNRS, 1957–61. *Cahiers/Notebooks.* Ed. Brian Stimpson, Paul Gifford, and Robert Pickering. Trans. Robert Pickering ("Ego Scriptor") and Norma Rinsler ("Poetry"). 2 vols. Frankfurt: Peter Lang, 2000.

Wellek, René, and Austin Warren. *Theory of Literature.* 1949. 3rd ed. New York: Harcourt, Brace & World, 1962.

Chapter 2

Genetic Criticism: Origins and Perspectives

Louis Hay

In 1966 Louis Hay helped the Bibliothèque Nationale acquire the Schocken collection of Heinrich Heine's manuscripts. To organize and study them, he assembled for the Centre National de la Recherche Scientifique a small group of French and German scholars. This became the nucleus of the Centre d'Analyse des Manuscrits (CAM), which steadily expanded, added other authors' manuscripts and scholars, and in 1982 became the Institut des Textes et Manuscrits Modernes.

As ITEM's founder, its director until 1985, and the editor of many important volumes, Hay has played a crucial role in the development of genetic criticism in France. His many publications have been central to the definition of the discipline in its contemporary form, and he is one of a handful of French geneticists to have already had an impact on Anglo-American textual criticism. His "Does 'Text' Exist?" published in 1988 by *Studies in Bibliography,* is widely cited for its overarching historical, comparative, and theoretical perspectives on the status of texts and avant-textes. A collection of his essays, *La Littérature des écrivains: Questions de critique génétique*, appeared in 2002.

The article translated here was originally an afterword to the 1979 volume *Essais de critique génétique,* itself a landmark defense and illustration of genetic theory and practice. Hay, ever a geneticist's geneticist, uses the essay to engage in an *Ur*-project that traces the origins and growth not of a set of literary manuscripts but of genetic studies itself. Emphasizing the roles played by poets and creative writers rather than critics, he sketches the background history since Romanticism of activities that were de facto "genetic" long before they were given the official rank of a scholarly discipline. Only a wide-ranging and erudite mind like Hay's could show how the rolling sea of modern genetic criticism was fed by such different streams as the national cultures of Germany, England,

America, and France, the methods and objects of various disciplines of the humanities, the vagaries of literary theories, and the creative forces of individual writers and critics.

> Now, let us go backstage, see the workshop, the laboratory, the internal mechanism . . .
>
> —Baudelaire [1]

At the very moment, 1979, that this first volume of the series *Textes et Manuscrits* is appearing,[2] a neologism is entering into the French lexicon, "manuscriptology," separated from its ancestor, "manuscript," by one dictionary entry and several centuries. In this interval, and in the relationship between a material object and a method, the destiny of a new field of research has been and is being played out: genetic studies, that is, studies dealing with the production of writings, especially of literary texts.

Of all the fairy godmothers present at the birth of genetic studies, no doubt the most powerful is the one we will encounter at every turn, the spirit of paradox. To begin, genetic analysis has the appearance of being entirely new. Whether evoked under the auspices of a new philology, a new poetics, or even a new anthropology, the attribute of newness is its invariable mark. Yet its history, or at least its origin, brings us back to the dawn of the contemporary epoch; for something so new, it has had quite a long destiny. Moreover, we are dealing with a kind of research that is famous for its erudition, or even its scientificity, and yet the people who first became interested in it were poets—long before those who were critics by trade. Finally, the inspiration for genetic research is generally attributed to France. While it is true that today our country originates much of it, France was nonetheless one of the last countries to become engaged in it, and indeed one must look elsewhere for the origins of genetic criticism.

In the aesthetics of German idealism, we find the modern source of reflection on what Goethe first called the "genetic evolution" of a writing. As early as the end of the eighteenth century, Novalis noted in his *Schriften*: "To penetrate the secret of its elaboration is to give the means to write the total history of poetry."[3] Goethe, whose work inspired this remark, wrote in turn in 1803: "One cannot embrace the works of nature and art when they are finished; they must be taken on the wing, in the nascent state, if one wishes to comprehend them."[4] And the next year Friedrich Schlegel declared: "One can only claim to have real understanding of a work, or of a thought, when one can reconstitute its becoming and its composition. This intimate comprehension . . . constitutes the very object and essence of criticism" (*Thoughts and Opinions of Lessing*). In Germany these shattering intuitions left a wake through poets' criticism all the way from Kleist's essay "Über die allmähliche Verfertigung der Gedanken beim Reden" (1806) to Benn's communication on the *Problems of Poetry* (1951). One can follow the same thread through English letters, from Coleridge's 1817 *Biographia Literaria* to T. S. Eliot's 1948 "From Poe to Valéry," passing through Poe's 1846 "The Philosophy of Composition." In France, which echoes with the thunder of so many literary manifestoes, this reflection emerges last—it was probably not until Valéry that it was really written into French poetics.

Although this last observation is of interest to those who wish to understand the evolution of French literature, it is not my subject. For me the essential fact is that from the beginning poets have followed the path opened up by Schlegel and his contemporaries, while for a long time critics were unable to do so. This historical gap, for which there are profound reasons, enlightens us about the conditions of all genetic study. There are two kinds. First, to analyze work habits, we must be able to "go backstage," to enter into "the workshop, the laboratory" of the writer. Next, to be able to interpret the meaning of what we discover there, we must also be equipped with sufficient theoretical intelligence about these "internal mechanisms." It is clear that these conditions have been fulfilled only relatively recently. For a long time, artists kept the doors of their workshops carefully guarded. With little generosity, Poe describes this attitude in "The Philosophy of Composition":

> I have often thought how interesting a magazine paper might be written by any author who would—that is to say who could—detail, step by step, the processes by which any one of his compositions attained its ultimate point of completion. Why such a paper has never been given to the world, I am much at a loss to say—but, perhaps, the authorial vanity has had more to do with the omission than any one other cause. (743)

It is true that where Poe finds a reflex of authorial vanity, the "shudder at letting the public take a peep behind the scenes," a peep that would compromise the fiction of the poet's "ecstatic intuition," Mallarmé attacks, by contrast, the "contemporary astonishment, not very informed about what one could easily call the theology of letters" and denounces the "pedantry there always is, for the writer, when speaking in public . . . about technique" ("Notes—1895" 856). This controversy has not cooled—great writers have taken it up again in our time—and a good deal remains to be said about the relation between writers, their works, and the public, that cannot be said here. I will limit myself to one purely historical observation: writers were not the ones who brought criticism into their workshops. It slipped in by the detour of another paradox—the transformation of laboratories into museums. I am referring to the construction of literary-manuscript collections that have, for the first time, given onlookers access to writers' works—despite the fact that this was far from the original intent of the collections.

The history of this cultural phenomenon brings us back to Romantic-era Germany. Exalting the national tradition, Romanticism gave such prestige and authority to the documents of German literature that patriotic and enlightened benefactors began to collect them on the same level as Greek and Latin manuscripts. By the middle of the nineteenth century, Germany was home to about a hundred important collections—four times more than France at that time. At the end of the century, this movement culminated in the inaugural ceremonies of the Weimar "Goethe- und Schiller-Archiv"; the modern manuscript had become a national monument. It is not surprising that this archive started to attract critical attention, nor that it produced the first series of works devoted to genetic studies. Although these productions are forgotten today, they nonetheless provide a remarkable, albeit negative, illustration of the theoretical necessities for such research. In such a new enterprise, triumphantly positivist academic criticism spontaneously tended to borrow the tools it lacked from its powerful scientific neighbors, above all from natural science. We may smile at the candor it took to think of literature "biologically" or "geologically," but the failure of such attempts carries with it a still valid lesson about method: it puts us on guard against transferring concepts from one domain to another in purely metaphorical fashion. It also had an historical effect; for nearly fifty years criticism avoided these literary manuscripts that were decidedly embarrassing for it. Critics abandoned them to philologists, who did a very useful job; they uncovered documents, made great editions, and perfected methods of increasingly demanding erudition. Still, on the whole, philologists' works have had little influence on the course of literary studies.

We had to wait until the second half of the twentieth century to witness a renaissance whose center, this time, really was in France. This new current also had precursors, and it is interesting to note that one of the first, Jean Prévost, was both a writer and a critic. The example he set with the 1942 *La Création chez Stendhal* was followed after the war by the works of some of his academic colleagues: Robert Ricatte, Guy Robert, Marie-Jeanne Durry, and others. It was the quarrel over the *nouvelle critique* at the beginning of the sixties,[5] however, that signaled the decisive turning point, a fact that is not the least of our paradoxes: the first wave of structuralism brought to criticism the analysis of closed systems and clearly bounded sets—the exact opposite of genetic study. Yet the lances broken in this fenced-off field were not all in vain. Supported by the advances of both structural anthropology and modern linguistics, text-based criticism progressed in France beyond the previous givens of New Criticism and *Werkimmanente Interpretation*.[6]

Even if such was not their intention, the first works of immanent criticism did establish the prerequisite concepts for all genetic reflection. By studying both the structures and the internal workings of texts, they managed to shed light upon the relations that form among, and give meaning to, all the elements of the text. Following this, more attention was paid to the phenomena of representation and textualization at work in writing. The concept of textualization, which has played an important role in the emergence of a reflection on genesis, was finally opened to the reality of a *temporal* unfolding—a historical dimension of the text itself. Thus was shaken the image of a fixed structure, crystallized in the unchanging surfaces of the text. In the depths of texts, we started to glimpse a process of becoming in which textual systems were juxtaposed, shoved around, or replaced in the manner of soap bubbles.

This historical evolution, which developed, inflected, and at times inverted basic critical positions, itself suggests the trajectory of a genesis, for it underwent the pressures of its time and reacted upon its own cultural environment. To bring us into the present perspectives on genetic analysis, then, the surest path may be the detour—a survey of the intellectual landscape in which it is inscribed and of which, so as not to divagate too far, I will signal only the nearest points of reference.

I can only begin to mark out the territory of the "human sciences" in which textual studies are rooted. There are the disciplines that bring new perspectives to genetic analysis, such as the study of cognitive processes in psychology; those that bring theoretical support, such as the work done by logicians in philosophy; and others that bring methodological support, for example, recent mathematical and computer-science models. There are also evolutionary progressions in confluence with our work. One such case is linguistics, where generative and transformational perspectives have exerted a direct influence on the study of discourse and the phenomena of homology and transformation. The relation between these new linguistic procedures and the practices of textual analysis has been examined elsewhere; there is therefore no reason to linger on the point here.[7] By contrast, it is necessary to note a cultural fact of the highest importance: the coincidence of writers' and critics' concerns. Above, we have already pursued the conjunction between a literature that deals with its own practice and a criticism that explores the mechanisms of literary works. Perhaps this conjunction justifies the dream of a return to sources and an end to a long schism; personally, I take from it whatever pertains to genetic studies. This is more than just my prejudice: writing or the production of text always organized thought in the works of Aragon (*Les Incipit,* 1969), Elsa Triolet (*La Mise en mots,* 1969), and Francis Ponge (*La Fabrique du "Pré",* 1971;

Comment une figue de paroles et pourquoi, edited by Jean Ristat in 1977). The same is true for writers of the following generations, as evidenced by writers' interviews and collections published in the United States, Germany, and France during those years. A specific new field was delimited in which writers' criticism and critics' criticism were intermingled.

It is a new field because it deals with a phenomenon proper to the times. Wishing to discover a plurality of virtual texts behind the surface of the constituted text, this is a criticism that is clearly connected to a contemporary literature in search of open forms, attentive to what Julien Green described as the "novel that could have been," to the elements that are always fermenting in an existing novel, and to what Julien Gracq called the "phantoms of successive books" (*Lettrines* 2: 151) that have disappeared along the way and forever haunt the finished compositions. And yet, are literature and criticism really only breathing in the air of modern times? Their complicity beneath the garments of modernity (and sometimes current fashion) manifests, it seems to me, a more durable reality—the deep relation between writing and reading in all texts, the relation between the textualization of a writer's private representation and what one might call the verbal simulacrum, that is, the textual simulation that is later operative in the reader's representations. As Jean Bellemin-Noël writes in his study "Lecture psychanalytique d'un brouillon de poème: 'Été' de Valéry," "At two ends of the chain of poetic operation, there are representations" (123).[8] Here we are brought back again to Novalis's original intuition: "Authentic productions must reproduce their own production. From the engendered the engendering is reborn."[9] Since then, much has been written about the way writers' words speak both to themselves—in order to "render present and to awaken the attention of precisely that forgotten interlocutor one has in oneself," as Mallarmé said in his notes ("Notes—1895," 856)—and to others, by awakening a different echo in each reading of an identical text. Bellemin-Noël speaks about these "subjects that are both clear and confused," and I can only recall here one relevant lesson: from the perspective of textual genesis, it appears that studies of the production of a text and its reception are complementary rather than concurrent approaches. Certainly, this observation is not immediately obvious because the methods and even the theoretical or ideological implications of these approaches have provoked controversies between the representatives of these two schools. Still, the observation seems to me to be symptomatic. Today, in a whole series of domains, genetic analysis allows us to glimpse a transcendence of the contradictions that have sometimes divided modern criticism. It is this aspect that I would like to privilege here, and it is from this point of view that I propose to take up again the study of the present perspectives in genetic studies. And since these can only be brief remarks, I will limit myself to three observations.

First of all, studies of texts have led us to distinguish among a number of aspects: a rhetorical (generic, tropological) or thematic code, a narrative or descriptive organization. These elements have given rise to specific investigations. Yet while genre studies, poetics, thematics, or narratology have produced remarkable works, they have also increasingly accentuated their autonomy. Genetic analysis makes us question this development because it confronts us with a text in movement. The diverse givens that are acting upon it—ideas, representations, phantasms, as well as formal, rhythmical structures and linguistic constraints—react upon each other in the movement that carries the text forward. And the transformations that make it move from one state to another manifest themselves as a totality. A transformation of metaphors affects the organization of the narrative; a change on the thematic level may affect the choice of a genre. This is how critical categories become shaken up. Bernard Brun's text shows how a genesis transgresses the delimitation of genres; Proust's *Contre Sainte-Beuve* moves from theoretical essay to autobiographical narrative before finally giving birth to an entirely new form, the *Recherche du temps perdu.* And the work of Raymonde Debray Genette explicitly articulates the problems any poetics has when faced with forms in movement. Her reflection meets up with Henri Mitterand's when he writes at the end of his study: "Genesis and structure are not contradictory but solidary notions."

This kind of study also encourages us to question another type of binarism—the opposition between text and context, between the study of writings and of cultures. In this regard, the work on Zola's personal writing files is very enlightening. It reveals the stages of a writer's real appropriation of sociocultural givens—and also shows how these givens themselves deflected the initial project and impacted upon the finished work. Such observations can be decoded in an opposite sense. To say that the text is marked by social structures, ideologies, and cultural traditions is to say that it continues to speak of them, that in its warp and woof we can read, at every moment, the truth of the time. Or rather a certain truth since the cultural imprint is inscribed in each text in a specific fashion. This means that a study of a text is simultaneously a study of its specificity, a questioning of the opposition between "historical criticism" and "immanent criticism" and an actualization of the first proposition in Friedrich Schlegel's 1804 *Thoughts and Opinions of Lessing*:

> One can rebuild an idea by starting from solid givens procured in a mass of historical facts, but one can also . . . reconstitute the formation of the idea, from its origin to its complete development, and enable it in this way to appear alongside

the complete history of its own internal genesis. Both procedures allow one to *characterize* and thus to fulfill the supreme function of criticism.[10]

To undertake this project with the modern weapons of genetic analysis is to start down the path of cultural studies of literary texts. This "sociocriticism," to take up Claude Duchet's term, will incidentally be presented in a forthcoming volume.[11] Rather than pursue this here, I would like to examine a last type of contradiction that emerges directly from it because it deals with the relation between individuals and collectivities. Today it is the subject of a debate that has overwhelmed the field of literary studies and extended itself to the whole epistemology of "human sciences." Genetic analysis appears to be capable of bringing an original contribution to it.

We know that the *nouvelle critique* defined itself in part by reacting against the biographical tradition of literary studies. In the debates of the 1960s and 1970s, certain of its representatives suddenly disputed whether there is any sense at all in attaching a text to an author or in including the writing subject in the study of the literary object. It is interesting to confront a position so extreme with the thoughts of writers during the same period. Two observations emerge from the variety of available testimony, observations made successively and sometimes simultaneously by very different authors. The first is that there are pressures and constraints that ceaselessly shape writing and impose themselves constantly upon whomever holds the pen. Wolfgang Koeppen speaks of a "voyage through the night, straying often from a route that is never traced in advance" (Bienek 61). The second, contradictorily, is that the writer is present at the very heart of this process; Hans Erich Nossack tells of his effort to "watch that the characters do not wander onto the wrong road, do not wander into an impasse" (Bienek 98). The writers' care is in opposition to the forces working upon their texts, and Nossack writes: "Maybe this tension is what makes the book live" (Bienek 98). It is in the manuscripts that genetic analysis picks up the trace of this productive confrontation that testifies to the work process involved in writing. I have already signaled Mitterand's example: his work locates many echoes of "collective language" resounding in a novel's genesis from start to finish. At the same time, it attests to Zola's continued intervention, for he transgresses the collective language and reorganizes it into an utterly new discourse. It is this innovation, both ideological and formal, that makes of *L'Assommoir* something other than one text among others—a *book* that continues to "live" thanks to the very "tension" that engendered it. In this way, genetic experience nourishes and perhaps renews a reflection on the specificity of literary texts, whose static structures have not so far been sufficient to define "literariness" completely.

We return again to the ambition of the first precursors, which was to *characterize* literary productions in their fullness.

Is it possible to think that today's research is ushering in a new golden age of criticism accomplishing yesterday's dream of achieving the harmony of contraries? In its own field, genetic analysis is renewing the project of a totalizing criticism. Yet conditions have obviously changed: previous intuitions have given way to the difficult exploration of a reality so complex that the whole apparatus of modern research cannot entirely account for it. Constant questioning is the one quality that unites works of genetic criticism. Confronting the study of language in its real uses, the linguist says that it "complicates studies of genesis and maybe renders them obsolete or impossible." Invoking "the image of the unconscious at work in a nascent state," the psychoanalyst observes that, thanks to genetic study, "it is easier both to see clearly and to fall into traps." To appreciate the meaning of such remarks, it is not enough to invoke origins and perspectives; it is necessary above all to confront actual *problems* in genetic studies. That is, to all evidence, the affair of a book, and not of these few pages, and this lesson alone is important to me. Engaged in still-unexplored realms, genetic analysis uncovers in a single movement both new perspectives and problems hitherto unknown—problems for which it has yet to find answers. That is proof at least that it is moving.

Source: "La Critique génétique: Origines et perspectives." In *Essais de critique génétique*, ed. Louis Hay. Paris: Flammarion, 1979. 227–36.

Works Cited

Aragon, Louis. *Je n'ai jamais appris à écrire, ou les incipit.* Geneva: Albert Skira, 1969.

Baudelaire, Charles. *Œuvres complètes.* Ed. Claude Pichois. Pléiade ed. 2 vols. Paris: Gallimard, 1976.

Bellemin-Noël, Jean. "Lecture psychanalytique d'un brouillon de poème: 'Été' de Valéry." In Hay, ed., *Essais de critique génétique*, 103–50.

Benn, Gottfried. *Probleme der Lyrik.* Wiesbaden: Limes, 1951.

Bienek, Horst. *Werkstattgespräche mit Schriftstellern.* 1965. 2nd ed. Munich: Deutscher Taschenbuch Verlag, 1969.

Brun, Bernard. "L'Édition d'un brouillon et son interprétation: Le Problème du *Contre Sainte-Beuve*." In Hay, ed., *Essais de critique génétique* 151–92.

Coleridge, Samuel Taylor. *Biographia Literaria, or, Biographical Sketches of My Literary Life and Opinions.* 1817. Ed. James Engell and W. Jackson Bate. Princeton, N.J.: Princeton University Press, 1983.

Debray Genette, Raymonde. "Génétique et poétique: Le Cas Flaubert." In Hay, ed., *Essais de critique génétique* 21–68.

Duchet, Claude, ed. *Sociocritique: Colloque organisé par l'Université de Paris-VIII et New York University.* Paris: Nathan, 1979.

Eliot, T. S. "From Poe to Valéry." *To Criticize the Critic.* London: Faber and Faber, 1965. 27–42.

Fuchs, Catherine et al. *La Genèse du texte: Les Modèles linguistiques.* Paris: CNRS, 1982.

Goethe, Johann Wolfgang von. *Sämtliche Werke, Briefe, Tagebücher, und Gespräche.* Sect. 2, vol. 5. Ed. Volker C. Dörr and Norbert Oellers. Frankfurt am Main: Deutscher Klassiker Verlag, 1999.

Gracq, Julien. *Lettrines. Œuvres complètes.* Ed. Bernhild Boie. Pléiade ed. 2 vols. Paris: Gallimard, 1995. Vol. 2.

Hay, Louis, ed. *Essais de critique génétique.* Paris: Flammarion, 1979.

Kleist, Heinrich von. "Über die allmähliche Verfertigung der Gedanken beim Reden." In *Sämtliche Werke und Briefe*, ed. Helmut Sembdner. 2 vols. Munich: Hanser, 1952. 2: 319.

Mallarmé, Stéphane. "Notes. II—1895." In *Œuvres complètes.* Ed. Henri Mondor and G. Jean-Aubry. Pléiade ed. Paris: Gallimard, 1945. 854–56.

Mitterand, Henri. "Programmes et préconstruits génétiques: Le Dossier de *L'Assommoir.*" In Hay, ed., *Essais de critique génétique* 193–226.

Novalis (Friedrich von Hardenberg). *Schriften.* Ed. Paul Kluckhohn and Richard Samuel. 4 vols. Vols. 2–3. *Das Philosophische Werk I–II.* Ed. Richard Samuel. Stuttgart: Kohlhammer, 1960.

Poe, Edgar Allan. "The Philosophy of Composition." *Graham's Magazine* (April 1846). In *The Norton Anthology of Theory and Criticism*, ed. Vincent B. Leitch et al. New York: Norton, 2001. 739–50.

Ponge, Francis. *Comment une figue de paroles et pourquoi.* Paris : Flammarion, 1977.

———. *La Fabrique du "Pré"*, Geneva: Albert Skira, 1971. *The Making of the Pré.* Trans. Lee Fahnestock. Columbia: University of Missouri Press, 1979.

Prévost, Jean. *La Création chez Stendhal: Essai sur le métier d'écrire et la psychologie de l'écrivain.* Marseilles: Sagittaire, 1942.

Proust, Marcel. *Contre Sainte-Beuve; Suivi de Nouveaux mélanges.* Paris: Gallimard, 1954. *Against Sainte-Beuve and Other Essays.* Trans. John Sturrock. London: Penguin, 1988.

Schlegel, Friedrich. "Lessings Gedanken und Meinungen." In *Kritische Friedrich-Schlegel-Ausgabe*, ed. Ernst Behler, with Jean-Jacques Anstett and Hans Eichner. Vol. 3. Ed. Hans Eichner. Munich: Ferdinand Schöningh, 1975.

Triolet, Elsa. *La Mise en mots.* Geneva: Albert Skira, 1969.

Further Works by the Author

Hay, Louis. "À la recherche des manuscrits d'Henri Heine." *Revue de Littérature Comparée* 2 (1962).

———, ed. *Carnets d'écrivains 1.* Paris: CNRS, 1990.

———. "Le Cas Heine ou à quoi sert la critique génétique?" *Œuvres et Critiques* 25 (2000): 164–80.

———. "Ces Manuscrits ont échappé à la Gestapo: Henri Heine à la Bibliothèque Nationale." *Nouvelles Littéraires* (December 8, 1966): 6.

———. "Critiques de la critique génétique." *Genesis* 6 (1994): 11–23.

———, ed. *De la lettre au livre: Sémiotique des manuscrits littéraires.* Paris: CNRS, 1989.

———. "Des Manuscrits, pour quoi faire?" *Le Monde* (February 8, 1967), "Le Monde des livres" Supplement, p. 6.

———. "Édition et manuscrits." *Die Nachlassedition / La Publication des manuscrits inédits.* Bern: Peter Lang, 1979. 12–20.

———. "Genetic Editing, Past and Future: A Few Reflections by a User." Trans. J. M. Luccioni and Hans Walter Gabler. *Text* 3 (1987): 117–33.

———. "Histoire ou genèse?" *Études Françaises* 28 (1992): 11–27. "History or Genesis?" Trans. Ingrid Wassenaar. *Yale French Studies* 89 (1996): 191–207.

———. *La Littérature des écrivains: Questions de critique génétique.* Paris: José Corti, 2002.

———, ed. *Les Manuscrits des écrivains.* Paris: CNRS/Hachette, 1993.

———, ed. *La Naissance du texte.* Paris: José Corti, 1989.

———. "Papiergeschichte, eine Hilfswissenshaft?" *L'Histoire du papier: Une science auxiliaire historique.* 23rd Congress of l'Association Internationale des Historiens du Papier. Leipzig: IPH Editions, 1996. 17–22.

———. "Pour une sémiotique du mouvement." *Genesis* 10 (1996): 25–58.

———. "Le Texte n'existe pas: Réflexions sur la critique génétique." *Poétique* 85 (1985): 147–58. "Does 'Text' Exist?" Trans. Matthew Jocelyn and Hans Walter Gabler. *Studies in Bibliography* 41 (1988): 64–76.

Hay, Louis, and Jean Glenisson, eds. *Les Techniques de laboratoire dans l'étude des manuscrits.* Paris: CNRS, 1974.

Hay, Louis, and Péter Nagy, eds. *Avant-texte, texte, après-texte.* Paris: CNRS; Budapest: Akadémiai Kiadó, 1982.

Chapter 3
Psychoanalytic Reading and the Avant-texte

Jean Bellemin-Noël

For the first fifteen years of modern French genetic studies, Jean Bellemin-Noël was a dominant figure. His 1972 book *Le Texte et l'avant-texte: Les Brouillons d'un poème de Milosz* introduced the concept of "avant-texte" to literary theory and was an important contribution to, and model for, genetic criticism at the moment when the discipline was taking shape. His 1977 essay "Reproduire le manuscrit, présenter les brouillons, établir un avant-texte" helped define some of the basic theoretical issues in modern genetic studies. Over the years he has invented other influential concepts—such as the "unconscious of the text" ("l'inconscient du texte") and "textoanalysis" ("textanalyse")—and has pursued an extremely productive research program whose core tenets, adapted from psychoanalysis, are nearly unique among geneticists.

The text translated here, "Psychoanalytic Reading and the Avant-texte," was published in 1982 and summarizes the basic Freudian logic underlying much of Bellemin-Noël's work. It explains, in particular, two interrelated hypotheses that are among his most original and recurrent: first, the idea that literary works themselves have psychoanalytical structures only distantly related, or relatable, to the lives of their authors; second, the idea that the avant-textes of a given work can function as compensatory material for the associations that play such an important role in psychoanalysis.

Given genetic criticism's reputation in the Anglo-American world for casting a wide net and tracing sources in many contexts, the implications of those two ideas will certainly raise eyebrows. Not only do authors' original intentions for, and opinions of, their own writings no longer have any analytic value, according to Bellemin-Noël, but neither do the larger literary movements and cultures in which they participated. What do count in this psychoanalytic-genetic approach are the subtle relations of alterity that texts and avant-textes maintain with each other. Their interactions, like those between different structures of a psyche or between parents and their children, can be analyzed for the complex play they reveal between words, images, fantasies, and desires that are both conscious and unconscious, expressed and unexpressed.

Each half of this essay's title needs an explanation, and the two halves must be taken together to be understood. The idea of a *text* exists only for a *reading*, and of all the interpretive approaches to literature that seek meaning independently of the conditions in which texts were produced, the so-called "reading" with the best chance of attaining its objective in a pure or radical way is a Freudian one. Freudian theory deals with the relation between the text and the reader without requiring the reader to have any prior knowledge other than that of the writer's own "language"—that is, a common cultural foundation and idiom, however these are acquired.

I will here assume that many of the delicate problems raised by psychoanalytic reading have been resolved, or at least validated, by previous work. Instead of attempting to pin the method down by studying a published and supposedly definitive text and seeing how it relates to its prepublication writings, it seems better to set forth, through the notion of the "avant-texte," the things that underpin such endeavors. So, as I justify using this term I will also describe the psychoanalytic method and explain some of the reasons for choosing it. This, in turn, will allow me to elucidate the advantages—and inconveniences, too—of that method for exploring the phenomenon of *writing*, that is, the activity of the writer, understood both as the time when a work is brought forth and as an original way of treating language. To be clear, what follows concerns the genesis of artworks much more than the general problematic of art, although that is inevitably in the background.

When chance first presented me with an opportunity to study the documents of a writer's composition, I was embarrassed by a terminological difficulty. The French language gave me a choice between two words to designate these documents: *le manuscrit* [the manuscript], quite literally the sheets of paper covered with signs traced by the hand of the writer, and *les brouillons* [the rough drafts], that is, the materializations of an unfinished, prospective discourse, sometimes rejected but more often transformed through a process of development. The first word posed few problems; one could easily restrict its meaning to the tangible media of the writing process, those objects destined to be preserved by the generosity of authors and the admiration of lovers of belles-lettres. One could use the second term, it seemed to me, to qualify what was written on the manuscripts. *Rough drafts* would then include the following:

(1) everything that had ever played a part in the composition of a work but had not attained publishable status: the preliminary dossier, the worksheets, and the portfolio of accessory notes; (2) the *drafts properly so called,* that is, the first draft and its metamorphoses (additions, corrections, erasures, and substitutions) up to the final state of first publication. This last state could again be transformed by print modifications, called "variants" [*variantes*].

The term "rough draft(s)" [*brouillon*(*s*)] bothered me for two main reasons. First, it connoted something tangled [*embrouillé*] or un-straightened [*non-débrouillé*], that is, a process of groping. It therefore implied that authors have a presentiment of a perfect state that they are reaching for, whereas in reality their words, at first, are potentially acceptable formulations. Only afterwards do authors discover that they are dissatisfied with their words; only then do they return to work on them. It is too idealistic to assume that somewhere a perfect Text already exists that writers must find like a treasure; nor, theoretically, from the perspective of how writers work, can one assume that the Meaning of a given writing exists and that writers need only obtain the most appropriate words for it, as if through recipes. A second problem was that historians of literature commonly used the term "rough draft(s)" to refer to authorial intentions; historians have never been able to place literary works in different contexts without at least considering the original authors' ideas about their own works. Yet for a reading, especially one hoping to reconstitute the unconscious values of texts, what writers wanted to say or thought they were writing is of no interest. What counts for me is what the text itself says "literally and in every sense," as Rimbaud's formula has it.

You understand that at first I tried to take only the rough drafts into account. The more peripheral and circumstantial documents, amounting to a commentary on the author's understanding of the work, did not hold my attention. When I then considered the semantic and historical weight of those two words "rough draft"—the ways they were historically and ideologically charged—it caused me to coin the term "avant-texte" as a substitute. With that neologism, I joined up with a theory of "text" that had had great success in France at the end of the 1960s and has continued to leave its mark on the 1970s. Still, the value of the prefix "avant" ("pre") does need a few words of clarification. I do not endorse a sort of primitivism in which anteriority would imply clumsy sketch (as it does in Lucien Lévy-Bruhl's nonchalantly baptized "prelogic" [*prélogique*] in his 1922 *La Mentalité primitive*). Nor would I give to preliminary writing the prestigious and inaugural character of being a text's first intuition, localizable in a native state, such that the later work would amount to a mere embellishment upon it. No, what is *before* the published *text* is *already text* and *already the text.* The text in the imperfect tense can be read; it is not devoid of structure and it is not a paraphrase of the text in the future tense. Of course, one can also see preliminary writings as texts in the conditional or in the subjunctive, but one must nonetheless treat them in their present tense.

Let us examine this. I am calling "avant-texte" the totality of the material written for any project that was first made public in a specific form. Since the term "textual" designates the closed field where a reading meets a writing so as to make the latter signify its unexpected and unpredictable possibilities, regardless of the author's intentions and the pressure of social and biographical history, I will say that to attend to an avant-textual document is *to read, continuously with the text and without any presuppositions, the totality of formulations that, as previous possibilities, have become part of a given work of writing.* Several things are self-evident: (1) this ensemble is not always all there is (whatever could be formulated in thought without being written on paper is missing, at any rate); (2) the order of successive stages is not necessarily revelatory (I do not reconstitute the sequential history of a creation, I explore an environment of words); (3) the information provided by the process of inscription (graphic marks, marginal ornamentation, technical intrusions, etc.) does not interfere with the written material and, as a result, such material enjoys no special privilege (what was once written is neither more prestigious and revelatory nor less significant for having been blotted or crossed out); (4) the primary interest of this reading consists, finally, in surrounding the final text with a halo, that is, with verbal materials that radiate from it while resonating with it, whether such verbal spokes are parallel, oblique, or perpendicular to it. Since the writing process is itself a production governed by uncertainty and chance, we absolutely must substitute spatial metaphors for temporal images to avoid reintroducing the idea of teleology. We must never forget this paradox: what was written *before* and had, at first, no *after,* we meet only *after,* and this tempts us to supply a *before* in the sense of a priority, cause, or origin.

Saying that an avant-texte cannot be read as the origin of a text introduces us imperceptibly to the problem of the unconscious and therefore to my psychoanalytical view of how texts *signify.* Avant-textes are no more and no less the origins of texts than mothers are the origins of children. Of course, mothers exist *before* their children (and they all continue to live side by side); yet children, from their first cries, are autonomous beings who will constitute their own pasts and construct their own origins for themselves. If, for example, texts are adults, old enough to reproduce and participate in public life, then avant-textes are children, youths, or adolescents, but not mothers. Avant-textes are texts *as* children; texts are not avant-textes' children. Moreover, "who I was" until my maturity is both myself (thanks to the memories I claim as mine) and an infinity of other selves I have forgotten, no longer understand, and would not recognize if I ran into them. (I need only think of what happens when I look at my own children.) Thus I could say that my past "I" is *my other,* the alterity of which is rooted in the very first Other I ever met without really realizing it, my mother. And psychoanalysis tries precisely to explain this rootedness in an Other that was later reinscribed in me—while for her, for her alone and not for me since I didn't exist, I was part of her "before" being. This relation ties the profound desire for being—for being alive and happy, as we were in the beginning, since beginnings leave lasting impressions—to the Other, a desire that has always lived in me and will always live in *my other* without my being conscious of it. And this relation is also what, in a particular language, Freudian doctrine takes as its object of study and calls "the unconscious." Let us say then, in a figure of speech, that the avant-texte is the text's other and that the text is attached to what brought it into the world only as it would be to the Other. Let us also see why I, as a reader considering a text—a text that is also my text—might find it advantageous to confront it with its childhood.

Before undertaking my task, I will offer a few words about the history of the relationship between psychoanalysis and literature in order to help state my position succinctly. Ever since Freud's analysis of Wilhelm Jensen's novel *Gradiva,* psychoanalysts have been attracted to the project of painting authors' portraits from the psychological hints contained in their works. Using the theory of the unconscious, psychoanalysts have essentially tried to accomplish what Sainte-Beuve attempted with traditional psychology. Marie Bonaparte, for example, has reconstructed the hidden psyche of Edgar Allan Poe by studying his life and fiction, and today this procedure lives on in what is called psychobiography. In the 1950s, Charles Mauron, proceeding not as an analyst but as a critic—this is significant because it means that he treats writing as writing rather than as a symptom—developed a rigorous method for locating those key elements in a work that seemed to refer to a particular structure of desire. This approach is called *psychocriticism;* it proceeds by "superimposing texts," and most of us recall examples of it based on Mallarmé or Racine. Mauron's procedures were especially suited to "listening" to the discourse of the unconscious in the works themselves. Indeed, he believed that biographical facts were valuable only in confirming his own conclusions. Nevertheless, he could not resist consolidating his conclusions into what he called "the personal myth of the writer."

I do not deny the interest and apparent fascination of such studies. As long as one is concerned with the history of writers or with the mysterious and even disquieting relations between an artist's private life and artistic creations (genius is close to madness), they are indispensable. But my point of view demands that the works themselves, taken in isolation, reveal their structures of meaning. This prevents me from asking about the human authors as well as about the intellectual movements in which their aesthetic projects were written. My problem, instead, is this: can we reconstruct the configurations of unconscious desire that allow themselves to be seen (when one has the means to render them visible) in a work that one treats as a text? Then, most importantly, since we are behaving as literary critics and not as analysts (exactly who would one *analyze*, in the clinical sense of the term?), what can we know of the way unconscious discourse slips into conscious discourse? Are we not dealing here with one of the kinds of information that, in the absence of the fascination exerted by the writer as a person, might explain what we call the success, beauty, charm, or genius of a given work?

Without recourse to difficult technical terms and precise examples, I can go no further in describing my work. It seems more judicious in the present context to explain in a rapid summary how this reading method helped me when I applied it to the documents of a writing process. And rather than insist in a general way on the benefits—undeniable as they are—of this operation, I will emphasize one point and try to explain why it is of primary importance in this type of research.

The fundamental problem of psychoanalytic research is this: when I read a text with the aim of locating those failures or distortions of discourse (gaps, forgettings, supplements, etc.) that reveal the pressure of an unconscious desire, I lack the essential ingredient that allows a practitioner to work on such material: the patient's *associations.* Without them, I risk producing a merely symbolic "translation." The analyst can interpret a dream, for example, only if the person on the couch says in all freedom what a particular word, character, setting, or detail makes him or her think about. Now a text cannot respond to questions with words other than those that constitute it. Its sentences are all fixed and cannot be supplemented, but their linkages, inflections, and rhetorical effects are open to question. This situation has its difficulties because critics constantly regret not being able to extrapolate from one verbal series to another; they feel the limits of appealing to other words of the text when they substitute their own concatenations for those that they find lacking. This is a perilous exercise in which we are never sure that we are not, in trying to put ourselves in the place of the text, indulging in our own "fantasies" at the text's expense. While, luckily, there are certain correctives for these uncertainties (which in no instance go beyond the uncertainties found in other humanities disciplines), for the researcher nothing is more valuable than a new word, one that extends a series and brings an added clarity to it. Such a word, in general, has been repressed; it is nowhere to be found, at least not as a readable, visible whole. And it happens that the avant-texte can permit us to discover this lost word. As in the case of people who as children pronounced or heard pronounced a name in such painful circumstances that they no longer wish to remember it, so too a formulation that a writer has erased in favor of another can put us onto the path of a missing link; then the play of associations is no longer left entirely to the reader's diligence and discretion. Readers, no matter how much confidence they have (never very much, in these situations), quake at the thought of being fooled by appearances, and, this time, there is a solid guarantor and thus a faster and surer path towards an illuminating hypothesis. It may be a name, a scene, a syntactical figure, a lost adjective, a recurring letter, a syllable, or some other minuscule detail carrying an immeasurable significance.

Since this kind of research does not yet have rich past experience to work from, even small discoveries are very valuable. It is encouraging to find in avant-textes the supplementary pieces that allow us to render the puzzle of the unconscious less obscure, a puzzle that (by definition) will never be solved. Such discoveries also open the door for other research, other imaginative ideas, and further theoretical reflection. Even a minor point can admirably demonstrate the interest of studying manuscripts, rough drafts, and other avant-textes, and in such studies we can recognize, I think, both the promise of new findings and the justification for seeking other ways to look at texts.

Source: "Avant-texte et lecture psychanalytique." In *Avant-texte, texte, après-texte,* ed. Louis Hay and Péter Nagy. Paris: CNRS; Budapest: Akadémiai Kiadó, 1982. 161–65.

Works Cited

Bonaparte, Marie. *Edgar Poe, étude psychanalytique.* 2 vols. Paris: Denoël et Steele, 1933. *The Life and Works of Edgar Allan Poe: A Psycho-Analytic Interpretation.* Trans. John Rodker. London: Imago, 1949.

Freud, Sigmund. "Delusions and Dreams in Jensen's *Gradiva.*" 1907. In *Standard Edition of the Complete Psychological Works of Sigmund Freud.* Ed. James Strachey, trans. James Strachey et al. 24 vols. London: Hogarth Press, 1953–74. Vol. 9. 1–95.

Lévy-Bruhl, Lucien. *La Mentalité primitive.* Paris: Félix Alcan, 1922. *Primitive Mentality.* Trans. Lilian A. Clare. New York: Macmillan, 1923.

Mauron, Charles. *Des Métaphores obsédantes au mythe personnel: Introduction à la psychocritique.* Paris: José Corti, 1962.

———. *Introduction à la psychanalyse de Mallarmé.* Neuchâtel: La Baconnière, 1950. *Introduction to the Psychoanalysis of Mallarmé.* Trans. Archibald Henderson, Jr. and Will L. McLendon. Berkeley: University of California Press, 1963.

Further Works by the Author

Bellemin-Noël, Jean. "Foundations and Problems of 'Textoanalysis.'" *American Imago: Studies in Psychoanalysis and Culture* 56 (1999): 221–34.

———. *Gradiva au pied de la lettre: Relecture du roman de W. Jensen dans une nouvelle traduction.* Paris: Presses Universitaires de France, 1983.

———. *Interlignes: Essais de textanalyse.* Lille: Presses Universitaires de Lille, 1988.

———. "Lecture psychanalytique d'un brouillon de poème: 'Été' de Valéry." In *Essais de critique génétique*, ed. Louis Hay. Paris: Flammarion, 1979. 103–149.

———. *Psychanalyse et littérature.* Paris: Presses Universitaires de France, 1989.

———. "Reproduire le manuscrit, présenter les brouillons, établir un avant-texte." *Littérature* 28 (December 1977): 3–18.

———. *Le Texte et l'avant-texte: Les Brouillons d'un poème de Milosz.* Paris: Larousse, 1972.

———. "'Textoanalysis' and Psychoanalysis." Trans. Ronald P. Bermingham. *Substance* 18 (1989): 102–11.

———. *Vers l'inconscient du texte.* Paris: Presses Universitaires de France, 1979.

Chapter 4
Toward a Science of Literature: Manuscript Analysis and the Genesis of the Work

Pierre-Marc de Biasi

Pierre-Marc de Biasi's French audience knows him as an artist, a textual critic, a journalist, and a literary theorist. A Flaubertian above all, having published a groundbreaking edition of Flaubert's notebooks, de Biasi's extensive practical and theoretical experience with canonical texts and avant-textes is especially visible in the 1985 essay chosen for this volume: "Toward a Science of Literature: Manuscript Analysis and the Genesis of the Work" (translated here from its revised appearance in the *Encyclopaedia Universalis Symposium 1989*). Written as an encyclopedia entry on genetic criticism, it provides a thorough exposition of the major critical premises, techniques, and methodologies of the discipline and has become extremely influential.

De Biasi begins with the idea that textual genetics has two main critical assignments: to render avant-textual materials readable and to analyze the logic of their evolution. To perform these complex tasks, the geneticist must navigate a host of related practical and theoretical problems. Patiently describing these, de Biasi addresses many of the questions that nag the general reader about this kind of criticism. Some are theoretical: is geneticism compatible with other isms? Can one be a "genetic" New Historicist, Marxist, or psychoanalytic critic? Others are more practical: given the state of the publishing industry, will we ever see *complete* genetic editions of our favorite literary works in print? If not, what compromises will be made? And computers? Can they help solve any of genetic criticism's problems? Most of the questions, however, are commonsense ones: how useful is it, really, to study 2,500 pages of avant-texte for a single story? Supposing one has the energy for a full-blown genetic project, how does one find all the materials, put them in order, analyze them intelligently, learn something important, and communicate the results in an interesting way to nonspecialists?

Underlying all these questions is de Biasi's deeper one: what can be systematic or scientific about the study of avant-textes? More than we might think, he answers, as he brings his Aristotelian, ordering mind to the sprawling field and sorts out the pullulating methods and documents for which it has become notorious. For naysayers who carry the image of genetic studies as all trees and no forest (and of geneticists as groping blindly among leaves on the forest floor), he offers a moral tale drawn from the critical history of Flaubert's manuscripts. He shows how "internal" genetic criticism—the study of a series of drafts of a single fragment of text—has certain alchemic powers, as when it overcomes manuscript illegibilities that were long thought insuperable. He also demonstrates, through a sample transcription, that even the dense, matted material of avant-textes can be intelligibly communicated to nonspecialists.

Throughout the essay, de Biasi gradually charts the history of genetic studies, starting with the early days in source-seeking criticism and influence study and ending with the newer, more dynamic forms that seek to render visible the various logics of avant-textual development. He also explains how the critical senses of some key terms have evolved and analyzes the way the discipline of manuscript studies has transformed the very idea of a literary work. What was once usually understood and examined as a finished, neoclassical, structured, and concrete book has become today a dynamic, temporal, moving object—a text.

Nearly every technique of literary criticism operates on the published text of a literary work. Although this object of study has long been thought of as a discrete whole, recent developments in literary research have revealed a more and more perceptible rupture inside it. The originality of the present situation derives from the fact that this rupture was not produced by any particular questioning of critical procedures but rather by the placement of them in a "historical" or, more precisely, genetic perspective. The object-text has been torn from the closure of the "in-itself" and enriched with a new temporal dimension.

One rather banal observation suffices to suggest what is involved: the definitive text of a published or publishable work is, with very few exceptions, the result of a process, that is, a progressive transformation, an investment of time that the author has devoted to researching documents, writing, correcting and recorrecting, etc. The literary work, closed in its perfected form and in a state of equilibrium that seems to be the immediate expression of its own internal necessity, nonetheless remains the mediated product of its own genesis.

Next to the text, and before it, there exists a more or less developed set of "draft documents," gathered, produced, and sometimes kept by the author: these are generally called the "manuscripts" of the work. This set of manuscripts (which must first of all be found and preserved) obviously varies in quantity and type according to the work and author under consideration. The dossier of manuscripts of a work can include, besides documentation gathered by the writer, a more or less diverse series of draft documents that bear witness to the evolution of the work: there are *outlines* [*plans*], *scenarios* [*scénarios*], *sketches* [*ébauches*], *rough drafts* [*brouillons*], edited *clear copies* [*mises au net*], a *final manuscript* [*manuscrit définitif*], corrections on proofs, etc. In sum, there is a whole history from which the work issues and whose aesthetic culmination it appears to be, but this history is sometimes so different from the definitive result that one must also see in it a dimension of the work. Certainly the production of a text can be understood teleologically, but the process of its development reflects a logic intersected by many possible becomings. A work's manuscripts are clearly distinct from the text; although they lead to the text, they also keep reminding us that they are prior and external to it. To grasp the vast movement that, with increasing precision, produces the final text, without covering up the many divergences operating inside its transformation—such is the critical work of manuscript analysis. This means changing the critical status of the holograph dossier from undifferentiated "manuscripts of the work" to "avant-texte." Following from a good deal of other preparatory work, this operation represents the essential stakes of the scientific bet introduced by "genetic" textual criticism.

The Origin and Program of "Textual Genetics"

Taking the existence of manuscripts systematically into account and demanding a coherent method for establishing and constituting them as avant-textes delimits a new research space and a new viewpoint on the question: "What is writing?" Concretely, this means examining the operation by which a text, notably a literary text, is invented, sketched, amplified, exploded into heterogeneous fragments, and condensed until it is finally chosen from among and against several other written materializations. Fixed in its stable form, it becomes (at least traditionally) publishable as the finished text of the work.

Such is the problematic for which manuscript analysis provides both a new object and a demand for new methods. A new object, because, as paradoxical as this may appear, the set of extant literary manuscripts still represents, with very few exceptions, a material field of analysis that is almost totally unexplored. A demand for new methods since in the nearly complete absence of scientific experience in this domain the first task is to construct the necessary operative concepts for grasping the recalcitrant object of writing in its nascent state. From this situation it results that, at the very moment it is seeking to constitute itself scientifically as the genetic study of literary texts, manuscript analysis finds itself confronted with the hypothesis of a maximal opening of its space of definition—the genetic study of all written expressions of thought and especially of textual production. Thus, although it was first limited to the space of literature, textual genetics today finds itself at the source of a research stream capable of renewing linguistic studies and the history of ideas and cultures.

The thought of such a renewal may be surprising because the study of an author's manuscripts does not in itself appear to be an entirely new critical procedure. It is a new one, however, and with enough clarity that it is not an exaggeration to speak of rupture. Something has radically changed, and very recently, in our understanding of the manuscript object. Until now it was first and foremost a collector's object, jealously preserved in public or private cabinets as a guarantee of the authenticity of the work and occasionally consulted as documentary evidence of the artist's work process. Now, without losing this value of "symbolic possession," the manuscript has been given the entirely different cultural value of an object of scientific study, a transformation that has also broadened our conception of the object. Above all, the collector's manuscript used to be the Manuscript of the work: the definitive manuscript, the one the author recopied at the end of the writing process in order to provide a readable version for the copyist or the printer (or even to offer a "nice" manuscript to an admirer). Yet the manuscript of most interest to the researcher in textual genetics, the manuscript-object of study, is not usually this definitive clear copy. Although it can be beautiful, precious, and moving, most often it offers a very fixed image of the work. Rather, it is in the rough drafts, the handwritten documents of the writing process, that one concretely glimpses writing in the act of being born. Seen in this way, manuscripts are not yet an established cultural reality. Their value and meaning must be constructed and explored, and thus they offer an inside perspective on one of the main ways our very culture is fashioned. We can evaluate this reversal of manuscript status by examining the conditions on which it rests, that is, the practical and theoretical methods that are necessary to analyze manuscripts.

We are dealing with nothing less than a mutation, one reflected, incidentally, in the late 1970s French neologism *manuscriptologie,* a term that defines the horizon of a coherent and systematic scientific discourse in the matter of manuscript analysis. This current striving for systematicity clearly reflects the innovative character of the research projects undertaken in this realm over the last few years. It also indicates the kind of rupture they have introduced into the relationships between texts and manuscripts.

Indeed, contemporary genetics of literary texts has little to do with the traditional kinds of genetic study that have sporadically reoriented critical discourses and erudite editions along the lines of positivism since the end of the nineteenth century. The bulk of most traditional studies were dedicated to researching texts that might have explicitly "influenced" the author of the work under consideration ("sources" for a work). Yet within the limits of such a "source critique," very few of the so-called erudite research works relied on a serious list of bibliographical or documentary references provided directly by the writer's manuscripts. Even when they were easily available, the work's "dossiers" (including, for example, the handwritten notebooks for reading notes and commentaries) were seldom considered to be essential elements of research; at best, they were used partially and allusively. As for the idea of going to look at a rough draft, at the writing process itself, for the eventual trace of a source that the author might have been led to hide in the definitive text, virtually nobody thought of it.

Aside from this source-seeking, the old study of genesis traditionally devoted itself to a tentative stylistic evaluation. In general, the methods and results were not very penetrating: the most daring enterprises of this kind tended to present a more or less voluminous selection of "variants," chosen without any precise criteria from among those best suited for illustrating what one already intended to make of them. The customary project produced a list (rarely exhaustive) of the corrections (suppressions and additions of detail) made to the Manuscript, that is, to the definitive clear copy, obviously much easier to read than the rough drafts, which were ordinarily considered undecipherable from the start.

In such a climate, which above all displayed critical indifference to literary manuscripts, some notable exceptions (still, only since the 1950s) stand out as signs of an entirely new exigency: most notably the works of Robert Ricatte (*La Genèse de "La Fille Élisa"*), Marie-Jeanne Durry (*Flaubert et ses projets inédits*), René Journet and Guy Robert (*Le Manuscrit des "Contemplations"*), Pierre Clarac and Alain Ferré (for the edition of the works of Marcel Proust), Jean Levaillant (*Anatole France*), and Claudine Gothot-Mersch (*La Genèse de "Madame Bovary"*). These publications, and a few others of the same type, theorized—sometimes explosively—an entirely different path for genetic studies. Nonetheless, far from helping to develop a united procedure, these pioneering research projects remained isolated initiatives until very recently. No doubt because of the positivist presuppositions that were still attached to this type of work, everything has in fact happened as if textual genetics, in order to unify itself as a coherent method and free itself of the prejudices weighing upon it, had to find itself at some point rejected by contemporary developments in literary criticism. Paradoxically, the paths of criticism inaugurated at the beginning of the 1960s marked the decisive turning point. Starting then, and for ten years or more, what would become the structuralist current more and more clearly oriented criticism toward an approach that was diametrically opposed (at least in appearance) to the genetic hypothesis, that is, toward closed systems, or sets analyzable according to their internal logic.

If the successes of structuralist criticism were bound, however, to eclipse the still tenuous and intermittent lights of the new studies of genesis, the sum total of this formalist period was a profit for future textual genetics. Developments in structural anthropology and formal linguistics made it possible, in the fields of textual criticism and semiological research, to define new projects that in France have resulted in intense efforts at conceptualization, notably in the theory of text (see Roland Barthes's encyclopedia article on "the text").[1] Besides the new paths that such an overhaul was able to pencil into a completely redrawn critical panorama, this period of theorization wound up developing and working with a number of concepts capable of grounding a coherent approach to the problems posed by genetic studies.

Structuralism allowed us to specify the decisive character of certain processes at work in writing, notably the phenomena of representation and textualization, for three reasons: it insisted upon describing the formal processes at work in texts, it studied texts as the structural site of production of meanings, and it demonstrated the internal laws that operate in a purely relational manner in texts qua systems. Research advances in semiology culminated in a more dynamic analysis of these structural processes, making the text the center of a theatricized process of meaning that had to be understood in terms of "signifying practices" and "productivity," all according to a logic in which the text was the site of an intertextual deconstruction-reconstruction. Finally, in the same period sweeping theoretical revisions redefined historical discourses (especially Marxist) and research projects (especially psychoanalytic) in terms of the logic of the signifier and the theory of the subject. It is likely that textual genetics would never have been able to constitute its own theoretical foundations had it not been able to ground itself upon such critical underpinnings. In many ways, the requirements for a reflection on the genesis of the text have only been satisfied since the moment when, with gains made in the theory of text, it has become possible to pose the problem of a text's temporal production in terms of internal systematics. Of course, the theory of structural analysis, once dominated by a synchronic obsession with form, had to be opened up to the exteriority of a diachronic unfolding. Yet precisely because it insists on theorizing a historical dimension inside writing, textual genetics places itself at the endpoint of structuralist research and insists upon a point of view that was cruelly lacking from formal analyses—the unexplored expanse of a new object structured by time.

Defining its research domain as one of systematically studying manuscripts to restore the genesis of written works, textual genetics does not claim in any way to be a substitute for different critical approaches to the text. The best proof is that among geneticists analyzing different dossiers of manuscripts since the end of the 1970s, we find represented, with none summarily excluded, most of the great orientations of contemporary critical discourse. It must be added that researchers, as geneticists, do not see themselves as constrained to abandon the point of view that was and remains theirs in criticism of the text. Just the opposite is true because the theoretical presuppositions of genetic study are the same as those that govern analyses of texts. Depending on the case, a genetic study of a work's dossier will therefore be either exclusively or jointly constructed on the criteria of narratological, sociocritical, semiotic, psychoanalytic, linguistic, or other kinds of observation.

It is in fact essential to distinguish the genetic from the critical dimension: both claim to use scientific procedures and therefore to be complementary but not competitive or mutually exclusive.

Textual genetics does not in itself have a criterion of critical evaluation. It has a double objective that consists, on the one hand, of rendering technically readable and analyzable the before-the-text [*antérieur-du-texte*], its evolution, and its internal workings up to the definitive form. On the other hand, it must reconstruct the logic of this genesis. For the first aspect of the genetic objective, one must adopt a specific technique for internal and external manuscript analysis. For the second, the study of a text's genesis or, if one prefers, the attempt to establish an avant-texte, one can only succeed if one applies a selective critical procedure. This procedure will reconstruct the genesis from a chosen point of view, for example, desire (psychoanalysis), inscription of sociality (sociocriticism), or the very conditions of its own poetics (narratology).

This does not mean that genetic study gives itself over to the arbitrariness of an exclusive aim: nothing prevents the same avant-texte from becoming multiply reconstructed. Nor does anything prevent each of the avant-texte's logics from being analyzed and then redeployed in relative autonomy and, when possible, reconnected to synthetic hypotheses that establish a more integrated image of the writing process. Yet even if genetic study must consider this synthetic finality, the fact remains that to establish an avant-texte one must choose a precise critical point of view, or method, in order to reconstruct a continuity between everything that precedes a text and that same text in its definitive form. Without such an initial choice, the avant-texte is not (any more than the text, and perhaps less than it) susceptible of being understood scientifically.

Only upon this construction, that is, upon precise criteria of observation, conceptually harmonized with a preexisting analytical system, can the avant-texte be constituted as an object of research. Still, as the earliest and latest works of textual genetics all attest, this fact has not stopped genetic researchers from frequently transforming or reconsidering critical presuppositions that inadequately account for the temporalized phenomena of writing. Appropriate new notions and criteria are then elaborated, and today one of the most dynamic aspects of textual genetics resides precisely in the permanent methodological vigilance that it provokes in textual criticism.

In a general way, the situation comes down to making the divisions that Jean Bellemin-Noël recommends.[2] Analyzing the manuscripts and the genesis of a work schematically implies taking three distinct objects into consideration, each of which has different objectives and calls for particular treatment:

- The Manuscript of the so-called "definitive" work. This manuscript authenticates the text (published or not) and belongs in the library curator's jurisdiction. It is culturally endowed with the value of a symbolic possession, and it must be fixed, reproduced, and published.
- The manuscripts of the work. This is the dossier (as complete as possible) of the rough drafts and other draft documents that were used to conceive and produce the work. This dossier, which must be collected, deciphered, transcribed, and presented, belongs in the literary historian-geneticist's jurisdiction.
- An avant-texte (or a study of genesis.) This represents a certain reconstitution of the genetic operations that precede the text. The avant-texte is no longer a set of manuscripts but an elucidation of the logical systems that organize it, and it does not exist anywhere outside the critical discourse that produces it. It lies in the jurisdiction of the critic-geneticist who establishes it using the results of the manuscript analysis.

Manuscript Analysis

What, then, are the chief scientific operations performed by geneticists when they face the most typical research materials, that is, the manuscript dossier of a published work? In most cases, these operations present themselves in a relatively constraining order as a series of technical and theoretical procedures fixed in advance. These procedures are produced, first, by the demands of deciphering and classification (manuscript analysis properly so called) and second, by the final goal of the study of genesis.

To establish a work's avant-texte (to reconstitute its genesis) presupposes that the essential analytical work has produced a dossier that is transparent both as a whole and in each of its elements. Yet when geneticists sort out the manuscript dossier in the initial phase of work, it is obvious that they already have in mind the ulterior objectives of genetic study. Thus a good portion of the avant-texte will already be established when they finish analyzing the rough drafts and other draft documents. Conversely, when geneticists then devote themselves to synthetically reconstructing the logic of the operations involved in genesis, they are often required to decide whether hypotheses are verified everywhere or only in portions of the avant-texte. In these circumstances, it often happens that the study of genesis, returning to one aspect or another of the preliminary analysis, leads them to reexamine or even correct an inexact detail in decoding or classifying. This back-and-forth play in the research is a permanent characteristic of textual genetics, which presupposes at all times the possibility of systematic recourse to verification and retroactive correction. For this reason the relatively constraining order of the analytic procedures corresponds well, as we will see, to a nonpermutable series of operations, but only insofar as each of these operations, effectively united with all the others, undergoes the permanent test of verification from top to bottom. Thus if the manuscript analysis unfolds in several distinct and globally successive stages, the necessities of systematic backchecking often result in such a solidarity that several research phases can only be tackled head on, that is, in parallel and simultaneous fashion.

Nonetheless, successful analyses reveal that some technical imperatives have a general structure. Ordinarily, one can distinguish five essential phases, each one corresponding to a key research operation:

- Constituting (gathering and authenticating) the whole dossier of the available manuscripts of the work in question.
- Specifying and classifying each folio of the dossier.
- Organizing (checking over, partially deciphering, and arranging in a teleological order) the dossier of rough drafts and other draft documents.
- Deciphering and transcribing the whole dossier.
- Establishing and publishing an avant-texte.

These five operations constitute the work of the geneticist and establish the possibility of genetic study. Some precise examples, borrowed from a genetic analysis of the manuscripts of a text by Gustave Flaubert ("La Légende de saint Julien l'Hospitalier") will allow us to follow this analytic procedure through all its phases and define its specific practices.

1. Constituting the Dossier

The first phase of research consists of gathering and authenticating the objects that materially condition the very possibility of analysis, that is, the manuscripts belonging to the work to be studied. The initial objective is therefore to constitute (or to "reconstitute" if the constitution has already been done) the whole dossier of available manuscripts. It is therefore necessary that these manuscripts exist (that they not have been totally destroyed or lost) and that they are available, that is, that it is possible to consult them for a sufficient time, either directly by reading the originals or indirectly by reading reproductions (for example, photographed/photocopied versions or projections and enlargements in microfilm). In all these cases, it is necessary for the manuscripts to be found, conserved (maintained in a state of legibility, that is, fixed in their medium, protected, and ultimately restored), and accessible to the researcher in a private or public collection.

Over the last several years, public, municipal, and national collections (notably the famous Department of Occidental Manuscripts in the Bibliothèque Nationale in Paris) have received numerous manuscript dossiers of great scientific value and made them directly available for research. Several large private collections have also generously offered to make important new documents available to researchers. But it is still true that in France, as elsewhere, many private collections of manuscripts still remain totally inaccessible. In several cases it has even become impossible to determine the actual location of documents whose existence is indubitable but whose trace has been lost through anonymous public and private commercial processes.

Nonetheless, thanks to greater vigilance by public officials and the personal initiative of certain people in charge of manuscript conservation as it relates to national heritage, the situation seems to be developing favorably. In France the publicly acquired and preserved collections today represent a considerable scientific capital (one that must now be made productive). Thus when textual-genetic researchers seek to reconstitute and authenticate the manuscript dossiers of French literary works, in many cases they can confidently rely upon the work of curators who have constructed a complete catalogue of the documents available in their holdings. In such cases, researchers merely need to acquaint themselves with the manuscripts and verify, with the aid of specialized library curators, whether the known totality of the manuscripts is gathered there or if other documents pertaining to the writing of the work (perhaps held in other public collections) must be consulted elsewhere. In more uncertain cases, researchers will be forced to undertake a real quest to find the traces of the different manuscripts of the dossier and to collect all its elements. In such a case, it often takes several years to constitute the dossier, especially when there are private holdings and collectors, sometimes in different countries, to be found and persuaded.

After the preliminary job of assembling the dossier (in whatever conditions), the researcher produces as precise a description of its elements as possible. At first, the description follows the model of library catalogues but uses refined criteria to summarize the gathered documents. This means (1) grouping the documents in large categories, for example, manuscripts, rough drafts, other draft documents, reading notes, documentary pieces, outlines, etc.; (2) materially analyzing and authenticating them (nonholograph manuscripts are sometimes interspersed in a dossier); (3) identifying them (a single work's dossier may include handwritten manuscripts from very different time periods); (4) classifying them according to material criteria, for example, characteristics of the medium (analysis of the paper: dimensions, quality, color, thickness, type, watermark, distance between chain-lines);[3] analyzing their chemistry (the ink, the pencil, etc.); and identifying and dating the writing. For material research, the geneticist may have recourse to the technical and scientific resources of laboratories specializing in codicology.

Thus the dossier of a work's manuscripts is constituted when the geneticist has finished identifying the material elements and has available a set of documents clearly redistributed in homogeneous subsets. This is merely a first and general form of presentation, yet upon this initial organization all the later divisions of research rest because it is what allows for different analytic treatments (for example, between the subset "rough drafts" and the subset "reading notes"). This preliminary effort at clarification is all the more necessary since a manuscript dossier (especially one without gaps) can have dimensions considerably vaster than the definitive work.

Thus, to take the example of a dossier whose constitution did not pose any major problems, the essential manuscripts are held at the Bibliothèque Nationale, and which dealt with a short text by Gustave Flaubert—"La Légende de saint Julien l'Hospitalier" (written in 1875–76 and published in 1877 in *Trois contes*), all the known and available documents could, after the initial survey, be divided up in the following way:

- Manuscripts held at the Bibliothèque Nationale: the definitive manuscript (27 sheets, holograph recto); the copyist's manuscript (41 nonholograph sheets, recto); the rough drafts (74 holograph sheets, recto and verso); reading notes from 1856 (holograph, but in a different hand, twenty years older than that of the other manuscripts in this dossier; 24 sheets, recto or recto/verso); the work notes from 1875 (6 holograph sheets, recto or recto/verso); the outline in five parts from

Figure 1. Gustave Flaubert, "La Légende de saint Julien l'Hospitalier." BN N.A.F. 23 663-2, f. 429. Courtesy of the Bibliothèque Nationale de France.

1856 (1 holograph sheet, in 1856 hand, recto); the plot, in three parts, from 1875 (3 holograph sheets, recto).

- Documents held at the Bibliothèque Historique of the city of Paris: notebook 17 [*carnet 17*], consisting of reading notes (20 holograph sheets dealing with the planned text, 10 of which are recto/verso).
- A manuscript held by a private collector (who insists on anonymity): the Laporte manuscript, that is, the second version of the definitive manuscript (27 holograph sheets, recto).

This survey (reduced here to its minimal specifications) gives a fairly typical image of the manuscript dossier of a Flaubert work. For a text of about forty pages in the current editions, there are more than three hundred pages (in general, 220 by 340 mm.) of avant-texte. For other writers, the constituted dossier may be entirely different, either because working techniques are different (for example, a dossier may have no documentary notes, or the rough drafts may be reduced to one, two, or three versions, etc.) or because the dossier has more or less significant gaps (certain documents destroyed, lost, or not available). Besides this, some dossiers offer—though this does not make them deficient—the characteristic of having very few handwritten documents. In the case of Balzac's last works, for example, geneticists have little to analyze other than the "corrected proofs," that is, the evolution of the text as it was being printed. Indeed, genetic research has proven that as Balzac progressed in the *Comédie humaine*, he tended to replace rough drafts and manuscripts with series of proof corrections. He wrote and provided the printer with a schematic rough draft that, once printed, became the object of various additions before being printed and transformed again until the series of proofs reached a state that Balzac deemed satisfactory. In a case like this, the dossier is constituted when one has managed to gather all the proofs together (from five to twenty versions). This set of printed and hand-corrected manuscripts evokes rather directly what draft documents [*documents de rédaction*] are today: typed manuscripts, whether or not they include handwritten corrections. Textual genetics unhesitatingly construes all draft documents as relevant to "manuscript analysis," whatever their medium and technical mediation may be. This includes cassette tapes on which an author has orally fixed a "rough draft" and computer disks on which the progressive development of a text is stored.

2. Organizing the Draft Documents

Several categories therefore appear in a constituted dossier and from these the geneticist will separate out the "draft documents," a set composed of outlines, plots, and drafts that represents the central research element.

This category of manuscripts can provide (in a more or less complete and continuous manner) an analyzable image of the mediations of writing by which the author carries the work forward from the initial to the definitive version of the text. To succeed, genetic analysis requires classification and transcription. Yet, usually before it can even reach that point, the set of documents must first be reorganized. Indeed, it happens rather often (for technical reasons that will be discussed under the third heading, "Specifying and Classifying") that these manuscripts have been bound together, and thus fixed, in an unsatisfactory form. The problem is not yet how to classify them but how to "arrange" them according to a general, teleological principle, and this means performing a two-part reorganization. First, an initial approximation of the relative genetic situations among the different elements of the group "draft documents" must be made. At first glance, how do the different categories of manuscripts (outlines, scenarios, rough drafts) follow each other along the hypothetical axis of genesis? It is understood that this arrangement must be carefully reviewed at a later time and that for the moment the problem is one of sketching the broad lines of a provisional organization. Finding an outline does not guarantee that one has grasped the starting point of the genesis. It happens rather often that an outline—far from being the first element—is only a way for the author to sum things up, that is, to summarize the work done during the draft process. (This is often the case, for example, with Flaubert.)

The second aspect of the reorganization—the most important in this second phase—consists of arranging the elements of the rough drafts themselves. At first, one must not attempt to orient this still-formal arrangement along the genetic axis. Rather, one must simply align it with a teleological principle, the problem being to relate each draft page to the definitive text while acting as if all the drafts were aiming for that result alone. It is clear that in many cases this teleological principle will falsify the perspective. An author may not even decide upon the focus of the definitive text until very late in the writing process, after working for a long time on passages that have no place in the final project. Such a problem cannot be resolved at this level of analysis and must be deferred until the genetic classification; thus geneticists will proceed for the moment as if the teleological arrangement were sufficient. Partially deciphering rough draft pages (by visual survey—top, center, bottom of the page), they will, as precisely as possible, assign them places relative to the definitive text. A given page of the rough draft will contain in embryonic form the elements contained, for example, on pages 10, 11, and 12 of the printed text; another page of the rough draft will present a passage relative to page 10, etc. Again, at this point the analysis will not try to account for divergent contents such as paragraphs or passages missing from the definitive text that the author includes at first but later removes. Once this job of teleological arrangement has been completed, geneticists can align each page (and more precisely each paragraph) of the final text with a variable number of pages (or page fragments) of rough draft. One page of the printed text will have been worked out on something like five pages of rough draft, another on eight pages, etc. To produce the most efficient teleological arrangement, it is practical for geneticists to refer to the most "spacious" editions of their final texts and to break up that text paragraph by paragraph and sometimes even sentence by sentence.

Once this arrangement has been completed, it is possible to redistribute all the rough draft pages by groups corresponding to segments on the axis of the printed text. Still, although a segment allows us to group the rough-draft versions, nothing yet allows us to define the order in which these versions succeeded each other in the writing process. To discover this, it is necessary to move from arranging to classifying.

3. Specifying and Classifying Rough Drafts

Once we have constituted the dossier and arranged the rough drafts teleologically, we have a first description for each page of rough draft. In fact, we now have two descriptions, a material one and a teleological one that follows the pagination of the definitive text. These two descriptions are the results of the two first phases of analysis, and with refinements they make possible a tabular recapitulation that is not a true genetic classification but is a static classification of all the givens.

3a. Official Numbering of the Folios

The first classification is made in the order that the dossier itself suggests, according, when possible, to the official numbering affixed on the sheets by the library where the manuscripts are kept. Each sheet possesses a number that allows one to identify that particular page in a set of manuscripts: the page with this number is considered the *recto,* and the other side the *verso.* One can therefore relocate any document in a dossier by identifying it with this number, and one speaks not of pages but of *folios.* In this way, all the rough drafts of "La Légende de saint Julien l'Hospitalier," held at the Département des Manuscrits in the Bibliothèque Nationale under the general heading B.N. N.A.F. 23 663-2, comprise seventy-three sheets numbered from 408 to 480, all written on recto and verso with the exception of 450 verso (f. 450v), which is blank. This set of rough drafts therefore comprises one-hundred-and-forty-three written pages numbered in this order: 408, 408v, 409, 409v, 410, 410v, etc.

Of course, this official numbering is often arbitrary. It does not determine a logical order but gives a means of unimpeachable formal identification. Thus folio 409, just cited, is identifiable and will not be confused with folio 410 (which has some of the same content). Yet, conversely, nothing proves that it precedes folio 409v (the verso of the same sheet) or folio 410 in any logical or chronological sense (and, in fact, analysis proves that they follow each other only formally). For the most part, large public libraries have rationalized their numbering in dossiers by gathering sets of manuscripts together by genre: in general, we find the definitive manuscript gathered in one ordered and continuous series, the rough drafts in another, the documentary notes in a third, etc. Yet even with the greatest critical vigilance, it is not rare that, perhaps for material reasons, the person in charge was not able to number the folios systematically. An author may have used one sheet of paper to outline one part of the work but at another moment in the writing process used the other side of the same sheet for the rough draft of another portion of the text. It is clear that since the recto of a folio is materially connected to the verso, the choice must be made to place this sheet somewhere—yet it is arbitrary whether to place it with the "rough drafts" or the "outlines." Even worse, at the moment when the curator has to make this decision, nothing indicates which side of the sheet was really the author's recto. Perhaps it was the partial outline, perhaps the rough draft? In short, the official numbering (folio number with the recto/verso designation) does not provide a classification, but rather a formal identification of the dossier's elements placed in a more or less homogeneous series. It is nonetheless an indispensable principle of identification since it offers researchers a common and indisputable code.

3b. Static Classification

Thus the job of classification begins with the attempt to tabularize the characteristics of each folio's rough drafts according to the official numbering. This first classification is static in the sense that it does not offer a hypothesis about the logical and chronological evolution of the rough drafts. Each folio, identified by the official, "external" numbering, is therefore described in terms of its material characteristics, and to this is added, when necessary, both the folio's "internal" numbers (handwritten by the author) and the teleological identification of the fragments of definitive text to which it is related. Finally, identifying the type completes and refines the static classification; it amounts to evaluating the approximate stage to which each folio belongs in the evolution of the writing process.

If teleological identification makes it apparent that several different folios of rough drafts may be aligned with the same fragment of definitive text, then identifying the type consists of grouping together those six folios according to whether they belong to this or that phase of the textual development. The group that appears to be the furthest from the definitive result is distinguished, for example, from the group that approaches it perceptibly and from the group that culminates in the manuscript. Types of rough drafts vary considerably (in number and nature) according to writers' diverse writing practices and, for the same writer, according to the specific work under consideration. It even happens rather frequently that writing practices evolve because of the demands produced by the writing of a specific work. In that case, it is necessary to create categories on the spot that are appropriate for the processes being studied. A writer such as Gustave Flaubert, justly famous for the breadth and duration of his writing process, possessed rough drafts that were particularly developed, and it was not rare for one page of his definitive manuscript to require the mediation of ten or more folios of rough drafts with different versions. In such a case, to determine the *types* one must specify the phases of textual development. Flaubert had five: the initial scenario, the developed scenarios, the sketch-drafts, the corrected fair copies, and the definitive fair copy. If we accept that the first scenario (and the initial outline when it exists) and the definitive clear copy (or definitive manuscript) do not belong, strictly speaking, to the group "rough drafts," then each folio will therefore belong to one of three intermediate types: developed plot, sketch-draft, or corrected fair copy. This specification is essentially a first genetic evaluation, but it remains relatively imprecise because fairly often in the rough drafts, for one page of definitive text, there exist one, two, or three developed plots, two or three sketch-drafts, and two or three corrected fair copies. Once this succession of phases has been grasped, at least approximately, the internal succession of each phase remains to be determined. That is the essential objective of the genetic classification—to present the rough draft folios in the order they were developed.

3c. Genetic Classification

To reclassify all the rough drafts according to the operational logic proper to the writing process, geneticists compare the static classification with the results obtained by exhaustively deciphering the folios (particularly results concerning the relative classification of folios of the same type). This task, which represents the central objective of all research in textual genetics, is pursued throughout all the analyses and can only make progress and become conclusive if it parallels the discoveries provided by completely elucidating the manuscripts: upon this scheme rests the possibility of establishing an avant-texte of the work, that is, a synthetic reading that follows the order of genesis. Unlike the initial static description, genetic classification is characteristically dynamic. The general idea (when the draft dossier is not too incomplete) is to fill out a synoptic table with two sets of coordinates. The vertical side of the table provides the axis of definitive text according to the sequence of sentences, paragraphs, chapters, and other parts of the printed work. Vertically, therefore, the table begins at the top with the first words of the text and extends downward, segment by segment (depending on the text, segments may be sentences, paragraphs, or several paragraphs) until the last phrase of the fixed, revised work.

The horizontal axis of the table will give the genesis for each segment; from left to right, one will arrange the paradigm of different successive versions of the same fragment (this is the axis of similarity). The final result will therefore consist of a table showing simultaneously the genetic organization of the rough drafts according to the order of the definitive text (from top to bottom) and the different strata of the writing process (from left to right). At the far left side of the table appears the original folio—for example, the first scenario—which is followed, from left to right, and in the chronological order of their writing, by the developed plots, the sketch-drafts, and the corrected fair copies, ending up, at the far right of the table, with the corresponding folio in the definitive manuscript and the corresponding segment in the printed text (pagination—paragraph—phrase).

Thus, to give an example borrowed from the genetic classification of the rough drafts mentioned above, a section of the synoptic table provides, for the genetic evolution of what will result in the fifteenth page of the first edition of the text (Charpentier, 1877), the paradigm figured in the table below.

Initial scenario	*Developed scenarios*	*Sketch-drafts*	*Fair copies*	*Definitive manuscript*	*Printed text*
SI	SD 1, 2, 3	EB 1, 2, 3	MN 1, 2	MD	Page
SI 492	SD1 SD2 SD3 408v 415v 418	EB1 EB2 EB3 EB4 423v 421v 422 421	MN1 MN2 420v 479v	MD 36	p. 15

As one may imagine, perfecting such a table presupposes a considerable number of verifications and corrections, including the very latest results of deciphering and transcription.

4. Deciphering and Transcription

In textual genetics, deciphering accompanies each stage of research, from the first contact with a new manuscript dossier to the last corrections of detail in the edition and the critical study. To constitute a dossier and to authenticate, identify, specify, and classify its elements presupposes, to varying degrees, localized, partial, or exhaustive recourse to deciphering. Rapid explorations of the folios, precise forays into the depths of the rough drafts, continuous deciphering of draft documents: geneticists spend the largest amount of research time reading the manuscripts, becoming familiar not only with the handwriting and its internal codes, but also with the way the author appropriates the medium. Authors individualize themselves by their form of writing, their particular use of abbreviations, their personal way of using the material space of the pages they write on, and their manner of progressively organizing the growing set of written pages.

To read or to decipher is to reduce the illegible to the legible (using the appropriate technical and theoretical means), but it is also to reconstitute (on a given folio, or from one folio to another) the capricious and unpredictable line of a microchronology of writing. Often the line is broken by cross-outs and suppressions or unsettled by a juxtaposition or divergence of additions . . . sometimes the very space is clogged by several rounds of corrections.

4a. Reducing the Illegible

As for deciphering, the current ambitions of textual genetics no longer have anything in common with the evaluations offered by ancient manuscript explorers. Their almost unanimous habit of merely listing variants of the definitive manuscript inspired excessive prudence in most of them. Often, when it became necessary to try to discover something in the rough drafts (which were then called "sketches"), it led them to give up. In famous critical editions, it was not rare to find on this subject, in the chapter "Sketches of the Work," some acknowledgment of total impossibility: "Sketches absolutely undecipherable . . . illegible not only because of cross-outs but also because it is almost impossible to restore the sequence and because there are too many gaps" (Dumesnil in Flaubert, *Trois contes*). Coming from one of the most eminent Flaubert critics, this judgment dealt with the same 143 pages that have been chosen as an example for this essay—the rough drafts of "La Légende de saint Julien l'Hospitalier." Such an initial admission of failure is all the more interesting because it gives us a way to gauge the stakes of deciphering. It is not just a difficult reading process, sometimes requiring a magnifying glass. Above all, it is a work of reconstitution that, as Dumesnil sensed, must (and can only seriously) be done alongside a classification process that allows for the evaluation of the continuous or discontinuous character of the draft documents. Classification and deciphering are research operations that complement each other to a great extent. Deciphering provides the hypotheses that are indispensable for restoring (by internal criticism) an order in the writing process, and the provisional classification that results from it (and relies, perhaps, on the external criticism of authors' numbering) allows most of the apparently insoluble problems of deciphering to be solved. Deciphering illegible portions in turn offers new elements (of internal criticism) that refine hypotheses and permit more precise classification. Of course, this give-and-take demands much patience and imagination, but it is not without profit. The manuscripts that the critic deemed "indecipherable," impossible to classify, and plagued with too many gaps are a good example. Recent genetic analysis has allowed us to demonstrate that they did not have gaps and were not discontinuous; deciphering them has allowed us to reduce the illegibilities to a negligible proportion (3 to 4 percent). From the general classification of the rough drafts has emerged a perfectly clear image of the complex but quite logical and continuous way Flaubert managed his draft documents. Since the classification provides the key to the author's writing technique, in this case we might say that it solved the problem of deciphering the illegible.

If Dumesnil and his contemporaries were not able to decipher these manuscripts, it is because they were mistaken about the general structure of the rough drafts. Indeed, at first glance this group of manuscripts presents a mysterious characteristic: over half of the folios are crossed out with a large cross covering the whole page. This characteristic allowed critics to believe that Flaubert had written two successive sketches. Hypothesizing that the crossed-out folios represented the first version, critics concluded that the set of uncrossed-out folios contained the second sketch. (Dumesnil affirmed that there were "two absolutely indecipherable sketches of this story.") Yet the two-sketch hypothesis was incorrect: Flaubert did not write his text from start to finish before starting over. He wrote fragment by fragment, following the order and suggestions of his first scenario. After deciding to write a given passage, he produced five, six, or seven versions that enabled him to reach a definitive result—a very repetitive process.

How exactly did Flaubert write? First, at intervals on a blank folio, he put markers of the plot fragment that he wished to develop. Once the whole page was marked with these rudiments of narrative logic, he began filling the large interlinear spaces with passages that amplified and linked the initial suggestions together, a process that further developed those suggestions. His technique of recopying remained the basic principle of the text's growth. After editing each folio, Flaubert recopied it, removing erasures and integrating additions. As soon as this was done (and often even during the recopying), a new round of erasures and additions began. Yet once he had recopied the preceding version, he had no more need of it and, to keep things clear, he crossed it out at once with a large cross. This explains why there are so many crossed-out folios. As the writing proceeded, Flaubert crossed out the rough draft folios whose most developed forms he recopied as fair copies; this permitted him to ignore the previous states of the text. To understand the crosses is to understand the dynamic of repetition that animated the whole genesis; for the geneticist, this dynamic helps solve the enigma of undecipherables. The repetitive procedure by which Flaubert recopied his corrected versions one after the other gives the manuscript reader a precious means of regressive and progressive reading. A given erasure, rendered virtually illegible by the thickness of the ink stain, becomes clear if it is aligned with the immediately previous textual state where the suppressed part was written clearly. Conversely, an interlinear addition so faint that it is almost impossible to decipher always finds itself clearly integrated in the next state of the text.

At first a hypothesis, but subsequently verified, this repetitive dynamic (which is not unique to Flaubert) gives to internal criticism (criticism of the contents of a writing process) a very safe criterion by which to overcome the apparent illegibility of certain folios. It also allows critics to establish unambiguously the genetic sequences that allow for biaxial classification. And this is why the task of gradually perfecting the classification is inseparable from the tasks of deciphering and transcription. Analyzing the Flaubert manuscripts makes it clear that the formula of repetitive writing simultaneously complicates the appearance of documents and gives the key to their elucidation.

4b. Transcription

Transcription is the clear (and publishable) transposition of deciphered, "restored" manuscripts and their major characteristics. It is accomplished thanks to a code that allows the situation (linear, interlinear, marginal, etc.) to appear along with the status (written, added, crossed out, added and then crossed out, etc.) of each folio's contents. Because of the relatively recent character and diversity of its objects, textual genetics has not yet defined a common code for all transcriptions. While harmonizing the current codes remains an unrealized objective, it is already certain that a unified code would have to adapt to the very diverse demands placed on it by different manuscripts. Yet besides the problem of its ability to represent faithfully all the modalities of a writing process, the transcription code also always raises the question of readership. Must the fixed results of deciphering remain scientific documents reserved for specialists, or can they be made more widely accessible? In this second hypothesis—which appears to be much more productive—shouldn't a good transcription code be both efficient and subtle? Experience has proven that certain very simplified codes allow complex manuscripts to be made directly readable without compromising the exactness of deciphering. Current efforts at harmonization are oriented in that direction.

The example of transcription proposed in the following pages (see the table, draft documents, and illustration) uses a code with only nine conventional signs.[4]

Transcription code with 9 conventional signs

Italics	everything written by the author
Roman, in parentheses	all marks added by the transcriber for clarification (especially for indicating the placement of a folio's marginal additions)
< >	interlinear additions
~~xxx~~	crossed out, erased, blotted
~~<xxxx>~~	added, then crossed out
<~~xxxxx~~>	crossed out within an interlinear addition
" "	marginal addition
(?) in roman	probable but hypothetical transcription
(illeg.)	illegible word

Transcribed below with the help of this code is draft document folio 492 from the manuscript dossier cited in this article: Flaubert, "La Légende de saint Julien l'Hospitalier" (B.N. N.A.F. 23 663-2). This is the first scenario for the first part of the work:

(A stroke of the pen crosses the upper half of the folio diagonally until "How the taste for hunting comes upon him"; that paragraph is crossed out by seven pen strokes.)

I

Jamais il n'y eut meilleurs parents. ni d'enfant mieux élevé que le petit Julien.

Ils habitaient un chateau, sur une montagne boisée, ensemble dans le paysage.– enceinte, tours, jardin, verger, mail, chapelle, pigeonnier etc. Le tout ~~dans~~ peu fortifié, & dans une enceinte de haies d'épines. vue en pente & d'un seul coup d'œil comme un plan. aspect doux (?) *un <e> ~~homme~~ sentinelle sur la courtine. mais inutile.*

Le père de Julien. <pelisse> costume et occupations <apaise les querelles de ses voisins>

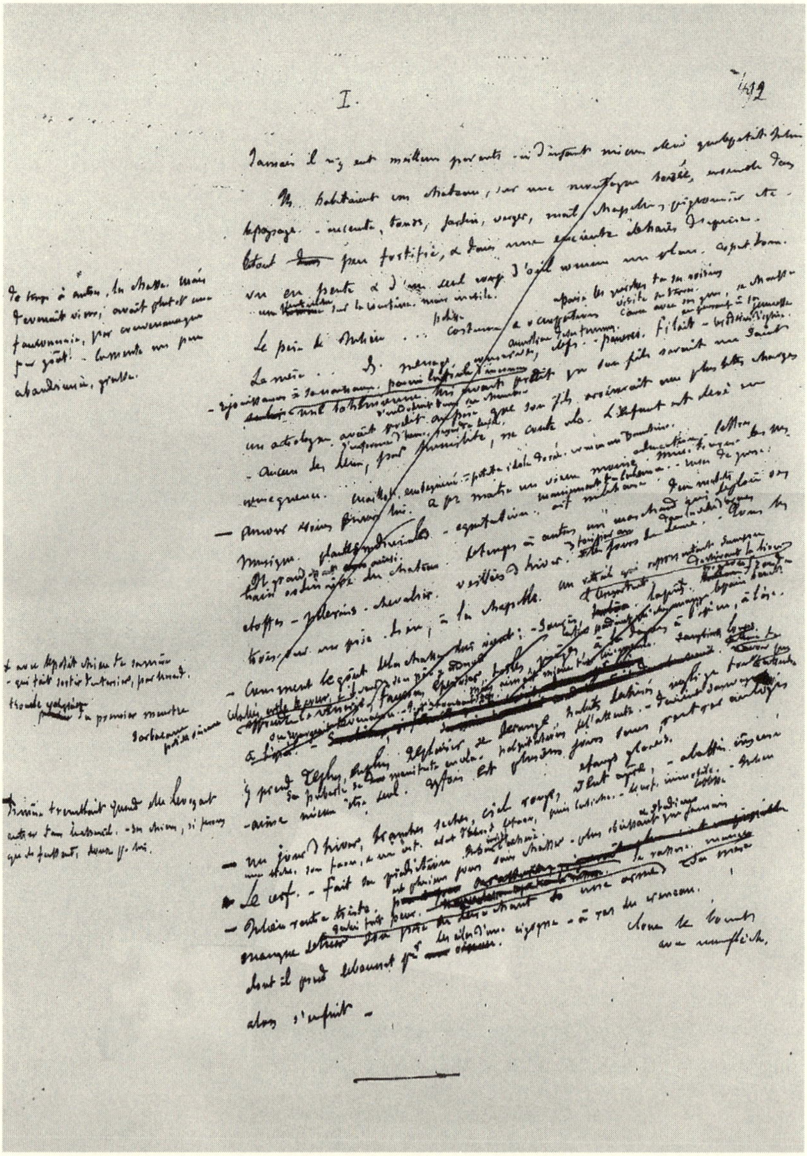

Figure 2. Gustave Flaubert, "La Légende of saint Julien l'Hospitalier." BN N.A.F. 23 663-2, f. 492. Courtesy of the Bibliothèque Nationale de France.

<visite ses terres.> <cause avec ses gens. se chauffe> <en pensant à sa jeunesse> "(à gauche*) De temps à autre, la chasse. mais devenait vieux, avait plutot une fauconnerie, par convenance que par goût. La meute un peu abandonnée, grasse."*

La mère. . . & ménage, conserves, clefs.–pauvres <au milieu de ses femmes> filait–broderies d'église. <– réjouissances à sa naissance. parmi la foule d'inconnus> ~~au lit~~(?) *une bohémienne. <s'introduit dans sa chambre–> lui avait predit que son fils serait un saint un astrologue : <s'informa d'heures–regarda le ciel> avait prédit au père que son fils arriverait aux plus hautes charges*

– Aucun des deux, par humilité, ne conte cela. L'enfant est elevé en consequence.
– Amour & soins envers lui <maillot, embeguiné. petite idole dorée. comme un Bambino.> A pr maître un vieux moine <éducation, lettres>. miniatures.–les ms. musique. plantes médicinales–équitation. art militaire <maniement de la lance.–ruses de guerre> <Il grandissait [illis.] *ainsi.>*

train ordinaire du chateau. de temps à autres un marchand <deux mulets> qui déploie ses etoffes.–pèlerins. chevaliers. veillées d'hiver <3 fois par an> les jours de dîme. <dans la salle d'armes>. Tous les trois sur un prie-dieu, à la chapelle. Un vitrail qui représentait Samson <déchirant le lion> <il le regardait>

– Comment le goût de la chasse lui vient : souris ~~la tue~~ <la tue pendant qu'elle mange le pain bénit> lapins "(à gauche, en bas) *avec le petit chien de sa mère qui fait sortir du terrier, par hasard" ~~plaisir~~ <trouble voluptueux> du premier meurtre." "Sarbacane, petits oiseaux" ~~hibou?~~ <pigeon> fronde. <Cela lui enfle le coeur, & il veut> apprendre la vénerie, <son père ~~s'y adonne~~> faucon, épervier, toiles, pièges, à la dague, à l'épieu, à l'arc, à l'épée. ~~ses chiens, si féroces qu'ils soient, doux pr lui~~ ~~sa mère tremblait quand il entrait dans le chenil~~ <on regorgait de venaison –. J. n'y touchait pas. Mais aimait mieux tuer lui-même.> ~~<sangliers>~~ <loups> <pleure de n'avoir pu l'atteindre>* (fin du fragment barré de 7 traits)
Y prend de plus en plus de plaisir, se derange, habits dechirés, neglige tout <sa puberté se ~~d...~~ manifeste en cela–palpitations de l'attente.–devient sauvage.> "(à gauche en bas*) Sa mère tremblait quand elle le voyait entrer dans le chenil.–Ses chiens, si féroces qu'ils fussent, doux pr lui.>*"

– aime mieux être seul. Qqfois est plusieurs jours sans rentrer au logis.
–un jour d'hiver, branches seches, ciel rouge, vent âpre, <etangs glacés>,–abattis insensé. <une biche, son faon, & un cerf. abat d'abord le faon, puis la biche.–le cerf immobile.–Julien le blesse>
– Le cerf.—fait sa prédiction. Julien <irrité> l'achève.
– Julien rentre triste. ~~peu à peu se rassure, n'y croit plus. c'est impossible~~ <est plusieurs jours sans chasser–plus obéissant <& studieux> que jamais> manque de tuer son père n décrochant ~~so~~ une arme <ça lui fait peur> <~~Une incantation [?] le prêtre le rassure~~> <se rassure.> <manque>–sa mère dont il prend le bonnet pr ~~un oiseau~~ <les ailes d'une cigogne>

– à ras du creneau. <cloue le bonnet avec une flèche.> alors s'enfuit.

I

There had never been better parents, nor a child better raised than little Julian.

They lived in a castle, on a forested mountain, together in the countryside.–the enclosure, towers, garden, vineyards, walkways, chapel, pigeonhouse etc. The whole ~~in~~ not very fortified, & in an enclosure of thorny hedges. view of a slope & in one glance as on a map. pleasing appearance (?) a ~~*man*~~ *sentinel on the rampart. but unnecessary.*

Julian's father . . . <fur cloak> dress and occupations <calms the quarrels of his neighbors> <visits his lands> <talks with his people, warms himself> <thinking of his youth> "(to the left) *From time to time, hunting. yet was becoming old, kept a falconhouse, more out of tradition than taste. The hounds a little neglected, fat.*"

The mother . . . & household, preserves, keys.–the poor <surrounded by her women> *spun–church embroidery. <– revelries at his birth. among a crowd of unknown people>* ~~*at bedside*~~(?) *a gypsy. <enters his room–> had foretold that his son would be a saint an astrologer: <asked about the hour–looked at the sky> had predicted to the father that his son would reach the highest office.*

–Neither of the two, because of humility, recount that. the child is raised accordingly.
–Love & care for him <vest, bonneted. a little golden idol. like a Bambino.> Has old monk fr teacher
<education, letters>. miniatures–manuscripts. music. medicinal plants–horse-riding. military arts <use of the lance, war strategy> <he was growing up (illeg.) *this way.>*

ordinary routine of the castle. from time to time a merchant <two mules> who shows his wares.–pilgrims, knights, winter watches. <3 times a year> tithing day. <in the weapon room>. All three on a prie-dieu, in the chapel. A stained-glass window representing Samson <destroying the lion> <he looked at it>

–How the taste for hunting comes upon him: mouse ~~*kills it*~~ *<kills it while it eats the communion bread> rabbits* "(to the left, at the bottom) *with his mother's little dog which by chance flushes them from their burrow"* ~~*pleasure*~~*<confused excitement> of the first kill." Pea-shooter, little birds"* ~~*owl?*~~ *<pigeon> sling. <this fills his heart, & he wants> to learn venery, <his father*~~*is devoted to it*~~*> falcon, hawk, nets, traps, with a dagger, with a lance, with a bow, with a sword.*~~*– his dogs, as ferocious as they are, gentle w him his mother would tremble when he entered the kennels*~~ *< an extreme abundance of venison –. J. didn't touch it. But preferred killing it himself.>* ~~*<wild boars>*~~ *<wolves> <cries because he could not kill it>* (end of fragment crossed out with 7 strokes)
Takes more and more pleasure in it, mind becomes deranged, habits broken, neglects everything <his puberty is ~~*d...*~~ *this manifests–palpitations of expectation.–becomes wild.>* "(to the left at the bottom) *His mother trembled when she saw him enter the kennels. His dogs, as ferocious as they were, gentle w him.>*"

–prefers being alone. Smtimes is several days without returning to lodging.
–one winter day, dry branches, red sky, bitter wind, <frozen ponds>,–mad slaughtering. <a doe, its fawn, & a stag. First kills the fawn, then the doe.–the stag is immobile.–Julian wounds it.>
–The stag.–makes its prediction. Julian <irritated> kills it.
–Julian returns saddened. ~~*slowly reassures himself, no longer believes it. it's impossible*~~ *<goes several days without hunting—more obedient < & studious> than ever> almost kills his father while taking down a weapon <this scares him> <*~~*An incantation (?) the priest reassures him*~~*> <reassures himself.> <nearly>–his mother whose bonnet he mistakes fr* ~~*a bird*~~ *<the wings of a stork>*
–at the top of the battlement. <nails the bonnet with an arrow.> then runs away.

Genetic Editions and the Genesis of the Work

Manuscript analysis therefore claims to reconstruct, in various forms depending upon the texts studied, as exact a prehistory of the text as possible. From this point of view, the final goal of research projects in textual genetics is, almost indissociably, to enable studies of genesis—by establishing critical avant-textes of the works—and to make clear and ordered transcriptions of genetic documents public. Geneticists are well placed to be the first critical users of the material they analyze, yet they also have the scientific objective of making the results of their analysis available to many critical readings. To this extent, the genesis of the work is merely a heuristic dimension—inside the work and next to it—that is open to any theoretical reading occasioned by writing in a nascent state.

This means that the essential objective of textual genetics is to produce genetic editions. Two basic kinds are possible: one can try to publish either an exhaustive collection of a work's manuscripts or an edition of the text enriched by an important selection of genetic documents.

1. Exhaustive Genetic Editions

The project of publishing the draft documents of a text in extenso (outlines, scenarios, rough drafts, manuscripts, etc.) does not seem realistic, given the actual conditions of publishing and the existing norms in the marketplace of books, except in the case of short works (short stories, novellas, poems, etc.) that do not have very developed genetic material. When it is feasible, two publishing formulas may be adopted: the diplomatic edition, which consists of giving a transcription of each folio and reproducing as clearly and faithfully as possible the topological aspect of the document. This is the formula chosen by Giovanni Bonaccorso for his edition of "Un Coeur simple." In this case the reader has available, with a more or less complex code of usage, the whole of the genetic dossier deciphered and reclassified; the whole is clarified by genetic studies proposing different interpretive paths for establishing the avant-texte. Another kind of diplomatic edition has recently been prepared by Jeanne Goldin. Treating a well-known passage from *Madame Bovary*, she gives, in readable (typographical) form, an "identical" reproduction of the original rough drafts (including the blots of ink). The indisputable advantage of this presentation is that it requires almost no code; however, a nonspecialist may be disconcerted by the density that this kind of reproduction inherits from the original.

The teleological edition is a second imaginable formula for exhaustively presenting draft documents, and it adopts a different strategy. It does not try to transcribe all the documents folio by folio, but instead tries to capture the genetic movement sequentially. This type of edition provides transcriptions of all the avant-textes leading to the definitive text: the complete series of successive versions of each paragraph of the final text is given in the order of its writing, from the first draft to the final manuscript. Such a publication explodes the unity of the folio and redistributes the transcriptions sequentially. The advantage of this formula is that it offers the nonspecialist reader an immediately available image of the genetic evolution for each moment of the text. On the other hand, teleological editions imply two other things: (1) that the genetic classifications on which they rest have been unambiguously demonstrated and (2) that their presentation of the avant-textes will allow readers to reconstitute—perhaps with the help of a biaxial table—both the unity of each folio and its relative place in the genetic development.

2. Editions Inspired by Genetic Criticism

Although exhaustive publications of manuscript dossiers are still rare, the contributions of textual genetics to the renewal of contemporary editions are now too numerous to count. In reality it is a mutation, one that affects not only the specialized milieu of critical and erudite editions but also, much more generally, a great number of new editions of literary texts. Thus numerous scholars from universities or the Centre National de la Recherche Scientifique (CNRS) have felt called upon to implement a new conception of textual editing in which the work's genetic dossier has a more and more important place. There, too, the strictly genetic publication (even partial and selective) of avant-textes still remains a rather rare publishing phenomenon. Some recent cases bear witness nonetheless to a positive evolution in this direction (Marcel Proust, *Matinée chez la princess de Guermantes,* genetic edition of a manuscript by Henry Bonnet and Bernard Brun, and Jules Romains, *Dossiers préparatoires des "Hommes de bonne volonté,"* the initial project and the elaboration of the first four volumes presented by Annie Angremy). Numerous editions with a large print run are also now starting to carve out a nonnegligible place for the genetic perspective of literary texts. Teams of researchers are attempting (in collections of the type Bibliothèque de la Pléiade, or even in pocket collections of the type Folio or Garnier-Flammarion) to forge a compromise between material demands (book dimensions, publication costs) and the new possibilities offered by publication, in appendix form, of a selection of unpublished draft documents of works. Among other works of this type, we must mention, for French literature of the nineteenth century, the editions of Zola (by Henri Mitterand), Balzac (under the direction of Pierre-Georges Castex),

Michelet (by Robert Casanova), Flaubert (notably by Claudine Gothot-Mersch for the collection Folio and by Guy Sagnes and Gothot-Mersch for the new Pléiade edition), Hugo (by Pierre Albouy, Jean Gaudon, and Jacques Seebacher), Nerval (by Claude Pichois), and Vigny (by André Jarry). For French works of the twentieth century, an important editing movement has begun to undertake genetic presentations of vast works: notably works of Céline (by Henri Godard), Giono (by Pierre Citron and Robert Ricatte), Proust (under the direction of Jean-Yves Tadié for the new Pléiade edition and Jean Milly for the Garnier-Flammarion Edition), and Sartre (by Michel Contat and Michel Rybalka). All these editions have in common the fact that they provide, parallel to the text, a genetic dossier that is as "meaningful" as possible. Of course, this can only be a very partial selection of draft documents because, even if the publisher accepts the hypothesis of an "important" dossier, it will always be within limits that materially exclude a real genetic evaluation (the draft dossier for a novel like Flaubert's *L'Éducation sentimentale* comprises 2,500 pages). So the obligation to choose and divide (in general about five or ten percent of available genetic material) sometimes makes it difficult to decide upon criteria. Yet by and large, and despite these material limits, something about the edition of literary texts is now irreversibly changing. Traditional procedures of presentation (and notably the apparatus of "variants") are progressively being abandoned to the benefit of a much more dynamic point of view that makes the logic of the avant-texte appear in its proper dimension. Since textual genetics is resolutely engaged in this transformation, editing is a natural space of application for it. This activity offers the added advantage of opening research up to the public and to the realities of contemporary reading.

Editions of letters represent a special phenomenon since the manuscripts do not appear to be independent from the epistolary objects—almost always handwritten—to be published. Even in this case, however, the demands for exactness and analysis seem to have evolved (taking, by the way, in the research sector, a lead of about a decade on recent developments in textual genetics). The control over original manuscripts (no longer retransmissions of preceding editions) and the demand for precise dating, for completeness, the restitution of punctuation, etc., have progressively transformed the conception of editions of letters, such as those of Honoré de Balzac (*Correspondance* and *Lettres à Mme Hanska,* editions established and presented by Roger Pierrot), George Sand (*Correspondance* by Georges Lubin, Garnier), and Gustave Flaubert (*Correspondance* by Jean Bruneau). Within this perspective, it has been possible, with the collaboration of different groups of researchers, for vast projects of re-editing (and editions of as yet unedited letters) to be undertaken. An example is the *Correspondance* of Zola (edited by Bard H. Bakker, Colette

Becker, Owen Morgan, and Henri Mitterand with the collaboration of Alain Pagès and Albert J. Salvan).

Organization and Perspectives for Research

Since a great portion of the studies in textual genetics emanates from the academic sector, it would be impossible to overstate the importance that the 1976 foundation by the CNRS of the Centre d'Analyse des Manuscrits (CAM)—transformed into a laboratory in 1982 under the name Institut des Textes et Manuscrits Modernes (ITEM)—has had on originating and developing these research projects. Growing out of work begun as early as 1968 by the "Heine team," this research structure developed very rapidly under the impetus of Louis Hay, who directed it until 1986. In 1987 the results of work undertaken at CAM were already sufficiently convincing for the writer Louis Aragon to donate all his manuscripts to the state on the condition that their scientific analysis be entrusted to that group. Today, ITEM acts as a coordinating, centralizing structure for some 120 researchers (mostly university-based) who work in the framework of about a dozen different teams.

Besides a specifically literary subset that includes programs of genetic study on the works of various authors (Heine, Joyce, Flaubert, Proust, Valéry) and programs of critical editions (Zola, Nerval, Sartre), ITEM comprises three transversal research programs (manuscripts and linguistics, manuscripts and genetic criticism, manuscripts and culture) and three operations of collective interest (computerized manuscript research, automatic writing analysis, codicology). This laboratory, equipped with a center for specialized documentation, represents an irreplaceable tool for a research that, essentially begun in France, is now developing internationally and being applied in more and more diversified sectors.

Textual genetics appears to be increasingly open to different sectors of cultural, technical, and scientific actuality. In a rather surprising way, for example, genetic studies have contributed to modifying the relations between creators and researchers. Since the end of the 1970s, several writers (for example, Louis Aragon, Francis Ponge, Claude Simon) have personally taken part in ITEM research. Others (for example, Michel Butor, Jean-Paul Sartre, Michel Tournier) have requested that research be done on their work. Paralleling literary studies, the genetic approach has initiated research projects in the arts (musicology, plastic arts, theater) and in other domains in which researchers must analyze written documents and study the processes of conception. Indeed, basically under the effect of interdisciplinary exchange, textual geneticists are broadening their objects of research to include every phenomenon of textual and genetic production. The only limiting condition is that these phenomena must be concretely analyzable in manuscript form. Thus a certain number of researchers have been tempted to try their work methods on manuscript dossiers from the histories of ideology or science, insisting on the possibility of modeling the processes of conception that have produced "new" things in those fields. They start with the hypothesis that these phenomena of rupture can be tracked, at least partially, in terms of the effects of writing in a nascent state.

1. Automatic Analysis of Writing

An interdisciplinary program bringing together ITEM and the Duffieux laboratory in Besançon is working on using optic imagery to analyze manuscripts. Combining the resources of a laser beam, a hologram, a computer, and some mathematical models, this research has made it possible to bring scientifically rigorous answers to fundamental problems in textual genetics. It has become possible to detect forgeries, determine whether a manuscript has been written by one person only, determine whether it has been written in a continuous or discontinuous fashion, and follow the aging process of a given handwriting and thus date manuscripts in an automatic manner. The manuscripts of Heine, Claudel, and Nerval have been analyzed, and the results of this optical/numerical treatment have enriched, and sometimes modified, the understanding that literary critics had had of their works. Methods range from optical/numerical hybrid treatment for large samples (for example, a page) to computerized syntheses of tracings for small samples (for example, a single letter, sets of letters, or a signature). Hybrid treatment consists of passing a manuscript's microfilm negative through a homogeneous light: the resulting diffraction image, containing all the individual characteristics of the writing, is then captured by an electronic camera, digitized, and numerically analyzed.

2. Computerization of Manuscript Research

The transformations that occur during a given genesis are often so numerous and complex that a direct approach is useful only for a small corpus. The tasks of memorizing and analyzing these transformations, however, lend themselves admirably to the abilities of computers, whatever the size of the textual corpus. By schematizing these genetic operations along two axes, one paradigmatic (for textual variants) and one syntagmatic (for sequences of text), it has been possible to construct several software programs capable of generating the first "automatic editions" of manuscripts and the first "substitution dictionaries." The current objective is to complexify the initial model and to introduce necessary topological, chronological, and other parameters into it to make exhaustive manuscript analyses possible. From now on, much more than traditional editions, which are limited by size and logical means, computerized approaches appear to offer the best perspective for developing research on large textual samples; they should allow us to develop the basis for a real calculus in genetic matters. The direct approach used on smaller samples has already allowed us to imagine some models for quantitatively evaluating certain genetic phenomena (for example, a standard profile of the development of a draft process). The creation of databases large enough to exploit numerous genetic documents should culminate in the near future in a complete overhaul of studies of the "style," that is, the systematic calculation of transformations, and the structures of literary works. On the horizon as well, probably, are a large number of technological applications for systematic analyses of writing in general.

Source: "Vers une science de la littérature: L'Analyse des manuscrits et la genèse de l'œuvre." In *Encyclopaedia Universalis Symposium 1989.* Paris: Encyclopaedia Universalis, 1989. 466–76.

Works Cited

Anis, Jacques, ed. *Les Signifiants graphiques.* Special issue of *Langue Française* 59 (September 1983).

Balzac, Honoré de. *La Comédie humaine.* Ed. Pierre-Georges Castex et al. 12 vols. Paris: Gallimard, 1976–81.

———. *Correspondance.* Ed. Roger Pierrot. 5 vols. Paris: Garnier, 1960–69.

———. *Lettres à Madame Hanska.* Ed. Roger Pierrot. 4 vols. Paris: Bibliophiles de l'originale, 1967–71.

Barthes, Roland. "Le Texte." *Encyclopaedia Universalis,* vol. 15. 1973. 1013–17. "Theory of the Text." Trans. Ian McLeod. In *Untying the Text: A Post-Structuralist Reader,* ed. Robert Young. Boston: Routledge, 1981. 31–47.

Bellemin-Noël, Jean. "Reproduire le manuscrit, présenter les brouillons, établir un avant-texte." *Littérature* 28 (1977): 3–18.

——— *Le Texte et l'avant-texte: Les Brouillons d'un poème de Milosz.* Paris: Larousse, 1972.

Bonaccorso, Giovanni, ed. *Corpus Flaubertianum* 1. Paris: Les Belles Lettres, 1983.

Céline, Louis-Ferdinand. *Romans.* Ed. Henri Godard. Paris: Gallimard, 1974–88.

Charraut, Daniel, Jacques Duvernoy, and Louis Hay. "L'Analyse automatique de l'écriture." *La Recherche* 184 (January 1987): 49–59.

Debray Genette, Raymonde, ed. *Flaubert à l'oeuvre.* Paris: Flammarion, 1980.

Durry, Marie Jeanne. *Flaubert et ses projets inédits.* Paris: Librairie Nizet, 1950.

Espagne, Michel, Almuth Grésillon, and Catherine Viollet, eds. *Écriture et contraintes.* Special issue of *Cahier Heine* 3 (1984).

Flaubert, Gustave. *Bouvard et Pécuchet, avec un choix des scénarios du Sottisier, L'Album de la marquise et Le Dictionnaire des idees reçues.* Ed. Claudine Gothot-Mersch. Collection Folio. Paris: Gallimard, 1979.

———. *Correspondance.* Ed. Jean Bruneau. Pléiade ed. 4 vols. Paris: Gallimard, 1973–97.

———. *Œuvres complètes.* Ed. Claudine Gothot-Mersch and Guy Sagnes. Pléiade ed. Paris: Gallimard, 2001–

———. *La Tentation de saint Antoine.* Ed. Claudine Gothot-Mersch. Collection Folio. Paris: Gallimard, 1983.

———. *Trois contes.* Ed. René Dumesnil. Paris: Les Belles Lettres, 1957.

Fuchs, Catherine et al. *La Genèse du texte: Les Modèles linguistiques.* Paris: CNRS, 1982.

Genèse du texte. Special issue of *Littérature* 28 (December 1977).

Giono, Jean. *Œuvres romanesques complètes.* Ed. Robert Ricatte with Pierre Citron et al. Paris: Gallimard, 1971–83.

Goldin, Jeanne. *Les Comices agricoles de Gustave Flaubert.* 2 vols. Geneva: Droz, 1984.

Gothot-Mersch, Claudine. *La Genèse de "Madame Bovary".* Paris: José Corti, 1966.

Grésillon, Almuth, and Michael Werner, eds. *Leçons d'écriture: Ce que disent les manuscrits.* Paris: Minard, 1985.

Hay, Louis. "Eléments pour l'étude des manuscrits modernes." *Codicologica 1: Théories et principes.* Ed. A. Gruys and J. P. Gumbert. Leiden: E.J. Brill, 1976. 91–109.

———, ed. *Essais de critique génétique.* Paris: Flammarion, 1979.

——— et al. *Le Manuscrit inachevé: Écriture, création, communication.* Paris: CNRS, 1986.

Hay, Louis, and Jean Glenisson, eds. *Les Méthodes de laboratoire dans l'étude des manuscrits.* Paris: CNRS, 1984.

Hay, Louis, and Péter Nagy, eds. *Avant-texte, texte, après-texte.* Paris: CNRS; Budapest: Akadémiai Kiadó, 1982.

Herschberg-Pierrot, Anne. *Répertoire des manuscrits littéraires français (XIXe–XXe siècles).* Paris: Bibliothèque Nationale, 1985.

Hugo, Victor. *Œuvres complètes.* Ed. Jacques Seebacher with Guy Rosa, by the Groupe inter-universitaire de travail sur Victor Hugo. Paris: Laffont, 1985.

L'Inconscient dans l'avant-texte. Special issue of *Littérature* 52 (1983).

Jacquet, Claude, ed. *Genèse de Babel: Joyce et la création de "Finnegans Wake."* Paris: CNRS, 1986.

Journet, René, and Guy Robert. *Le Manuscrit des "Contemplations",* Paris: Les Belles Lettres, 1956.

Lebrave, Jean-Louis, and Almuth Grésillon, eds. *Manuscrits-Écriture, production linguistique.* Special issue of *Langages* 69 (March 1983).

Levaillant, Jean. *Anatole France.* Paris: Collège de France, 1955.

———, ed. *Ecriture et génétique textuelle: Valéry à l'oeuvre.* Lille: Presses Universitaires de Lille, 1982.

Michelet, Jules. *Œuvres complètes.* Vol. 20: *1866–1871: La Montagne, Nos fils, La France devant l'Europe, Articles.* Ed. Linda Orr, Françoise Puts, and Robert Casanova. Paris: Flammarion, 1987.

Nerval, Gérard de. *Œuvres complètes.* Ed. Jean Guillaume and Claude Pichois. Paris: Gallimard, 1984–93.

Pierrot, Roger. "Les Écrivains et leurs manuscrits: Remarques sur l'histoire des collections modernes." *Bulletin de la Bibliothèque Nationale* 4, 4 (1979): 165–77.

Proust, Marcel. *A la recherche du temps perdu.* Ed. Pierre Clarac et André Ferré. Paris: Gallimard, 1954.

———. *À la recherche du temps perdu.* Ed. Jean Milly, Bernard Brun, and Anne Herschberg-Pierrot. Paris: Flammarion, 1984–87.

———. *À la recherche du temps perdu.* Ed. Jean-Yves Tadié. Pléiade ed. Paris: Gallimard, 1999.

———. *Matinée chez la princesse de Guermantes: Cahiers du "Temps retrouvé".* Ed. Henri Bonnet and Bernard Brun. Paris: Gallimard, 1982.

Ricatte, Robert. *La Genèse de "La Fille Elisa".* Paris: Presses Universitaires de France, 1960.

Romains, Jules. *Les Dossiers préparatoires des "Hommes de bonne volonté".* Ed. Annie Angremy. Paris: Flammarion, 1983–87.

Sand, George. *Correspondance.* Ed. Georges Lubin. 25 vols. Paris: Garnier, 1964–91.

Sartre, Jean Paul. *Œuvres romanesques.* Ed. Michel Contat and Michel Rybalka, with Geneviève Idt and George H. Bauer. Paris: Gallimard, 1981.

Vigny, Alfred de. *Œuvres complètes.* Ed. François Germain and André Jarry. Paris: Gallimard, 1986–93.

Zola, Emile. *Carnets d'enquêtes: Une Ethnographie inédite de la France.* Ed. Henri Mitterand. Paris: Plon, 1987.

———. *Correspondance.* Ed. Bard H. Bakker with Colette Becker, Owen Morgan, Henri Mitterand et al. 10 vols. Montréal: Presses de l'Université de Montréal, 1978–95.

Further Works by the Author

de Biasi, Pierre-Marc. "Editing Manuscripts: Towards a Typology of Recent French Genetic Editions, 1980–1995." Trans. Helene Erlichson. *Text: An Interdisciplinary Annual of Textual Studies* 12 (1999): 1–30.

———. "Flaubert: Dynamique de la genèse." *Annali della Scuola Normale Superiore di Pisa: Classe di lettere e filosofia* Ser. 4 Quaderni 5 (1998, Quaderni 1): 87–102.

———. "Flaubert lecteur de Flaubert, ou la lecture endogénétique." *Le Letture / La lettura di Flaubert.* Ed. Liana Nissim. Milan: Cisalpino, 2000. 61–77.

———. *La Génétique des textes.* Paris: Nathan, 2000.

———. "Horizons for Genetic Studies." Trans. Jennifer A. Jones. *Word and Image* 13, 2 (April-June 1997): 124–34.

———. "Le Manuscrit spectaculaire: Réflexions sur l'esthétique hugolienne de la mise en page autographe." In *Hugo: De l'écrit au livre,* ed. Béatrice Didier and Jacques Neefs. Saint-Denis: Presses de l'Université de Vincennes, 1987. 199–217.

———. "Qu'est-ce qu'une rature?" In *Ratures et repentirs,* ed. Bertrand Rougé. Pau: Université de Pau, 1996. 17–47.

———. "What Is a Literary Draft? Toward a Functional Typology of Genetic Documentation." In *Drafts,* ed. Michel Contat, Denis Hollier, and Jacques Neefs. Special issue of *Yale French Studies* 89 (1996): 26–58.

Flaubert, Gustave. *Carnets de travail.* Ed. Pierre-Marc de Biasi. Paris: Balland, 1988.

———. *L'Éducation sentimentale: Histoire d'un jeune homme.* Ed. Pierre-Marc de Biasi. Paris: Seuil, 1993.

Chapter 5
Flaubert's "A Simple Heart," or How to Make an Ending: A Study of the Manuscripts

Raymonde Debray Genette

Since the early 1970s, Raymonde Debray Genette has been a Flaubert scholar and a chief proponent of narratological genetics. She has taught at the Université de Paris VIII and published numerous studies using genetic material to analyze narrative modes, figural language, and such structural components as the beginnings and endings of narratives. In 1979 she founded the still-thriving Flaubert research program at the Institut des Textes et Manuscrits Modernes.

In "Flaubert's 'A Simple Heart,' or How to Make an Ending: A Study of the Manuscripts," first published in 1984, Debray Genette characteristically sifts through a dozen avant-textual strata to examine one of literature's most recurring and complex narratological questions: when authors end their stories with familiar events like the death of the main character, how do they deal with well-known literary and cultural models? If, like Flaubert, they do not wish simply to affirm or echo the givens of their culture, if they wish instead to control those homogenizing forces or transform them in their creative work, then how do they do it?

Tracing Flaubert's negotiations with the models his culture provided as well as the ones he himself had previously written, Debray Genette paints an unexpected picture of the creative process. Rather than a fluid, dialectical method of invention, erasure, and reinvention, Flaubert's technique was one of extracting a text from preexisting and competing imagistic, linguistic, and narrative examples. Trying to write the death of Félicité's famously simple heart, Flaubert slowly made his ending by ignoring or integrating key elements from pagan, Christian, baroque, beatific, Romantic, mystic, scientific, saintly, and other stories and pictures of death.

As she reads and compares the avant-textes, Debray Genette manages to identify and diagnose some of the major narrative and stylistic blockages Flaubert faced as he wrote. She also shows how intimately interconnected these different orders of difficulty were for Flaubert and how the methods he used to overcome them were sometimes more obstinate than efficient. Near the end of his writing, stymied by a metaphor so hermetically conclusive that his whole text was asphyxiating, he tried to manipulate the meanings of his work through stylistic and syntactic rather than semantic forms.

By the end of this essay, we might suspect that some of Flaubert's famous experiments in prose—his play with tropes, ellipses, sound patterns, and the lengths of phrases—were really strategies of writing that helped delay and distract him from the ending. What is beyond suspicion, however, is that such trademark features of his writing as antiromanticism and impersonality were not the starting points but the end results of a long, laborious construction.

One could, and in a sense one must, assume that a textual study of a literary work, in part or as a whole, presents a coherent set of methodological and even theoretical problems and reflections. That is the spirit in which I am going to examine the series of manuscripts leading up to the final paragraph of "Un Coeur simple." A practical and theoretical study of this *excipit* inspires me, however, from the start to point out more divergences and deviations than identities.[1] The hazards of genetic evolution are not exactly the risks of the finished text, any more than the impasses of the first are the necessities of the latter.

It seems that no matter what stage of work they have reached, when writers try to end a story they always have the same goal. I wouldn't say that they try to recapitulate, "sum up," or put the finishing touches on what they have written. Rather, they simply try to signify that they have nothing left to say, that they cannot or do not wish to say anything else. In fact, an *incipit* is fundamentally different from an *excipit,* and all *incipit* studies fall prey to the same paradox: no matter how random it may be, an *incipit* always retains the character of being decisive and (in every sense) primordial. It is possible to reverse this paradox in the case of the *excipit* and say that no matter how programmed it may seem to be because of the beginning and the progress of the narrative, it nonetheless retains its arbitrary character—to the point where it can sometimes disappear, forcibly or by choice, without harming the reputation and the efficiency of the story (random examples: Urfé, Marivaux, Novalis, Stendhal). There are stories without tails, but none without heads or something headlike. Reversing the paradox, we see, makes it difficult to equate the functions of these two narrative extremities. Moreover, it designates the functional specificity of the *excipit*: it has a high probability of being programmatic, and yet it also concedes a good deal to arbitrariness or, more precisely, to diversity or even diversion.

This explains the fact that we find so many divergences between the developmental and the final states of the text, although the goal of both was the same. Readers are subjected to many different effects and are led down paths that writers, who have recourse to very diverse, seemingly freely chosen means, will never again find. This is the case for "Un Coeur simple." We will see that the banality and predictability of the final moment (the death of a character) authorizes certain gestational avatars: predicative and circumstantial scaffolding, invasion of internal models from Flaubert's own *œuvre,* visual models, ideological and cultural stereotypes, and numerous stylistic "tryouts," as if in simplicity great flourishes lay hidden. "Valincour's theorem" applies to this *excipit*: the worth of a paragraph is defined by the difference that remains after one subtracts its motivation from its function.[2] We will actually move from an overmotivated ending to one that is "plausible" or has "an implicit motivation" and that completes the general function.

Once again genetic study raises the ever-living question of the closure of the text (if not of all text). Here again, Barthes's "Where to begin?" does not exactly find its counterpart in "Where to end?" The text's structure has already been installed and has its range and maximum capacities. In their very conception, structural analyses take into account the ends of stories. But if in so doing they privilege the idea of closure, then they are using an idea of organism rather than organization: they favor the possible developments over the stoppages in a sequence. In a way, then, the assumption of a (or any) closure(s) frees one from fetishizing *the* closure as such.

Restricting ourselves to the classic narratives that are the forerunners of Flaubert's *Trois contes,* we might think that the most accomplished stories are the ones whose endings coincide with their main objectives.[3] It is then that the semantic effect (telling the ending) and the semiological effect (signifying the ending) meet, or rather combine together. Looking at "Un Coeur simple," we see that Flaubert, in the final text, did indeed tell the ending, although he used a euphemism: "she breathed her last."[4] He also signified the end of the narrative (later we will see the marks of this), but as Philippe Hamon indicates, he avoided the closure of meaning and thus the closure of the narrative.[5] Besides this, there is also a kind of willful asymmetry between, on the one hand, the *incipit* and the rest of chapter 1 and the *excipit* and what precedes it in chapter 5. The first chapter and its famous sentence—"For half a century, the good ladies of Pont-l'Évêque envied Mme Aubain her maidservant Félicité" (17)[6] [*Pendant un demi-siècle, les bourgeoises de Pont-l'Évêque envièrent à Mme Aubain sa servante Félicité*]—are uttered from the vantage point of a history still to come (despite the fact that Flaubert erased the dates "From 1810 to 1852"), and they paint the portrait of a servant, "a wooden woman functioning automatically" (18).[7] Félicité is an effective, invariable, and enviable object in every possible way. She is a finished object. Chapter 5, by contrast, evokes a particularly individualized subject brought to ultimate maturity through her experiences and the original way she takes control of her own death. One cannot say that the ending completes the beginning. It seems rather to know nothing of it, or, if one wishes to stress the asymmetry, to contradict it. The *incipit* multiplies the signs of closure while the *excipit* multiplies the signs of opening. (From this point of view, the three deaths that end the *Trois contes* are expansive deaths.) In the published narrative "Un Coeur simple," there is something, even *in fine*, that resists ordinary systems of closure.

This is even truer if we consider the avant-texte.[8] In general, compared with reading a final text, reading an avant-texte is a partial and piecemeal process, but it is also open-ended or even tentacular. As we have said, it is less predictable, and disruptions play a more essential role. We go from consistencies to resistances and from resistances to changes. To this general description may be added a particularity of the *excipit*. In practice, it is a place where diverse codes (among others, the ones Roland Barthes speaks of in *S/Z*) confront each other, codes that are themselves overdetermined by the narrative genre to which they belong. Stereotyped elements—as much social, aesthetic, and cultural as properly literary—tend to abound. They are productive only if they are refined and overcome or converted and integrated. The avant-texte we are considering is a good, one might say an exemplary, example of this. A final question remains, always of first importance and invoked as a last resort: that of the author's intentions. Despite what one might imagine, the experience of manuscripts allows us to be sure of these even less than published texts do, even when authors give instructions to themselves. The factory overpowers the factory-worker. Manuscripts show it well: writers are apprentices, and writing is their master.

This is what we will examine closely once the whole corpus has been presented.[9] There are twelve different documents: three plans or résumés (the word *résumé,* which in French means summary, does not necessarily mean a final stage for Flaubert), three scenarios, a subscenario, two rough drafts, two fair copies, and the copyist's manuscript. The word *scenario,* borrowed from Flaubert's correspondence, implies a writing in sequences, usually with an underlined title, made up of notations, with verbs usually in the present tense, and with Flaubert's directions to himself occasionally mixed in. Theoretically, the rough draft looks for syntax and style. The subscenario participates in both the scenario and in the rough draft. It is sometimes difficult to decide the order and the importance of the plans or résumés that are often written at the same time or after the scenarios and even the rough drafts. Yet we will see that for the *excipit* in question, there is no serious problem of classification.

Since the finished story is of most interest to everyone, I recall here the ending of the final text. Distancing himself once more from the idea that the writer had made it predictable, Flaubert willfully placed it into a separate paragraph. Only at the very end of the gestation period did he write: "I must end my Félicité in a splendid way" (letter to his niece Caroline, August 7, 1876).[10] The story was written after "La Légende de saint Julien l'Hospitalier," from mid-February to August 16, 1876. As usual, Flaubert ends the preceding paragraph on a detail that establishes a metonymic continuity with the beginning of the following one:

Et les encensoirs, allant à pleine volée, glissaient sur leurs chaînettes.

Une vapeur d'azur monta dans la chambre de Félicité. Elle avança les narines, en la humant avec une sensualité mystique; puis ferma les paupières. Ses lèvres souriaient. Les mouvements de son coeur se ralentirent un à un, plus vagues chaque fois, plus doux, comme une fontaine s'épuise, comme un écho disparaît; et quand elle exhala son dernier souffle, elle crut voir, dans les cieux entr'ouverts, un perroquet gigantesque, planant au-dessus de sa tête.

And the censers, swinging at full tilt, slid up and down their chains.

A blue cloud of incense was wafted up into Félicité's room. She opened her nostrils wide and breathed it in with a mystical, sensuous fervor. Then she closed her eyes. Her lips smiled. Her heart-beats grew slower and slower, each a little fainter and gentler, like a fountain running dry, an echo fading away. And as she breathed her last, she thought she could see, in the opening heavens, a gigantic parrot hovering above her head. (56)

For clarity of reading and for ease of reference, I give here the numbered list of the folios in which the development of this *excipit* appears:

Rouen municipal library, MS g[8] 226:

1. f. 195r. "Perroquet" (Initial plan)

Bibliothèque Nationale, MS 23663:

2. f. 87v. Proto-scenario or detailed outline (crossed through with a long diagonal mark)
3. f. 394. Scenario
4. f. 381r. "Résumé" in 7 basic parts (beginning crossed through with a diagonal slash)
5. f. 340v. Scenario (crossed out with an X)
6. f. 349v. Subscenario (crossed out with an X)
7. f. 376. Outline in 5 parts

8. f. 352. Rough draft
9. f. 353r. Rough draft
10. f. 268r. Clear copy (MS 1)
11. f. 30r. Clear copy (MS 2)
12. ff. 140–41r. Copyist's manuscript

1st Occurrence

Number 1 (f. 195r) is a manuscript classified at Rouen in the *Bouvard et Pécuchet* archive.

As in the case of "Saint Julien" (1856 outline), we possess here an initial outline, entitled "Parrot," which is really half-outline, half-scenario. Alberto Cento has tried to date it and places it between 1853 and 1854.[11] The outline is centered on the relations between a parrot and Mlle. Félicité (these connections are already metonymico-metaphorical):

la couleur de sa peau grise semblable à la couleur des pattes du perroquet

the color of her gray skin similar to the color of the parrot's feet

The main action: the parrot is sick and dies. Long dénouement: the after-parrot, the stuffing, the emotion of Corpus Christi and its altar, and the attack:[12]

à l'hopital <vision mystique. Son perroquet est le St Esprit>
elle meurt saintement.
"il m'a semblé que les chaînettes des encensoirs étaient le bruit de sa chaîne. — est-ce un péché mon père
— non mon enfant.
& elle expira

at the hospital <mystic vision. Her parrot is the Holy Spirit.>
she dies in saintly fashion
"it seemed to me that the little chains of the censers were the noise of its chain. — is this a sin my father
— no my child
& she expired

This first outline-scenario (we will see that two answers in the dialogue are essential to the narrative strategy) carries two semantic systems in it at the same time, two different isotopic lines that will enter into conflict and provoke a constant disruption of meaning that only the last folio will resolve. In the manuscripts the places of disruption will change, but never disruption itself as the motivation for textual production. In fact, on first reading, the final meaning intended here is not in doubt. It is the death of a saint. The words *simple* or *simple heart* do not appear (just "heartbeats-apprehension"), with all the ambiguity that the idea of mental simplicity linked to simplicity of the heart brings with it. Nor is there any reference made here, and none will survive, to the words of the Evangelist: "Blessed are the poor in spirit . . . Blessed are the pure in heart . . ."[13] The underlying cultural model is what we would call the "mystic death," that is, the *beatific death*. It is characterized here by the complete identification of the transitional with the absolute object, rendered by this addition: "mystic vision. Her parrot is the Holy Spirit." For a mystic, there is no gap between the terrestrial and the celestial; and we can even say that the slippage from the sublimated copulation to the copula is a natural one. That is what the verb *to be* expresses in its clumsiness and, I would say, its purity. The outline could well end on this thematic, narrative, and symbolic closure.

Yet in this same outline there is another semantic chain that, contrary to the first, is open and therefore susceptible to various extensions and variations. In this text (from this point forward there is always full textualization), it is made up of three elements: first a modalization ("it seemed to me") from which the idea of doubting is kept, then the establishment of metonymic spatial relationships between the chain of the parrot and the little chains of the censers, between the human domestic space and the religious space of the Holy Spirit. These metonymic relations allow for the immediate resemblance of signifiers ("chain," "little chains") and the potential metaphoric coalescence of metonymic signifieds: the parrot is the Holy Spirit. This also explains, perhaps, the grammatical oddity: "the little chains of the censers *were the noise* of his chain" [*les chaînettes des encensoirs étaient le bruit de sa chaîne*]. We go from copresence to forced imaginary coincidence.

In this outline, Félicité is not deaf; she is myopic. Whence her tendency to confuse things visually, a tendency further exaggerated by her sensitive hearing. The initial addition, which makes one notice the resemblance between her gray skin and the color of the parrot's feet, comes from the same system and reinforces it. Told this way, the story would allow one to move from the progressive analogy between the servant and the object of her desire to the identification of the object with the value that authorizes and sanctifies this confusion. If Félicité senses that this confusion is a sin, it is because the confusion between the profane and the sacred poses a problem. The priest erases the doubt in vain, for the discordance remains in the mind of the reader. We note that what is essential is said in dialogue. The experience of Flaubert's manuscripts teaches us that the lines of dialogue written *in the scenarios* are almost always the places where invention, in the rhetorical sense of the word, is at work. They are argumentative and narrative developments of sorts. It is the opposite in the final text ("hatred of dialogue"). A third and last textual element—after the dialogue, Flaubert feels the need to rewrite the death of Félicité: "and she expired" [*et elle expira*]. For the moment, it is more a euphemistic than a technical term, yet it is slated for great expansion.

As early as this outline, then, there is textual activity [*mise en texte*], not only because the formulations are more than telegraphic notes and there is a story, however thin, but especially because they are organized into networks that play on the motivations and details (of signifier and signified) on which the color of the narrative depends. We have here a perfectly Flaubertian construction: the microstructure tailors, even governs the macrostructure. Yet Flaubert has already written many endings, especially deaths. As we have said, narrative endings are overdetermined, and it is not surprising to find clichés, stereotypes, and other more general models in them. First of all, Flaubert's own models. We know that as a creator Flaubert was very sensitive to the situation of personal rewriting. He had a fear of repeating the same effects from one work to the next. And in a sense, he did, or almost did, because, just as Proust's narrator tells Albertine with regard to Vinteuil's "phrase-types," "the great writers have only completed one work" (Proust 3: 375).

He was especially worried when he was finishing a novel (*Salammbô, La Tentation de Saint Antoine*). This is because at that point the battle begins between the specificity of the narrative and the influence of the model that allows us to predict the ending, or rather to recognize it. (Here we know perfectly well that Félicité is going to die.) As it happens, death is the commonplace par excellence, the tomb of received wisdom, and the drawer of sleeping euphemisms. Gussied up or overripe, it arouses, as Claude Duchet might say, the sociality more than the individuation of the text. From a more theoretical point of view, an author's rewriting of the same "passage" from one work to another belongs to the study of hypertextuality, where each previous work partially becomes the hypotext of the ongoing hypertext.[14] The fact that this is a case of autotextuality does not change the phenomenon or its laws very much.

With Flaubert, the variations on the theme of death throes begin in nearly obsessive fashion, with the works of his youth. Let us put aside the classic (or romantic if you prefer) fantasies of the agonies of the man enclosed alive in his tomb ("Rage et impuissance," December 1836). From the same period, we find death throes of more interest to this essay since they amount to a profane version of the beatitude. In "Les Funérailles du Dr. Mathurin," the skeptic Dr. Mathurin decides, like Félicité, to die in the middle of the summer, surrounded not by angels but by his disciples: "He bathed just before dying in a bath of excellent wine, bathed his heart in a nameless beatitude, and his soul went straight to the Lord, like a wineskin full of happiness and liquor" [*Il se plongea avant de mourir dans un bain d'excellent vin, baigna son coeur dans une béatitude qui n'a pas de nom, et son âme s'en alla droit au Seigneur, comme une outre pleine de bonheur et de liqueur* (Flaubert, *Œuvres complètes* 11: 585)]. Here we see two fundamental clichés working together: the first, ancient and pagan, of the cup of life being emptied (reinforced by the Stoic imagery of the Senecan suicide in the bath), and the second, Christian, of the ascension into a welcoming heaven.

All indications are that in this case the Christian cliché becomes ironic in relation to the pagan. When Flaubert returns, in the first Outline, to the system of the double register or double version (beatific death/profane death; vision/confusion), he again takes a generative model of meaning but transforms it to suit his needs. The system is one of *transposition* or *serious transformation* (Genette, *Palimpsests* 28). This reprise of oppositional, or simply contradictory, cliché-models that play against or with each other attests to Flaubert's fidelity to the problematic of writing the already seen, heard, and perceived (see Herschberg-Pierrot and also Felman). In the example cited, the analysis of the transformational media is complicated by the fact that the process of quoting is already a kind of playful parody. In the different stages of the *excipit* of "Un Coeur simple," we will see ludic playful parody disappear and become parlayed into serious parody and transformation. Generally speaking, only the context allows one to qualify the development of a model as positive or negative. Before finishing with the role of autotextuality as a form of hypertextuality, I must first quote an example, this time of imitation, and thus of pastiche, or of double pastiche. Emma Bovary (and Saint Julian after her) has certain visions at the moment when she believes she will die from love and abandonment:

> Alors elle laissa retomber sa tête, croyant entendre dans les espaces le chant des harpes séraphiques et apercevoir en un ciel d'azur, sur un trône d'or, au milieu des saints tenant des palmes vertes, Dieu le père tout éclatant de majesté, et qui d'un signe faisait descendre vers la terre des anges aux ailes de flamme pour l'emporter dans leurs bras. (246)

> She let her head fall back, thinking she heard the music of angelic harps coming to her through boundless space: and on a golden throne in an azure sky, amid saints holding green palm branches, God the Father appeared in all His majesty, motioning angels with wings of flame to descend to earth and bring her back in their arms.[15]

This text imitates all the writings of sacred death and ecstasy. Of course, it imitates even more, as we will see, the formless Saint-Sulpician evocations of a degenerate baroque. All the harps are "angelic," the sky "azure," and the angels have "wings of flame." Here some of the same material already used in "Saint Julien" has a very different connotation.

The language takes on an ironic value solely because we know that Emma is living in mental confusion and transferring to God the surges of passion that Rodolphe has rejected. This pastiche of what is already a pastiche of mystic ecstasy and beatitude will return in quoted form in the plots and rough drafts to follow. There Flaubert will cite himself citing clichéd writing and images. Thus the procedures of autotextuality are efficient in the genetic development of a hypertext whether they are produced by the transformation of a genre or by the imitation of a written work. Efficient, that is, in the sense that they rework the genesis of the *excipit*, sometimes sending it forward and sometimes entangling it. The feature common to nearly all these Flaubertian beatific deaths will recur in all the manuscripts we are studying—the copresence, indispensable for textual development, of on the one hand a simple reading founded on saintliness and the immediate fusion of the profane and the sacred, and on the other hand a complex reading founded on doubt, the misalliance of the profane and the sacred, mental confusion, and a kind of sin. These two readings are analogous in their component parts, but incompatible in the way they refer flesh and charity to different orders, in the Pascalian sense of "order." When Flaubert takes this original outline up again, probably more than twenty years later, he will seek in his rewriting to melt this binary structure into a perfect indetermination, one that nevertheless will still bear the trace of the models and attempts implied in it.

2nd Occurrence

It is generally agreed (Willenbrink, Bonaccorso) that the first stage, in February-March 1876, is a detailed Outline or Proto-scenario (f. 387v). It is numbered "2" and is the first of an incomplete series of scenarios, the first of which is lost.[16] Relatively detailed on the nephew, Father Colmiche, and the Parrot, it is laconic about the ending:

maladie et mort de Félicité. <u>Le perroquet St Esprit</u> à la fête dieu sur un reposoir

illness and death of Félicité. <u>The parrot Holy Spirit</u> on an altar of repose at Corpus Christi

This outline almost regresses when compared with the original one on this point. The parrot on an altar indicates neither the final vision nor the dying. One can already anticipate a partial conclusion: whenever there is a proper outline, Flaubert contents himself, for the *excipit*, with a few neutral words. This ending leaves no intermediary between nomination, its expansion, the textual organization, and the overall placing of things. Either you tell, or you construct so as "to show."

3rd Occurrence

This last is what happens in the folio 394 (recto) scenario that formed the basis for all the remaining scenarios because it is designated XI, overwritten by E, and finally overwritten by III. It presents two orders of writing, one of the scenario and one of the rough draft:

L'encens monte jusqu'à Félicité par la fenêtre ouverte.
Elle confond le St Esprit et le Perroquet, planant sur elle
dans les cieux — & meurt

Et quand elle exhala son dernier souffle... quand (une phrase
très longue) cette vie terrestre s'éteignit... elle crut voir
...comme un St Esprit
le Perroquet planant audessus de sa tête
~~Rêverie sur le St Esprit. Dans sa maladie finale~~
~~+ l'avoir préparé~~
~~par ironie qq'un a dit en parlant de lui~~
~~"comme le St Esprit"~~
"~~par la grâce~~ du St Esprit"

The incense rises up to Félicité through the open window.
She confuses the Holy Spirit and the parrot, hovering over her
in the heavens — & dies

And when she exhaled her last breath... when (a very long
sentence) this earthly life went out... she thought she saw
...like a Holy Spirit
the parrot hovering above her head.
~~Revery about the Holy Spirit. In her final sickness~~
~~+ have prepared for it~~
~~by irony someone said speaking of it~~
~~"like the Holy Spirit"~~
"~~by the grace of the~~ Holy Spirit"

The resumption of style and phraseology after the dividing line may have been done at a different time. Also, the remark about the preparation of the parrot, which incidentally is crossed out. Three phenomena predominate:

- First is the reactualization of the model already seen in the original Outline, that of the beatific death. The last phrase, "hovering above her head," remains unchanged in all the versions to come. It inscribes the call to rise to a protective and welcoming heaven. We will see this celestial part expand and retract, but this nucleus will always remain.

- In a second, seemingly contradictory, phenomenon, Flaubert affirms the confusion and then, in his organizational notes, takes it upon himself to construct the effect. He hesitates between two motivations. He thinks first of a verbal motivation, the reactivation of the formula "by the grace of the Holy Spirit." Now, among all the graces that the Holy Spirit grants and that Flaubert, incidentally, noted, there is—height of irony for the taciturn Félicité—the gift of languages, the gift with which parrots are endowed. He will finally explore a motivation that is, narratively speaking, much better integrated: reverie. It is the scene of catechism, and it will be written into the Outline in seven parts, but only in the margins. Here Félicité takes the words of the Evangelist literally; that is, she confuses the sign with its referent and attempts to picture the physical person of the Holy Spirit. To this will be added later the Épinal image in her room, across from the parrot.[17] This reactivation of religious clichés makes banal, as much as it authorizes, whatever would be miraculous and exceptional about the dying woman's vision.
- Then, in the third phenomenon, Flaubert works on syntactic and stylistic stereotypes in order to take the "she expired" motif up again. I refer to the construction of "a very long sentence," whose length is also designated as a signified, or rather as a diagram. Of what? First of all, of a solemn slowing-down of the "magnificence" of which he will write a little later. There is an attempt to reach meaning through semantically empty forms such as lengths of phrases, ellipses, anaphora, metaphorical words, and a climax ("she thought she saw"). Here, if anywhere, "the form has dictated the thought" (Riffaterre 75), but in a contradictory way. Whereas Flaubert grammatically deploys the ecstasy of the vision, he introduces a modalizer analogous to that of the original Outline—"it seemed to me"—but this time it bears on vision and not on hearing—"she thought she saw." Moreover, the metaphorical euphemisms "exhaled her last breath" and "this earthly life went out" signify the physical gentleness as much as the grandeur of this death.

4th Occurrence

What Flaubert entitles "Résumé" (f. 381r) no doubt belongs here, for in fact it is like an outline whose seven chapters are looking for their proper places. Chapter III, which will become V, is entitled:

	<procession de la Fête-Dieu>
<u>mort</u> de Félicité	apothéose du Perroquet

<Corpus Christi procession>
death of Félicité apotheosis of the Parrot

Nothing very new here, unless it is the emphasis on the apotheosis of the parrot rather than on the death and the vision. Nothing decisive.

7th Occurrence

That is why we can turn immediately to the last outline (f. 376r), which gives a clearer summary. Although it must be classified as rather late, it indicates the last of the five parts in just as laconic a fashion:

V. La Fête-dieu
<agonie>
~~mort~~ de F.
vision du Perroq.

V. Corpus Christi
<death throes>
~~death~~ of F.
vision of the Parr.

"Death throes" is more precise than "death"; "vision" restates the main idea without detailing it. Therefore the only certainty is that Flaubert wishes to detach this episode and that he is relying on the rough drafts to work out not only its details but also its central meaning.

5th Occurrence

The next folio (340v, crossed out) is again a scenario, very detailed as far as the procession and its sequence go, but also more worked out than the 394 (recto) scenario. Most of the verbs are in the present tense, but the surge of details makes a properly textual reading necessary:

It would be impossible to comment on everything, so we will follow a few threads already begun to see if there is anything new. What is striking at first is that Flaubert amplifies and varies a series of metaphorical expressions that convey the *passage* from life to death and parallel the "supreme confusion": life goes out, the soul departs, or the link is broken. More than euphemisms, Flaubert needs to erase every gap between the accelerations of the heart and its last beat. Flaubert continually affirms "the confusion"; it is natural that he should write and affirm that "she saw" [*elle voyait*]. Let us note the imperfect tense, which, if kept, would have been the ending of all three stories—a sort of infinite imperfect quite contrary to the diegetic contemporaneity here. Flaubert

<ne parle plus. accélération de sa poitrine
de ce coeur qui n'avait
battu pr rien d'ignoble>

La procession se rapproche xx bruit des chaînettes des encensoirs.
L'encens monte jusqu'à Félicité ~~gest~~ le hume. sensualité

<~~Son coeur qui n'avait~~
~~jamais battu pr rien d'ignoble~~>

<en exhalant son dernier souffle>
et quand s'exhala son dernier souffle... dans la suprême confusion du
<immédiat> <le dernier lien de sa> se rompit crut voir entre
<lors du> départ de l'âme... quand ~~s'éteignit cette~~ vie terrestre, elle ~~voyait~~
<resta sur le dos elle & le
souriante> <les Anges>
<~~le Paradis~~ >
<un gigantesque> <qui était le St Esprit>
le <~~Saint Esprit~~> perroquet planant au dessus de sa tête

<speaks no longer. acceleration of her chest
of this heart which had
never beaten fr anything ignoble>

The procession approaches xx noise of little chains of the censers.
The incense rises up to Félicité ~~gest~~ inhales deeply. sensuality

<~~Her heart which had~~
~~never beaten fr anything ignoble.~~>

<While exhaling her last breath>
and when she exhaled her last breath... in the supreme confusion of the
<immediate> <the last link of her> broke thought she saw b
<during the> departure of the soul... when <~~this~~> earthly life <~~went out~~> she saw

<remained on her back her &
smiling> <the Angels>
<~~Heaven~~>
<a gigantic> <that was the Holy Spirit>
<~~the Holy Spirit~~> parrot hovering over her head

returns right away to "she thought she saw" [*elle crut voir*], a perfect tense that both leaves us with the possibility of doubting the vision and gives the story its ambiguity. In a more general way, Flaubert tries to modulate the equation parrot = Holy Spirit by two rather decisive stylistic features: he adds the adjective "gigantic," which mythifies the object, and he moves from the definite article (*the* parrot of the story) to the indefinite (*a* parrot, which will not exactly be Loulou), which invites all sorts of fantasy. In this case, the heavy translation "who was the Holy Spirit" flattens the text once again and blocks the expansion of meaning. We see here a perfect example of invention at work: it is a question not so much of stylistic work as of the range and reach of the story, of all the meaning that flows towards this *excipit.* Surfacing here at last is a new notation that will engender, as we will see, something more than a theme, a veritable bridge giving access to the final resolution.

For the moment, Flaubert writes "*acceleration of her* chest," a purely physiological notation. But in parallel fashion he also twice affirms (once crossed out in the margin): "of this heart that had never beaten for anything ignoble." This is a clear-cut value judgment that clashes with the more generally adopted impersonality. Félicité would no longer be a simple heart, but a pure heart full of charity, with no dark shadows whatsoever. This is indeed one side of the story ("for such souls the supernatural is simple"), but it is not the only one. There is also the metonymy or synecdoche of the physical and the moral that creates a loosely controlled play on the word "heart."[18] Thus Flaubert has not yet seen the importance of his simplest resources. That is probably why he works on the second part, the vision (which is not, contrary to what Juliette Frølich has said, put in place right away, aside from the "hovering over her head"). He turns his attention to various models from visual arts outside of the text. The first is the image of a stone statue on a tomb: she "remained on her back, smiling." I add right away the elements that reappear in the next three folios:

Elle était à plat comme une statue sur un tombeau couchée. Un sourire (f. 349v)
elle se tenait comme une statue sur un tombeau—souriante ~~béate~~ (f. 352r)
~~Elle se tenait comme une statue sur un tombeau~~ (f. 353r)

She was flat like a statue lying on a tomb. A smile (f. 349v)
she held herself like a statue on a tomb—smiling ~~beatific~~ (f. 352r)
~~She held herself like a statue on a tomb~~ (f. 353r)

The last one is completely crossed out. This model is archaic, almost archeological, and above all it is a cultural reference that cannot be assimilated to Félicité's imagination, or even to the universe of the story. Nor is there a tomb statue in the church of the catechism. Yet it is a received figuration of beatific death. The other model has a very wide plasticity: religious paintings or simple color prints depicting Christ, a pious image from hymnals, the figuration of God witnessing a dying person, or a good soul rising into the sky. As I did for the statue, I will now gather together all its occurrences up until its final effacement:

entre elle et ~~le Paradis~~ les Anges (f. 340v)
entre des ~~nuées~~ nuages d'or . . . ψ entre Jésus et le Père (f. 349v)
~~entre parmi des nuages d'or, à la droite du fils, à la gauche du père~~ (f. 352r)

between her and ~~Heaven~~ the Angels (f. 340v)
between the radiant clouds . . . ψ between Jesus and the Father (f. 349v)
~~enters among radiant clouds, to the right of the son, to the left of the father~~ (f. 352r)

This is very close to the *Madame Bovary* pseudo-death-throes imagery that we have cited. Between Emma and Félicité, there is only the size of a heart. Both of them bring to mind pious, Saint-Sulpician imagery and a kind of degenerate classical baroque for the masses. It may be that this model appears and starts growing at the moment when Flaubert has the idea of placing an image of the Holy Spirit in the room across from the parrot (f. 391). All these pious images, after being inflated, will simply resolve into those purely allusive "opening skies" that leave the reader in suspension even as every imaginable image-cliché rushes in. The emphasis will be placed elsewhere. But for the moment these inscriptions confirm quite well the relationship that each of these three stories has with representations from the plastic arts (images, stained-glass windows, and sculptures). Ultimately, these relations are always the subordinate effects of a writing capable of suggesting without ever translating or copying.[19]

While he keeps and even nourishes the idea of a beatific death, Flaubert maintains the idea of confusion on the one hand and sensuality on the other, each of these elements being badly integrated. Three rough drafts follow, the first two containing maximum stylistic developments. Everything, then, competes and intersects.

6th Occurrence

f. 349v

The most noticeable hesitation occurs in the attempt to produce confusion on one hand and consciousness on the other: whence "the interval of a lightning flash."

Besides the Épinal print of Christ that I have mentioned, there is also here, in the margin, a clear development of the tomb statue model. This time it comes to life: the nostrils breathe, the lips quiver, either from pity or from pain. We still have the two interpretations, one beatific, "either she prayed mentally," and the other physiological and realistic, "or it was convulsive." If it is true that the image of the beatific death seems to predominate over the "convulsive" one, Flaubert does try to maintain a suspension of meaning because after having written "she saw," he crosses it out again and

~~Le St Esprit comme~~
audessus de sa tête.

Ψ entre Jésus et le Père

< Fel. (son portrait)
Elle était à plat comme une
statue de tombeau couchée. Un sourire. narrines aspiraient le parfum.
Ses lèvres vibrantes. soit qu'elle priat <mentalement> ou que c'était
convulsif.>

au dernier moment de sa vie — pendant la
Et ~~en exhalant son dernier souffle~~ ~~dans la confusion du départ~~
<rupture de l'âme et du corps>
~~de l'âme~~ ~~quand~~ en exhalant son dernier souffle
— ~~pendant que le dernier lien de la vie se rompait~~ . . .
~~dans l'intervalle d'un éclair~~ ~~couchée sur~~
~~le dos~~ et ~~priant mentalement~~
conscience crut
dernier ~~mouvement~~ de sa pensée elle ~~voyait~~ voir Ψ ... entre des
nuages d'or
~~nuées~~ un gigantesque perroquet qui était le St Esprit, planant

at the last moment of her life — during the
And ~~exhaling her last breath~~ ~~in the confusion of the departure~~
rupture of body and soul
~~of soul~~ ~~when~~ exhaling her last breath
— ~~while the last link to life was breaking~~ . . .
~~in the interval of a lightning flash~~ ~~lying on~~
~~her back~~ and ~~praying mentally~~
consciousness thought she saw
last ~~movement~~ of her thought she ~~saw~~ Ψ. . . between the
radiant clouds
~~clouds~~ a gigantic parrot that was the Holy Spirit hovering
~~The Holy Spirit as~~
over her head

Ψ between Jesus and the Father

<Fel. (her portrait)
She was flat like a
statue lying on a tomb. A smile. Nostrils were breathing the scent.
Her lips vibrating. either she prayed <mentally> or it was
convulsive.>

writes "she thought she saw." The smile, still a feature of the statue, has not yet been integrated with the sensuality of the nostrils, or with the quivering lips of a prayer or frown. We have momentarily lost the beating of the heart. Félicité is all body or else all head—sensuality or saintliness.

A phenomenon appears which is new here but frequent in Flaubert's manuscripts, one that, I believe, has been somewhat misunderstood. Flaubert notices phonic repetitions, and he is already testing the sonorities of his text by shouting his words aloud "at the gueuloir."[20] He underlines the French "è" sound in "gigantesque perroquet qui était." The trees hide the forest from him. In fact, we are more sensitive to the chattering of the three k sounds than to any bellowing, open "è" sounds. Now it seems to me in a general way (I've tried to show this elsewhere for a Francis Ponge text[21]) that when writers are bothered by something, a word, a sound, it is almost always another contiguous phenomenon that is really at stake, not the one stumping them. Here it is the copula itself: "A gigantic parrot that was the Holy Spirit." This absolute identification, too clear, stops the play of the text. That is where the blockage is. I say "the text" because it is obvious that we are dealing more and more with an extremely complex network, overdetermined, in full conversion and expansion. Yet everything remains open, precisely because everything is thwarted by this equation: parrot = Holy Spirit.

There are two rough drafts left to examine. The first is more developed syntactically, but both have in common not only the typical saturation of the left margin but also a kind of paradigmatic push toward the bottom right, where Flaubert tries out some equivalences by writing a few columns. Two series of paradigms will compete. The first concerns the beatific death that attains the apogee of its representation. The other concerns what we will call, with Frølich, the "gentle death," that is, a gentle physiological expression of death. To get to the second we must first undergo the pains of death throes and a realistic death.

8th Occurrence

f. 352r

It is difficult to extract the essential facts from such hesitation and competition. This is the last time that the sculptural models of the supine tomb statue and especially the glorious heaven of which we have spoken appear. They are at their point of maximum amplification. Thus we must question their disappearance. It is also remarkable that Flaubert has never tried so many metaphors to express the passage from life to death. Yet most of these metaphors are clichés that express brutal rupture or slippage and progressive dénouement, a circumstance that gives us two very different readings. First, the coils break down or tear apart, and we have a rupture of soul and body. Flaubert even goes so far as to evoke "the hiccup" and "the supreme nausea." There would thus be a certain continuity between the horror of these death throes and the delirium, cold sweat, cough, frothing at the mouth, and trembling evoked earlier.

pendant que se cassaient ~~à la fois~~ rompaient à la fois toutes
les derniers ressorts de la vie pendant que se déliaient les dernières au départ de son
~~le hoquet~~ et ~~au dernier moment~~ de sa vie, pendant la rupture de l'âme
dans la nausée suprême attaches de la vie<dans le dernier souffle>
au ~~dern~~ départ de son âme
et du corps- en exhalant son dernier souffle
~~entre~~ — la dernière conscience
elle se tenait comme de sa pensée, elle crut voir ~~parmi des nuages d'or à la droite du fils,~~
une statue sur un ~~perroquet~~ ~~monstrueux~~
~~tombeau~~. Souriante ~~à la gauche du père~~ un ~~gigantesque~~ perroquet ~~qui était le St Esprit~~
~~béate~~ planant au dessus de sa tête démesuré
ses narrines gigantesque
[et pendant que
~~s'arrachaient~~ se mouvements
cassaient à la fois ses lèvres... puis les pulsations saccadées de son coeur de plus en plus
les derniers tous ——————————lents comme
les ressorts de la vie]
~~s'exhala~~ dans les cieux entr'ouverts
~~et quand ell exhala~~ son dernier
à la place du
les souffles souffle elle crut voir dans les St Esprit
et au dernier cieux qui s'ouvraient
(souff) un ~~*gig*~~ perroquet
sur
un perroq. gigant planant au dessus de dém
sa tête
l'absolvant de
dans les cieux qui
qui s'ouvraient
un peu dém
planant au dessus
de sa tête

There would also be a similarity with all the deaths that have preceded Félicité's in the story. On the other hand, something exceptional happens that prepares the vision: all the lines are cast off, quite naturally, until the exhalation of the last breath. Both types of cliché are telling but are brought low and written in a common language, as are the imagery or imageries invoked. Either Flaubert rewrites Emma's death here, or he installs a pious image, totally beatifying, which does not accord with the realistic register maintained throughout the narrative and initiated at the start. "Un Coeur simple" is a double tissue with a novel of manners on the front and a hagiographic story on the back. Now, the double aspect of religion, partly sensual, even sexual, and partly sublime, was always copresent in Flaubert's thinking about mysticism. (The words "sensuality" and "mystical love" are written a few lines earlier, when Félicité breathes the scented cloud.) There is a very early passage, to which Flaubert often returned, in *Pensées intimes* from 1840, in which he makes explicit a thought that would never leave him: "I'd love to be a mystic; it

while the last springs of life
were breaking ~~at the same time~~ at the same time they all broke
while the last lines of life were being cast off
~~hiccup~~ and ~~at the last moment~~ of her life, during
in the supreme nausea rupture of soul and body
the departure of her
she held herself like ~~her~~
~~in the last last breath~~ at ~~last~~ departure of her soul
a statue on a tomb. Smiling
exhaling her last breath - the last consciousness of her thought,
~~beatifically~~ ~~between~~
she thought she saw ~~among between the radiant clouds to the right of the son,~~
her nostrils ~~*parrot*~~ monstrous
~~to the left of the father~~ a ~~*gigantic*~~ parrot ~~*that was the Holy Spirit*~~
[and while hovering above her head immense
~~torn away~~ gigantic
the last springs
of life were all broken
at the same time.] movements
her lips... then the jerky pulsing of her heart slower
——————— and slower like
~~breathed out~~ in the opening skies
~~and when she exhaled~~ her last
the breaths instead of the Holy Spirit
breath she thought she saw in the
and at the last a ~~gig~~ parrot
(breath) opening skies
on
a gigant parr hovering above imm
her head
absolving her of
in the opening skies
rather imm
hovering above
her head

must give you a wonderful feeling to believe in paradise, to drown in waves of incense . . . it is a much more refined sensualism than the other; these are pleasures, thrills, raptures of the heart" (22–23) [*Je voudrais bien être mystique; il doit y avoir de belles voluptés à croire au paradis, à se noyer dans les flots d'encens . . . c'est un sensualisme bien plus fin que l'autre, ce sont les voluptés, les tressaillements, les béatitudes du coeur* (599)]. Félicité breathes the incense that rises from the street with such sensuality that Flaubert writes nostrrils [*narrines*] with two r's in the last copy. It is his traditional writing of this word, but sometimes it may be better to see spelling mistakes as symptoms rather than as blunders.

Another sticking point on this page is the groping attempt to move from parrot to Holy Spirit. This time Flaubert underlines the ends of "gigantic" [*gigantesque*], "parrot" [*perroquet*], and "was" [*était*], but one can see that this great search for assonance and repetition is not purely a stylistic phenomenon: the insistence is a heaviness and redundancy of meaning rather than of sound. If the parrot is "gigantic," "immense," even "monstrous," this should suffice to characterize it as a divine, supernatural phenomenon without having to write for the fifth time "that was the Holy Spirit" (incidentally, it is crossed out this time) or "instead of the Holy Spirit." I note the concomitant, surreptitious return of the original Outline—"is this a sin my father"—in the form of the "absolving" parrot. Félicité, like Saint Julian, cannot die as a saint unless she has sinned, here by confusion, or "brahmanism," as Flaubert puts it in a note.

~~Puis elle ferma~~ ~~Elle se tenait comme une statue sur un tombeau~~
~~les yeux ses~~ Puis elle ferma les paupières. Sa figure souriante. du coeur
~~lèvres étaient~~ ses narrines... ses lèvres souriaient. Les mouvements ~~saccadés de son coeur~~
~~ses~~ [*illis.*] ~~sa bouche~~
s'affaiblirent
~~de plus en plus lents~~ comme l'écho affaibli - vibration
~~sa figure souriait~~ et quand ~~se~~ s'exhala son dernier souffle
~~lents de plus et au dernier~~
elle crut voir dans les cieux qui
perroquet gigantesque
entr'ouverts un ~~immense~~ audessus de
~~s'ouvraient~~ ~~un gigantesque~~ planant ~~sur~~ sa tête
se ralentissaient
dernier
2 1
se ralentirent un à un, plus lents, chaque fois chaque fois
~~chaque fois plus éloignés~~ plus doux ~~comme~~ éloignés
comme une fontaine s'épuise comme toujours
un écho disparaît s'affaiblissant
~~s'en va~~ étant plus lents
~~diminue en s'épuisant de plus en plus~~
se firent - un à un - plus lents chaque fois
plus doux
plus longs chaque fois
~~un à un~~
~~plus lents~~
~~presque insensiblement~~
~~plus doux~~
d'argent
Comme les vibrations d'une corde sur
~~comme les flots~~ laquelle on a joué, ou bien l'écho
~~s'apaisent~~ tombant au fond d'un précipice
et les encens se balançant
~~écho~~
comme une fontaine s'épuise
comme un écho disparaît

~~then she closed~~
~~her eyes her~~
~~lips were~~
~~her~~ [*illeg.*] ~~her mouth~~

~~her smiling~~
~~face~~

~~She held herself like a statue on a tomb~~
Then she closed her eyelids. Her smiling face. of the heart
her nostrils... her lips smiled. The movements ~~jerkings of her hea~~

weakened
~~slower and slower~~ like the weakened echo - vibration

and when she exhaled her last breath
~~slower more - and to the last~~
she thought she saw in the
gigantic parrot
opening an ~~immense~~
skies which ~~were opening~~ ~~a gigantic~~ hovering ~~on~~ her head
above slowing down
last

2 1
slowed down one by one, slower, each time
~~each time farther apart~~ softer
as a fountain runs dry as
an echo fades
~~goes away~~
~~diminishes while tiring more and more~~
were - one by one - slower each time

each time
~~as~~
always
weakening
~~being~~ slower

softer
longer each time
one by one
~~slower~~ ~~almost imperceptibly~~
~~softer~~

of silver
~~like waves~~ Like the vibrations of a string which has
~~calming~~ been plucked, or else the echo
falling to the bottom of a precipice
and the incense in suspension
~~echo~~
as a fountain runs dry
as an echo fades away

A last, most important remark, that brings us to the final rough draft: in linking the sensual nostrils and lips by a long stroke of the pen, Flaubert suddenly discovers a contiguity and a metonymic (or rather synecdochic) continuity with the "pulsing" or "jerky movements of her heart . . . slower and slower like." We await a comparison or comparisons. The heart is therefore going to become the constitutive link between the expression of the body and that of the soul, the metonymic liaison of suffering and its metaphorical equivalent in the register of death, no longer beatific, but gentle.[22] That is what the next folio accomplishes.

9th Occurrence

f. 353r

The image of the tomb statue, inscribed one last time, disappears. There is no longer any need for a model external to the writing to support the literary production of meaning. All the metaphors of the rupture of soul and body are also effaced, and we are back to the "when she exhaled her last breath" of folio 394r (3rd occurrence) without the anaphoric repetition of "when" or "while." The idea of a long sentence is transferred to the extension of the movements of her heart, which are linked to the smile and detached from the vision itself. There is thus a double attenuation, or rather oblivion: that of the range of images that evoke a purely beatific death and that of the indications of a hiccuping, nauseated, or violent death in the realist version. The two annul themselves to the benefit of a sort of poetic simplification of agony. Flaubert starts working in columns, constantly moving the pieces of the puzzle. On the one hand, we see a gradual slowdown accomplished by adverbs ("always—each time—more and more") and by predicates about which he cannot make up his mind: "Longer—slower—softer" [*plus longs—plus lents—plus doux*], always binary terms. On the other hand, there he is again returning to what has always eaten him up, metaphors and comparisons. We are compelled to notice that he falls again into the romantic clichés, worthy of Chateaubriand and even the much-detested Lamartine that one can easily locate in his own youthful works.[23] Examples: "Like the vibrations of a string of silver which has been plucked, or else the echo falling to the bottom of a precipice." He is falling into Bovaresque excesses well out of place for a character of a deliberately softened tone like Félicité.[24] These slips of the pen toward excess and cliché betray the writer's, and certain of his characters', fascination for the "pohetico-religious" trappings that he claims to mock or hold himself distant from. We are instantly tempted to refer to the *Dictionnaire des idées reçues*: "Harp: Gives out heavenly harmonies. In engravings, is only played among ruins or on the edge of a torrent" (in *Three Tales*, trans. Baldick 309) [*Harpe: produit des harmonies célestes—Ne se joue, en gravure, que sur des ruines ou au bord d'un torrent.*] In writing these purple formulas, a little too "splendid," Flaubert drains away all stereotypical language and cleans, so to speak, his mind and pen of the "already said and written" disease. Whence the rage of the vertical erasures that overwhelm his attempts. In the corner of the opposite left margin, he keeps himself to the essentials: "as a fountain runs dry, as an echo fades." In a pastoral register that is not at all out of place, these two comparisons render both the liquid flow and the sonority of the heartbeats.

10th Occurrence

As Bonaccorso has noted, what is inappropriately called manuscript 1 is the fair copy before the manuscript. Folio 268 shows some decisive precision and other options left open:

vers
Une vapeur d'azur monta dans la chambre de Félicité. Elle avança les narrines
~~joie~~ sensualité
en la humant, avec une ~~sensualité~~ mystique. Puis / elle / ferma les paupières. Sa
lèvres volupté
~~figure~~ souriai<en>t les mouvements de son coeur se ralentirent - un à un - plus
vagues ~~lents à~~ ~~plus faibles~~
~~longs~~ chaque fois plus doux, - comme une fontaine s'épuise, comme un
écho disparaît. - & quand elle exhala son dernier souffle, elle crut voir dans
les cieux entr'ouverts un perroquet gigantesque planant audessus de sa tête

toward
An azure vapor climbed into Félicité's room. She advanced her nostrrils
~~joy~~ sensuality
while breathing it in, with mystic ~~sensuality~~. Then/ she/ closed her eyelids. Her
lips sensuousness
~~face~~ smiled while the movements of her heart slowed - one by one -
vaguer ~~each~~
each time ~~slower~~ ~~weaker~~
~~longer~~ softer, - as a fountain runs dry, as an
echo fades away. - & when she exhaled her last breath, she thought she saw
in the opening skies a gigantic parrot hovering above her head.

After several hesitations over "slower, longer, weaker," Flaubert hits upon "vaguer" and keeps "softer." "Slower" is contained in "slowed down." Instead of emphasizing the beatific death, its attendant clichés, and physiological precision, Flaubert has accentuated a hazy simplicity, sudden, peaceful, and gentle, orchestrated more by an alternating binary/ternary rhythm than by tropes:

3	2	3	2
[*un à un*]	[*plus vagues*]	[*chaque fois*]	[*plus doux*]
one by one	vaguer	each time	softer

12th Occurrence

On this point, the final edition and especially the copyist's manuscript (ff. 140–41r) with its oddities do not make visible the six dashes of the last phrase of the final manuscript (that is, the 11th occurrence). These are the scars of the work that we have just described and the respiration of the text.

11th Occurrence

f. 30r

Les mouvements du coeur se ralentirent—un à un—plus vagues
chaque fois, plus doux—comme une fontaine s'épuise, comme un écho
disparaît,—et quand elle exhala son dernier souffle, elle crut voir
dans les cieux entr'ouverts—un perroquet gigantesque—planant audessus
de sa tête

The movements of the heart slowed down—one
by one—vaguer each time, gentler—as a fountain runs dry, as an echo
fades away,—and when she breathed her last breath, she thought
she saw in the opening skies—a gigantic parrot—hovering above
her head.

To summarize: in the original outline, Flaubert starts from two elements that coexist both in his general thought on religion and in the initial scenario: the sensual impulses that animate all religiosity (he will hesitate until the end before clarifying the differences between joy, sexual feeling, and sensuality) and the threadbare asceticism that permits him to achieve a gentle form of mysticism in this text. The passage from one to the other rests on the expression of the confusion between the corporal and the spiritual register. Passing through a series of saturations and social preconstructions, extraliterary models, models from the visual arts, and stylistic effects, he goes from expansion to blockages and from blockages to displacements. Finally, it is by playing on the word "heart," by reinscribing, so to speak, his title (discovered very early) in his ending that he invents a third term that includes both the realist and the spiritual reading. It is thus impossible for the reader to decide for one or the other. The reader is led to make *both* readings. Thus questions about Flaubert's irony, or about his dedication to Félicité, are no longer to be asked. Every trace of such judgments as "in saintly fashion" or "either she prayed mentally or it was convulsive" is erased to the benefit of what one would like to call "an exact incertitude." In this, the *excipit* of "Un Coeur simple" is perhaps exemplary and marked by the double function of a novel's end: to close the plot and to open reflection. It also avoids, once more, the foolishness of trying to conclude.[25] If every conclusion is born of foolishness, and thus lives by it—that is, deals in it—nevertheless it does not die of it because there can never be a final word. It is therefore immortal, and that is all the felicity that one can wish for in a novel and its readers.

Source: "'Un Coeur simple': Ou comment faire une fin." In *Gustave Flaubert 1.* Paris: Revue des Lettres modernes, 1984. 105–33. The essay was also published as "Comment faire une fin" in Raymonde Debray Genette. *Métamorphoses du récit: Autour de Flaubert.* Paris: Seuil, 1988. 85–112 (copyright © 1988 Éditions du Seuil).

Works Cited

Barthes, Roland. "Par où commencer?" *Poétique* 1, 1 (1970): 3–9. "Where to Begin?" Trans. Richard Howard. In *New Critical Essays.* New York: Hill and Wang, 1980. 79–89.

———. *S/Z.* Paris: Seuil, 1970. *S/Z.* Trans. Richard Miller. New York: Hill and Wang, 1974.

Bellemin-Noël, Jean. *Le Texte et l'avant-texte: Les Brouillons d'un poème de Milosz.* Paris: Larousse, 1972.

Bonaccorso, Giovanni. *Corpus Flaubertianum, "Un Coeur simple".* Paris: Les Belles Lettres, 1983.

Cento, Alberto. "Il 'Plan' primitivo di 'Un Coeur simple'." *Studi Francesi* 13 (January–April 1961): 101–3.

de Biasi, Pierre-Marc. *Édition critique et génétique de "La Légende de saint Julien l'Hospitalier".* Thèse du 3e cycle, Paris-VII, 1982. Part 3, chapter 6.

Debray Genette, Raymonde. "Génétique et poétique: Le Cas Flaubert." In *Essais de critique génétique,* ed. Louis Hay. Paris: Flammarion, 1979. 21–67.

Duchet, Claude, ed. *Sociocritique: Colloque organisé par l'Université de Paris-VIII et New York University.* Paris: Nathan, 1979.

Fairlie, Alison. "La Contradiction créatrice: Quelques remarques sur la genèse d' 'Un Coeur simple.'" In *Essais sur Flaubert,* ed. Charles Carlut. Paris: Nizet, 1979. 203–31.

Felman, Shoshana. "Gustave Flaubert, folie et cliché." In *La Folie et la chose littéraire.* Paris: Seuil, 1978. 159–69. "Gustave Flaubert: Living Writing, or Madness as Cliché." In *Writing and Madness.* Trans. Martha Noel Evans and Shoshana Felman, with Brian Massumi. Ithaca, N.Y.: Cornell University Press, 1985. 78–100.

Flaubert, Gustave. *Correspondence.* Trans. Geoffrey Wall. New York: Penguin, 1997.

———. *Intimate Notebook, 1840–1841.* Trans. Francis Steegmuller. Garden City, N.Y.: Doubleday, 1967.

———. *Madame Bovary.* Livre de Poche. Paris: Librairie Générale Française, 1983. *Madame Bovary.* Trans. Lowell Bair. New York: Bantam, 1989.

———. *Œuvres complètes.* 20 vols. Paris: Club de l'Honnête Homme, 1971–75.

———. "A Simple Heart." *Three Tales.* Trans. Robert Baldick. London: Penguin, 1961. 17–56.

———. "A Simple Heart." *Three Tales.* Trans. A. J. Kreilsheimer. London: Oxford World's Classics, 1991.

Frølich, Juliette. "Battements d'un simple coeur: Stéréographie et sonorisation dans 'Un Coeur simple' de Flaubert." *Littérature* 46 (May 1982): 28–40.

Genette, Gérard. *Palimpsestes: La Littérature au second degré.* Paris: Seuil, 1982. *Palimpsests: Literature in the Second Degree.* Trans. Channa Newman and Claude Doubinsky. Lincoln: University of Nebraska Press, 1997.

———. "Vraisemblance et motivation." In *Figures II: Essais.* Paris: Seuil, 1969. 71–99. "Plausibility and Motivation." Trans. John D. Lyons. In Marie-Madeleine de Lafayette, *The Princess of Cleves: A Norton Critical Edition,* ed. John D. Lyons. New York: Norton. 1994. 178–85.

Hamon, Philippe. "Clausules." *Poétique* 24 (1975): 495–526.

Herschberg-Pierrot, Anne. *La Fonction du cliché chez Flaubert: La Stéréotypie Flaubertienne.* Thèse du 3e cycle, Université de Paris III, 1981.

Proust, Marcel. *À la recherche du temps perdu.* Pléiade ed. 3 vols. Paris: Gallimard, 1973.

Riffaterre, Michael. "Fonctions de l'humour dans *Les Misérables.*" *Modern Language Notes* 87, 6 (November 1972): 71–82.

Simon, Claude. *Les Géorgiques.* Paris: Minuit, 1981. *The Georgics.* Trans. Beryl and John Fletcher. London: John Calder; New York: Riverrun, 1989.

Willenbrink, George A. *The Dossier of Flaubert's "Un Coeur simple".* Amsterdam: Rodopi, 1976.

Further Works by the Author

Debray Genette, Raymonde. "La Chimère et le sphinx: Texte et avant-texte dans *Madame Bovary.*" *Littérature* 64 (December 1986): 47–61.

———. "Description, dissection: Par les champs et par les grèves." In *Flaubert: La Dimension du texte,* ed. P. M. Wetherill. Manchester: Manchester University Press, 1982. 141–56.

———. "Du Mode narratif dans les *Trois contes.*" *Littérature* 2 (1971): 39–70.

———. "L'Empire de la description." *Revue d'Histoire Littéraire de la France* 81 (1981): 573–84.

———. "Flaubert: Science et écriture." *Littérature* 15 (1974): 41–51.

———. "Histoire littéraire et critique génétique." *Revue d'Histoire Littéraire de la France* 95, 6 (Supplement) (November-December 1995): 157–62.

———. "Intertextualité, autotextualité: Proust et Balzac." In *Voix de l'écrivain,* ed. Jean-Louis Cabanès. Toulouse: Presses Universitaires du Mirail, 1996. 247–60.

———. *Métamorphoses du récit: Autour de Flaubert.* Paris: Seuil, 1988.

———. "Profane, Sacred: Disorder of Utterance in *Trois Contes.*" Trans. Susan Huston. In *Flaubert and Postmodernism,* ed. Naomi Schor and Henry F. Majewski. Lincoln: University of Nebraska Press, 1984. 13–29.

———. "Un Récit autologique: Le Bonheur dans le crime." *Romanic Review* 64 (1973): 38–53.

———. "Some Functions of Figures in Novelistic Description." Trans. Barbara Benavie. *Poetics Today* 5 (1984): 677–88.

———. "Thème, figure, épisode: Genèse des aubépines." *Poétique* 25 (1976): 49–71.

———. "Traversée de l'espace descriptif." *Poétique* 51 (September 1982): 329–44.

Debray Genette, Raymonde, and Jacques Neefs, eds. *L'Œuvre de l'œuvre: Études sur la correspondance de Flaubert.* Saint-Denis: Presses Universitaires de Vincennes, 1993.

Chapter 6
With a Live Hand: Three Versions of Textual Transmission (Chateaubriand, Montaigne, Stendhal)

Jacques Neefs

Primarily a Flaubert scholar, Jacques Neefs is an exception among genetic critics in that he is also at home in many other manuscript dossiers. Besides editing *Madame Bovary* and Georges Perec's *Cahier des charges de "La Vie, mode d'emploi,"* he has written about Stendhal, Hugo, Pascal, and many others and was instrumental in producing *Drafts*, a 1996 *Yale French Studies* volume devoted to manuscript studies. A longtime professor at the Université de Paris VIII, he has also been teaching at Johns Hopkins in recent years.

"With a Live Hand: Three Versions of Textual Transmission" was first published in 1986 and is a project in the field of comparative manuscriptology. This exacting discipline understandably sees only rare contributions, for it is difficult enough to make sense of the story of a single dossier of manuscripts, let alone several. Neefs illustrates some rewards unique to comparison by contrasting the vastly different attitudes toward writing and communicating that Chateaubriand, Montaigne, and Stendhal inscribed in their avant-textes and texts.

Readers seeking a treatment of theoretical issues in genetic studies will be especially interested in the essay. Not only does Neefs raise many complex questions about genesis, but as he answers them, he demonstrates that avant-textes carry the traces of authors' attitudes toward specific literary projects or general processes of writing and also toward life, death, the community, and even time itself.

Neefs theorizes that an inherent mobility of writing is what ultimately denied Chateaubriand's attempt to control, or authorize, his own death and publication through a single, final, definitive gesture. Yet the same textual restlessness that so frustrated Chateaubriand was celebrated and affirmed by Montaigne, an author who, as Neefs tells it, wished all of his writings well and democratically welcomed each one, from fragment to published edition, into the world with a handshake and a smile. Where one author passionately cherished the priority of the Text over the avant-texte, the other felt that all his texts were created equal.

Like Chateaubriand, Stendhal wrote for a time that would follow his death, and like Montaigne, he did not see writing as a preliminary or transitory stage on the way to more perfect or unitary works. Neefs juxtaposes Stendhal's desire to write for a community of kindred spirits in the distant future with his habit of inscribing the immediate physical and environmental conditions into his avant-textes. This odd play of immediacy and eternity even resulted in the hybrid textual form sometimes preferred by Stendhal—Neefs calls it the "manuscript-volume." The form is heterogeneous and unfinishable in principle, filled with notes, comments, narratives, fragments, empty spaces, personal remarks, and other things, but it is singular and personal enough to overcome time and communicate with the future.

With the brilliant acuity he brought to things seen, Victor Hugo described René de Chateaubriand's death chamber on July 4, 1848: "The window blinds opening onto a garden were closed. A little daylight entered through the door, just ajar, to the living-room." In the shadows of this already-deserted space, abandoned forever to an anterior time, two things still stood out:

> At M. de Chateaubriand's feet, in the angle made by the bed and the wall of the room, there were two white wooden cases placed on top of each other. The larger one contained the complete manuscript of his *Mémoires,* divided into forty-eight copybooks. Of late there had been such disorder around him that one of these copybooks had been found that very morning by M. de Preuille in a dirty, black little corner they used for cleaning lamps. (Hugo 7: 1106)

It is as if the manuscripts, and the work itself, were waiting to be gathered up—waiting for Chateaubriand himself to slip into the immortality of books.

Until this day when it was (seemingly) finalized, the text of the *Mémoires d'outre-tombe* had grown ever more "definitive."

Chateaubriand took great care watching over his manuscripts, so that at his death, and only at his death, the text would be published the way he wanted.[1] He made meticulous preparations for the way the manuscript was to become a book, so that the great edifice of the *Mémoires* might be delivered as it was conceived, strictly orchestrated and controlled even postmortem. Chateaubriand had prevented any untimely publication and had managed everything so that the published text of the *Mémoires* would be exactly what was left at his death. He even devised a legal apparatus and a complex system of deposit boxes, drawers, and keys for the manuscripts. He attempted to ensure two things: (1) that the publishing company (which by an agreement reached in 1836 guaranteed financial and, it seemed, publishing security to Chateaubriand) would receive at Chateaubriand's death a complete and exact text of the *Mémoires* to be published as a book; and (2) that he would, first, retain complete freedom to finish and transform his work as he wished and, second, be guaranteed scrupulous fidelity in future editions.

At the very frontier of writing, the writer had taken on the world of time. Chateaubriand's management of his manuscripts reflects his will to keep absolute control over the text to be printed, control he brought to the limit of death itself. Maurice Levaillant, in the centenary edition of the *Mémoires,* has reconstituted and luminously described the manuscripts' amazing fate. I recall the important points here.

The 1836 contract gave the publisher the rights to Chateaubriand's *Mémoires* "such as they exist from the deposited manuscript and such as they will exist at his death as the result of any modifications or additions that he would choose to make before then." The same contract also provided for the delivery in 1840 of four volumes, not yet written, dealing with "the time of the war with Spain." Besides this, Chateaubriand gave the publishing company "the right to acquire by privilege any works that M. de Chateaubriand might compose in the future."

A system of "copies" and deposits was put into place. Two "control copies . . . containing the portion written as of now" (in 1836 there were eighteen portfolios, that is, the text of the *Mémoires* at the time of the contract signing) were to be kept, each in a box "locked" by three different keys. One key was to be held by the notary and another by the editor. Chateaubriand was to keep the "original manuscript" for himself. As the editing progressed, the "control copies" were to be augmented and ultimately revised to correspond strictly to the text desired by Chateaubriand. Yet provision was also made for the two "control copies" to be eliminated on the day of Chateaubriand's death. In fact, only the author's original manuscript was to be considered authentic; only that text was to be published.

In this gap between a text already deposited but provisional and a text that was to be considered definitive upon the death of its author, Chateaubriand constructed a space for a process of free writing and incessant revision. Indeed, the writing of the rest of the *Mémoires* coincided with the revision of what already existed. Sunday after Sunday, regular readings at the house of Madame Récamier allowed intimate friends to become acquainted with the transforming and still-confidential text. Chateaubriand worked out his general Conclusion (much more somber than he had first conceived of it in 1834, when its title was "The Future of the World"). He also corrected the "Verona Congress" "in order to insert it into the *Mémoires.*" (At this point Chateaubriand declared, "I now judge this work to be impartial. *Mémoires* is my real title, and business, in the future.") This process of writing and rewriting lasted until 1841. The *Mémoires* was then considered finished.

The year before, "no doubt when beginning to write his Conclusion," remarks Levaillant, Chateaubriand had burned his drafts and sketches, except for the beginning of the first manuscript. Such a gesture isolated the "definitive" manuscript in its completeness, in its finishedness, and gave it the force of an absolute original. Apparently the edifice of the *Mémoires* could not tolerate the existence of approximations and approaches: all "previous" writing had to be destroyed in order to affirm the finished text, to produce once and for all the splendid clarity of a perfectly orchestrated and definitive whole.

All was not, however, to have this superb decisiveness. Some copied and corrected pages escaped destruction (and were later found in private collections). Above all, time intervened in the writing of the work, in the form of a long delay. Most likely the date of November 16, 1841, signals the end of the conception of the *Mémoires* as Chateaubriand wanted it. In a striking effect, the last sentence of the Conclusion inscribed into the very text of the work—with a carefully rhythmed pause—the connection between the end of writing and the suspension of life: "I behold the light of a dawn whose sunrise I shall never see. It remains only for me to sit down at the edge of my grave; then I shall descend boldly, crucifix in hand, into eternity" (*Memoirs* 375). Yet although the curve of the work was closed by this suspension of text, the writer's manuscript work would continue for another seven years. The work itself continued to be "provisional." It was augmented in a virtual way by whatever memorable things happened; moreover, its details were transformed above all by the revisions and corrections so patiently and endlessly brought to it.

Thus the manuscript adventure of the *Mémoires* continued, tormented and devouring. When in 1844 the future publication of the work was threatened—negotiations took place for the work to appear serially in magazines before the publication in book volumes—Chateaubriand entertained the idea of himself preemptively undoing, in certain places, the unity he had so scrupulously constructed for publication. He gave this idea up, but in order to keep control of the exact composition of the text to be printed from his manuscripts, he did make the effort to authenticate, while still revising, the manuscript text of the *Mémoires.* At the beginning and end of each book, he put the notice "reviewed February 22, 1845" followed by his signature. He worked at this from the end of 1844 to October 1845 (thus the date of February 22, 1845, is curiously "theoretical"). Yet this work of authentication amounted to a new plunge into the work, a new reading that included numerous corrections and, above all, important subtractions. To become "definitive" again, the *Mémoires* manuscript had to be reworked, reproportioned, and resized once more.

Materially, this new manuscript is composed of pages from the 1841 manuscript: in these pages are crossouts, corrections, and recent notes and additions. Yet there are also numerous suppressions. It is a manuscript in several hands, in which variations introduced by time are marked by the successive strata of textual intervention. The sheets of 1841—that is, the copy made by a first secretary, Pilorge—were crossed out and corrected by Chateaubriand, and they were accompanied by more recent notes and a small number of additions copied by a new secretary, Danièlo. Once again there was a "definitive" manuscript and a new reading, and, as with the previous states of the *Mémoires*, a confidential reading before the faithful of l'Abbaye-aux-Bois. "We reread the *Mémoires*," writes Ballance, on October 16, 1845, "but just among ourselves, and in the most complete intimacy."

Thanks to this public presentation, the text became immediately modified. Far from being fixed by its oral exposition, the manuscript opened up once more to corrections, nuances, and attenuations. Chateaubriand took listeners' comments into account as well as the scruples of Madame de Chateaubriand, herself a reader of the manuscript, and once again the "definitive" manuscript stopped being definitive. Indeed, at this point considerable modifications were made: some dealt with the political interpretation of events (Madame de Chateaubriand suggested that he soften his criticisms of the Bourbon monarchy), and others dealt with his comments on his contemporaries (Madame Récamier, for example, asked him to abbreviate the volume devoted to her). This revision of the *Mémoires* ran from the end of 1845 to the end of 1846.

At this point Chateaubriand was worried about the exactness of the control manuscripts deposited with the notary, and he had his new secretary—Maujard, who would stay with the *Mémoires* to the end—copy over the first twelve books. Moreover, as the revision advanced, Chateaubriand continued to ensure that as texts became incomplete or obsolete they were replaced by copies conforming to his personal manuscript.

This personal manuscript was itself a new version of a "definitive" manuscript: composed of pages from the 1841 manuscript, reworked in 1845, it was copied by Pilorge, revised again by Chateaubriand, and new fair copies of certain pages were made by Maujard. Finally, Maujard established a continuous copy of the fourth part of the *Mémoires* as it had just been revised and, especially, toned down or abbreviated in certain places. Thus there exists, again, a "definitive" and authentic manuscript; at the end of each book of this manuscript there is the handwritten notice "reviewed in December 1846" followed by Chateaubriand's signature. Finally, to protect this "authentic" manuscript, Chateaubriand kept it with him in a box with two locks, a box that stayed with him until his death.

In March 1847 this new version of the *Mémoires* was offered in its turn to the close friends at l'Abbaye-aux-Bois during reading sessions organized by Madame Récamier. However, some notations, for example, "reviewed in 1847" (which make it into the printed text), bear witness to the fact that Chateaubriand had already reviewed this new "definitive" text and indeed would do so until his death. The manuscript, still open in this uncertain time that awaits closure, was endlessly remodeled into itself.

Chateaubriand's enterprise is marked by his anxiety about his signature and his vigilance over the definition of his text. Yet this care and vigilance met with uncertainty at the final moment, at the very instant when his death should have authenticated the text. Until that moment, his heartbeat rendered virtual the real end of the *Mémoires*. Work on the manuscript was like a furtive and continuous postponement of an expiration date. The text of the *Mémoires* was torn between the decision to ensure completeness and finishedness, and the freedom, accorded as if a reprieve, to modify it at will. The manuscript apparatus promoted this double attitude until the very end.

On April 27, 1847, as he sent a new "definitive" copy to replace the old, obsolete manuscript in the boxes with three keys, Chateaubriand wrote to M. Mandaroux-Vertamy, the notary charged with the scrupulous execution of the contract:

> Here are all my manuscripts, generally collected under the name of *Mémoires*. They begin with these words: *As it is impossible for me to predict the moment of my end*, and end with these *It remains only for me to sit down at the edge of my grave; then I shall descend boldly, crucifix in hand, into eternity*. Forty-two books constitute these manuscripts. . . .

The letter ends with a formula that repeats, more prosaically, the final sentence of the *Mémoires*: "I end my work at the moment of leaving this world; I am preparing to seek the eternal rest that I have always desired in the other." It is signed "Chateaubriand." The text, from its beginning to its end, miming the path that led from its conception to its completion, reposed, awaiting its exact publication.

Yet toward the end of the same year (1847), Chateaubriand took another precaution. He sent this letter to M. Mandaroux-Vertamy:

> Monsieur,
> I hasten to inform you that I have entirely reviewed and corrected my *Mémoires*. I have placed the copy that must serve for printing, at the fulfillment of my

> contract, in a white wooden box and I am sending you the key. You will be so kind, Sir and friend, to unite this key with the record of my testament already in your hands. I hope that after I am gone you will find that I have neglected no precautions so that the publication of my *Mémoires*, which I have entrusted to my testamentary executors, will be accomplished with the strictest fidelity.

This "original" draft is not, however, the very last state of the *Mémoires*. As Levaillant stresses, Chateaubriand "had kept, as was his right, one key to the box; and even then he sometimes took a copybook, had it read to him, and dictated one or two corrections to Maujard." It is to these still-open "white wooden boxes" and to one of these copybooks that Hugo alluded on July 4, 1848.

"The publication . . . will be accomplished with the strictest fidelity": the published work was to obey the author's absolute decision; it was to be composed only of that formulation deemed perfectly "definitive" by Chateaubriand himself. Yet at the juncture between the manuscript, that is, the work's reserve, and the monumental dispersion of the printed book, Chateaubriand placed his own death. The activity of writing and the public fate of the edited work thus slid into each other, imperceptibly, at the very instant of the author's erasure. The situation mimed in the very words of the text, in the last sentence, is also what ultimately decided the real achievement of the text of the *Mémoires*. This text, ceaselessly reworked and authenticated in manuscript revision by Chateaubriand, became "definitive" only when it intersected with death; death was entrusted with the definitive authentication. As the final erasure renders the text "definitive," the mortality of the writer slid into the work and into its public future.

By an arrangement that made a signature of death itself, the space of the manuscript was thus kept open as if it were a long postponement. This written text, so inhabited by the time period it was meant to relate, this work memorializing the vanishing of an epoch ("one could even say that the old world is ending and the new one beginning"), folded into the margins of a life. The author, who was also the subject matter, gave birth to it in the very act of disappearing; his erasure marked the end of both text and manuscript. Was not the density of such a conjunction part of the work itself? Was not the managing of this text, exposed from the outset to the process of rewriting, finally brought to the precise moment when the finished work transfigured into itself and suddenly appeared, born into the timeless time of books? There is an anxious strategy animating the passage from writing mastered by the hand (that is, manuscript writing) to the "definitive" definition of the printed work. It is a strategy that wishes to control with absolute mastery the question of the afterlife of the work as well as the instant that signs the passage between handwriting and publication: the dead hand continues to sign a text that has become whole and untouchable.

(During the postponement of the *Mémoires*, Chateaubriand wrote the *Vie de Rancé*. The strange, trembling sharpness of this text reveals the afterlife that Chateaubriand was attempting to reach, at the very frontier of time, or to liberate in his work. This text also confronts writing with its very own gesture; indeed the act of writing becomes "a quivering of time." To allow one's own hand to be led—a phrase in the *Vie de Rancé* is "Time has taken my hands in its own"—to the point of creating a work, or a book, out of the moment when the individual death resonates at last as a written portion of the printed matter, this is also a means of allowing the work to resonate with everything that the hand no longer controls, everything that creases the text with the infinitudes that it welcomes in advance.)[2]

Nevertheless, the printed text of the *Mémoires* would not have the "fidelity" that was so carefully prepared. A new history of variations begins. Despite Chateaubriand's precautions, the *Mémoires d'outre-tombe* is basically a series of compromises made with manuscripts. In fact, at Chateaubriand's death, the edited text of the *Mémoires* was doubly unfaithful. First, the printers used the control copies that did not have all the original manuscript's corrections and revisions; second, the will's executors who held the original manuscript truncated certain parts of it, suppressing the circumstantial developments and stylistic audacities that they thought would make the work hard to sell. The architecture in "books" that Chateaubriand had planned was also defeated; the series of brief chapters comprising the text of the *Mémoires* was published in "volumes" (a strictly typographical unit).

Only during the long period of the work's eventual destiny was a more "complete" text of the *Mémoires* able to be unraveled. Yet this was only achieved by recourse to a group of remaining manuscripts—in particular by the editing and publication of those earlier manuscripts rendered obsolete by the "original" and definitive manuscript. The floating multiplicity of texts that Chateaubriand had wished so terribly to avoid was nevertheless exactly what was necessary to restore to the *Mémoires* the fullness of their writing and the wholeness of their intent.

This monument-work was only "restored" in an era that went back to look at the manuscripts, that is, by Maurice Levaillant's "centenary edition." Editing the *Mémoires* meant retracing the internal work of its variations and rediscovering the genetic involution of a text that had undergone perpetual modification. Paradoxically, considering Chateaubriand's project of textual definition, it meant giving a new public presence to that which the progressive finalization of the *Mémoires* was supposed to absorb or destroy.

Editing means reconstituting a text on the basis of the existing manuscripts, at least those that have been somehow preserved. In the case of Chateaubriand, it means, first of all, the "1826 manuscript," or the 103 discontinuous, signed pages that escaped Chateaubriand's own destruction. Under the title of the first page of this manuscript, Chateaubriand himself notes: "This is the only part that remains of the first manuscript of my *Mémoires*, written in my own hand. All the rest, corrected and erased, was burned after Hyacinthe made a complete copy of it. (Note written in 1840 at the moment when I have just burned my papers.)"

The text of the *Mémoires* consumed itself, a pattern that held thereafter: "1834 manuscript," "1840–1 manuscript," "1847 manuscript," "1847–8 manuscript." All these followed, but as Maurice Levaillant emphasizes, "on the whole, and speaking materially, . . . these various manuscripts, from 1830 on, really formed just one: the manuscript delivered into the hands of the author after the 1836 agreements, enriched by new books until 1841, and shortened from then on by the effect of regrettable suppressions in 1845, 1846, and 1847. The text was endlessly corrected by Chateaubriand and ceaselessly reworked under Pilorge's care. Whenever a page was too covered with erasures, corrections, and second thoughts, the indefatigable secretary made a new clear copy." Yet not every eliminated page was destroyed; different states of this autoengendering manuscript, constructed on its own rewriting and created by the removal of previous versions of each passage, have survived. Traces remain of these fluid moments of writing, these corrections and alterations. Sheets that were kept or given away by Chateaubriand himself, condemned pages that were preserved or copied by secretaries, and loose pages (the intentions for which were still unclear) that somehow slipped away.

There were also parts of the manuscript that Chateaubriand himself had given away as he removed them from the "definitive" text, for example, the pages devoted to Madame Récamier or the chapters on Venice. To Madame Récamier, Chateaubriand gave the manuscript of the fourth part (such as it existed before the last revisions and suppressions) as well as the book in the 1845 manuscript that concerned her. Only in this way was it possible to produce a text of the *Mémoires*—an anamorphosis from the perspective of an indefinitely "definitive" elaboration, as it were—such as it was, more or less, in its most "complete" moment. Perhaps, too, it was at this moment (the "1841 manuscript") that the writing of the *Mémoires* was most free; in the subsequent period, as we have seen, suppressions and cautionary measures were very numerous. The editorial finishing of the work (one of its possible public manifestations) was paradoxically the restitution of a single stage of its elaboration and the reestablishment of the rejected fragments' right to be published.

The *Mémoires* therefore had a second life. In the long, projected time of edition, they became the composite image of what might have been a given moment of the manuscript. The editor himself stresses this virtuality, which he approached by examining "all the manuscripts" he found: "We attempted to restore the text of the *Mémoires d'outre-tombe* such as it was presented in the 1841 manuscript. At least, since this integral restitution no longer seemed possible, we approached it as an ideal." Does not this ideality of the text always persist, visible in the double perspective in which it is formed, that is, in the time of its genesis (in the reserved space of the manuscript) and in the long, indeterminate, unmasterable time of its editions, in the series of books that are made from it?

The text of the *Mémoires*? Chateaubriand wanted it to be fixed, defined as authentic by the instant of its definitive interruption. Yet this writing of time did not seem to be able to envisage being affected by the very time of its elaboration. For Chateaubriand the strict definition of the text of the work to be published meant the refusal of all the "earlier" pages made provisional by the very fact of rewritings, revisions, additions, and suppressions. The thought involved in these phases—thought that has no other destiny than that of total absorption in newer writing and destruction in a gesture that consumes or rejects them—is considered obsolete as soon as new formulations modify their consistency. It is the mobility proper to writing, and to its elaboration in time, that Chateaubriand seems to have wanted to efface in the clarity of an ever more definitive writing.

Thus this work so intimately wrought of the thinking of what is done and undone in time was submitted to the aesthetic demands of a totally controlled and "definitive" formulation. Chateaubriand seems to have wanted to deliver the text from its own anterior states—once they were rendered approximative by an ultimate formulation. In this conception of the "finished" work reigns the classical ideal of the absolute unity of the work, of its definition without variations.

Reacting to the future serial publication of the *Mémoires,* Chateaubriand was especially indignant about the public dispersal and the fragmenting of the work:

> It has been announced that everything I've written will be published, without respect for my absolute will, without deference for my memory, and that my ideas will be sold in lots so that, as with merchandise, the method of distribution will bring the sellers a maximum profit.

Fragmenting, public dispersion—for Chateaubriand these are two sides of the same crumbling, the crumbling of unity as authority. Mere shards of a becoming they do not control, the author and his work are swept into modernity's dispersion:

> Today the tragedies of Racine and Corneille and the funeral orations of Bossuet would be put into wax paper and promptly devoured like the crêpes they sell in cabbage leaves for the little brats to eat as they scurry over Pont Neuf.

This scattering goes hand in hand with modern aesthetic misunderstanding:

> In vain could I declare here that everything that will be published by me is not my finished manuscript such as it exists today in my very own hands; does there exist today as there once did a public that really wishes to know about things and would distinguish the finished picture from the early sketch? Certainly I do not claim to have made a masterpiece, but I was raised in another school and I would not like to be judged by my laborious, lifelong pains and my half-started sketches.

The concern for the monumental, aesthetically finished work is reinforced by the rejection of provisional states of the text:

> Will anyone listen to me when I say that I renounce the sketches that could be published under my name, and that I accept only those works entirely finished? Who are the judges today? Would they prefer, over the pieces that I claim as mine, the lines I traced merely to serve as guides a long time ago?[3]

In order for the death of the author to give absolute birth to the work, it seems that the work must be detached from its own genesis. It must be torn from anterior attempts, that is, from the approximations that are made provisional by the very fact of being anterior to the decisive instant of the end, to the "ultimate" state of the text. This requirement joins up with the aesthetic demands of "finished" works, that is, works delimited by the absolute authority of their authors. But it is sensitive, also, to the way works modernize, to an interest (devalued and discredited by Chateaubriand) that is perhaps new. Could not the dispersal and fragmentation of the writings become forms of works? Could not those very texts that have been rendered provisional be readable too? Could they not be read, precisely, for what is recognizably offered in them as an effort to think and speak? The terms of Chateaubriand's reprobation are on this point particularly sharp.

(At the same time, has not Chateaubriand himself also carefully controlled the byways that allow certain rejected pages to appear elsewhere much later? One thinks of how the "complete" manuscript of the fourth part was offered to Madame Récamier while the "original" manuscript had numerous suppressions. Did he not also show confidence in the length of time it takes for works to develop? Witness this codicil to his testament, written as early as 1837 to the attention of his posthumous editors: "If there are some pages that one could not now publish, they would allow them to be cut, with the certitude that these pages would be reestablished sooner or later.")

Rejection of variants and early attempts, organized mastery of the definitive text—it is very much to the authority of the author that Chateaubriand tends to give substance in the transmission of a manuscript reputed to be the only "original." Also to the banishment of every "anterior" version: the system of the work is affected by this, even if the editorial destiny of the text of the *Mémoires* has reestablished its successive strata and given it back its dimension as a fluid work developed in time.

At the other extreme of this demand for finitude and finishedness, one finds the mobility cultivated by Montaigne, a mobility molded in the space of variation that characterizes invention. In readable fashion, the text of his *Essais* is composed of the superimposition of moments of its own development. Here the time of thought's own flow becomes the juxtaposition of texts: neighborhoods of commentary communicate among themselves, making the separate moments of their formation overlap. Montaigne composed in time the work made of the variations brought by time itself. Successive editions and a mode of inflating the text with additions allowed the activity of thought to become the written trace. To the first two books of the 1580 edition of the *Essais*, the 1588 edition added, we know, a book III but it also enriched the first two books with numerous additions and corrections. Montaigne worked on this text, already impregnated with its own transformations, continually until his death in 1592. He performed a continuous commentary-rereading, placing alterations and additions into the margins of a copy of the 1588 edition (called the "Bordeaux copy"), which served as the original for future editions.

With his organized cohabitation of the differences woven of time, with his linkages that turn dialogue into a kind of freedom, with his relentless hand that continually "stuffs" the printed text with marginalia for more editions, Montaigne invents the textual (and editorial) form of the activity of writing. It is text made of its own movement ("Anyone can see that I have set out on a road along which I shall travel without toil and without ceasing as long as the world has ink and paper" [*Essays* 1070]). A book that carries such a text must welcome all the versions of this movement. Whatever of life passes into the work, whatever slips out softly to meet distant "others," it is this force of saying that animates the writing, it is this free coming and going of thoughts. A text made of its own additions, revisable until the very end, is the ultimate example of this. Here the end spreads out everywhere, almost surreptitiously, as a simple cessation of additions and commentaries. Silence strikes the whole of the text; the multitude of texts already present are left to battle it out.

Far from placing the subject-author in the perspective point of the ending—of the text, of the writing—where his effacement will decide (ultimate, exorbitant power) upon the legitimacy of the text, as was the case for the *Mémoires*, Montaigne disperses in each essay, in each version of a reflection, the incidental apparition of a voice, as if in suspension.

Such a form of cohabitation ensures the free existence of varied states: "Reader, just let this tentative essay, this third prolongation of my self-portrait, run its course. I make additions but not corrections" (1091). What then reigns is a sort of communal chance given to each utterance, to each formulation:

> My book is ever one: except that, to avoid the purchaser's going away quite empty-handed when a new edition is brought out, I allow myself, since it is merely a piece of shoddily constructed mosaic, to tack on some additional ornaments. I am really just throwing a little extra in, and this does not condemn the original version but does lend particular value to each subsequent one through ambitious bits of precision. (1091; translation altered)

Notions of sketches and drafts have no meaning here; or rather, to write is always to sketch a truth in the movement that attempts it, to pursue it without capturing it in any "definitive" formulation. And to turn the whole supply of additions, revisions, and variant possibilities into text is to welcome a sort of equality among the diverse, attempted utterances: "this does not condemn the original version." Is there not here the opening of a space favorable to the differences which are the living, always-displaced divisions of an incessant activity, the differences that compose the mobility of thoughts? Divisions without any overarching rule are what open up the possibility of a free thought.

To allow the text to be constructed in time, to allow differences to become encounters, combinations, and minute depths gained in the temporal vastness of variation—variation itself becoming an actor in the text—this would be the ambition of a text enriched by its own development, adding "particular value to each subsequent one through ambitious bits of precision" (1091).

Patchworked, the development of the text becomes the very text of the change through which the truth must be made to pass. One would have to deposit into writing's *revisable* space (for example, successive editions and manuscript additions) the discrepancies that give variety and life to a thought and that make room for readings to meet freely. Montaigne constructs a relationship between the act of writing and the printed book that allows the successive strata of thought to associate progressively with each other. This relationship becomes the printed space of the variants and of the internal dialogue conducted by the hand that is writing.

The afterlife that Montaigne develops in his work is the live opening toward time that is the activity of writing. It is the chance for thoughts to make their mobility known, to throw themselves into unforeseen encounters. For Montaigne, to depict "the passage" was also to invent, using successive editions and additions, a material space of writing that would preserve the place of passage.[4] Rather than erasures and destruction of earlier states, equal survival is accorded to each phrase and to each instant of a formulation. In the tomb-work, the intersections of thought are actively traced out.[5] And in this transmission of writing, there are no stops where we can fix the "definitive" text. No stops, at least, other than the simple, nearly subordinate, and accidental interruptions of rereadings and additions, the end of the dialogue of thought with writing, and the stopping of the hand that writes.

A third version of the relation between texts still in the hands of their authors (texts still revisable by possible rereading and rewriting, still modifiable in the authors' remaining lifetime—little matter whether they are signed manuscripts, copies, sets of proofs, or successive editions) and the postmortem edition of texts rendered "definitive" by their public fate, and of the controlled articulation of this relation with the limit that is the death of the writer, a version closer historically to Chateaubriand, and even singularly concurrent with him, is offered by Stendhal.[6]

In Stendhal, two opposing behaviors meet. On the one hand, certain of his texts seem to have been consumed by their passage into a book, indeed at the very moment of his dictation of the manuscript. This is the case with *Le Rouge et le noir* and *La Chartreuse de Parme,* both of whose manuscripts seem to have been destroyed after publication. On the other hand, Stendhal made books out of his own unfinished manuscripts: these volumes were composed and registered for a completely hypothetical publication. *Lucien Leuwen* and *Vie de Henry Brulard* are exemplary instances of such manuscript-volumes.[7]

Manuscript-volumes are composed of the following elements: the entirety of the writing (handwritten) done for the work in question, in numbered folios (sometimes there are several superimposed numberings) with gaps left in the text; blank folios; other folios very unequally filled. Side by side on these pages one finds the writing of the text itself (fast, cursive writing), variants, and, especially, many "notes": outlines, plans, considerations of the effects to be produced and of the narrative development, and sketches of episodes or actions. But these notes belonging to the genesis of the text also encounter a great deal of the "marginalia" so often evoked by Stendhal critics: indications of the date and the hour of the writing of the page, of the speed of the writing, of the weather, of the spatial location ("near the window," "next to the chimney"), and of nearby activities (meetings, trips, shows . . .). The circumstantial sphere of the writing, its immediate depth, is thus fleetingly but intensely transcribed, in both long dashes and rapid traces: "December 3. Head grew heavy at three o'clock because of the North wind's light coolness"; "climate: December 3, worked an hour with the window open" (*Lucien Leuwen*, R. 301, vol. III, ff. 287, 294). In the free space of the manuscript, Stendhal festooned the text that he was writing—he even gave himself material space for this freedom by leaving blank sheets for the episodes in which he interrupted himself or for the developments he suspended—with a memory of the gestures, movements, fevers, boredoms, and jubilations that participate in the advent of the text. The genetic space of the writing bustles with minute circumstances that are the concrete presence, on the page itself, of all that accompanies the act of writing, of everything to which the writing cannot remain indifferent. All these "small things"[8] to which Stendhal gives, in the text of his works, such a new aesthetic and ethical power, find an amazingly active inscription in his manuscript-volumes, in the nearness to the text that is born in them. (One thinks here of Nabokov and of his ethics of detail: "This capacity to wonder at trifles—no matter the imminent peril—these asides of the spirit, these footnotes in the volume of life are the highest forms of consciousness" [374].)

These pages of the manuscript-volume are only the surface of a fabulously agile dialogue among the figures that the writer invents for himself in the space of the writing—"self"-reflections multiplied by the divisions of speech: "about me," "about the character of Dominique," "about the author," etc. The author comments: "*For me*: you are only a *naturalist*: you do not choose the models, but always take Métilde and Dominique for love. 13 July 34 and 18 September" (*Lucien Leuwen*, R. 301, vol. 1, f. 306v).[9] Phrases are also found for the difficulty of writing: "18 December 1835. At 4 (O'Clock) 50, lack of daylight. I stop. / 18 December 1835 from 2 (O'Clock) to 4:30, twenty-four pages. I am so absorbed by the memories unfolding before my eyes that I can hardly form my letters. Fifty-two years and eleven months" (*Henry Brulard*). Thus in the manuscript Stendhal engraved—inscription, more or less cryptic, is one of the motifs of Stendhal's texts, in particular in *Henry Brulard*—a multiple presence of things and of himself. He also gave an equal written existence to the "text" carried out by rapid improvisation in the folios and to the "marginal" notations that are the very acuity of a life being transformed into writing—he retained, that is, the presence of the little signals that still make up things and thoughts.

Into these manuscript-volumes, again, Stendhal slipped many testaments and engravings meant not so much to illustrate the text as to give a value to the volume itself. Ironically accompanying the uncertain future of the writing, these testaments predict contradictory fates for their text:

17 Feb 1835, *Testament* (Gift of the present book to Mme Pauline Perier-Lagrange, at the house of M. Colomb, 35, Godot-de-Mauroy).

If the heavens call me to take pleasure in the reward of my virtues before this novel is printed, I fear that these volumes might be cheated of a fair trial and may fall into the hands of some merchant who, mercenary by nature or intent, will use this paper to light his green wood. In order to give these volumes some worth in the eyes of fools, I placed some etchings in them. (*Lucien Leuwen*)[10]

He also foresees a sort of random afterlife:

I bequeath and give this manuscript *Vie de Henry Brulard* etc. and all manuscripts relative to the history of my life, to M. Ab[raham] Constantin, ch[evali]er in the Legion of Honor, and, if he does not print them, to M. Alphonse Levavasseur, bookseller, place Vendôme, and, if he dies before me, I bequeath it *successively* to Mssrs. Ladvocat, Fournier, Amyot, Treuttel and Wertz, Didot, on this condition: 1) before printing this manuscript they change all the women's names: where I have Pauline Sirot, they will put Adèle Bonnet. It will suffice to substitute the names from the next jury list: in short, absolutely all the proper names of women, and no names of men, must be changed.

Second condition: send copies to the libraries of Edinburgh, Philadelphia, New York, Mexico City, Madrid, and Brunswick. Change all the women's names, a condition *sine qua non*.

Civita-Vecchia, 29 November 1835
H. Beyle. (*Henry Brulard*)

Thus, lightheartedly and in its unfinished state, the text was hazarded in the direction of a still-uncertain future. Yet it was the totality of the manuscript-volume that moved toward the possible destiny of a finished work. It was a text with surroundings, hesitations, gaps, and concurrent versions—the private text of an incessant dialogue. Even the decision to finish becomes part of the manuscript text: "31 [sic] April 1835—tomorrow May 1st, one year ago I started this. The canvas is covered; I've known it for two days (suppression of Omar)" (*Lucien Leuwen*).[11] Stendhal leaves behind a text that has itself rejected the idea of a "definitive" text—a text that is still murmuring with the singularity of a writing, a behavior, and a solitude as well.

Yet it is precisely this irreducible singularity that has a chance of passing from the manuscript-volume to those unknown, yet already friendly, readers—rare people who can be touched by a happy meeting: "With luck, I may well be read in 1900 by the souls I love, the Madame Rolands, the Mélanie Guibers, the . . ." (*Henry Brulard*). No doubt one of the most precious of Stendhal's inventions was his willingness to conceive of the manuscript-volume as a form of precious singularity capable of dialoguing with the indefinite time of readings. "I buy a lottery ticket whose grand prize is basically this: to be read in 1935." Staying in the open cockpit of the manuscript-volume was a form of confidence in the life of works and encounters to come. Elias Canetti has well described the liberty opened up by Stendhal, this new form of literary immortality made of an encounter in time, an encounter freed from the weight of the present and even from the concern for the work:

> Without pitying himself, he was content to write for a few, but he was certain that in a hundred years he would be read by many. Nowhere in modern times is a belief in literary immortality to be found in a clearer, purer and less pretentious form. (277)

Nestled inside such a conception of the work and of writing is the multiple presence of all things and the affirmation of presence before the living:

> Not only does he abjure killing, but he takes with him into immortality all who were alive with him here, and it is then that all these, the least as well as the greatest, are most truly alive. (278)

To inhabit the manuscript-volume and to let it go forth into an uncertain future—this has certainly been the most extreme form of an open trust in possible recognition across time. The aesthetics of interruption and the active unfinishing that characterize the works of Stendhal rupture completely with the classical aesthetics of imperiously finished works (a rupture Stendhal had already theorized in *Racine et Shakespeare*) and are carried out by the very development and transmission of the manuscripts. The idea is that the work and its gestures, the singular attention to details and to the little things that form a life inseparable from the text of the work, can pass into the time of publication (but this is a wide-open, distant time into which the present is disseminated).

In the gamble on the future that Stendhal took, there was enough necessity—could one say truth?—for it to be effected. Or more exactly, its accuracy comes from the fact that it continues to be achieved. Although the executor of the will (the "faithful Colomb," says literary history) preserved the manuscripts that Stendhal had constructed and bound into books, he never could have conceived of them as publishable, so far were they from the finishedness required for even the idea of a work. He published only that part of *Lucien Leuwen* that Stendhal had dictated directly to him, in his time, under the title *Le Chasseur vert* in 1855.

The very time that Stendhal had given himself (since he wrote "for the reader of 1880, 1900, 1935") had to elapse before the manuscripts became books. In 1890, Casimir Stryienski naively emphasized this effect of having the work completed in the time of its edition: "By a marvelous intuition, Beyle, in this *Vie de Henry Brulard* addresses the readers of

1880, and writes for them—he had foreseen that it was necessary to wait; we may well be ten years late, but what is that when we remember that the *Memoirs* of Benvenuto Cellini were published 150 years after his death."[12] The editions elaborated from the manuscripts by Stryienski in 1890 for *Henry Brulard* and by Jean de Mitty in 1894 for *Lucien Leuwen* are still texts conforming to the unifying idea of the finished work: they truncate the manuscripts, build bridges where there are gaps, and make a continuous, presentable text of the echo chamber invented by Stendhal.

Only very gradually was the precious infinitude of these manuscripts able to be converted into printed books. Little by little the successive editions restored the abundance of Stendhal's texts: Henry Debraye in 1913 and Henri Martineau in 1927 for *Henry Brulard*; Debraye in 1926 and 1927 and Martineau in 1929 for *Lucien Leuwen*. The manuscript sketches of *Henry Brulard* appeared only in the 1927 edition (and even then they were only published in part). Even now the "marginalia" continue to be treated as decidedly secondary texts to be stored away in notes. The more recent editions of these manuscripts, in particular that of *Henry Brulard* by Victor del Litto in the Pléiade edition, tend to restore the manuscript as it is, with its multiple cohabitations, but in a manner still quite controlled by the classic disposition of a book (in particular, even now, by the rejection of the "marginalia" to the status of notes). It would seem that Stendhal's creativity has exceeded, so far, the conception that editors can form of a nineteenth-century book.

The audacity and the freedom that Stendhal projected into the space of his manuscripts still call for actualization in books better conforming to the infinite vivacity that the manuscripts attempt to transmit. No doubt they are not reaching for the future of Literature, but for the infinitude of a freedom carried by writing and the friendly recognition that the gesture of a hand can evoke.

Is it possible to see, all at once, the idea of a work that inhabits a manuscript, the material management of a given writing and its transmission, and the way a book becomes a work in the history of its editions? No doubt each of these faces, or moments, has its own autonomy and its own history and specific habits (an aesthetic conception that rules the form of the work, some material conditions of writing and edition, and a cultural history of editorial practices). Yet the three versions sketched above also indicate how much texts, slipped by their authors into the envelope of time, can join in composing two of their own distinct variations: that of their genesis—in the manuscripts, where the hand of the writer reigns—and that of the long time of their successive published editions. During the latter period, their very transmission is controlled by a prevailing idea of works and books, an idea that the works themselves slowly transform, by means of their own exigencies and by means of those possibilities to which they so often, from so far away, make appeal.

Source: "De Main vive: Trois versions de la transmission des textes." *Littérature* 64 (1986): 30–46.

Works Cited

Blum, Claude. "La Peinture du moi et l'écriture inachevée." *Poétique* 53 (February 1983): 60–71.

Canetti, Elias. *Masse und Macht.* Hamburg: Claassen, 1960. *Crowds and Power.* Trans. Carol Stewart. New York: Viking, 1963.

Chateaubriand, François-René, vicomte de. *Les Mémoires d'outre-tombe: Édition du Centenaire.* Ed. Maurice Levaillant. Paris: Flammarion. 1982. *The Memoirs of Chateaubriand.* Trans. Robert Baldick. London: Hamish Hamilton, 1961.

———. *Les Mémoires d'outre-tombe.* Ed. Jean-Claude Berchet. Paris: Classiques Garnier, 1989–98.

———. *Œuvres.* Ed. Maurice Levaillant. Pléiade ed. Paris: Gallimard, 1951.

Garavini, Fausta. "*Les Essais* de 1580, ou 'la mort par publication.'" *Littérature* 62 (May 1986): 104–15.

Hugo, Victor. *Œuvres complètes.* Ed. Jean Massin. 17 vols. Paris: Le Club Français du Livre, 1967–70.

Levaillant, Maurice. *Deux livres des Mémoires d'outre-tombe.* Paris: Delagrave, 1936.

Marin, Louis. "Le Tombeau de Montaigne," In *La Voix excommuniée: Essais de mémoire.* Paris: Galilée, 1981. 133–56.

Montaigne, Michel de. *The Essays of Michel de Montaigne.* Trans. M. A. Screech. New York: Penguin, 1991.

Mouchard, Claude. "Deux secondes vies." *Le Temps de la Réflexion* 3 (1982): 145–70.

Nabokov, Vladimir. "The Art of Literature and Commonsense." In *Lectures on Literature.* Ed. Fredson Bowers. New York: Harcourt Brace Jovanovich, 1980. 371–80.

Neefs, Jacques. "Stendhal, sans fins." *Le Manuscrit inachevé.* Paris: CNRS, 1986. 15–44.

Stendhal. *Lucien Leuwen.* Ed. Jean de Mitty. Paris: E. Dentu, 1894.

———. *Lucien Leuwen.* Ed. Henry Debraye. Abbeville: F. Paillart, 1926. Revised ed. Paris: Le Divan, 1927.

———. *Lucien Leuwen.* Ed. Henri Martineau. Paris: Le Divan, 1929.

———. *Œuvres complètes.* Ed. Henri Martineau. Paris: Le Divan, 1927–37.

———. *Œuvres intimes.* Ed. Victor del Litto. Pléiade ed. 2 vols. Paris: Gallimard, 1981–82.

———. *La Vie de Henry Brulard: Autobiographie.* Ed. Casimir Stryienski. 1890. New ed. Ed. Casimir Stryienski. Paris: Emile-Paul frères, 1923.

———. *La Vie de Henry Brulard: Autobiographie.* Ed. Henry Debraye. Paris: H. and É. Champion, 1913.

Further Works by the Author

Contat, Michel, Denis Hollier, and Jacques Neefs, eds. *Drafts.* Special issue of *Yale French Studies* 89 (1996).

Debray Genette, Raymonde, and Jacques Neefs, eds. *Romans d'archives.* Lille: Presses Universitaires de Lille, 1987.

Didier, Béatrice, and Jacques Neefs, eds. *Chantiers révolutionnaires.* 2 vols. Saint-Denis: Presses de l'Université de Vincennes, 1992–93.

———, eds. *Diderot: Autographes, copies, éditions.* Saint-Denis: Presses de l'Université de Vincennes, 1986.

———, eds. *Éditer des manuscrits: Archives, complétude, lisibilité.* Saint-Denis: Presses de l'Université de Vincennes, 1996.

———, eds. *La Fin de l'Ancien Régime: Sade, Rétif, Beaumarchais, Laclos.* Vol. 1 of *Manuscrits de la Révolution.* Saint-Denis: Presses de l'Université de Vincennes, 1991.

———, eds. *Hugo: De l'écrit au livre.* Saint-Denis: Presses de l'Université de Vincennes, 1987.

———, eds. *Manuscrits surréalistes: Aragon, Breton, Éluard, Leiris, Soupault.* Saint-Denis: Presses de l'Université de Vincennes, 1995.

———, eds. *Le Manuscrit surréaliste.* Saint-Denis: Presses de l'Université de Vincennes, 1994.

———, eds. *Penser, classer, écrire: De Pascal à Perec.* Saint-Denis: Presses de l'Université de Vincennes, 1990.

———, eds. *Stendhal: Écritures du romantisme.* Vol. 1. Saint-Denis: Presses de l'Université de Vincennes, 1988.

Flaubert, Gustave. *Madame Bovary.* Ed. Jacques Neefs. Paris: Le Livre de poche, 1999.

Neefs, Jacques, ed. *Configurations d'archives.* Special issue of *Cahiers de Textologie* 4 (1993).

———. *Madame Bovary de Flaubert.* Paris: Classiques Hachette, 1972.

———. "Marges." In *De la lettre au livre: Sémiotique des manuscrits littéraires,* ed. Louis Hay. Paris: CNRS, 1989. 57–88. "Margins." Trans. Stephen A. Noble. *Word and Image* 13,2 (April-June 1997): 135–57.

Perec, Georges. *Cahier des charges de "La Vie, mode d'emploi."* Ed. Hans Hartje, Bernard Magné, and Jacques Neefs. Paris: CNRS, 1993.

Chapter 7
Genetic Criticism and Cultural History: Zola's *Rougon-Macquart* Dossiers

Henri Mitterand

Henri Mitterand is a semiotician, lexicologist, and genetic critic who has particularly emphasized the social and cultural dimensions of avant-textes. Retired from the Sorbonne, he is currently a professor at Columbia University and the world's leading authority on Émile Zola, whose complete works he edited and whose definitive three-volume biography he began publishing in 1999.

The 1989 essay translated here showcases Mitterand's ability to identify and analyze concrete examples in the broad field of cultural genetics, an expanding discipline that examines the way avant-textes interact with or reflect their cultural surroundings. Readers who think of genetic studies as too hermetically self-contained or microfocused on the development of a single text to be of general interest are apt to be surprised at the ambitious and open-ended nature of the questions Mitterand puts to manuscripts.

Among other things, he wonders what led Zola, after his youthful works, to conceive of and write his massive cycle of *Rougon-Macquart* novels, the most far-reaching novelistic project since Balzac's *Comédie humaine*. What aspects of the mid-1860s Parisian and French politico-cultural landscape can be detected in such an apparently private process of creation and how can one detect them? During this tumultuous period, Zola was simultaneously active on several fronts: fighting private battles over ideology and literary technique with Taine, Balzac, and the Goncourt brothers; sharing in the public reception of fashionable ideas from French physiologists, psychologists, sociologists, and Darwinians; and rethinking, with his nation, the political future of France.

Mitterand demonstrates that to understand the way so many historical textures—sometimes as opaque as a dawning Zeitgeist—can be embedded in an avant-texte, one must read at once "internally" and "externally," respecting and remaining sensitive not only to the author's evolving literary expression but also to the most diverse extra-authorial phenomena. This necessarily speculative technique has wide applicability since it presumes that all avant-textual documents or fragments—from all authors everywhere—may contain the heterogeneous echoes of both individual creations and larger social discourses, evolutions, and trends.

To address the technical question of *how* avant-textes can record, reflect, or even instigate such broader movements, Mitterand examines Zola's reading notes and early drafts. He then creates suggestive links between various cultural phenomena and Zola's own transforming ideas, for example, his theory of character, narrative logic, and the forms of mimesis he installed between his texts and his times. He shows that if it is always difficult to grasp the dialectic between a set of avant-textes and their surrounding environment, it is especially so when an author has great social stature and creative power. Yet Mitterand refuses to simplify the matter; Zola neither imposed a vision upon French society nor received one from it. Rather, the author, the *Rougon-Macquart* texts, and many cultural forces all mutually pushed, pulled, and reinforced the still-nascent but spreading psychological, encyclopedic, and scientific tendencies of the time and cocreated the realist/naturalist movement that became a leading trend in late nineteenth-century France.

Genetic criticism often scrutinizes something so close to what germinates or is born in thought and writing that it understandably tries to grasp, in the very first draft of a manuscript and beyond the author's individual expression, both the symptoms and earliest traces of transformation in the surrounding culture's thought, collective ideals, and tastes. Only with infinite prudence, however, can this tendency, both justified and perilous, produce a cultural genetics—a complement to cultural history in the way that literary genetics (the study of every aspect of the genesis of literary works) is a complement to literary history.

On the one hand, the tendency is justified because, as we well know, any individual's language, especially in its experimental phases, feeds on its environment and on the preimpositions and presuppositions of collective discourse: each person's words are necessarily the words of others. Looking ahead to distinctions cherished by Zola in 1868, we could say that there is no such thing as an innate semantics; no language is entirely new. Instead there is a hereditary semantics, inherited from parents, teachers, and classmates in every sense of the word "class." Thus, thanks to their relative spontaneity and their freedom from later constraints and restructuring, avant-textual materials, for example, the first lines of a sketch or a scenario, are the most direct and—because they lack the flourishes of the finished work—often the most candid and raw contacts with what is "being said" or "murmured about," that is, the very things that might be announcing new themes in the wider social discourse. When, in 1884, at the beginning of his *Germinal* sketch, Zola wrote: "I wish to describe the uprising of the laborers against capital," he was expressing not so much a fact as a fantasy, one he then shared with many of his contemporaries.

On the other hand, it is a risky tendency. Giving this dimension to genetic analysis may broaden it in an exciting way, but it also incurs great risks, mainly because there exists an infinite textuality of relevant reference. Where could limits be imposed? Where should pertinent links and intersections be sought? How should the space of previous and contemporary writing be mapped out? How can the impact of an isolated language on a collective language be measured? How can the concept of intertext, so seductive and yet so imprecise, be harnessed for work if one wishes, on the one hand, to avoid lapsing into a critical romanticism and falling prey to a dizzying array of cultural constellations, and, on the other, to do more than merely offer a meticulous and myopic account of authenticated sources?

Genetic criticism does provide some guard rails. Indeed, as does archeology, it carries the material strata of history out into the open; it brings the history of a thought, or a language, into the materiality of its words and configurations and therefore functions as a guarantee against uncertainty and divagation. If genetic criticism has had some success in our time, it is thanks to this exacting philological method. These days we are all still recovering, to some extent, from many great, brilliant, and improbable generalizations that proved to be neither verifiable nor falsifiable.

If we agree to use the term "genetic," despite its homonymy with the altogether different science of biology, and despite the fact that we literary geneticists are not able to to do any "genetic experiments" on literary objects (such as conceive of a work in vitro), and if we agree that there exist at least two kinds of literary genetics—(1) a "scenaric" or avant-textual genetics that studies any and every manuscript document that plays a role in the conception and preparation of a work and (2) a manuscript, scriptural, or textual genetics that studies variations among the written manuscripts—then it seems to me that (1) offers the best resources for a reflection on the relationship between genetic criticism and the history of culture. It is at this level that one can seize the generative relations that unite the different series of historical facts, discourses, and productions of text in a synchrony immediately anterior to the birth of a work.

The constitutive documents for the general project of the *Rougon-Macquart* cycle, which Zola wrote during the winter of 1868–69, are fertile terrain for this kind of work. Hidden in the shadows cast by the finished works and by the journalistic campaign that Zola carried on at the same time, these avant-textes have received very little study. Only Roger Ripoll has shown real interest in them, in his thesis *Réalité et mythe chez Zola.* His work is a convenient starting point for new research.

The documents in question can be found at the end of volume 5 of the Pléiade edition of the *Rougon-Macquart.*[1] In the order provided in that

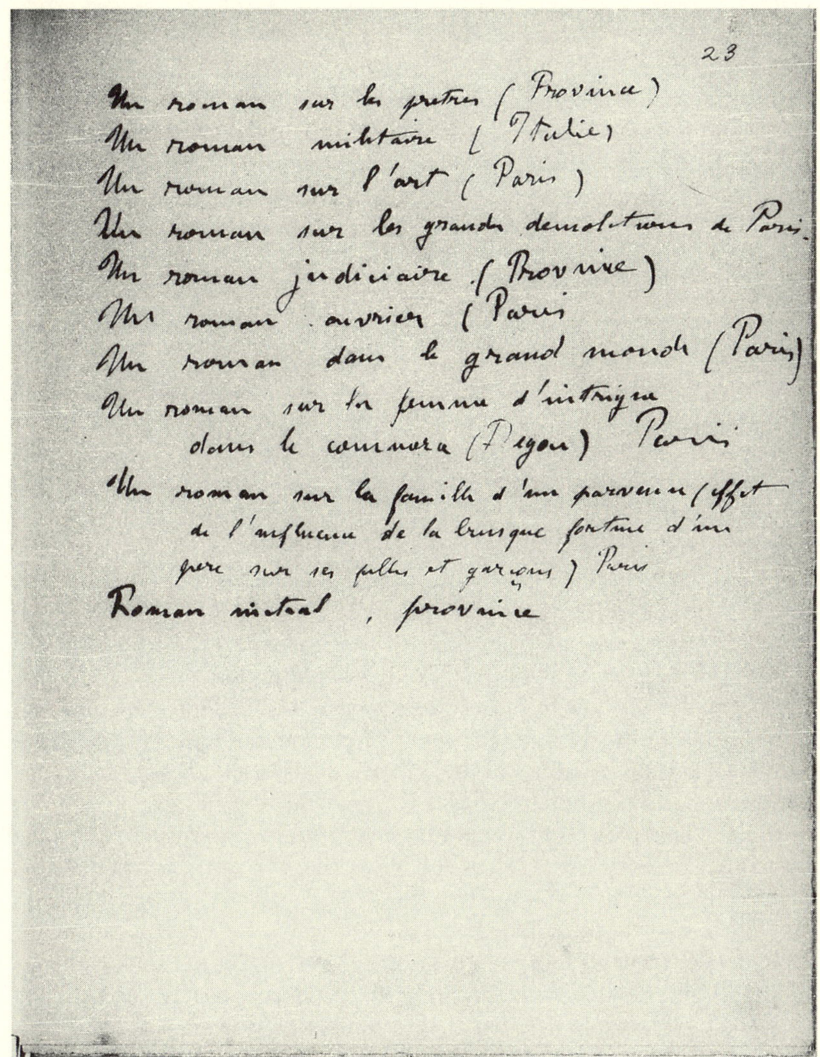

23

Un roman sur les prêtres (Province)
Un roman militaire (Italie)
Un roman sur l'art (Paris)
Un roman sur les grandes démolitions de Paris.
Un roman judiciaire (Province)
Un roman ouvrier (Paris)
Un roman dans le grand monde (Paris)
Un roman sur la femme d'intrigue dans le commerce (Pegou) Paris
Un roman sur la famille d'un parvenu (effet de l'influence de la brusque fortune d'un père sur ses filles et garçons) Paris
Roman initial, province

Figure 1. Émile Zola, "Projet de dix romans." BN N.A.F. 10345, f. 23. Courtesy of the Bibliothèque Nationale de France.

edition, we have the following materials: a series of titles of works on physiology and psychology; reading notes and a summary of *Physiologie des passions*, by Charles Letourneau (Paris: Baillière, 1868); reading notes and a summary of the *Traité philosophique et physiologique de l'hérédité naturelle* by Dr. Prosper Lucas (Paris: Baillière, 1847–50); *General Notes* on heredity and on the future structure of the cycle, in particular an early list of ten novels; a text of two handwritten sheets entitled *Différences entre Balzac et moi*; a text of four handwritten pages entitled *Notes générales sur la nature de l'œuvre*; a detailed outline for the first novel (this will be *La Fortune des Rougon*, published in 1871); a second detailed outline of this book, followed by a summary of nine other novels planned at that time; and, finally, two genealogical trees for the future Rougon-Macquart family. To this we must add the reading notes taken from Dr. Ulysses Trelat's *La Folie lucide* and from Dr. Moreau de Tours's *La Psychologie morbide*, which were not reproduced in this Pléiade volume but which Zola wrote down as early as 1868–69. They were eventually used in *La Conquête de Plassans* in 1873 and *La Faute de l'abbé Mouret* in 1874. Generally speaking, we have traces of Zola's readings in science, his general notes for his works, and his first outlines.

All these avant-textes, which are stored in the Bibliothèque Nationale in Paris, are undated. From internal allusions we know that they are later than *Madeleine Férat*, published in November of 1868. Of course, they are earlier than Zola's first drafts of *La Fortune des Rougon*, written in the spring of 1869.

In his thesis Ripoll criticizes the order in which I had chosen to publish these texts in 1967. Except for one or two details, I am won over by his arguments. He contrasts the apparent logic of classification (readings, general notes, and outlines) with the real work of genesis, and this debate clarifies the basic givens of our problem today.

Essentially the debate is over two points: (1) the internal order of Zola's general notes and (2) the genetic placement of these general notes with respect to his readings in the sciences or para-sciences of physiology of passions and psychopathology. Let us put the outlines to one side, for by all evidence they seem to have been written later than the rest of the material. The most likely genetic order for the rest of the dossier can be reconstituted in the following way.

First of all there is a list of ten novels (MS 10345, f. 23), a list that reflects the pains taken by Zola, after writing *Thérèse Raquin* and *Madeleine Férat*, to give a more sociological expansion to his program for novelistic production and to organize the production as a whole composed of complementary units—the way Balzac gave structure to his *Comédie humaine* after the fact. Zola planned a novel about a preacher, a military novel, a novel about art, a novel on the great demolitions of Paris, a novel to start the series, etc. Again the example of Balzac—probably the prologue to *La Fille aux yeux d'or*—suggested to Zola the idea of rationalizing this disparate list by reclassifying the subjects according to a more systematic paradigm. He did so in his famous list of worlds:

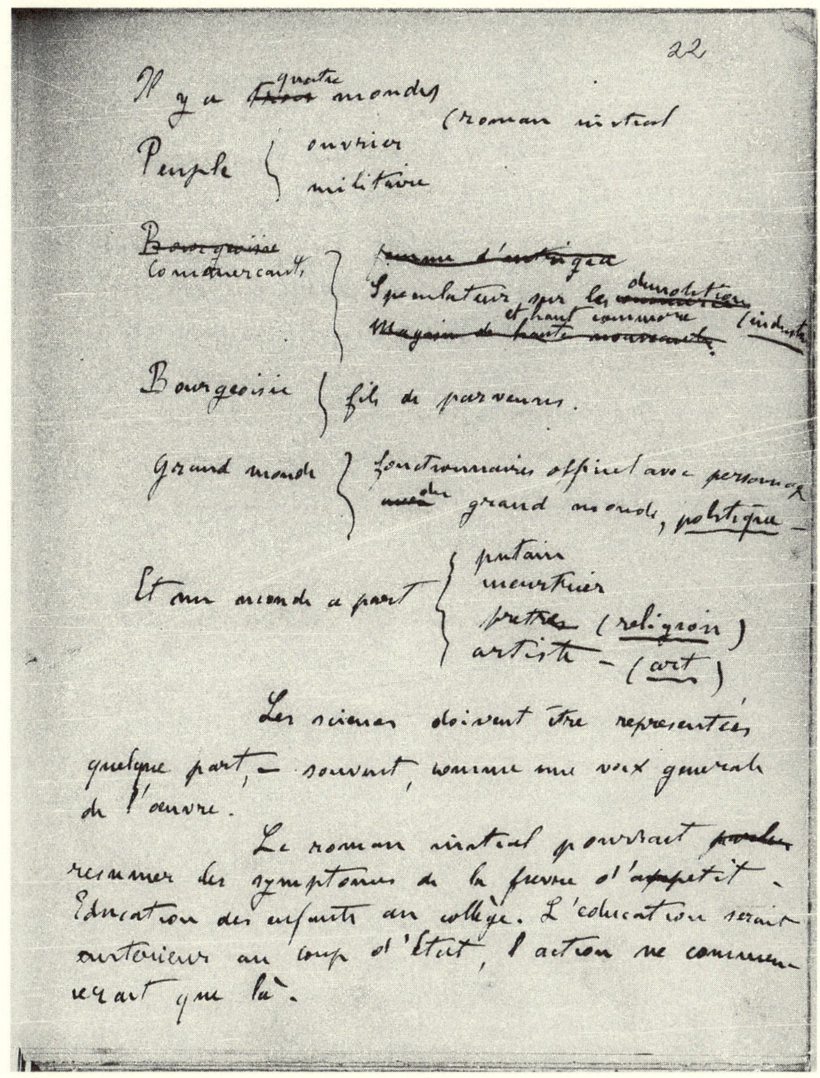

22

Il y a ~~trois~~ quatre mondes

(roman initial

Peuple { ouvrier
militaire

~~Bourgeoisie~~
Commerçants { ~~femme d'intrigue~~
Spéculateur sur les ~~commerce~~ démolitions
et haut commerce (industrie
~~Magasin de haute nouveauté~~

Bourgeoisie { fils de parvenus.

Grand monde { fonctionnaires officiel avec personnage
~~avec~~ du grand monde, politique –

Et un monde à part { putain
meurtrier
prêtre (religion)
artiste – (art)

Les sciences doivent être représentées quelque part, – souvent, comme une voix générale de l'œuvre.

Le roman initial pourrait ~~parler~~ résumer les symptômes de la fièvre d'appétit. Éducation des enfants au collège. L'éducation serait antérieure au coup d'État, l'action ne commencerait que là.

Figure 2. Émile Zola, "Fiche sur 'Les Mondes.'" BN N.A.F. 10345, f. 23. Courtesy of the Bibliothèque Nationale de France.

There are four worlds: the people (workers, soldiers), the businessmen (speculators in the demolitions and high commerce), the bourgeoisie (sons of parvenus), the high society . . . and a world apart (prostitute, murderer, preacher, artist). (MS 10345, f. 22)

There is also the first novel, apparently located outside the "worlds." If we count carefully and include this first novel, then we also find that

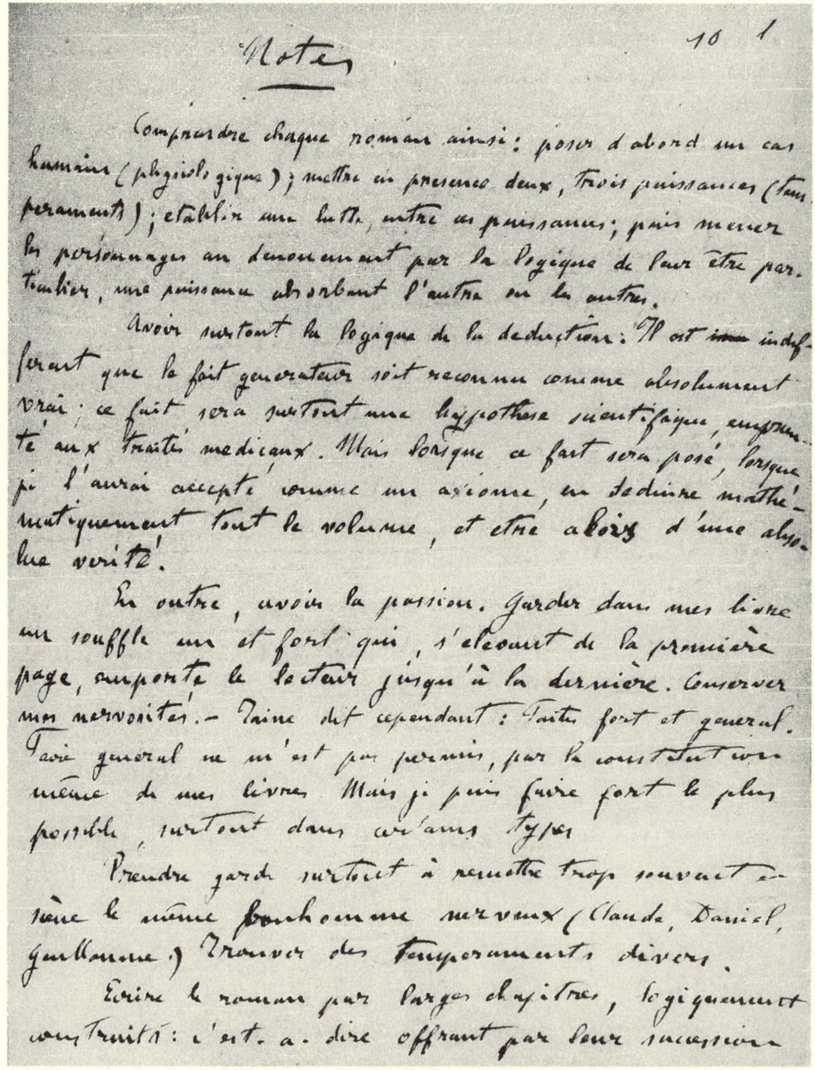

Notes 10 1

Comprendre chaque roman ainsi: poser d'abord un cas humain (physiologique); mettre en présence deux, trois puissances (tempéraments); établir une lutte, entre ces puissances; puis mener les personnages au dénouement par la logique de leur être particulier, une puissance absorbant l'autre ou les autres.

Avoir surtout la logique de la déduction: Il est indifférent que le fait générateur soit reconnu comme absolument vrai; ce fait sera surtout une hypothèse scientifique, empruntée aux traités médicaux. Mais lorsque ce fait sera posé, lorsque je l'aurai accepté comme un axiome, en déduire mathématiquement tout le volume, et être alors d'une absolue vérité.

En outre, avoir la passion. Garder dans mes livres un souffle un et fort qui, s'élevant de la première page, emporte le lecteur jusqu'à la dernière. Conserver mes nervosités. — Taine dit cependant: Faites fort et général. Faire général ne m'est pas permis, par la constitution même de mes livres. Mais je puis faire fort le plus possible, surtout dans certains types.

Prendre garde surtout à remettre trop souvent en scène le même bonhomme nerveux (Claude, Daniel, Guillaume). Trouver des tempéraments divers.

Écrire le roman par larges chapitres, logiquement construits: c'est-à-dire offrant par leur succession

Figure 3. Émile Zola, "Notes, première page." BN N.A.F., f. 10. Courtesy of the Bibliothèque Nationale de France.

there are eleven characters or category-types in this new distribution, not ten. The difference can probably be explained by the fact that at this stage the worker novel and the prostitute novel are one and the same. As we see, the peasants are forgotten; we are dealing with Parisian worlds only.

Ripoll is surely right to say that at this moment Zola had not yet read Dr. Lucas and that, meditating on the advice that Taine had given him after reading the two earlier novels—"be more general"—his sole intention was to add a sociological model to his original model, or even substitute one for it.

His original plan, in conformity with Taine's teachings as they were taken over and vulgarized in 1864 by Emile Deschanel in *Physiologie des écrivains et des artistes,* was to balance two fundamental components of modern novelistic character: temperament and milieu. Presumably Zola felt that "milieu" had been defined too informally: his new project would reconceptualize it and expand it to the frontiers of profession and class.

As early as this first phase of the genetic process, a process that is far from being finished, we see a change on the intertextual front. After Zola's narrow and scholarly reading between 1866 and 1868 of Taine's *Essais de critique et d'histoire* (and also of Michelet's *La Femme*), which inspired *Thérèse Raquin* and *Madeleine Férat,* there followed, at Taine's suggestion, a freer and more supple inspiration, nourished no doubt by new and continued readings in the *Comédie humaine.* These two little programmatic sheets appear prima facie to be small things, but they attest to a notable transformation of Zola's intellectual space and surely, beyond this, a transformation of what one might call the Zeitgeist. Why should we not correlate these two lists, which from here forward visibly dominated Zola's classifying and unifying mentality, with the signs of a contemporaneous development of a new encyclopedic spirit? Pierre Larousse's 15-volume *Grand Dictionnaire universel,* an alphabetical panorama of all the knowledge, stereotypes, dreams, and myths of the time, started appearing in 1865, Littré's four-volume *Dictionnaire de la langue française* in 1863. And Zola responded, as if in echo: "I am going to devote ten volumes to the natural and social history of a family during the Second Empire." In a manner more historically exact than a mere reading of the finished novels will allow (recall that the novels did not start appearing until 1871), we grasp here the surfacing of a cultural ebb and flow that between 1865 and 1870 traversed and nourished diverse discursive structures of reception, from dictionaries to novelistic projects. The cultural demands of 1869 were not those of 1865; something had changed in mentality and curiosity, and the very first preparatory notes for the *Rougon-Macquart* novels bear witness to it. The new work would be didactic and totalizing: "There are four worlds," wrote Zola, and this word "world" was indeed a key word of the day.

To this must be added the political and polemical component that is perceptible, for example, in the novel about the speculator in Parisian demolitions. French political judgment was in the middle of a transformation away from the current régime and Bonapartism. The time of the "Authoritative Empire" was over. From 1868 on, Zola would participate in an intense campaign of political and moral opposition. Around and through him everything connected to endow the novel with a modality of political satire that the genre had not had since Stendhal.

So much for the basic apparatus. There were to be ten novels, each complementing the others in an organized system representing "worlds"—Balzac would have called them social "spheres." Does this mean that Zola was gearing up for a "remake" of the *Comédie humaine*?[2] Absolutely not. While Balzac certainly helped liberate him from the code of the physiologists, Zola still had to differentiate himself from Balzac. One should read in this regard the *Notes générales sur la nature de l'œuvre,* probably written immediately after the list of ten novels. Here Zola takes care of two debts. First, a debt to Balzac (Zola's rejection of the "current analysis of Balzac" is a rejection of fatalism—"fatalism is an old tool"—and of philosophy as well: "It has been said that there was never a great novelist who was not also a philosopher: yes, but an absurd philosophy, like Balzac's. I prefer to be just a novelist"). Next, a debt to the aesthetic doctrine of the Goncourt brothers. In a certain way, Thérèse Raquin had been Germinie Lacerteux's sister; there was the same fatalistic determination of behaviors by temperament, the same search for artistic detail. Yet the Goncourt school had already closed, too, for the winds had turned: "It is useless to devote oneself ceaselessly to the dramas of the flesh." Or again: "Now everybody succeeds in the analysis of detail" (subtext: the authors of *Germinie Lacerteux* excel at this, for they know nothing else); "one must react by constructing solid masses using logic, the thrust of chapters, and a breath of passion that animates the whole and runs from one end of the work to the other" (MS 10345, ff. 10–13; *Les Rougon-Macquart* 5: 1742–43). This is also true for the way Zola distanced himself from Balzac. Tension would overwhelm extension.

This was a liquidation. It was also the announcement of a new novelistic skill, and maybe even the intuition of a new "horizon of expectation." A new age of novelistic reading was arriving, building itself on the ruins of artistic romanticism; it was surrounded by the inchoate constructions of other forms of knowledge, experience, sensibility, and pathos. Of course, Zola still remembered his Taine period: "First posit a human (physiological) case; bring two or three powers (temperaments) to light; establish a battle between these powers; then lead the characters to the dénouement using the very logic of their particular being, one power absorbing the other or others." Yet here a sort of Darwinian imaginary started to overlay the substratum of positivistic determinism and assign to the forthcoming works an utterly new dynamism, expressed, hereafter, in terms of power, force, mass, pressure, passions, battles, and conflicts. "The Goncourts will be so well crushed by the mass, the length of the

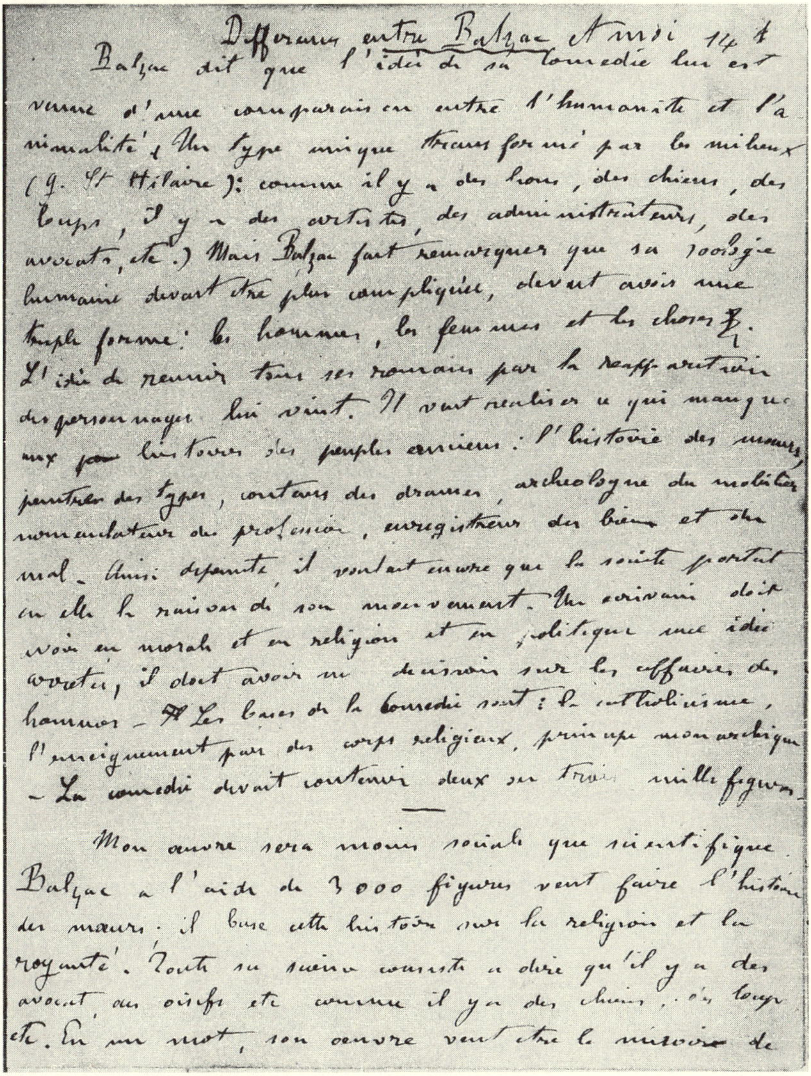
Différences entre Balzac et moi 14

Balzac dit que l'idée de sa Comédie lui est venue d'une comparaison entre l'humanité et l'animalité. (Un type unique transformé par les milieux (G. St Hilaire): comme il y a des lions, des chiens, des loups, il y a des artistes, des administrateurs, des avocats, etc.) Mais Balzac fait remarquer que sa zoologie humaine devait être plus compliquée, devait avoir une triple forme: les hommes, les femmes et les choses. L'idée de réunir tous ses romans par la réapparition des personnages lui vint. Il veut réaliser ce qui manque aux histoires des peuples anciens: l'histoire des mœurs, peintre des types, conteur des drames, archéologue du mobilier, nomenclateur des professions, enregistreur du bien et du mal. Ainsi dépeinte, il voulait encore que la société portât en elle la raison de son mouvement. Un écrivain doit avoir en morale et en religion et en politique une idée arrêtée, il doit avoir une décision sur les affaires des hommes. — Les bases de la Comédie sont: le catholicisme, l'enseignement par des corps religieux, principe monarchique. — La comédie devait contenir deux ou trois mille figures.

Mon œuvre sera moins sociale que scientifique. Balzac à l'aide de 3000 figures veut faire l'histoire des mœurs. il base cette histoire sur la religion et la royauté. Toute sa science consiste à dire qu'il y a des avocats, des oisifs etc comme il y a des chiens, des loups etc. En un mot, son œuvre veut être le miroir de

Figure 4. Émile Zola, "Différences entre Balzac et moi." BN N.A.F. 10345, f. 14. Courtesy of the Bibliothèque Nationale de France.

chapters, the breath of passion and the marching logic that nobody will dare to accuse me of imitating them." Hereafter the nodal scheme of the Zolian novel held fast to an energetic and conflictual vision of psychic and social existence. "To study men as simple powers and register the shocks between them."—Was this a sign of the times? Must we invoke, as does Michel Serres, the rise to power of the model presented by thermodynamics?

Baudelaire died in 1867, Jules de Goncourt in 1870. Artistic modernity was no longer a sufficient ideal for Zola, even one accompanied by *nervosisme* (which brought the physiology of temperaments and the seduction of medical discourse into harmony in the decade of the 1860s). Another modernity had to be invented, and for this, too, some distance from Balzac had to be taken. Zola devoted himself to this exercise in his two other general notes, *Notes sur la marche de l'œuvre* and *Différences entre Balzac et moi*, and used new intellectual equipment, more precise and specialized than Taine's concepts and metaphors: Dr. Lucas's discourse on heredity and Dr. Moreau de Tours's discourse on madness. In short, the introverted imagination of nervosity ("Be especially careful not to put the same nervous gentleman on the scene too often") was succeeded by a neurotic imagination more attentive to that Other that is installed in the subject from the start and gnaws at its identity; installed as well in society, it contradicts its unity. Alterity of blood, alterity of class: such things were starting to be thought about during these years.

I cannot comment in detail here on the *Notes sur la marche de l'œuvre* (MS 10345, ff. 1–7; *Les Rougon-Macquart* 5: 1738–41). Here are its first lines: "A central family which has at least two families acting on it. Growth of this family in the modern world, in all classes." We can see here, in embryonic state, the Rougons, the Macquarts, and the Mourets. If Ripoll is correct to hypothesize that Zola's writing of the note about the work's progress, unlike the note on the work's nature, postdates his reading of Lucas, then it permits us to isolate the contribution of the theory of heredity to the genesis of the *Rougon-Macquart* cycle. Essentially, it would amplify and restructure the family model, while confirming and specifying the orientation implied by the list of ten co-associated novels. The system of these ten novels would be articulated, then, not only by a coherent distribution of professional and social categories, but also, and at the same time, by a kinship structure, thereby adding an anthropological dimension to the sociological one. This was neither a light retouching nor a modest supplement. Rather, it was a veritable mutation of the project, a second genetic state of the transforming novelistic cycle, and, perhaps, another reflection of a network of cultural symptoms. Zola was no longer working inside a familial circle that was flat (as all circles are) and cramped—wife, husband, lover, and minor characters. Instead, he was preparing to construct a multidimensional universe in which the play of family alliances and lineages would infinitely increase the circulation of vital fluids, of objects of desire and energies, and the very scale of novelistic combination.

The degree of scientificity in Lucas's observations and theses on heredity is of little matter. What counts here is the generative power of the hereditary, or hereditarist, scheme on the levels of imagination and narrative structure. Between the writing of *Madeleine Férat* and *La Fortune des Rougon*, the whole system of the Zolian novel was transformed. One example is the character system: the Rougon-Macquart genealogical tree, conceptualized at about the same time as the general notes, now ensured that the system would be progressively enriched. Another is the narrative logic, its temporality, and its relation to the surrounding society. And indeed the most basic dynamic: the *Notes sur la marche de l'œuvre* show that the technique of borrowing knowledge and imaginative elements from an author such as Lucas was in perfect harmony with the power and richness called for and begun in the previous note. The succession of generations was itself a figure for the expansion of vital drives.

> I am studying the ambitions and appetites of a family thrown into the modern world, making superhuman efforts but failing because of its own nature and other influences. The family nearly succeeds but falls back, and ends up producing real moral monstrosities (the preacher, the murderer, the artist). . . . I wish to paint, at the beginning of a century of liberty and truth, a family which thrusts itself toward immediate gain and which runs off track because of its very own thrust, precisely because of the dim light of the moment—the fatal convulsions of a world being born.

It seems to me that at this precise moment and in this very language the epic dimension of what would become Zolian naturalism appeared—and that through this one may glimpse one of the most powerful currents in the modern novel.

I put to one side the note entitled *Différences entre Balzac et moi* (MS 10345, ff. 14–15; *Les Rougon-Macquart* 5: 1736–37). Zola had reread the foreword to the *Comédie humaine* and had no difficulty seeing the consequences of the structural choice that he had just made. He was in no way trying to become the zoologist of humanity, the historian of morals, "the cataloguer of professions"; nor, either, was he to "have" political and religious "principles," to claim like Balzac "to have a decision to make about human affairs, to be a politician, a philosopher, and a moralist." In contrast to the global, horizontal, and extensive strategy of the Balzacian novel, Zola expanded in depth and focus: "I wish to paint not contemporary society but just one family." This expansion lent itself more immediately and more intensely to the diffusion of branches of the genealogical tree throughout the "worlds" and it helped meet the obligations of the dramatic process. "Balzac says that he wishes to portray men, women, and things. While I admit that there are natural differences, to me men and women are one and the same. I subordinate them to things."

We are far indeed from those eternal truths in light of which Balzac understood himself to be writing: monarchy and religion. Subordinated to things, Zola's men and women were nothing less than alienated, in the Hegelian sense of the term. The laws of heredity, such as Zola understood them, were not laws that benefited the human species: they made all being subservient to the matter of its genes and endowed it forever with an original fissure. Zola's reading of Moreau de Tours, as Ripoll has shown, would complete and accentuate this aspect of the lessons learned from Lucas by linking the fissure to deviant, abnormal, morbid, and pathological effects that were just as innate as they were inherited. "Exhaustion and failure: the family will burn as matter devouring itself, it will nearly wear itself out in one generation because it will live too fast." Everything suggested that evil was transmitted from one generation to another more certainly than wealth, and madness more easily than reason. We could certainly find many examples of this general tendency in the *Rougon-Macquart* cycle.

This, briefly retraced, was the path that Zola seems to have followed during the few months that separated the last of his youthful novels from the first of the *Rougon-Macquart* cycle. It was a great path of rupture and innovation: rupture with the inherited model that had governed the writing of *Thérèse Raquin* and *Madeleine Férat* and invention of a novelistic dimension undoubtedly better suited to the new needs of knowledge and emotion.

Another question, which I will not be able to develop here, would be to ask what happened to this genetic program throughout the long history of the entire cycle. The genesis of the *Rougon-Macquart* must be grasped in both the short and the long term. The short term is important because the general project, as we have just seen, germinated in the space of a few months and left only a few brief manuscript traces. The long term is also significant since the production and publication of the twenty novels of the cycle took almost twenty-five years and left behind thousands of pages of avant-texte. What correlations should be made between the pregenesis of 1868–69 and the long, discontinuous genesis formed by regular deposits during the following quarter of a century? How can we appreciate the residue of the original program's genetic energy? I do not have anwers to these questions. At least they demonstrate that genetic criticism, in a case such as this, must become dynamic, differential, and perspectival. Certain motifs—notably the genealogical motif—momentarily faded, only to reappear in the novel-summary that is *Le Docteur Pascal*. Others, such as the dualism of *élan vital* and fissure, kept their vitality over the long term. All of this is to be studied in the details of the text.

Let us return to archeology. What do these literary museum pieces, these notes from 1868–69, allow us to think about the correspondences between the text and its genesis—what I would be tempted to call the "genoscript," or the genotext if Julia Kristeva hadn't used this word in another sense—and the surrounding culture? Because of a lack of historical and philosophical competence, my conclusions are disappointing. At any rate, we cannot reasonably interpret these preparatory avant-textes unless we start from our own knowledge of the massive work in question. Only this knowledge permits us to grasp the work's place, role, meaning, originality, range, and insertion in a developing system. A project like this only becomes interesting when it has succeeded, and its cultural significance and historic importance can only be appreciated in tandem with the *Rougon-Macquart* cycle as a whole.

Nevertheless, as I have gone along, I have tried to reveal some points of rupture, some points of connection, some specific paths, and some new modes of sensitivity in thought, imagination, and narrative ability. These are all indications of the convergence of Zola's and his public's evolution, and thus of an atmospheric change on the contemporary horizon. Was this, to borrow an expression from Bernard Groethuysen, "the pathos of a new generation"? Perhaps, more simply, at least with Zola, it was a recomposition of the intellectual and rhetorical settings or a change of discursive configurations. In this theater of shadows where only the director's words are heard, this prologue before the curtain is raised on the *Rougon-Macquart* fortunes, there are entrances on stage, exits into the wings, and other movements and adjustments on the stage. The Goncourt brothers are sent off. Taine and Deschanel, still present in the first act, are gradually pushed into the background. The décor of physiological realism is replaced by social fresco. Balzac has changed his role. And here come two characters whose individual identity matters little, but whose professional and cultural membership is significant: two doctors, one a specialist in genetic biology, the other in psychiatry. Dr. Freud is still waiting in the wings, but his time will come.

As for the political voices, they can hardly be heard. Nevertheless, the first *Rougon-Macquart* novel will be the indictment of a coup d'état. Most likely what happened is that between the writing of the notes that I have just commented upon and the actual production of the first work of the series, the general opinion, if not the cultural discourse, was once again transformed. The image of the imperial institution was degraded, and the critical examination of the behavior of the governing class was accentuated. If the manuscript notes of 1868–69 do not carry an explicit trace of this, then one must look in the articles that Zola gave to the *Tribune*, the *Cloche*, and the *Rappel*.

Thus the biological imaginary (emerging from a medical discourse which itself relayed Taine's and Deschanel's "natural criticism") and the political imaginary (emerging from liberal and republican polemics) converged with the public expectations of 1868–70 in the texts underlying the *Rougon-Macquart* cycle. What was this public tired of? What was it already curious about? What returns of the repressed was it about to accept? These questions remain alive.

Nonetheless, future research will have to account for the fact that the biological imaginary emerged from a history of events and from scientific and philosophical concepts with a long range, whereas the political imaginary grew out of a political history with immediate significance—and yet it too rested on a rhetoric and mythology that extends beyond the view of history. With this I have insisted sufficiently, I think, on the necessity of carefully locating and measuring the mediations that bind, as well as separate, the genetic avant-texte and its sociocultural space.

Source: "Critique génétique et histoire culturelle: Les Dossiers des *Rougon-Macquart*." In *La Naissance du texte*, ed. Louis Hay. Paris: José Corti, 1989. 147–62.

Works Cited

Kristeva, Julia. *La Révolution du langage poétique: L'Avant-garde à la fin du XIXe siècle, Lautréamont et Mallarmé.* Paris: Seuil, 1974. *Revolution in Poetic Language.* Trans. Margaret Waller. New York: Columbia University Press, 1984.

Ripoll, Roger. *Réalité et mythe chez Zola.* Thesis, University of Paris IV, 1977. 2 vols. Lille: University of Lille III; Paris: H. Champion, 1981.

Zola, Émile. *Les Rougon-Macquart: Histoire naturelle et sociale d'une famille sous le Second Empire.* Ed. Armand Lanoux and Henri Mitterand. 5 vols. Pléiade ed. Paris: Gallimard, 1960–67.

Further Works by the Author

Mitterand, Henri. "The Calvary of Catherine Maheu: The Description of a Page in *Germinal*." Trans. Julia Bloch Frey. *Yale French Studies* 42 (1969): 115–25.

———. "The Genesis of Novelistic Space: Zola's *La Bête humaine*." Trans. Anne C. Murch. In *Naturalism in the European Novel: New Critical Perspectives*, ed. Brian Nelson. New York: Berg, 1992. 66–79.

———. *Littérature, textes et documents.* Series directed by Henri Mitterand. 9 vols to date. Paris: Nathan, 1986–.

———. *Le Regard et le signe: Poétique du roman réaliste et naturaliste.* Paris: Presses Universitaires de France, 1987.

———. *Le Roman à l'œuvre: Genèse et valeurs.* Paris: Presses Universitaires de France, 1998.

———. "The Scarlet Vision of the Revolution . . ." Trans. Robin O. Bodkin and Roland H. Simon. In *Unfinished Revolutions: Legacies of Upheaval in Modern French Culture,* ed. Robert T. Denommé and Roland H. Simon. University Park: Pennsylvania State University Press, 1998. 43–63.

———. "Toward a Sociocriticism of Totalities: The Year of 1875." Trans. Catharine Randall. *Sociocriticism* 1 (1985): 83–101.

———. *Zola.* 3 vols. Paris: Fayard, 1999–2002.

———. *Zola et le naturalisme.* Paris: Presses Universitaires de France, 1986.

———. *Zola: l'Histoire et la fiction.* Paris: Presses Universitaires de France, 1990.

Zola, Émile. *Carnets d'enquêtes: Une Ethnographie inédite de la France.* Ed. Henri Mitterand. Paris: Plon, 1986.

———. *Les Rougon-Macquart: Histoire naturelle et sociale d'une famille sous le Second Empire.* Ed. Armand Lanoux and Henri Mitterand. 5 vols. Pléiade ed. Paris: Gallimard, 1960–67.

Chapter 8

Paragraphs in Expansion (James Joyce)

Daniel Ferrer and Jean-Michel Rabaté

"Paragraphs in Expansion (James Joyce)" was coauthored by the literary theorists and Joyce scholars Daniel Ferrer and Jean-Michel Rabaté. Rabaté has written numerous books and articles—many available in English—on such Modernists as Joyce, Beckett, and Pound and on topics in psychoanalysis, poststructuralism, and visual art. Since 1992 he has been a professor of English and Comparative Literature at the University of Pennsylvania. Ferrer is also a scholar of Modernism, especially Joyce and Woolf, and a theorist of postmodernism. Above all, he is a versatile geneticist: at the Institut des Textes et Manuscrits Modernes, which he directed from 1994 to 1998, he was and is a leader in the Joyce group and a pioneer in the use of hypertexts and computers in genetic studies. He is also a member of the team currently engaged in editing Joyce's *Finnegans Wake* notebooks.

In this essay, first published in 1989, the authors pursue a question that at first may seem better suited to rhetoricians than geneticists: What is a paragraph? Few literary critics have given the topic much thought, and yet it is far from obvious just what paragraphs *do* in texts. Certainly they divide, organize, interrupt, build, give texture, and formalize . . . but how? And *what* is the object of their activity? What do they cut off, cut into, or cut up? A text's *times* or *spaces*?

To answer these questions, the authors show how paragraphs act on and reflect different levels of voice, narrative, reader experience, page layout, sentence flow, and language itself. Being neither purely material nor purely ideal, paragraphs are also, paradoxically, both evanescent and permanent. They do not obviously belong to a text's signifying content, yet they *are* structures intended to transcend a given draft or graphic presentation. Thus, we learn, if to study the paragraphs in a published text is to scrutinize the complicated interfaces between content and form or thought and style, then to trace the dynamics of their expansion in the avant-textes is to interrogate the creative process itself.

The insufficiency (but also the swirling suggestiveness) of these answers leads the authors to pursue a genetic inquiry unlike any other in the present volume. Admitting that paragraphs cannot be understood solely on the basis of concepts of style, content, or layout, they aim instead to reflect on the semiotic implications of a set of quintessentially modernist avant-textes and to study, in Joyce, the actual evolution of a textual epiphenomenon common to all prose writers.

The essay rejuvenates and widens the paradiscipline of what one might call "paragraph theory" by giving it an analysis enriched by genetic detail, drawn from stylistically differentiated periods of Joyce's composition of *Ulysses* and *Finnegans Wake*, and by nuanced theoretical perspectives, drawn mainly from semiotics and poststructuralist theory. Brushing aside the commonplaces still offered up in composition manuals, for example, that good paragraphs express a "single" idea or taxonomize a clear and conscious presentation of thought, the authors invite us to read and feel paragraphs as indices of writing's rhythms, as dialogic techniques, as traces of writerly necessity that outstrip logic, and, memorably, as systolic mechanisms that digest the material on the margins of expanding texts.

Are paragraphs written? Do they belong to the text or to its layout? To introduce their evanescent status, there is no better starting point than "Ithaca," the strange penultimate chapter of Joyce's *Ulysses*. Here one finds the following transcription of a letter written by a very young child to her father, an example of the absorption of the nontextual by the text itself: "capital Pee Papli comma capital aitch How are you note of interrogation capital eye I am very well full stop new paragraph signature with flourishes capital em Milly no stop" (*Ulysses* 592; 17: 1792–94).[1] In the French translation, approved by Joyce but often rather normalizing, we read: "Petit père, grand pé, virgule, Comment grand cé, allez-vous point d'interrogation Je grand ji, vais très bien, point, alinéa suivant, signature enjolivée, Milly grand em, pas de point" (*Ulysse* 645). The translation, like the original version, tries to render *textually*, beyond the—slight—verbal matter, the graphic, orthographic, and para-graphic particularities of the child's missive. Also noticeable is a difference between the English and the French versions, negligible or substantial depending on one's point of view. From one version to the other, at the same time that a second punctuation mark, in a somewhat contradictory manner, breaks into the linguistic flow, the English "paragraph" is transformed into the French "alinéa." Does this mean that for an analytic consciousness, which the written French has trouble dispensing with entirely, a signature cannot, all by itself, constitute a paragraph? The notion of a paragraph would seem to imply a fullness of sense that would not be reducible to a simple movement to the next line.

Etymology suggests two different paths: for the Greeks, the "paragraph" is a marginal annotation, a critical sign or a punctuation mark announcing the beginning or the end of a written passage. Such is the meaning that still prevails in Aristotle's *Rhetoric*: the sentence should "be cut off with a long syllable and be a clear termination, not through the action of a scribe or the presence of a marginal mark [*paragraphê*] but through the rhythm" (238–39). The term "paragraph" is indeed Greek—as Leopold Bloom emphasizes when he thinks, "Par it's Greek: parallel, parallax" (*Ulysses* 126; 8: 111–12), in "Lestrygonians," an episode that immediately follows the newspaper scene in which he appeared so eager to get a "par" into print for his client: "But he wants a par to call attention in the *Telegraph*" (120; 7: 973–74). On the other hand, the word "alinéa" comes from Latin; it takes its origin in the injunction *"a linea"* (leave this line), said by a person dictating to a copyist.

On the one hand, therefore, one could read a diacritical sign that would serve as the equivalent of a rhetorical closure and signal the end of a rhythmic effect that breaks up meaning. On the other hand, one could hear a simple vocal command manifesting the good will of an author who knows very clearly where he wants to put breaks. Whereas the paragraph is oriented towards the diacritical mechanism of writing (we often symbolize it by a double S: "§"), the "alinéa" plays on the simple spacing of the page. Moving to the next line does not, by itself, make an "alinéa" because it can mark the difference between verse and prose. But in prose, we perceive an "alinéa" as a simple resting-place for the eye or ear, whereas the paragraph can, by itself, transform a monologic text into a dialogic one. This is precisely what happens in the "Ithaca" chapter's technique, which Joyce named "dialogue" in contrast to the famous "monologue" of Molly Bloom, which "alinéas" break into eight immense sentences without punctuation. In "Ithaca," the process of cutting text into small units of variable length permits the text to pose itself all sorts of questions, which are then followed at times by units disproportionately short or long—all of which contributes to the creation of a textual dialogue of a new kind.

From the point of view we are adopting here,[2] paragraphs do not appear to be a very promising subject since they are only marked, in modern texts, by a negative trace, indeed the interruption of a trace. Moreover, this absence cannot always be interpreted simply in the terms of binary opposition because one must—and this is not always easy to do in a manuscript—distinguish paragraph breaks *both* from simple line breaks (produced by the material constraints and dimensions of the surrounding medium) and from the blank "reserve" space of the page, itself destined to be filled in later by a fragment of a paragraph, a whole paragraph, or several paragraphs.

Paragraph breaks are, however, among the few elements of the material presentation of the handwritten page that are destined to survive as such onto the printed page (as opposed to such other graphic features as margins and other features of the draft's layout that are generally condemned to disappear during the typographic composition or even at each new stage of writing or of faircopying). Thus paragraphs reflect an intermediary stage between certain borders proper to linguistics (borders of words, sentences, even speech) and others that have only iconic meaning (like pages or lines).

The constraints dictating the length of paragraphs and the placement of their breaks appear to be nonexistent (or at least not formulated, unless as a form of loose rhetorical precepts),[3] and one could think that this would leave a writer free rein to be totally arbitrary. Yet avant-textes offer privileged access to the logic hidden beneath this apparent arbitrariness. In fact, by studying the fluctuations of paragraphs as entities, the forms of their expansion, and the stability or instability of their breaks, we will best be able to grasp their status.

The *expansion* of paragraphs is a dynamic notion that is concerned with more than graphic or logical entities, fixed on themselves, but it has the inconvenience of lacking any specificity, especially with respect to the question of the margin and the problem of the ending or the nonending of a manuscript. This vagueness, however, has a positive counterpart: it is also a topic that refuses, if one may say so, to remain marginal. Rather, it connects with, and spurs on, a good number of current research problems on the genesis of texts.

In this way, the margins of a manuscript at first present themselves as the natural place for the expansion of paragraphs, but this does not imply that they must be considered as mere subservient appendages. After all, it is the interruption of the flow of writing that makes the paragraph exist as it is. Yet this break, this blank that spaces out the written text, strongly resembles an internal border, a margin transported into the heart of the text. It is true that the differences are as remarkable as the similarities. Paragraph breaks are not constrained in the same way as the first and final cuts or the lateral margins that the writing must necessarily run up against. They are deliberate and somehow gratuitous because, as we have noted, they are prescribed by no clear rule. Above all, they are not a separation from the exterior but an inner separation. We are therefore dealing with a border, but an attenuated border, less irrevocable than the others. And what if their function lay precisely there; what if paragraphs only served to tame the margins? What if they were a means for the text to domesticate its own limits by engulfing them or covering them with its own substance?

The same relation of writing to its internal and external limits is also put into play, on a different scale, in the question of the incompletion of the manuscript. In working on the genesis of the literary text, one rapidly discovers that the progression that would go from the first to the second paragraph, then to the third, so as to end up with the final nth paragraph is either a myth or a rare exception. One observes in fact that between the first and second paragraphs new paragraphs come to be inserted—but also that the same process of expansion continues inside each paragraph. It is therefore clear that the problem of completion is not (only) that of the absence of the eventual n+1st paragraph where there is a paragraph n, but (also) that of the finishedness of each paragraph and that of what it is that might come to occupy the space of the break between paragraphs. In this view, the break that begins a paragraph appears as an echo, or an internal rhyme, of the major break that separates the work from the world (and which originates it as a work). And if one considers the finishing of the work to be a form of death, or cadaverization, for the work, then the interruption of the paragraph embodies a little death—there is no reason to reject the echo that insinuates itself here and which suggests that the scansion of paragraphs could always be regulated by a rhythm, if not necessarily orgasmic, then at least erotic or, at any rate, organic.

The practice of different writers being, in the matter, extremely varied, it seemed to us that our only hope for escaping from vague generalities was to hold ourselves, in the limits of this essay, to one author; and Joyce, who has offered us our entry into the subject, seems to us to be a particularly promising object of study, not only because of the very great variety of his avant-textes, but also because he puts deliberately and systematically into question the diverse borders of the text—breaks between words (with the portmanteau words of *Finnegans Wake*), breaks between sentences (with the uninterrupted flow of Molly Bloom's monologue), and even the limit between the work and external world (with the circular form of *Finnegans Wake* in which the last words are linked to the first). One may thus expect that he does not deal routinely with the apparently weaker borders of paragraphs. Yet paragraphs, or something that resembles them, subsist in the last chapters of *Ulysses,* even when all the signs of punctuation disappear, and one finds again in *Finnegans Wake,* the experimental work par excellence, the classical architecture of paragraphs regularly breaking up pages.

One look at the avant-textes of Joyce suffices to confirm that these paragraph cuts are neither capricious nor fluctuating, by contrast to what one may observe in Balzac or in the Flaubert of *L'Éducation sentimentale.* On the contrary, they are extremely firm and deliberate (which does not mean fixed), as is made evident, for example, by the curious persistence of paragraphs through what can appear to be the verbal disorder of *Finnegans Wake.*

Thus, in March 1927, Joyce starts to revise Book 1, Chapter 3 in his *Work in Progress* for the journal *transition.* We have a typescript of these pages with numerous interpolations and manuscript instructions. Joyce is using at this time notebook VI.B.18 (as numbered by the SUNY Buffalo Poetry/Rare Books Collection). On page 41 of this notebook, we find the first draft of a passage with several erasures and additions:

> Not otherwise Inn the days of the Bygning did the traveller <from Nan Sealand>, some lazy skald or maundering pote, lift wearliy his slowcut eyes to the <semisigns> of his zooteac and, lengthily lingering ~~ove~~r along flaskneck cracktcups, downtrodden brogue ~~starstuft~~ <turfsod>, ~~wet~~ <wild>broom, and stockfish ~~know~~ <longinly learn> that there herberged for him poteen & tea & praties ~~to~~baccy with wine & woman & ~~song~~ warbling ~~& smile to thank~~ & informally all but begin to smile & almost think. (*Archive* 33: 80)

The whole of this notebook is dated March–July 1927, which accords with the process of revision of the typed pages. Next Joyce inserts by hand a passage, which receives some modifications, indicating clearly that it must remain a separate paragraph:

> Paragraph [line above and below the word]
> Not olderwise Inn the days of the Bygning would our traveller from Nan Sealand, some lazy skald or maundering pote, lift wearywilled his slowcut eyes to the semisigns of his zooteac, and lengthily lingering along flaskneck, cracketcup, downtrodden brogue, turfsod, wildbroom, cabbageblad, stockfisch, longingly learn that there where herberged for him poteen and tee and praties and baccy and wine with woman with warbling: and informally ~~all but~~ <quasi> begin ~~to ami~~ <to presquesm'ile> to ~~almost~~ thin.
> Paragraph [line above and below the word] (*Archive* 45: 229; British Library MS 47472, p. 149)

Perhaps the secretary misread it, or else certain modifications were made after the typing, but whatever the case it is clear that the passage, including a few obvious errors, is added directly to the end of the preceding paragraph in the new typescript. Joyce doesn't seem to remember the status of the paragraph separated from this passage, and his corrections are limited, as is often the case, to the interlinear addition of words or fragments of phrases or to the correction of certain expressions. The new version of this passage results in this:

> . . . similar in origin and in effective to a beam of sunshine upon a coffin plate. Not olderwise Inn the days of the Bygning would our traveller <remote, unfriended,> from ~~New Sealand~~ van Demon's Land, some lazy skald or maundering pote, lift weariwill~~ed~~ his showcut <snobsic> eyes to the semisigns of his zooteac and lenghtily lingering along flaskneck, cracketcup, downtrodden brogue, turfsod, wildbroom, cabbageblad, stockfisch, longingly learn that there <at the Angel> were herberged for him poteen and tea and praties and baccy and wine with woman with warbling : and informally quasi begin to <presquesm'ile> to <queasi> thin. <Nonsense! There was not very much windy Nous blowing at a given moment through the hat of Mr Melancholy Slow!>
> But in the pragma . . . (*Archive* 45: 246; British Library MS 47472, p. 233)

Next, this is composed for *transition* without modification, as MS 47472, page 336 (in the British Library's numbering system; *Archive* 45: 257) shows. But when Joyce rereads the proofs, he rediscovers the internal necessity of a break, persisting through the transformations, and makes it resurface by inserting between "coffin plate" and "Not olderwise" a double slash stroke and the note "Paragraph" (*Archive* 45: 276; 47472, p. 354). This break is respected in the final text of *Finnegans Wake* (p. 56, ll. 19–20).

It is certain that Joyce would never have shown the flexibility of, say, a Faulkner on this point. Indeed, if one examines the history of the text of *Pylon*, one notices that in fact a long analepsis, originally written by Faulkner in the form of a single paragraph of several pages in order to distinguish it typographically from the dialogue in which it was hidden, was normalized, truncated by the editor into several paragraphs of average size.[4] Yet Faulkner did not reestablish the original continuity. Instead, he put a transitional sentence in the typescript to mark the passage from one temporal register to another and to make explicit the discontinuity that was no longer visually apparent as it was in the original version. This incident allows us to observe that the absence of a paragraph can have a positive value because the absence of this absence (third degree absence, since the mark of the paragraph is nothing other, as we have said, than an absence of text, a provisional interruption of the flow) requires the addition of another textual scrap, a supplemental commentary in another place in the text. Mainly, however, it demonstrates the contrast between the flexibility of Faulkner and the obstinacy of Joyce on this point (as on many others).

Finally, the last reason for our choice brings us back to the question of finishedness. One can say that the avant-texte of Joyce, in its monstrous proliferation, makes apparent, no doubt better than any other avant-texte, the state of what one could call the internal unfinishedness of the work (as opposed to the preestablished closure of a structure closed upon itself)—which has the effect of making paragraphs in expansion a strategic place of textual genesis and a privileged contact point for genetic criticism. The consequence of this textual inflation from the inside, which in the case of *Ulysses* transforms a simple novel into one totaling seven hundred pages, the consequence of this proliferation that short-circuits the very spatial limits that are supposed to contain the book, is that finishedness only intervenes as the effect of a scansion of another order or of a limitation that is almost necessarily temporal (because, if the dimensions of a human work are potentially infinite, the time of its writing is biologically limited). It is likely that *Ulysses* would never have been finished, or at least that it would have been much longer than it is, if Joyce, by superstition, had not decided that it should be finished the day of his 40th birthday. An arbitrary break, then, superimposed upon the writing—but it is not insignificant that this break was a birthday, that is, the echo of a birth or of an absolute beginning, a manner of both denying and emphasizing the finishedness and its mortal signification. . . .

Our first two examples belong to the "Aeolus" chapter of *Ulysses* and reproduce something of the overall structure on the level of the paragraph. We can first observe a primary form of the growth from sentence to paragraph: the expansion by simple inertia, verbal residue, or tendency of language to persist:

> Grossbooted draymen rolled barrels dullthudding out of Prince's stores and bumped them up on the brewery float. On the brewery float bumped dullthudding barrels rolled by grossbooted draymen out of Prince's stores. (*Ulysses* 86; 7: 21–24)

In the first version, the initial sentence ("Grossbooted draymen . . . float.") opened the chapter, and it seems that when the episode appeared in the *Little Review* the printer repeated it by mistake. Joyce, who was delighted by that kind of accident, took the idea for himself and kept the repetition—but it is remarkable that he also took advantage of the occasion to change the order of the words and to introduce a chiastic structure. The result of this modification is that the apparently minor paragraph break constitutes an echo of the opening of the episode.

At a later stage of the composition, however, this effect will be weakened because, textual material having been added in front of this passage, the opening of the chapter falls to the rank of simply being a new paragraph. In between these moments, the entire typographical and enunciative layout of the episode has been overhauled. Indeed, Joyce decided, very late since this work was done on the proofs made in 1921, to break up spectacularly a chapter written in a fairly conventional manner in order to give it the appearance of a series of articles in newspapers, each paragraph, or group of paragraphs, possessing an ironic or eye-catching headline. Inserting the headlines profoundly modifies the nature of the preexisting text, producing a real change in enunciative status and a move to a higher level of manipulation.

Now these additions, obviously textual but miming paratextual elements, these insertions that completely modify the visual aspect of the text, do not in any way upset the paragraph breaks: they insert themselves quite naturally between the paragraphs, a fact that tends to demonstrate indirectly that these breaks are not random and cannot be reduced to a simple need to space out or "whiten" the typography.

This remarkable stability of the paragraphs suggests that they are the result of a deliberate choice and tends to confer upon them the character of necessity. Thus, the counterexamples of fluctuation that we will find are all the more worthy of interest. The only passage in which the insertion of a journalistic headline divides a previously continuous paragraph is not insignificant:

> Hynes here too: account of the funeral probably. Thumping. Thump. [Paragraph broken here during a revision.]
>
> WITH UNFEIGNED REGRET IT IS WE ANNOUNCE
> THE DISSOLUTION OF A MOST RESPECTED
> DUBLIN BURGESS
>
> This morning the remains of the late Mr Patrick Dignam. Machines. Smash a man to atoms if they got him caught. Rule the world today. His machineries are pegging away too. Like these, got out of hand: fermenting. Working away, tearing away. And that old grey rat tearing to get in. (*Ulysses* 98; 7: 75–83)

This added typographical break, standing out here as an exception,[5] coincides with the other break that is very concretely evoked, that of a biological dissolution or an organic decomposition. A trace or rupture, a rupture of the trace, the "alinéa" is suddenly transformed into an iconic sign, but it signifies nothing other than the rupture of death, manifesting in this way the structural function that suggested itself earlier. We note without surprise that the redoubling of the interruption is accompanied by a process of filling in, taking the form of a heading sentence that occupies the hole opened up for it. The epitaph-headline both denies and draws attention to the rip that literally makes way for it.

In the "Scylla and Charybdis" chapter, we find a rather similar game of death and epitaph, of digging and filling a hole, on the occasion of another of these rare examples of paragraphs split open at a late stage in the process of rewriting.

—*Requiescat!* Stephen prayed.

What of all the will to do?
It has vanished long ago . . .

—She lies laid out in stark stiffness in that secondbest bed, the mobled queen . . .
(*Ulysses* 169; 9: 796–801)

These are localized examples, but one may ask whether one should draw more general conclusions, notably about the function of paragraphs in a text that advertises itself, at least in certain places, as an "interior monologue" and a "stream of consciousness." Shouldn't it be an uninterrupted flow? What can breaks mean if not death (since sleep, for Joyce, does not correspond to a blank, but on the contrary, if one believes *Finnegans Wake,* to a verbal pullulation)?

If the function of a paragraph break is really what we ordinarily assign to it, that is, the organization and serialization of ideas, then what can its role be in a genre founded on the non sequitur, which claims to reproduce, or at least to give the feeling of, an essentially unhierarchized pell-mell of ideas and diverse impressions? If "we consider that a paragraph corresponds to a theme—in a certain use of the term" and if "a displacement of theme is that which is normally expressed in the changing of a paragraph,"[6] then how can it keep its place in a discourse where this thematic displacement is constantly and continually occurring, along the thread of unpredictable associations?

It so happens that our first three examples belong to very different stages in the evolution of *Ulysses,* and it is obviously impossible in the perspective we are following here to neglect the history of the text. All the more because this evolution can be analyzed, in the case of *Ulysses,* as a series of creative renditions of avant-textes themselves. One could say that Joyce reread his own rough drafts and finished chapters in order to learn, from his own text, the implications of his writing. Such is the meaning of his stylistic "audacities" that certainly originate less in any innate radicality or desire to shock the public than in a patient progression of textual work; this is what pushed Joyce little by little to more and more daring stylistic experimentation.

This movement has been very well described in Michael Groden's *"Ulysses" in Progress,* which roughly distinguishes between three stages in Joyce's progression. A first stage, which Joyce called the "initial style" of the novel, corresponds to the first nine chapters. It presents the major characters by mixing rapid descriptions in the third person and the past tense with the first-person, present-tense flow of their current thoughts, that is, the "interior monologue," which we witness directly. This is still a classic novelistic procedure, one born of the fusion of two of Joyce's previous written networks, *Dubliners* and *A Portrait of the Artist as a Young Man*. The novelized autobiography preserves all of Stephen's traits and is content to follow his efforts toward creation, whereas Bloom is made distinct from the other Dubliners only by the effect of a symbolic complementarity because, although nothing makes it noticeable, he is already a Ulysses-figure seeking a Telemachus. This stage comes to a close at the end of 1918, when Joyce writes on his manuscript, on the last page of "Scylla and Charybdis": "End of the first part of *Ulysses*."

The second stage of writing signals a pause in the conventional narrative threads and corresponds to the introduction of independent linguistic strategies; the "Wandering Rocks," "Sirens," "Cyclops," "Nausicaa," and "Oxen of the Sun" episodes all shift the still-conventional narrative thread toward an encyclopedia of races, languages, and religions. The actions of the characters appear to be decentered, subordinate to a complex architecture that borrows procedures from particular techniques—labyrinthine structures, developed parodies, silly or grotesque insertions, absurd improvisations, a growing autonomy of language reworked and recreated from the inside in order to mime music or the gestation of idioms. The interior monologue no longer has priority; it is broken up and given the same treatment as cultural clichés.

Finally, the third period is contemporary with Joyce's hard work, exceptional in many ways, on the "Circe" chapter in 1920. Trying to resolve the problem posed by this series of theatrical hallucinations that run through the characters and the objects of the whorehouse, Joyce radically liberates the autonomy of language from its cultural and historical constraints and invents a text that perpetually comments upon itself. Conceiving and writing episodes two by two, "Circe" with "Eumaeus" and "Ithaca" with "Penelope," Joyce begins to deepen the meaning of the "monologue" and "dialogue" "techniques." All the elements of the text are reexamined and transcribed into a coordinate system that extends all the way to the cosmic level, as Joyce uses his linguistic advancements to rewrite certain of the earlier episodes.

Joyce's stylistic evolution appears very clearly in the manipulation of paragraphs through successive modifications. In each stage they maintain a relative stability. It is as if they were the smallest units of a writing that had to base its constant metamorphoses on these regulating elements that could be used as frames and that were made of writing itself, pure and simple. It is paragraphs, then, that allow the text to acquire in a progressive way the sense of language's independence, before or beyond characterization, mythic parallels, or the urge to universalize. Doing so, they do not function as full blocks, detachable sequences, or prefabricated textual atoms, since they show themselves to be open to fissures, scissions, and doubling. Their stability and their fissiparity are two sides of a single characteristic from which Joyce slowly elicits the huge consequence that their being is made only of language.

As a general hypothesis about the broad lines of this process, one could therefore schematize the way the text rewrites itself in the following way: the first stage corresponds to a practice of addition inside paragraphs, the size of which varies as a consequence; the second stage tends to be a practice of interpolating new paragraphs or additions between the paragraphs; and in the third stage, in "Circe" and "Ithaca" the paragraphs are devoured by the very typographic layouts themselves (theatrical or catechistic), whereas in "Eumaeus" and "Penelope" the sentences, which are lost, endless, or unpunctuated, display a deviant practice with respect to the norms of the internal scansion of text.

First, we will give an example of the first level of Joyce's work, in order to understand how relatively conventional a practice it is. It deals with one of the rare extant drafts corresponding to an extremely early stage of an episode, in this case nearly the first draft. In the manuscripts of the "Proteus" chapter, one can see Joyce's general practice of filling the pages from top to bottom and breaking each one into three masses by filling it with a tight handwriting that slowly drifted to the right until it doubled the size of the left margin.

Page 12 of this draft (Buffalo MS V.A.3; see *Archive* 12: 250–53) seems rather typical of these fairly precise drafts in which Joyce behaves as a good Jesuit student dividing his verbal material into three parts. We see that the first paragraph ends in a rhetorical and rhythmical closure: "I spoke to none: none to me." The second begins with an "objective" description of the movements of the dog given by the narrator: "The dog's bark ran towards him, ~~ceased~~ <stopped>, ran back." It continues with a resumption of Stephen's monologue; he speaks to himself: "For that are you pining, the bark of their applause?" Incidentally, this long central paragraph ends with a *clausula* rather similar to the first: "Water: bitter death: lost." The page itself functions as an iconic unit of rewriting, and its tripartition obeys both a poetic and a narrative logic. Points of view are readily switched in a style that, all things considered, is homogeneous and colored only by Stephen's poetic prose. Moreover, the insertions announced in the margins almost never destroy the initial unity of each paragraph.

Page 13 of this draft shows the same iconic disposition, and we see again that the margin is gradually filled up by interpolations, each of which is called into the text by the same sign, a sort of capital F. While page 12 gives only two lines to the third paragraph, entirely devoted to Stephen's thoughts, the first paragraph of page 13 returns to the narrator's description: "The dog ambled about a bank . . ." This description in the past tense is independent of Stephen's perspective. Page 14 shows how the paragraphs are added to Joyce's three-zone structure: another F indicates the insertion of a group from the margin. Lodged between various additions, this group does not fuse into the preceding paragraph since it shows Stephen's subjectivity expressed in the memory of a dream:

After he woke me last night same dream. Or was it? Wait. Open hallway. Street of harlots. Wait. Remember. I am almosting it <now>: wait ~~A~~ <That> man <le~~a~~d~~s~~ me, spoke. I was not afraid. ~~He~~ smiled: gave to me the melon <he had held>. That was the rule. In. Come. Red carpet <spread>. You will see.

The additions all seem to come from the same round of editing, and all the free space in the margin is taken up with this oneiric epiphany, very slightly developed in the final text.

Yet this practice is rarer than working in the margins to develop the paragraphs in the rough draft. Thus in the margin of page 15 we see first an addition ("What if I were suddenly naked? No, I am not") followed by a commentary that is not meant to be inserted—"L.B.'s letter: headache menstruous (monthly)"—because it deals with Bloom, who is not present in this scene and who will think as he receives Martha's letter that she must be having her period. Here the paragraph describes fluctuations of the sea and lunar rhythms as they affect women; Joyce makes a kind of note permitting him to link this passage to Bloom's speculations about women's periods. A little further the paragraph that begins "His lips lipped and mouthed fleshless lips of air: Mouth to her ~~moongmbh~~ moombh" readies to receive the insertion of a long phrase added in the margin below ("Oomb, ~~tomb~~<all>wombing tomb. His mouth moulded <issuing> breath, unspeeched, ~~oe to ah~~ <ooeeehah>, roar of cataractic planets, ~~balled~~, globed, blazing, roaring wayawayawayawayaway"). The margin contains a series of words noted one beneath another and right up against the paragraph; some of them are crossed out:

~~Moongb~~
~~Moongmbwb~~
~~moongbm~~
moongmb
moongbhmb
~~moongb~~
moongmbhb
moongbh
moombh

After writing "moongmbh," which probably didn't satisfy him, Joyce worked methodically on the permutations of the letters; it takes him no less than eight attempts to come to "moombh," which will be again modified in the Rosenbach manuscript, becoming simply "moomb." This tells us much about the kind of work that leads to such discoveries, at once onomatopoetic and poetic, rhyming "womb" (uterus, the maternal center), "tomb," "mouth," and "moon." But one may suspect that this hard work also produced the writing of the supplementary phrase ("Oomb, allwombing tomb") as it is inserted in the final paragraph. All of this demonstrates the dialectic interdependence of the margin and the paragraph, the one reloading or calling upon the other.

An example from the "Sirens" episode will allow us to understand exactly how Joyce's practice evolved in the so-called middle stage. We have a draft of the second half of the episode (Buffalo MS V.A.5), which probably dates from the beginning of 1919, and a typescript made from this draft in May or June of the same year. The draft was only one paragraph without breaks, while in the final text it produced five paragraphs, from "Bronze, listening" (233; 11: 1044) to "Philosophy. O rocks!" (234; 11: 1062). How shall we account for this systematic breaking by insertion? Here is the draft stage of the text:

> Bronze, listening by the beerpull, gazed far away. Soulful eyes. [F] What do they think about when they hear music. [Λ] Way to catch rattlesnakes. Night we got our box for *Trilby*, Michael Gunn. [A] Footlights glowering on the gilty work. Clove in her mouth account of the heat. Keep breath sweet. Her crocus dress she wore lowcut, full to be seen. Hypnotise. Told her what Spinoza says in that book of poor papa's. She listened, soulful eyes. Chap in dress circle staring down into her with his operaglasses. Philosophy. (*Archive* 13: 47; V.A.5 f. 28)

Prepared for places marked by the letters and symbols F, Λ, and A and coming from a margin that itself travels towards the verso of the preceding and the following pages because of the size and the chaotic, spontaneous character of the additions (*Archive* 13: 46–47; V.A.5 ff. 27v and 28f), the successive insertions superimpose all the motifs and thereby undo the essential originality of the earlier interior monologues, whether Bloom's or Stephen's. In this example, Bloom listens to the singers in the bar and looks at one of the two barmaids (Bronze). He asks himself what she's thinking about as she listens to the music, and this immediately evokes a memory of being at the opera with Molly. The unifying theme is the hypnosis exerted by the music, compared here with the sexual fascination felt by all the men who could see Molly's opulent chest.[7]

The final text moves toward fragmentation without renouncing the effects of superimposition:

> Bronze, listening, by the beerpull gazed far away. Soulfully. Doesn't half know I'm. Molly great dab at seeing anyone looking.

> Bronze gazed far sideways. Mirror there. Is that best side of her face? They always know. Knock at the door. Last tip to titivate.
>
> Cockcarracarra.
>
> What do they think when they hear music? Way to catch rattlesnakes.[. . .] Woodwind like Goodwin's name.
>
> She looked fine. [. . .] Met him pike hoses. Philosophy. O rocks! (*Ulysses* 233–34; 11: 1044–62)

We see the change from the first style: the narrator's third-person voice is still there (it describes the posture adopted by Bronze), but we can no longer distinguish it from the other musical effects of a text interspersed with ironic and occasionally affectionate commentaries. Thus a little further we find: "He bore no hate." Then after a paragraph break: "Hate. Love. Those are names. Rudy. Soon I am old" (234; 11: 1068–69).

Since this text is dedicated to imitating the appearance of music, it is tempting to call its scansion "musical." Yet the imitation of music is itself accomplished by visual and rhetorical means. This is especially true because the whole chapter deals much more with seeing and being seen than with hearing or singing. Scansion of this text, then, actually redistributes the motifs: it doubles the functions of hearing and sight in the case of Bronze, insists on the bygone beauty of Molly, and widens the spectrum of Bloomian memory.

The third and last stage of the creation of *Ulysses* begins with "Circe." Between the very first drafts and the final text, the paragraphs in the first pages of this chapter undergo a transformation much more profound than anything that we have seen yet. This rearrangement corresponds to a radical change in the status of discourse. In fact, what had previously presented itself in ordinary narrative form now takes the appearance of a theatrical script, including stage directions in italics and parentheses and responses identified by the names of the speakers in small capitals. The whole thing is carefully partitioned into separate paragraphs. Yet, as is often the case with Joyce, distinctions are subverted as soon as they are put in place, including the distinctions between the original narration and the scenic layout that replaces it and between the different discursive registers resulting from the new breaks. Indeed, the passage from a narrative to a dramatic form is readily accompanied, as we could have expected, by a change in focalization, but contrary to what should have been the case, it moves from a strict external focalization to a varying focalization.[8] To this major contradiction are added some contradictions of detail: the internal logic of the text implies that such or such a speech be attributed to a character who cannot utter it—the apparition of the character thus refers only to an absence. It becomes clear that entire scenes, far from assuming the objectivity and neutrality we might expect from the theatrical form, are in fact focalized by a few specific actors (this is what Joyce called the hallucinatory technique of "Circe"). One can therefore say that the new typography—notably the paragraph breaks—is contradicted by the substance of the text that it informs and that the distinctions it presupposes find themselves short-circuited. The enunciative status that it promises is abolished, or at least shaken, by another status that is imposed upon it. Or, if one prefers, the play of paragraphs abandons its traditional function of clarifying, distinguishing, and distributing voices and becomes another element in an extremely complex polyphony. While according to Roger Laufer, "the multivocal novelistic utterance of the nineteenth century could never have been written without the new typographic system, based on the 'alinéa,' the dash, and quotation marks" (55), modernism, which no longer aims at alternating but at stacking up voices, perverts this novelistic utterance of the nineteenth century by superimposing different typographical systems upon it. These systems are borrowed from the traditions of theater ("Circe"), journalism ("Aeolus"), catechism ("Ithaca"), or from the very ancient tradition of the text in dialogue with its own margins (in the "Lessons" chapter of *Finnegans Wake,* about which we will speak later).

Alongside this evolution of the text's appearance taken as a whole, it is interesting to consider the development of individual paragraphs. A page from a "Circe" typescript (*Archive* 15: 317; Buffalo TS V.B.13.h, p. 10) offers a nice example of the margin—of all available white space—being invaded by the somewhat monstrous growth of a paragraph. On the model of biblical genealogies, the insertion involves genesis, *begetting,* a genesis that despite its frankly parodic nature could possibly serve as an emblem for genetic studies insofar as it is not restrictive but indefinitely expansive. This expansion is even so virulent that one wonders what might eventually stop it. We are dealing with an enumeration, but since the paradigm is characterized by its heterogeneity, there is no reason that it should ever be exhausted.[9] The fact that the name of one of the ancestors attributed to Bloom is "Vingtetunieme" (Twenty-first) allows momentarily the illusion that a numbering is in progress, ordering in an invisible way this frenetic procession of begetters. A closer look reveals, however, that Vingtetunieme is 25th on the list, a fact that reinforces the sentiment of excess beyond all enumeration. This inflation of the paragraph beyond all measure (in the musical sense of the term) seriously perturbs the regulatory function of the play of the very paragraphs that are supposed to give order to this discourse by means of regular poses, both visual and conceptual.

It is true that the paragraph nevertheless manages to end. Why? One might think that it is an aesthetic criterion that ultimately imposes itself, a certain sense, despite everything, of measure in the immeasurable. The moment might have come when it was necessary to cease the game of excess, when to continue would have been merely weighty and maladroit insistence. What is such a moment? How can one define it? The question is particularly complicated if we consider "Eumaeus," the next chapter after "Circe." In fact, the aesthetic underway here is an aesthetic of ugliness. Supposedly reflecting the intellectual fatigue of the protagonists, the uneasiness and heaviness of style is deliberate, assiduously produced through the process of "correction." A page-proof strewn with additions in Joyce's hand offers us an example, beautiful in its plasticity, of this progress towards ugliness. One sees how the paragraph, increasingly coated and cluttered, is stuffed with indigestible material that it is forced to absorb well beyond the point of syntactic saturation. The first visual impression produced by this avant-texte, that of a paragraph radiating marginal additions, recedes, and we glimpse instead an aspiration, a movement toward a veritable black hole of thought in which verbal matter is to be engulfed.

This inversion of hollowness and fullness, this vacillation in which the paragraph abandons its role as an instrument for the analytic segmentation of discourse and becomes an abyss of confusion, can help us to perceive what is in play in a very different mode in *Finnegans Wake,* with its characteristic whirl of obscurity and meaning, hermeticism and illumination, and void and overabundance. The text and the avant-texte of *Finnegans Wake* are much too teeming and diverse, however, for us to be able to synthesize in a few pages Joyce's use of paragraphs in them. We will be content therefore with one example and a few general remarks.

The beginning of the first rough draft of Book 3, Chapter 4 (*Archive* 60: 5; British Library MS 47482a f. 4r) is a long single paragraph surrounded by marginal additions. At the top of the page is a brief first addition, signaled by a capital F linked by a hyphen to another F and ending by the sign ⊥, a siglum indicating that the sentence is to be attributed to the character Issy.[10] The second marker in the text is the siglum Λ, linked by a hyphen to an identical sign in the left margin. Now, this reference does not correspond to anything material: no text accompanies it. It is true that in the final text some thirty paragraphs are inserted in this location, but in the first draft, the sign refers only to itself. What might be the signification of this kind of auto-reference? It seems to us that it is threefold. The siglum designates the character of Shaun, under whose patronage the chapter is placed. Contrary to Issy in the first insertion, however, Shaun cannot be identified as the speaker of the inserted text—there is no insertion. Examining all of the avant-textes for this chapter reveals that the writing of this page coincided with Joyce's reading of the "Wolf Man" and with his discovery of the role played by the symbols V and upside-down V in the story of Freud's patient: they represented the open legs of a woman (and the absence that is revealed). Starting from this discovery, "Wolf Man" would become the nucleus of the chapter, whereas the link between the Shaun siglum and castration, and more generally lack, would become reinforced and more precise. Indeed, not only are the sigla of the children, ⊏ and Λ, graphically constructed from the parental E and Δ by the removal of one of their strokes, but the Λ sign is nothing other than the sign classically used to mark the place of an insertion when making additions to a manuscript or to proofs. It is a paratextual sign that is part of the process of writing but is destined to disappear in the final text. It is usually called the *caret* sign, from the Latin "it is missing." Here, therefore, this sign so heavily overdetermined from the narrative, symbolic, psychoanalytic, and typographic perspectives, refers programmatically to itself or to the opening of the absence that it designates. This absence is incarnated, certainly, in the empty spaces of the numerous paragraphs that will be inserted in its place in the succeeding birth of the chapter but also in the very substance of the successive paragraphs. One could show that they can be analyzed as the injection of massive doses of obscurity. What can be read, then, as the indication of missing paragraphs, refers in the last analysis to this lack that the insertion of each paragraph will only emphasize further.[11]

It might be possible to prudently extend these remarks on the substitution of paragraphs, on elucidation and obscurity, on filling up and cutting away, to the function of paragraphs in *Finnegans Wake*, in Joyce in general, and maybe even in all writing considered in its genetic dimension.

Indeed, paragraphs *in expansion* force us to go beyond the regulated game of rhythmic alternation between fullness and emptiness. They are dynamic nuclei, triggering a reactivation of writing that cannot be reduced to thematic development. In the Mallarméan dream of the "livre expansion totale de la lettre" [the book as total expansion of the letter], paragraphs would play the role of mediation between the book, understood as a formal organization, and the proliferating letter of which they are, if one may say so, the very vessels of expansion.[12]

If the example of Joyce is particularly valuable for bringing this function into view, it is because the ambition of modernism is to extend the very process of potentially limitless expansion that avant-textes display into the printed text. *Finnegans Wake* goes very far in this direction, on the one hand by simultaneously dramatizing and abolishing the final cut, linking the last phrase to the first and thereby relativizing all the intermediate breaks and transforming them into stages of a perpetual restarting. On the other hand, it offers us in the "Lessons" chapter (Book 2, Chapter 2) a typographic disposition that presents paragraphs studded with peripheral texts and marginal commentaries, all of which recall the appearance of rough drafts.

One may even say that in the case of *Finnegans Wake* the expansion of the avant-texte into the printed text of the final work is destined to continue even further. In order to channel the unfolding of meaning and to make paths in the labyrinth, all readers tend to cover the margins of their copies with diverse glosses—which in turn have the honor of being printed if they are made by a professional scholar[13] or, better, by another artist. Indeed, a facsimile of Arno Schmidt's copy has been published, copiously annotated in his handwriting, a copy that his own readers will be able to annotate at their leisure, in a process of unlimited expansion of paragraphs . . .

Source: "Paragraphes en expansion." In *De la lettre au livre: Sémiotique des manuscrits littéraires*, ed. Louis Hay. Paris: CNRS, 1989. 89–114.

Works Cited

Aristotle, *On Rhetoric.* Trans. George A. Kennedy. Oxford: Oxford University Press, 1991.

Faulkner, William. *Novels 1930–1935; As I Lay Dying, Sanctuary, Light in August, Pylon.* Ed. Joseph Blotner and Noel Polk. New York: Library of America, 1985.

Ferrer, Daniel. "Archéologie du regard dans les avant-textes de Circé." *Scribble I: Genèse des textes.* Paris: Minard, 1988. 95–106.

———. "The Open Space of the Draft Page: James Joyce and Modern Manuscripts." In *The Iconic Page in Manuscript, Print, and Digital Culture,* ed. George Bornstein and Theresa Tinkle. Ann Arbor: University of Michigan Press, 1998. 249–67.

———. "'Practise Preaching': Variantes pragmatiques et prédication suspendue dans un manuscrit des 'Sirènes'." In *Writing its own wrunes for ever: Essais de génétique joycenne / Essays in Joycean Genetics,* ed. Daniel Ferrer and Claude Jacquet. Tusson: Éditions du Lérot, 1998. 11–43.

Fordham, Finn, "Sigla in Revision." In *Genetricksling Joyce,* ed. Sam Slote and Wim Van Mierlo. *European Joyce Studies* 9 (1999): 83–96.

Genette, Gérard. "Discours du récit." *Figures III.* Paris: Seuil, 1972. 67–267. *Narrative Discourse: An Essay in Method.* Trans. Jane E. Lewin. Ithaca, N.Y.: Cornell University Press, 1980.

Groden, Michael. *"Ulysses" in Progress.* Princeton, N.J.: Princeton University Press, 1977.

Hay, Louis, ed. *De la lettre au livre: Sémiotique des manuscrits littéraires.* Paris: CNRS, 1989.

Joyce, James. *Finnegans Wake.* 1939. London: Faber and Faber, 1975.

———. *The James Joyce Archive.* Ed. Michael Groden et al. 63 vols. New York: Garland, 1977–79.

———. *Ulysse.* Trans. Auguste Morel with Stuart Gilbert, Valery Larbaud, and James Joyce. 1929. Paris: Gallimard, 1948.

———. *Ulysses: A Critical and Synoptic Edition.* Ed. Hans Walter Gabler et al. 3 vols. New York, Garland, 1984; 1 vol. New York: Random House, 1986 (page references are to the 1986 edition).

Laufer, Roger. "L'Alinéa typographique du XVIe au XVIIIe siècle." In Laufer, ed., *La Notion de paragraphe.* 53–63.
———, ed. *La Notion de paragraphe.* Paris: CNRS, 1985.
Le Ny, Jean-François, "Texte, structure mentale, paragraphe." In Laufer, ed., *La Notion de paragraphe.* 129–36.
Mallarmé, Stéphane. *Œuvres complètes.* Pléiade ed. Paris: Gallimard, 1945.
McHugh, Roland. *Annotations to "Finnegans Wake".* Baltimore: Johns Hopkins University Press, 1980. 2nd ed. 1991.
———. *The Sigla of "Finnegans Wake."* London: Edward Arnold, 1976.
Mitterand, Henri. "Le Paragraphe est-il une unité linguistique." In Laufer, ed., *La Notion de paragraphe.* 85–95.

Further Works by the Authors

D'Iorio, Paolo, and Daniel Ferrer, eds. *Bibliothèques d'écrivains,* Paris: CNRS, 2001.
Ferrer, Daniel. "Clementis's Cap: Retroaction and Persistence in the Genetic Process." Trans. Marlena G. Corcoran. In *Drafts,* ed. Michel Contat, Denis Hollier, and Jacques Neefs. *Yale French Studies* 89 (1996): 223–36.
———. "The Freudful Couchmare of Shaun Λd: Joyce's Notes on Freud and the Composition of Chapter XVI of *Finnegans Wake.*" *James Joyce Quarterly* 22 (1985): 367–82.
———. "Hypertextual Representation of Literary Working Papers." *Literary and Linguistic Computing* 10 (1995): 143–45.
———. "Joyce's Notebooks: Publicizing the Private Sphere of Writing." In *Modernist Writers and the Marketplace,* ed. Ian Willison, Warwick Gould, and Warren Chernaik. London: Macmillan, 1996. 202–22.
———. "Le Matériel et le virtuel: Du paradigme indiciaire à la logique des mondes possibles." In *Pourquoi la critique génétique? Méthodes et theories,* ed. Michel Contat and Daniel Ferrer. Paris: CNRS, 1998. 11–30.
———. "Modo-Post: A Postmodern Reconsideration of the Avant-texte." In *Writing the Future,* ed. David Wood. London: Routledge, 1991. 30–36.
———. "Reflections on a Discarded Set of Proofs." In *Probes: Genetic Studies in Joyce,* ed. David Hayman and Sam Slote. *European Joyce Studies* 5 (1995): 49–63.
———. *Virginia Woolf and the Madness of Language.* London: Routledge, 1990.
Joyce, James. *The "Finnegans Wake" Notebooks at Buffalo.* Ed. Vincent Deane, Daniel Ferrer, and Geert Lernout. 9 vols. to date. Turnhout, Belgium: Brepols, 2001— .
Rabaté, Jean-Michel. "Back to Beria! Genetic Joyce and Eco's 'Ideal Readers.'" In *Probes: Genetic Studies in Joyce,* ed. David Hayman and Sam Slote. *European Joyce Studies* 5 (1995): 65–83.
———. *The Future of Theory.* Oxford: Blackwell, 2002.
———. *The Ghosts of Modernity.* Gainesville: University Press of Florida, 1996.
———. *James Joyce and the Politics of Egoism.* Cambridge: Cambridge University Press, 2001.
———. *James Joyce: Authorized Reader.* Baltimore: Johns Hopkins University Press, 1991.
———. *Joyce upon the Void: The Genesis of Doubt.* London: Macmillan, 1991.
———. "Pound, Joyce and Eco: Modernism and the 'Ideal Genetic Reader.'" *Romanic Review* 86 (1995): 485–500.

Chapter 9
Still *Lost Time*: Already the Text of the *Recherche*

Almuth Grésillon

Almuth Grésillon is a linguist and a longtime genetic scholar who, like Louis Hay and Jean-Louis Lebrave, first developed her expertise in manuscriptology by studying the texts and avant-textes of Heinrich Heine. She later played an important role in developing the Institut des Textes et Manuscrits Modernes, an institution that she directed from 1986 to 1994, and in 1994 she published the first systematic, booklength exposition of genetic criticism, the as-yet untranslated *Éléments de critique génétique.*

The essay translated here, "**Still** *Lost Time*: **Already** the Text of the *Recherche,*" elucidates Proust's complicated, fitful production of the opening to *À la recherche du temps perdu.* It thus complements Raymonde Debray Genette's genetic study in this volume of a famous French literary ending. Grésillon offers us an intriguing model in at least two other respects.

First, she demonstrates the value of a strictly empirical and linguistic approach to manuscript study. Through careful scrutiny of a set of Proust's avant-textes, she shows that while linguistic analysis cannot respond to every genetic question, it can uncover and give conceptual control over some important strata in the genetic process. Bracketing literary history, psychology, cultural study, and every other contextualizing framework for Proust's novel and using Benveniste's idea of a temporality inherent in language, she traces the draft evolution of specific linguistic elements—most notably the adverbial play of "already" and "not yet"—and shows how Proust's meticulous study of grammatical time-markers is an inchoate index, or "programmatic skeleton," of the profound and compulsive reflections on time that structure his novel as a whole. Indeed, we learn how deeply rooted Proust's famous technique of "memory-writing" was in both linguistic and biographical structures of time.

Second, this essay suggests that more nonspecialists should consider writing genetic articles, for it inspiringly gives the lie to the common idea that one must be a lifelong expert on an author to do good genetic work. On the contrary, Grésillon's nearly New Critical focus produces numerous insights that not only do not depend on arcane or in-depth knowledge of Proust's life and work, but actually owe something to the fact that she did not travel down time-worn critical paths.

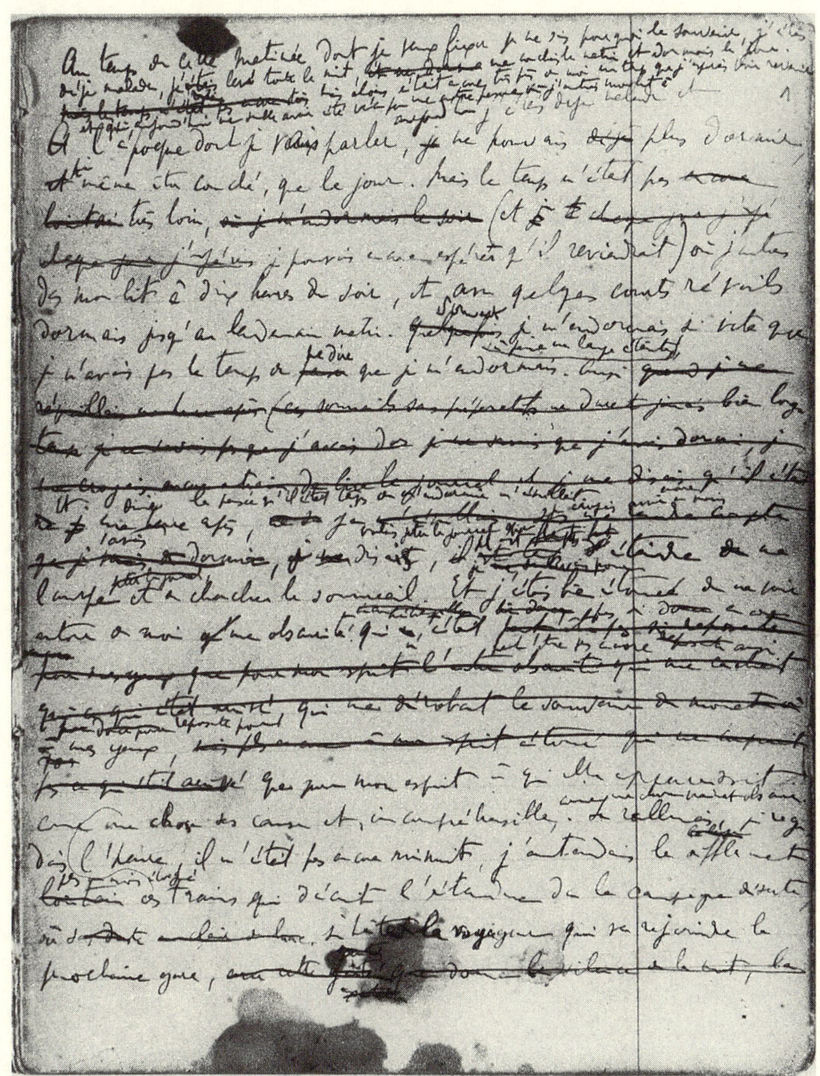

Figure 1. Marcel Proust, Cahier 1, f. 71v. Courtesy of the Bibliothèque Nationale de France.

Shall I tell here what is hardly even an anecdote, what is at best the bizarre experience of a linguist who, with eyes closed, wandered into a manuscript of Proust, an author of whom she had no knowledge other than that of a somewhat cultured nonspecialist? Having admitted my lack of competence, I will explain the circumstances of the story in question.

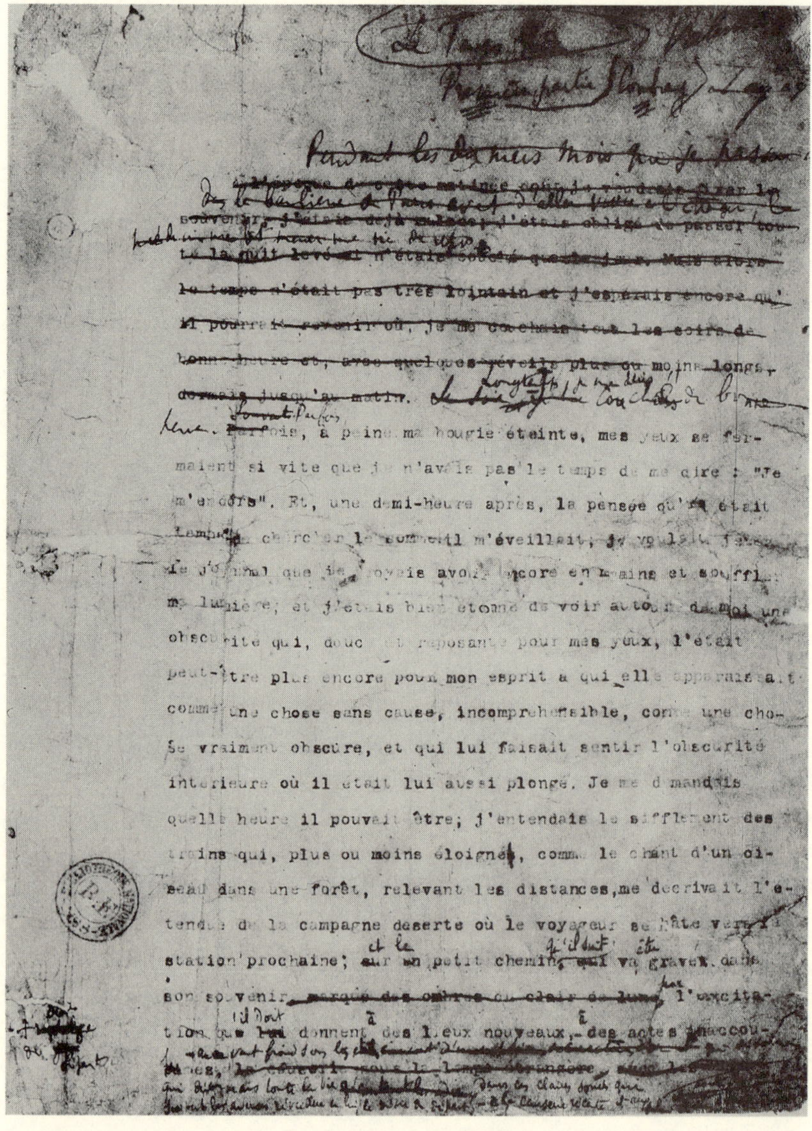

souvenir, j'étais déjà malade; j'étais obligé de passer toute la nuit levé et n'étais couché que le jour. Mais alors
le temps n'était pas très lointain et j'espérais encore qu'
il pourrait revenir où, je me couchais tous les soirs de
bonne heure et, avec quelques réveils plus ou moins longs,
dormais jusqu'au matin.

Parfois, à peine ma bougie éteinte, mes yeux se fermaient si vite que je n'avais pas le temps de me dire : "Je
m'endors". Et, une demi-heure après, la pensée qu'il était
temps de chercher le sommeil m'éveillait; je voulais [illegible]
le journal que je croyais avoir encore en mains et souffler
ma lumière; et j'étais bien étonné de voir autour de moi une
obscurité qui, douce et reposante pour mes yeux, l'était
peut-être plus encore pour mon esprit à qui elle apparaissait
comme une chose sans cause, incompréhensible, comme une chose vraiment obscure, et qui lui faisait sentir l'obscurité
intérieure où il était lui aussi plongé. Je me demandais
quelle heure il pouvait être; j'entendais le sifflement des
trains qui, plus ou moins éloignés, comme le chant d'un oi-
seau dans une forêt, relevant les distances, me décrivait l'é-
tendue de la campagne déserte où le voyageur se hâte vers la
station prochaine; sur un petit chemin qui va graver dans
son souvenir, marqué des ombres du clair de lune, l'excita-
tion que lui donnent des lieux nouveaux, des actes inaccou-
tumés, [illegible]

Figure 2. Marcel Proust, "Longtemps je me suis couché de bonne heure" addition. Courtesy of the Bibliothèque Nationale de France.

In those days I used to work on the texts and manuscripts of Heinrich Heine. Yet one day I found myself invited to explain to students of English the potential interest of a linguistic approach to literary manuscripts. Faced with the impossibility of turning to my usual examples (all in German), I took advantage of a simple proximity of work space and asked a Proustian colleague to show me one of "his" manuscripts.[1] It didn't matter which one, but preferably it would have many variants so as to illustrate, as best as possible, the great range of linguistic changes that can appear in the rough draft of a literary text. And thus I was plunged into a manuscript page of Proust. I knew nothing about its composition date or its eventual fate—nothing, even, about earlier or later drafts. So it was an enterprise entirely free of any of the "seriousness" that real "scientific" work would demand. If I choose nevertheless to speak about it here, it is because I found on its edges, laterally, as it were, a tale of heuristic interest that deserves to be told.

One Draft, One Hypothesis

First of all, the draft (N.A.F. 16641, notebook 1, f. 71r). I present the first half in a diplomatic transcription,[2] assigning, however, a number to each written line. Lines 1A to 4A are added in the upper margin to replace lines 1 to 4 (which Proust did not cross out); after 4A, the text continues to 5, "at ten at night."

Following my usual empirical method, I started by locating all the linguistic changes on this draft. I considered them to be traces of the writing process as it was preserved in the manuscript. Here are a few examples of such changes:

Syntax:

- one case of thematization (linked to a problem of determination):
  line 2–3: Mais le temps n'était pas très loin où . . . [But the time was not far off when . . .]
  line 3A: Mais alors était encore très près de moi un temps que . . . : [But then very near to me was a time which . . .]
- one case of embedding:
  lines 2–4: Mais le temps n'était pas très loin (et je pouvais encore espérer qu'il reviendrait) [But the time was not far off (and I could still hope that it would return), when . . .]
  line 3A: . . . un temps que j'espérais voir revenir [. . . a time which I hoped would return]

Verbs of modality:

- line 1: je vais / veux parler [I'm going to / I wish to speak]

[1A] Au temps de cette matinée dont je veux fixer je ne sais pourquoi le souvenir j'ét ais
[2A] déjà malade, j/e~~étais~~ levé toute la nuit et ~~ne dormais~~ me couchais le matin et dormais le jour
restais
[3A] ~~Mais le temps n'était pas encore très~~ Mais alors était encore très près de moi un temps que j'espérais voir r
[4A] et qui aujourd'hui me semble avoir été vécu par une autre personne où j'entrais dans mon lit à
aujourd'hui j'étais déjà malade et
1 l'époque dont je v/ais/eux parler, ~~je~~ ne pouvais ~~déjà~~ plus dormir
ni
2 ~~et~~ même être couché, que le jour. Mais le temps n'était pas ~~encore~~
3 ~~lointain~~ très loin, ~~où je m'endormais le soir~~ (et ~~j x chaque jour j'espé~~
4 ~~chaque jour j'espérais~~ je pouvais encore espérer qu'il reviendrait) où j'entrais
5 dans mon lit à dix heures du soir et avec quelques courts réveils
Souvent
6 dormais jusqu'au lendemain matin. ~~Quelquefois~~ je m'endormais si vite que
, à peine ma lampe éteinte,
me dire
7 je n'avais pas le temps de ~~penser~~ que je m'endormais. Aussi, ~~quand je me~~
8 ~~réveillais une heure après~~ (~~ces sommeils sans préparatifs ne durent jamais bien~~ long-
9 ~~temps je ne savais pas que j'avais dor je ne savais que j'avais dormi, je~~
10 ~~me croyais encore en train de lire le journal et me disais qu'il était~~
demi- la pensée qu'il était temps de m'endormir m'éveillait
11 ~~te j~~ une heure après, ~~ne sa~~, je ~~m'éveillais sans me rendre compte~~
voulais jeter le journal que je croyais avoir encore en mains
'avais il est ~~temps~~ temps ~~faut~~
12 ~~que je venais de~~ dormi~~r~~, ~~je me~~ dis/ant/ais, ~~il est temps d~~' éteindre ~~dx~~ ma
je me soulevais pour
~~jeter le journal~~
13 lampe et de chercher le sommeil.

[1A] At the time of that morning, the memory of which, for some reason, I want to fix, I was
[2A] already ill, I ~~was~~ up all night ~~and couldn't sleep~~ went to bed in the morning and slept during the day
stayed
[3A] ~~But the time was not yet very~~ But then very near to me was a time which I hoped would return
[4A] and which today seems to have been lived by another person when I entered into my bed at
today I was already ill and
1 the time of which I am going to/wish to speak, ~~I~~ was ~~already~~ unable to
nor
2 ~~and~~ even to be in bed, except during the day. But the time was not ~~yet~~
3 ~~distant~~ far off, ~~when I would go to bed at night~~ (and ~~I x each night I hop~~
4 ~~each night I hoped~~ I could still hope that it would return) when I would enter
5 my bed at ten at night and with a few short awakenings
Often
6 sleep until the next morning. ~~Sometimes~~ I went to sleep so fast that
, my light barely out,
tell myself
7 I had not even the time to ~~think~~ that I was going to sleep. Also, ~~when I~~
8 ~~Awakened one hour later~~ (~~this going to sleep without preparations never lasted~~ very
9 ~~long I didn't know if I had sle I didn't know if I had slept, I~~
10 ~~thought I was still reading the newspaper and told myself that it was~~
half- the thought that it was time to go to sleep woke me up
11 ~~you I~~ one hour later, ~~don't kno~~, I ~~woke up without realizing~~
wanted to put down the newspaper that I thought I still held
just it is time ~~it is necessary to~~
12 ~~that I had~~ gone to slee~~p~~, ~~I told/telling/ myself~~, ~~it is time to~~ turn out my
I got up to
~~put down the newspaper~~
13 light and try to sleep.

- line 1: je ne pouvais plus dormir [I was unable to sleep]
- line 2A: je restais levé toute la nuit [I stayed up the whole night]
- line 4: chaque jour, j'espérais / je pouvais encore espérer. [Each day, I hoped / I could still hope.]

Vocabulary:
- line 1: parler [speak]; line 1A: fixer le souvenir [fix the memory]
- line 1: à l'époque [at the time]; line 1A: au temps de cette matinée [at the time of that morning]
- lines 2–3: ne pas être très loin [to be not far off]; line 3A: être très près de moi [to be very near me]
- line 7: je n'avais pas le temps de penser / de me dire [had not the time to think / to tell myself]
- line 12: il est temps / il faut [it is time / it is necessary to]

Now, it was only in looking at the overall word choices—both what was changed and what was left unchanged—that a first intuition emerged: everything has to do with time.[3] Here are the elements in the order in which they appear in the draft:

time / time of that morning; today; memory; night; day; time; night; each day; at ten at night; short; next morning; sometimes; often; barely out; fast; not to have the time; one hour later; never to last very long; one half-hour later; it is time to.

This first intuition then focused on the adverbial play between *already* and *(not) yet* that runs like a fundamental axis through these lines.

Whence the sudden association with the title *À la recherche du temps perdu*. And the corollary question: does this rough draft have a genetic connection to the novel? Of what project is it a part?

I then learned that the passage in question is only one of the many phases of writing that ultimately led to the introductory sentence of the *Recherche*: "For a long time, I went to bed early" ["Longtemps, je me suis couché de bonne heure"].

Thus the sudden intuition of the linguist revealed itself to be true. But what was it founded upon? How to justify it after the fact? Before returning to this, it is necessary to recall schematically the full genesis of which the quoted draft is a part. In Part 2, I will indicate those of Proust's writing projects that underpin this genetic record. Then in Part 3, I will present excerpts from the manuscript dossier. These will corroborate the linguistic hypotheses to be elucidated in Part 4.[4]

At the Heart of the Writing Projects

Toward the end of November 1908, Proust began a study of, and against, Sainte-Beuve's method of literary criticism. Looking for an adequate format, he hesitated between an essay (of which I will not give an account here) and a narrative form in which the aesthetic discussion would be the major part of a morning discussion between the narrator and his mother. These sketches and beginnings are followed by the narrative "Sainte-Beuve," which Proust worked on during the winter of 1908–9 in a certain number of Notebooks [*Cahiers*] (held at the Bibliothèque Nationale; N.A.F. 16640ff). Proust never brought that project to conclusion.[5] Starting in March 1909, however, he did progressively metamorphose it into the novel that at the time of its first publication in 1913 would be given the title of *À la recherche du temps perdu.*

The complex genetic process leading from the initial project on Sainte-Beuve to the opening of the *Recherche* is recorded in a manuscript dossier whose various stages are spread out between 1908 and 1911 and whose rough draft (quoted above) constitutes the turning point. Thus in order to seize the broad lines of this development, I consulted the manuscripts, whose tenor I will rapidly try to sketch here.[6]

Notebook 3 (November–December 1908): The evocation of that singular morning that will become that of "the Conversation with Mama," in two contradictory modes: (1) an "I" *already ill,* who sleeps only during the day, has just gone to bed and awaits his mother's morning visit; it is dark; (2) there is a slippage between the peculiar dim light of morning and the chaotic reveries that are typical of any sleeping person who awakes in the middle of the night. A resolution of this contradiction by temporal dissociation is sketched at the end of this notebook; the memory of the period of nighttime sleeping is placed in a past of good health that is lost forever (see f. 18: "In the past, just like everyone else, I had known the sweetness of waking up in the middle of the night"), a past that contrasts with the present time of the morning narrative dominated by anxiety and illness.

Notebook 5 (Winter 1908–9): This notebook maintains the temporal dualism, with a few modulations, however. "The morning with Mama" is now only indirectly present ("At that time, I was already ill"), and the period of the "past" with its dreams and memories of childhood and adolescence is materialized at the same time that it is inscribed in a precise chronological frame ("Until the age of twenty, I slept through the night with only brief awakenings").

Notebook 1 (February–March 1909): The rough draft cited above constitutes the first lines; this notebook presents a text that is very much corrected, followed by what could have become the prelude to the morning dealing with Sainte-Beuve. But already the processes of reminiscence are multiplying ("sometimes," "occasionally," "most often"), and the room of awakening evokes all kinds of earlier rooms (at Trouville, Aix-les-Bains, Auteuil, Dieppe, Brussels). The memory becomes general and a textual generator.

In what way does this notebook occupy a pivotal position between the project on Sainte-Beuve and the future novel? Besides the development of memory-writing, which becomes entirely an illustration of an aesthetic theory and thereby removes the need for a focused discussion (planned for Sainte-Beuve), the variants and changes contained in the first lines of this notebook constitute the signs of the metamorphosis by which the "Sainte-Beuve" project was transformed into a novel about lost time. In fact, if the first draft phrase "At the time of which I wish to speak today" still seems to refer directly to the *words* of the conversation about Sainte-Beuve, this is not true for the sequence that replaces it. "At the time of that morning, the memory of which, for some reason, I want to fix" is a sequence that already announces the "involuntary memory." One addition contained in this same sequence also seems significant to me: "a time which I hoped would return *and which today seems to have been lived by another person.*"

Notebooks 8 and 9 (Summer 1909): These represent the first notebooks of the future novel; they already include in nearly definitive form the nocturnal recollections in the Overture to *Du côté de chez Swann.* Nevertheless, the problem of time divided between the *already-ill* of the morning and the *not-yet-far-off* of earlier dreams remains.

Typescript (1909–10): Proust has this typescript made from Notebook 9, whose beginning is at first copied word for word, maintaining the *already/not yet* balance. Proust reworks this typescript by hand, however. He crosses out the first lines—precisely those that, ever since their early origin in Notebook 3, had preserved the *already/not yet* dichotomy. In a first correction, he substitutes a sequence that certainly seems surprising but still preserves the idea of illness: "During the last months that I spent in the suburb of Paris before going to live abroad, the doctor had me lead a life of repose. At night, I went to bed early." This sequence is crossed out in turn, however, and replaced by a miracle-phrase that simultaneously eliminates the cumbersome morning,[7] the illness,[8] which has been an obsessive concern until now, and the push and pull between *already* and *not yet.* One element survives and incorporates all the rest—the *past* of memory: "For a long time, I went to bed early."

Another handwritten intervention in this typescript is the addition of a title: "Lost Time."[9] We can readily accept dating this addition to about the same time as the other revisions because it sums up this ultimate finishing touch that Proust brought to the novel's Overture. He will not find its definitive title, let us recall, until 1913.

Still/Already: A Genetic Journey

This brief review of the genetic history surrounding the draft that I had begun investigating is certainly piecemeal and perhaps even partial. I have omitted the gaps between the narrator and the "hero" as well as the chaotic textualization of the workings of memory—themes of great interest to literary critics. I have, however, attempted to make visible a temporal structure that stretches like an obsession through the whole of the dossier and will only be erased in extremis, just before Proust embarks on his long quest for a publisher.[10] This bias in favor of the temporal structure—in the linguistic and not the biographical sense of time—is of course governed by my first intuition about the eventual relation between *already/(not) yet* and something like a *programmatic skeleton of the Proustian novel.* Before pushing this hypothesis further, I will indicate here some simplified excerpts from the dossier, excerpts that all deal with the future beginning of the novel and are quoted simply to give words to what I have called the obsessive structure of the *already/(not) yet* binary. My mode of presentation is no longer a diplomatic transcription; I aim only to visualize as well as possible the units that interest me (they are in italics). Strike-throughs are used to indicate cross-outs; parentheses are in the original.

Cahier 3:

- ~~Comme j'avais *déjà* pris l'habitude de ne dormir que le jour on entrait chez moi~~ 8 heures, c'était le moment où maman entrerait me dire bonsoir (j'avais *déjà* pris l'habitude de ne dormir que le jour, je m'endormais après le premier courier) (f. 3r)
- maman ne tarderait pas à entrer dans ma chamber, car *déjà* je ne dormais que le jour (f. 5r)
- et à partir du moment où j'ai été malade (f. 6r)
- Depuis longtemps je ne dormais plus que le jour (f. 11r)
- ~~Depuis longtemps je ne dormais plus que le jour, mais cette nuit là j'eus pourtant~~ ~~Je m'éveillai après quelques minutes de sommeil seulement (depuis longtemps je ne dormais plus que le jour), mais surpris par~~ Je m'éveillai au milieu de la nuit après quelques minutes de sommeil (depuis longtemps je ne dormais plus que le jour) (f. 12r)
- Autrefois, j'avais connu comme tout le monde la douceur de m'éveiller au milieu de la nuit (f. 18r)

Notebook 3:

- ~~Since I had *already* acquired the habit of sleeping only during the day, people entered my house~~ 8 o'clock, it was the moment when Mama would come in to say goodnight to me (I had *already* acquired the habit of sleeping only during the day, I went to sleep after the first mail delivery) (f. 3r)
- Mama would not wait long before entering my room, because I was *already* sleeping only during the day (f. 5r)
- and from the moment when I was ill (f. 6r)
- For quite some time I had been sleeping only during the day. (f. 11r)
- ~~For quite some time I had been sleeping only during the day, but that night I had nevertheless~~ ~~I awoke after just a few minutes (for a long time I was sleeping only during the day), but surprised by~~ I awoke in the middle of the night after a few minutes of sleep (for a long time I had been sleeping only during the day) (f. 12r)
- In the past, I had known like everyone else the sweetness of awaking in the middle of the night (f. 18r)

Cahier 5:

- ~~A cette époque, j'avais *déjà* pris l'habitude de dormir le jour~~. ~~A cette époque j'étais *déjà* malade et ne pouvais plus me coucher et dormir que le jour. Mais je pouvais me souvenir comme d'un temps très rapproché, il est bien lointain *aujourd'hui*, où je me réveillais au milieu de la nuit, ce n'était pas pour bien longtemps et seulement pour prendre conscience un instant~~. A cette époque j'étais *déjà* malade et ne pouvais plus être couché et dormir que le jour. Mais ~~je me souvenais comme d'un temps assez voisin et que j'avais alors l'illusion de voir revenir~~ le temps *n'était pas* ~~bien~~ *lointain encore*—et je nourrissais l'illusion de le voir bientôt revenir—où ne faisant qu'un avec mon lit et ma chambre je dormais toute la nuit de conserve avec eux. (f. 114v)
- ~~Quand jétais jeune~~ jusque vers l'âge de vingt ans, je dormis la nuit (f. 113v)
- Jusque vers l'âge de vingt ans je ~~dormis~~ dormais toute la nuit avec de courts réveils (f. 111v)

Notebook 5:

- ~~At that time, I had *already* acquired the habit of sleeping during the day~~. ~~At that time I was *already* ill and could go to bed and sleep only during the day. But I could remember as if it were very recently, though very distant from me *today*, when I would awaken in the middle of the~~

~~night, not for very long and to be conscious for only a moment.~~ At that time I was *already* ill and could only lie down and sleep during the day. But ~~I remember as if it were a relatively recent time, one that I was then under the illusion would soon return~~ the time *was not yet* ~~very~~ *far off*—and I nourished the illusion that it would soon return—when becoming one with my bed and my room I would sleep the night through along with them. (f. 114v)

- ~~When I was young~~ until the age of about twenty, I slept at night (f. 113v)
- Until I was about twenty I ~~slept~~ used to sleep all night with only brief awakenings (f. 111v)

Cahier 1:

See above

Cahier 8:

- *Au temps de cette matinée dont je* ~~veux~~ voudrais fixer ~~je ne sais pourquoi~~ le souvenir, j'étais *déjà* malade, j'étais obligé de ~~passer~~ ~~rester debout~~ passer toute la nuit ~~debout~~ levé et n'étais couché que le jour. Mais alors le temps n'était *pas* ~~*encore*~~ très lointain, et j'espérais *encore* qu'il reviendrait, où j'entrais dans mon lit à dix heures du soir et avec quelques réveils plus ou moins longs dormais jusqu'au ~~lendemain~~ matin. Parfois, à peine ma lampe éteinte, je m'endormais si vite que je n'avais pas le temps de me dire "Je m'endors". Et une demie heure après . . . (f. 1r)

Notebook 8:

- At the time of that morning of which I ~~wish~~ would like to fix ~~I don't know why~~ the memory, I was *already* ill, I was obliged to ~~spend~~ ~~remain standing~~ spend the whole night ~~standing~~ up and go to bed only during the day. But then the time was *not* ~~*yet*~~ very far off, and I *still* hoped that it would return, when I would enter my bed at ten at night and with a few awakenings of various duration sleep until ~~the next~~ morning. Sometimes, my light barely out, I went to sleep so fast that I had not even the time to tell myself, "I'm going to sleep." And a half hour later . . . (f. 1r)

Cahier 9:

- ~~Au temps~~ A l'époque de cette matinée dont je voudrais fixer le souvenir, j'étais *déjà* malade, j'étais obligé de passer toute la nuit ~~debout~~

levé, et n'étais couché que le jour. Mais alors le temps n'était pas très lointain et j'espérais *encore* qu'il pourrait revenir, où ~~j'entrais dans mon lit à dix heures du soir~~ je me couchais tous les soirs de bonne heure et, avec quelques réveils plus ou moins longs, dormais jusqu'au ~~lendemain~~ matin. Parfois, à peine ma ~~lampe~~ bougie éteinte, ~~je m'endormais si vite~~ mes yeux se fermaient si vite que je n'avais pas le temps de me dire: "Je m'endors." Et, une demie heure après, . . . (f. 1r)

Notebook 9:

- ~~At the time~~ During the period of that morning of which I would like to fix the memory, I was *already* ill, I was obliged to spend the whole night ~~standing~~ up, and could sleep only during the day. But then the time was not very far off and I *still* hoped that it might return, when ~~I entered my bed at ten at night~~ I went to bed early every night and, with a few awakenings of various durations, would sleep until ~~the next~~ morning. Sometimes, my ~~light~~ barely out, ~~I went to sleep so fast~~ my eyes closed so quickly that I didn't have time to tell myself, "I'm going to sleep." And, a half hour later, . . . (f. 1r)

Typescript[11]

Le Temps Perdu
Première partie: Combray
~~Pendant les derniers mois que je passais~~

1 ~~A l'époque de cette matinée dont je voudrais fixer le~~
~~dans la banlieu de Paris avant d'aller vivre à l'étranger, le~~
2 ~~souvenir, j'étais *déjà* malade; j'étais obligé de passer toute~~
~~médecein me fit mener une vie de repos~~
3 ~~la nuit levé et n'étais couché que le jour. Mais alors~~
4 ~~le temps n'était pas très lointain et j'espérais *encore* qu'~~
5 ~~il pourrait revenir, où je me couchais tous les soirs de~~
6 ~~bonne heure et, après quelques réveils plus ou moins longs~~
Longtemps je me suis couché
7 ~~dormais jusqu'au matin~~. **~~Le soir je me couchais~~ de bonne heure**
~~Souvent~~ Parfois
8 ~~Parfois~~, à peine ma bougie éteinte, mes yeux se fermaient si vite que je n'avais pas le
9 temps de me dire "Je m'endors." Et une demi-heure après, . . .

Time Lost
First Part: Combray
~~During the last months I spent~~

1 ~~At the time of that morning of which I would like to fix the~~
~~in the suburb of Paris before going to live abroad, the~~
2 ~~memory, I was *already* ill: I was obliged to spend the whole~~
~~doctor had me lead a life of repose~~
3 ~~night up and go to bed only during the day. But then~~
4 ~~the time was not that far off and I *still* hoped that~~
5 ~~it might return, when I would go to bed every night~~
6 ~~early and, after a few awakenings of various durations~~
For a long time I went to bed
7 ~~sleep until morning.~~ **~~At night I went to bed~~** **early**.
~~Often~~ Sometimes
8 ~~Sometimes~~, my light barely out, my eyes closed so
fast that I had not the
9 time to tell myself, "I'm going to sleep." And a half hour later, . . .

Printed Text

Longtemps, je me suis couché de bonne heure. Parfois, à peine ma bougie éteinte, mes yeux se fermaient si vite que je n'avais pas le temps de me dire: "Je m'endors." Et, une demi-heure après . . .

For a long time, I went to bed early. Sometimes, my light barely out, my eyes closed so fast that I had not the time to tell myself, "I'm going to sleep." And, a half hour later . . .

Still/Already: A Linguistic Journey

Now, how to describe and interpret this game with time? Gérard Genette asked the same question about the *Recherche* and describes his own procedure as follows:

> So we can characterize the temporal stance of a narrative only by considering at the same time all the relationships it establishes between its own temporality and that of the story it tells. (155)

This method leads him to locate all kinds of discordances between narrative time, on the one hand, and "real," lived, biographical time on the other—discordances that in Proust's case lead to "narrative anachronies" (35) and even "to the threshold of achrony pure and simple" (79). This is not the approach that I will adopt. On the contrary, I will assume that the specific problems of time, as well as others linked to it (see below), can be treated in categories belonging to linguistics without recourse to anything extralinguistic. And I can only recall Benveniste, who advocated a temporality *inherent in language* in these terms:

> One could believe that temporality is an innate structure of thought. It is produced in and by enunciation. From enunciation proceeds the installation of the category of the present, and from the category of the present is born the category of time. The present is properly the source of time. It is this presence to the world that the act of enunciation alone renders possible, because, if you really think about it, we have no other means to live the "now" and to make it real than to realize it by putting language into the world. (83)

Antoine Culioli and Catherine Fuchs have often recalled the implication flowing from this position. Linguistic description does not analyze "events," a term that always evokes the experience of reality, but rather "processes," which are a representation of reality filtered by language. (See Fuchs and Anne-Marie Léonard, *Vers une théorie de l'aspect*, 51ff.)

To insert myself in the strict framework of linguistics in this manner in no way annuls the extralinguistic explanations that I supplied above; I will return to this at the end.

Thus I propose to examine the function of the *still/already* pair as it appears in the cited manuscript occurrences, and only that. I will neither explore all the possible uses of these two adverbs nor examine the other problems of linguistic time contained in the manuscript dossier.

Without recalling here in detail the numerous linguistic descriptions devoted to the *still/already* pair (see the bibliography), I will privilege the approach proposed by Fuchs (*Contribution*, "De quelques problèmes," and *Vers une théorie*) because she emphasizes from the start that *still/already* must be treated in terms not only of *time* but also of *aspect*. To illustrate the general difference between time and aspect, one can say, for example, about the French imperfect that, from the point of view of time, it marks a process that is transposed with respect to the moment of enunciation. From the point of view of aspect, it marks, just like the present, a process as it is unfolding, that is, not finished. Similarly, *still* and *already* mark a temporal coincidence with regard to the temporal relation between the moment associated globally with a process and the moment of enunciation, but an aspectual difference with regard to the precise moments of the process (beginning-unfolding-end) and the focal point from which this process is described.

I will thus base my interpretation entirely on the analyses proposed by Fuchs. Rather than present them separately, I will integrate them directly in the description of the Proustian occurrences of *still/already*. These have two common points: (1) They all belong to durative usage (as opposed to iterative usage, for example, "He repeated it to me again [encore]" or "I had already [déjà] gone last year"). (2) Except for one case of pluperfect, they are all in the imperfect. Are we dealing with a privileged homogeneity that could lessen the impact of the conclusions I will draw? No, that is not the case because the system of description adopted here is identical, whatever the implied verbal times and meanings (iterative or durative) may be.

Together the occurrences make up two series of processes, one marked by *already*, the other by *still*,[12] both locatable with respect to an identical moment T, which is different from the moment of the enunciation and identifiable in the different stages of the manuscript by:

- at that time
- during the period of which I would like to speak today
- at the time of that morning of which I wish to fix the memory

Remark. The following descriptions are all based on a general scheme: every process is associated with a closed interval to the left and, depending upon the case, an open or closed one on the right.[13] *Still* and *already* serve as expressions of the modifications in the system within these limits (see Fuchs and Léonard, *Vers une théorie* 243).

Already

(1) *I was already ill*

- The start of the interval associated with the process "being ill" is before T.
- The utterer is surprised by this anteriority;[14] he thought that "being ill" had not yet begun by T.[15] There is thus a gap between the situation described and the expected situation.

(2) *Since I had already acquired the habit of sleeping only during the day, people entered my house*

- The start of the interval associated with "acquiring the habit" is before T; moreover, the end is also before T. "Acquiring the habit" is a finished process, the habit has been acquired.[16]
- The utterer is surprised that the process of "acquiring the habit" had started so early that it has already been finished, that is, that even before T, "I" could only sleep during the day.

(3) *Already I could only sleep during the day*

- The starting point of "could no longer sleep except during the day" is before T.

- The utterer thought that the process had not yet begun at T and that it would start later.

Still

(1) *I still hoped that it would return.*[17]

- The endpoint of the interval associated with "hope that" has not been reached; it is later than T.
- The utterer is surprised that it is later; he thought that "hoping" would be finished by T.

(2) *The time was still very near to me when . . .*

- The endpoint of the interval associated with "to be near" has not been reached by the moment T.
- The utterer is surprised that this endpoint is later than T; he thought that it had already been reached.

Remark: In the draft process, utterance (2) changes places with (3) below. Because of the antynomy of the predicates, one might suspect a relation of synonymy between (2) and (3). As we will see, however, this depends on the type of analysis that we adopt for (3).

(3) *The time was not yet far off*

The problem with analyzing this utterance is linked to the negation. In one case, (a), we suppose *still (to be not very far off)*. In the other, (b), we will start from the fact that *not yet* is the current negation of *already*, which would result in (3A): *It is false that the time is already very far off.*

(a) *The time was not yet far off* (this is an attested variant).

- The endpoint of the interval associated with not being far off has not yet been reached at the moment T.
- The utterer is surprised that this endpoint has not yet been reached, thus that *not being far off* has not been finished.

(b) = (3A) *It is false that the time is already very far off.*

- It is false that the starting point of *being far off* is before the moment T.
- The utterer is surprised that this is false; he thought it was true that the beginning point of *being far off* was before T and thus that *being far off* had already started.

The two interpretations are very close. But (a) insists on the shift at the endpoint while (b) insists on the starting point. This proves that the surface correspondence between the negation of *already* and *not yet* actually conceals an aspectual displacement. That is why we ultimately privilege interpretation (a), and this all the more in that it confirms the supposed synonymy with utterance (2). In both cases, despite the lexical change, there is a shift in the endpoint.

To sum up, *already* is marked by the fact that the starting point is situated earlier than predicted; *still* marks the fact that the end point is situated later than predicted. Now, in our texts the two series of processes are correlated with a common point, T. Put otherwise, at the moment T, one process that in principle should have ended overlaps with another that in principle should not have begun. T is the concentric time when almost-elapsed and just-begun times coexist, and this to the greatest surprise of the utterer. The frontiers are displaced and disordered—but held nonetheless within the limited zone of moment T, a focal point marking the unfolding processes and situated in an open interval. It is this precariousness of the aspecto-temporal limits revealed by the function of *still/already* that permits us to confirm our first intuition after the fact. It can legitimately be understood as an underlying structure of language, as a formal mold, or as the programmatic skeleton of Proust's writing in the *Recherche.* Given the stakes of such a program, we can understand very well why the balance between *still* and *already* traverses in such an obsessive fashion the whole of the manuscript dossier.

The fact remains that Proust, in an ultimate stroke of the pen, erased this structural program to the benefit of "For a long time, I went to bed early." With this, a finished process (the closed series of "going to bed early") replaces unfolding processes with fluctuating limits: now the beginning and ending points have no more existence, and there is no interval in which the miraculous moment T, the sign of *still* and *already,* could appear. My aim is not to describe, comment upon, or interpret this inaugural phrase of the *Recherche.* I would rather emphasize this: the printed text certainly gives rise to all kinds of interpretations of the temporal problem in Proust. But it is the material presence of the *still/already* dualism, locatable only in the manuscript dossier, that contains *in nuce* the whole structural program of the novel.

One last word to return to the heuristic interest of this little journey. I admitted the literary naïveté with which I approached Proust's rough draft. It was strictly a linguistic intuition that pushed me to search in a direction that ultimately proved, it seems to me, to be full of interest. What does this say about method? What is the power of linguistics to intervene in the field of manuscript study? Certainly, the linguistic approach would not explain the overall genesis of a text. It can provide only a partial access to the mechanisms of production, the rest belonging to literary, historical, and psychoanalytical determinations. Yet in rendering certain latent linguistic structures of the manuscript explicit, the linguistic approach, with its specific tools, permits us to bring to light and to analyze pertinent paths leading from drafts to text.

Source: "**Encore** du *Temps perdu*, **Déjà** le texte de la *Recherche*." In *Proust à la lettre: Les Intermittences de l'écriture*, by Almuth Grésillon, Jean-Louis Lebrave, and Catherine Viollet. Tusson: Éditions du Lérot, 1990. 45–60. A somewhat different version appears in *Manuscrits-Écriture, production linguistique*, ed. Almuth Grésillon and Jean-Louis Lebrave. Special issue of *Langages* 69 (March 1983): 111–25.

Works Cited

Abraham, Werner. "Forschungsskizze: Temporales *noch*—Woher stammt *noch*?" *Klagenfurter Beiträge zur Sprachwissenschaft* 3 (1977): 1–24.

Benveniste, Émile. "L'Appareil formel de l'énonciation." In *Problèmes de linguistique générale*. Vol. 2. Paris: Gallimard, 1974. 79–88.

Brun, Bernard. "Le Dormeur éveillé: Genèse d'un roman de la mémoire." In *Études proustiennes*, vol. 4, *Proust et la critique anglo-saxonne*. Cahiers Marcel Proust 11. Paris: Gallimard, 1982. 241–316.

Doherty, Monika. "*Noch* and *schon* and their presuppositions." In *Generative Grammar in Europe*, ed. Ferenc Kiefer and Nicolas Ruwet. Dordrecht: Reidel, 1973. 154–77.

Fuchs, Catherine. *Contribution préliminaire à la construction d'une grammaire de reconnaissance du français*. Thèse de 3e cycle, Université de Paris VII, 1971.

———. "De quelques problèmes syntaxiques et lexicaux d'aspect." *Recherches Linguistiques* 5–6 (1978): 93–102.

Fuchs, Catherine, and Anne-Marie Léonard. *Vers une théorie de l'aspect*. École des Hautes Etudes en Sciences Sociales. Mouton: Le Haye, 1979.

Genette, Gérard. "Discours du récit." In *Figures III*. Paris: Seuil, 1972. 67–267. *Narrative Discourse: An Essay in Method*. Trans. Jane E. Lewin. Ithaca, N.Y.: Cornell University Press, 1980.

Hœpelman, J., and C. Rohrer. "'Déjà' et 'encore' et les temps du passé français." In *La Notion d'aspect*, ed. Jean David and Robert Martin. Paris: Klincksieck, 1980. 119–43.

König, Ekkehard. "Temporal and Non-Temporal Uses of *noch* and *schon* in German." *Linguistics and Philosophy* 2 (1977): 173–98.

Martin, Robert. "'Déjà' et 'encore': De la présupposition à l'aspect." In *La Notion d'aspect*, ed. Jean David and Robert Martin. Paris: Klincksieck, 1980. 167–80.

Nef, Frédéric. "Encore." *Langages* 64 (1981): 93–108.

Proust, Marcel. *Contre Sainte-Beuve; suivi de Nouveaux mélanges*. Preface by Bernard de Fallois. Paris: Gallimard, 1954. *Against Sainte-Beuve and Other Essays*. Trans. John Sturrock. London: Penguin, 1988.

Quémar, Claudine. "Autour de trois 'avant-textes' de l'Ouverture de la *Recherche*: Nouvelles approches des problèmes du *Contre Sainte-Beuve*." *Bulletin d'Informations Proustiennes* 3 (1976): 7–29.

———. "De l'Essai sur Sainte-Beuve au futur roman: Quelques aspects du projet proustien à la lumière des avant-textes." *Bulletin d'Informations Proustiennes* 8 (1978): 7–11.

Further Works by the Author

Grésillon, Almuth. "La Critique génétique: Entre philologie et théorie littéraire." *Bulletin des Études Valéryennes* 72–73 (1996): 147–55.

———. "Critique génétique et 'textual criticism': Une Rencontre." *Romanic Review* 86 (1995): 595–98.

———. "La Critique génétique: Origines et méthodes." *Annali della Scuola Normale Superiore di Pisa: Classe di lettere e filosofia*, Ser. 4 Quaderni 5 (1998, Quaderni 1): 15–22.

———. *Éléments de critique génétique: Lire les manuscrits modernes*. Paris: Presses Universitaires de France, 1994.

———. "Mise au net: Une Critique génétique sans brouillons?" In *Les Voies de l'invention aux XVIe et XVIIe siècles: Études génétiques*, ed. Bernard Beugnot and Robert Melançon. Special issue of *Paragraphes* 9 (1993): 227–32.

———. "Le Mot-valise et ses contraintes d'écriture chez Heine." In *Écriture et contraintes*, ed. Michel Espagne, Almuth Grésillon, and Catherine Viollet. Special issue of *Cahier Heine* 3 (1984): 29–64.

———. "Raturer, rater, rayer, éradiquer, radier, irradier." In *Ratures et repentirs*, ed. Bertrand Rougé. Pau: Université de Pau, 1996. 49–60.

———. "Ralentir: Travaux." *Genesis* 1 (1992): 9–31. "Slow: Work in Progress." Trans. Stephen A. Noble and Vincent Vichit-Vadakan. *Word and Image* 13, 2 (1997): 106–23.

Grésillon, Almuth, and Jean-Louis Lebrave. "Les Manuscrits comme lieu de conflits discursifs." In *La Genèse du texte: Les Modèles linguistiques*, by Catherine Fuchs et al. Paris: CNRS, 1982. 129–75.

———. "Manuscrits, linguistique et informatique." In *Avant-texte, texte, après-texte*, ed. Louis Hay and Péter Nagy. Paris: CNRS; Budapest: Akadémiai Kiadó, 1982. 177–89.

Grésillon, Almuth, Jean-Louis Lebrave, and Catherine Viollet. *Proust à la lettre: Les intermittences de l'écriture*. Tusson: Éditions du Lérot, 1990.

Lebrave, Jean-Louis, and Almuth Grésillon, eds. *Écrire aux XVIIe et XVIIIe siècles: Genèses de textes littéraires et philosophiques*. Paris: CNRS, 2000.

Chapter 10
Proust's "Confession of a Young Girl": Truth or Fiction?

Catherine Viollet

First and always a linguist, Catherine Viollet has also developed a keen interest and expertise in the burgeoning fields of gender studies and autobiography. In 1995, she co-founded, with Philippe Lejeune, a team at the Institut des Textes et Manuscrits Modernes to study the genesis of autobiographical writings of all kinds.

The 1991 article translated here, "Proust's 'Confession of a Young Girl': Truth or Fiction?" brings together all three of Viollet's areas of interest in a focused genetic study of two youthful stories by Marcel Proust: the 1893 "Avant la nuit" and its subsequent 1894 incarnation as "La Confession d'une jeune fille." Her thesis is that Proust was wrestling personally with how to express or confess his own sexuality and that this private struggle was complexly and perhaps unwittingly inscribed in the genesis of his fiction. It is precisely the kind of tantalizing mystery that many readers hope genetic criticism will be able to help solve. The essay will thus be of special interest both to those who—weary of presuming that the author is dead—are ready to rejuvenate biographical inquiry and to those who think of fiction writing as a gendered activity.

Viollet carefully elucidates how autobiographical, confessional discourse can sometimes speak between the lines of fiction, refusing to be erased. Through meticulous genetic work, she reconstructs the ways Proust wrote himself so deeply into his female character that he ultimately described "her" sexuality in unmistakably masculine terms. She reveals, too, that when Proust vacillated over the age and the sex of his transgressive fictional character, he may well have been struggling to understand and control the way such indices affect the social judgment of character in both his fiction and his life.

Viollet assumes, like Almuth Grésillon elsewhere in this volume, that linguistic observations can produce genetic patterns that call for wider theoretical synthesis. Methodically allowing her linguist's consciousness to meditate on such details as the gender of pronouns, the use of the first-person narrative, and the fluctuating subtleties of Proust's use of both intimate and general forms of "we," she demonstrates several strategies for interpreting different layers of texts that, as she shows, are somehow both "explicitly" fictional and "virtually" autobiographical.

This is a genetic project par excellence, for it deals with evidence available only in the avant-textes. It is thanks to the manuscripts that Viollet is able to identify and analyze the way Proust (unthinkingly?) misspelled past participles—parts of speech that in French reveal one's gender as *either* masculine *or* feminine. Proving that a strict binary matrix was already inadequate for Proust by 1894, Viollet uncovers an author whose genders were manipulated and mixed to suit himself and his audience, but whose pen did sometimes slip.

> You can say anything as long as you don't say "I."
>
> —Proust to Gide (Gide, *Journal* 1: 692)

> It is all laboriously fictive because I don't have any imagination.
>
> —Proust, Carnet 1 (1908)

On first reading, the short story that Proust called "La Confession d'une jeune fille" appears singular in many ways. The title, banal in itself, nonetheless has something intriguing about it: it is a confession, that is, a genre that deals with the production of "true" discourse. One thinks, for example, of Saint Augustine's or Rousseau's *Confessions* or of Musset's *La Confession d'un enfant du siècle.* Proust's youth and the singular form "confession" tend to orient the reading toward the idea of a mistake, a particular act, and not towards a "life summary."[1]

Yet we are dealing with the confession of a young girl; the narrative "I" cannot be identical with that of the author, Marcel Proust. If the confession, as an autobiographical act, is "a ritual of discourse in which the speaking subject is also the subject of the statement" (Foucault 61), then putting the title of the Proust text together with the identity of the author immediately excludes all autobiographical presuppositions. On the one hand, the term "confession" seems both to guarantee a kind of autobiographical discourse for the reader and to insist upon the truthful character of the theme. On the other hand, the "young girl" installs an obvious distance between the author and the narrator/character, instantly pulling the text in the direction of novelistic fiction.

Among other short stories of the period, "La Confession d'une jeune fille" seems to have a special status. It was probably written toward the end of the summer of 1894, when Proust, despite having some writing experience, was still a very young writer (not yet twenty-three years old).[2] It occupies a central place in the collection *Les Plaisirs et les jours,* which Proust published in 1896. Moreover, it is remarkable for being written in the first person while all the other short stories in the collection are in the third person.[3]

According to Anne Henry's hypothesis, this short story is a substitute for, and a more elaborate version of, another one entitled "Avant la nuit," which was written earlier but omitted from the collection.[4] Whatever the case, and even if these two short stories seem to have many evident points in common, Proust never said anything about the reasons for this eventual substitution.

Certain critics,[5] as well as contemporary readers and friends of Proust,[6] found autobiographical traits in "La Confession." Yet there is also a particularly marked fictional aspect. We find an extravagant plot and a melodramatic mood where pathos mixes with kitsch—and unrealistic things that can seem comical. No doubt this ambivalence provokes in the reader—especially the female reader—an undefinable unease.

The first part of this essay will help us understand this ambivalence by comparing the two stories and attempting to establish the places where they converge and diverge. The second part, a study of the avant-textes of "La Confession," will bring to light certain aspects of how the work was written and ultimately allow us to be more precise about the status of the story.

From "Avant la nuit" to "La Confession d'une jeune fille"

These two stories, "Avant la nuit" and "La Confession d'une jeune fille," have often been treated together by critics. To see how they might be related, it is important to examine the critics' arguments closely.

"Avant la nuit"

"Avant la nuit" appeared in 1893 in the *Revue Blanche,* a journal with advanced ideas in every field, in which Mallarmé, Nerval, Verlaine, and Henri de Régnier all published. In this story, Proust speaks explicitly for the first time on the theme, very much discussed in the 1890s, of homosexuality.[7]

Here is the plot: a male narrator, Leslie, recounts a dialogue with a young woman, Françoise, who, "pushed by an imperious need for truth" after a mysterious wound leaves her little hope of living, wishes to confess "a thing weighing on my conscience" to her best friend, Leslie himself.[8] Leslie resists at first, protesting with effusion of their warm friendship:

"Dear friend, I do not want to know this absurd confession." But Françoise insists on telling the truth. Her secrets are only hinted at because at first it is only a question of chastity:

—Leslie, . . . have you ever asked yourself, since I've been a widow since the age of twenty, if all this time I've stayed . . .
—Of course, but that is none of my business. (*Les Plaisirs et les jours* 168)

Next come whispered admissions, whose complex formulation (a supposition to which the interlocutor can only respond in the negative) is rather tasty:

—Listen, I don't know how to tell you this. It is even worse than if I'd loved you, for example, or even another, oh truly any other . . . (169)

Finally, there are more precise but still indirect confessions:

—Do you remember when my poor friend Dorothy was surprised with that chanteuse whose name I've forgotten . . . (169)

The confessions of Françoise stop there. We learn nothing else about this "thing weighing on my conscience" because the words that follow and that deal clearly with homosexuality, feminine and masculine, although they are spoken by Françoise, are in fact composed entirely of reported speech of which the author is none other than Leslie (a Leslie probably rather close to Proust):

—Do you remember when my poor friend Dorothy was surprised with a chanteuse . . . how you explained then that we shouldn't judge her harshly. *I remember your words*: . . . (169)[9]

Thus it is not Françoise who is speaking of her own tastes but rather the narrator who speaks through her; the "you" clearly designates Leslie, Françoise's interlocutor, who is also the narrator. This narrator also says "I" without parentheses, right up to the moment when it becomes clearly a question of homosexuality: the "I" then transforms into an "us." At first it is a deictic *us*, the first to bring together the two protagonists of the dialogue, and then it expands to become a wider referent: "you explained then that *we* shouldn't judge her harshly." It is this "us" [*nous*], sometimes expanding to the dimensions of a generic "anyone," which will take over. The use of "you, anyone" [*on*] has, on the one hand, the advantage of confusing the situation—the utterance pronounced by Françoise is in fact a quotation of an utterance previously pronounced by Leslie. On the other hand, it enlarges this last to the dimensions of an apologia:

Just because most people see objects considered to be red as red, *you* [*on*] cannot say that those who see them as purple are wrong. (169)

If *you* [*on*] can refine sensuality to the point of making it aesthetic—masculine and feminine bodies can be equally beautiful—then *you* [*on*] can see why a truly artistic woman might be attracted to another woman. (170)

Françoise—and, through her, the author—recalls several times that it is reported speech: "I remember your words," "you added"—in particular when the first person reappears:

Despite my revulsion for oysters, when *I* remembered (*you* were still telling me) the sea travels that their taste would evoke for me, they became . . . suggestively tasty. (170)

From the fact that this is Leslie's speech reported by Françoise, the words in italics (first person of the reported speech and second person in the direct speech) have only one referent: Leslie. The "I" therefore does not refer to the heroine, and the question of the oysters seems to have no direct link with it, despite what certain critics think (see Henry 78; Compagnon 1218). My interpretation is specifically contrary to Henry's, for whom "two voices mix and the friend who receives the supreme admission is only there to dramatize by his words and reactions the words of the dying woman" (74). An attentive reading shows that (1) the words pronounced by Françoise are really spoken by her interlocutor, Leslie, and (2) the character of Françoise and the dramatic staging have the principal function of putting this speech into context.

Three levels of enunciation are intertwined in this text: Leslie, the narrator who says "I," recounts the speech of a character, Françoise, who herself, acting as a sort of mirror, recalls to Leslie a conversation that they have already had.

Only after Françoise has recalled to the narrator his own (apologetic) words about homosexuality does he understand the import of the confession, blaming himself at that point for "his terrible responsibility." She finishes her confession by admitting that, "in one of these moments of despair that are so natural to all those who *live*" (Proust's italics), it was she herself who had tried to end her days. He then expresses his empathy, and both of them let loose a tearful flood of solidarity:

We wept together. . . . Our mingled pity now had an object greater than either of us and we willingly, freely wept over it . . . (*Les Plaisirs et les jours* 171)

Through the two characters in the story, Proust confronts two different attitudes and forms of expression: Françoise's confession and search for authenticity recall Saint Augustine, Dostoyevsky, and Tolstoy;[10] Leslie's melancholic contemplation of the countryside, mystical upliftings, aestheticism, elegance, and anglomania form a pastiche of decadence.

"La Confession d'une jeune fille"

The beginning of the text clearly recalls "Avant la nuit." Here it is no longer a male but a female narrator, one who, like the heroine of "Avant la nuit," finds herself dying after a suicide attempt by gunshot. The young girl, who is nameless, wants to die near her childhood home, a wish that allows Proust to introduce a flashback construction into the story. The text offers itself as a monologue, addressed to a "you" whose existence is not mentioned until the last paragraph and whose identity is never made precise: "this is not the last time that I'll tell *you*" (95).

The text is divided into four parts. The first two deal with the narrator's memories of childhood and early adolescence. The relationship with the mother takes the most space, and the heroine is the object of a sexual initiation by a boy, a "very corrupt little cousin." The third part, which corresponds to the young girl's sixteenth year, is devoted to her sexual waywardness and to her attempts, without much success, to resist those "guilty pleasures." The fourth and last part, which begins with "the winter of my twentieth year," shows how she repents and plans to marry when she commits during her engagement a last, and ultimately fatal, "mistake." Indeed her mother, having surprised her in the arms of her lover, dies on the spot from an apoplectic fit, a drama that in turn justifies the young girl's suicide.

Comparison of the Two Stories

A simple summary of the facts cannot of course account for the complexity of the two texts. Frequently linked by critics, with the second generally presented as a "rewriting" of the first, they have both similarities and differences:

Similarities

- Proust chooses a female protagonist for both stories.
- Both stories deal with sexuality.
- The construction of both texts plays on the same literary procedure: the confessional form, or the ritual of admission. Anne Henry aptly remarks that the use of this form is surprising in so young an author. Following Foucault, let us recall that "the confession was, and still remains, the general standard governing the production of the true

discourse on sex" (63). In both cases, Proust has clearly distanced himself from the classic form of the confession by choosing a female protagonist. Another indication of this distance is Leslie's answer in "Avant la nuit":

> Pardon me, Françoise, if I break the rules of the literary genre and interrupt a *confession* to which I should have listened in silence. (*Les Plaisirs et les jours* 168; Proust's italics)

- Staging a clichéd situation—an attempted suicide temporarily unsuccessful—is also common to both texts. The two confessions are situated therefore in a limited period of time preceding the forthcoming death of the heroine, and the choice of this moment emphasizes the gravity of the subjects they discuss. These scenes end the stories, so that suicide is evoked both at the beginning and at the end, giving a circular structure to both texts.

Differences

- "La Confession" is about twice as long as "Avant la nuit"; it is formally much more elaborate because it is divided into four parts with epigraphs carefully added by Proust.
- In "Avant la nuit" the protagonists have first names—Françoise and Leslie (incidentally, a name that can be masculine or feminine)—while the heroine of "La Confession" and her interlocutor do not.
- In "Avant la nuit" there is a dialogue with different levels of discourse, while "La Confession" contains only a monologue addressed to an anonymous interlocutor, ultimately just an abstract form. If homosexuality is associated with the dialogue form, then the monologue is linked to heterosexuality.
- We know almost no biographical facts about the heroine of "Avant la nuit"; the time covered coincides more or less with that of the conversation. By contrast the story of "La Confession" extends over a period of some ten years, and we see the heroine evolve from childhood to adulthood.
- The two suicides both show guilt, but they have different motivations. Françoise in "Avant la nuit" seems to have no other cause than the difficulty of living with her sexual orientation; the heroine of "La Confession," by contrast, is motivated by her (heterosexual) "mistakes" and the death of her mother that they cause.
- While the heroine of "Avant la nuit" appears (with the complicity of her interlocutor) to be responsible for her sexual orientation, the heroine of "La Confession" is presented as a victim of seduction, at

first by the "already very corrupt little cousin" and then by a "perverse and mean" young man who "induced her to act badly almost by surprise."

- In "Avant la nuit," however, the avowal is never really expressed as such and the secrets remain veiled. The text is centered on Leslie's theoretical explanations, the rest of it being just literary staging.[11] The gap is linked to the fact that Françoise has the role of mere spokesperson. The real source of the reported speech about homosexuality is Leslie, while, in parallel fashion, it really is Françoise who represents the "putting into practice."[12]
- In "La Confession" the avowals are more substantial and, although of a different resonance because they deal with heterosexuality, more concrete about the actions themselves:

> This little boy cousin . . . taught me things which made me shiver with remorse and sensuality. (85)

> We had locked both doors, and he, with his breath on my cheeks, squeezed me and his hands groped the length of my body. Then, while pleasure took hold of me more and more . . . (95)

- In "Avant la nuit" the subject of homosexuality is broached in a direct manner. The narrator proposes an explanation and openly defends it:

> there is no hierarchy between sterile loves and it is not less moral—or rather not more immoral that a woman should find pleasure with another woman rather than with a being of another sex. (169)

The indefinite article "of *an*other" sex is not as trivial as it seems and cannot equate to "of the other sex." Whether or not it alludes to the "third sex," in vogue at the time, the use of this indefinite article in fact represents a double transgression. "Of another sex" *contravenes* the linguistic norm (represented by "of the other sex") and subverts this norm: to escape the biological bipartition amounts to questioning explicitly the bi-categorizing system of thought.[13] "Of another sex" also has the effect of generalizing the range of the assertion by relativizing the sex of the subject himself: the sex of the people who exchange pleasure is, after all, unimportant. The choice of the article, generally a signifier of little value, seems to me to be of capital importance here.

"La Confession" unfolds inside a resolutely heterosexual frame, however, and "evil" only occurs because the heroine proves to be incapable of resisting "guilty pleasures."

While the two stories have certain points in common, other aspects seem to make them radically different. We are not dealing with a simple "rewriting"; the relation between the texts is much more complex than that. In order to make their kinship more precise, I suggest that it is useful to study their avant-textes. We have no avant-textes for "Avant la nuit," but those of "La Confession" offer a valuable site of investigation. They allow us to reconstruct different stages and metamorphoses of the story's genesis and to read certain clues about its ambivalent status between fiction and avowal.

The Avant-textes of "La Confession"

The Genetic Dossier

In this dossier are several documents that correspond to different stages in the writing:

- (A) a first, untitled, handwritten rough draft of the beginning that corresponds to the first paragraph of the published text (f. 75).
- (B) a handwritten version of the whole text (ff. 76r to 82r), comprising thirteen pages, numbered by Proust from 1 to 13, entitled simply "Stories." Rather than a rough draft, it seems to be a fair copy, including erasures and additions, in flowing penmanship. From f. 81v (numbered 10 by Proust), the writing changes; it is now much tighter and the interlinear space is clearly reduced (in similar format, 31 lines per page instead of 23).
- (C1) a first clear copy with the final title (ff. 83–109), established by a copyist, including corrections and numerous handwritten additions that sometimes cover an entire page (f. 102). The whole group is numbered in Proust's hand from 1 to 11, 11b and 11c, and then from 12 to 22.
- (C2) a second clear copy, established by another copyist, again with a certain number of handwritten corrections and additions both in the margins and in the text, inserted in Proust's hand into spaces left empty for them.

Certain clues suggest—but it is only a hypothesis—that C1 was actually copied, whereas C2 might have been dictated. We find in C1 some omissions in the transcription of additions (which Proust then reinserted). Certain spelling mistakes and above all some errors of agreement in participles (masculine instead of feminine) are maintained. In C2, not only have the spelling mistakes disappeared, but all the agreements—except for the last one, which will remain masculine even in the published edition—are rendered feminine. The copyist has therefore corrected these participles (for the most part with a silent "e") to agree with the feminine grammatical subject. The dictation hypothesis is reinforced by the fact that certain passages, left empty by the copyist at the request of the author, were then directly filled in by Proust.

As for the epigraphs, they do not figure into the handwritten version; in the two copies, they are added in Proust's hand on a separate sheet or in the margins of the text.

There are also three sets of page proofs, none of which has even the slightest correction. On the second set of proofs (*placard* 16), however, we find this dedication printed under the title: "To Count Robert Montesquiou Fezensac."[14] It was later removed.

Variations

The frame of the story is in place in the very first version of the opening sequence: a female narrator makes a failed suicide attempt, desires to return to the scenes of her childhood, and affirms the link to her mother.

Between the first and the second versions of this opening, the only notable difference is the transformation of the name designating the park where the heroine spent her childhood. The first version reads, "I would like to die at Blis," but in the second "Blis" is crossed out and replaced by "Oublis."[15]

There is no way to account exhaustively for the whole of the genetic process, so I will content myself with bringing to light some of the more revealing points of variance. The existence of variants means that for the writer several textual projects are possible and superimposed at one moment of writing.

(a) Age

The story is extended over at least ten years and structured by age indications (III: "During my sixteenth year, I underwent a crisis that made me suffer terribly"; IV: "The winter of my twentieth year, the health of my mother . . .") These markers fluctuate wildly, however, up until the last stages of the writing.

In the first version of the opening:

> I would like to go to Blis and die, in the park where ~~during my two week vacations~~ I spent all my summers until I was 16. (A)

This temporal indication occurs again in the second version of the opening:

> I would like to die at les Oublis in the park where I spent all my summers until I was fifteen. (B. f. 76r)

The age of the sexual initiation by the little cousin remains equally uncertain:

This little cousin ~~was very~~ who was only ~~my age~~ fifteen ~~thirteen~~ <fourteen> was already very corrupt . . . (B. f. 77v; C2. f. 116)

It's not my doing it's beyond me that ~~the s~~ my soul of ~~fi~~fourteen <14> years reawakens . . . (B. f. 78v. C1. f. 91)

If we choose to read the autobiographical stratum of the story, the imprecision of these dates would signify a surprising lack of memory.[16] The frequency of hesitation swings the text to the side of purely literary construction. An interlinear addition to the draft (f. 82r)[17] reinforces this hypothesis: it characterizes the death of the heroine's father as happening "already ten years ago,"[18] which means that she herself must be twenty-six at the time of the drama since the existence of the father is mentioned in the text when she is sixteen. This is no longer a very young girl; it is therefore not her *age* at the moment of the drama that can be the object of scandal.

(b) Gender

More troubling are the errors of participial agreement scattered throughout the draft. Their number and their location suggest that they are not simple mistakes on the writer's part. While the heroine's sex is clearly defined from the start, her grammatical gender varies[19]:

the day was approaching when I would be well enough for my mother to leave again, and until then I was no longer *suffering* [*souffrant*] enough for her not to return to her severity, the justice without indulgence of before . . . (B. f. 77r)

Often at les Oublis, *seated* [*assis*] with my mother by the waterside . . . (B. f. 78v)

If then . . . I kissed my mother a thousand times, I ran like a dog well in advance, or *stayed* [*resté*] indefinitely behind to gather poppies and blueberries . . . (B. f. 79r)

God's grace and the grace of youth, when so many wounds heal themselves thanks to the vitality of that age, had *healed* [*guéri*] me . . . (B. f. 81r)

The absence of my fiancé, who had gone to spend two days with his sister, and two of the young people who had *corrupted* [*débauché*] me being present at dinner . . . (B. f. 81r)

I was *wrong* [*trompé*] when I said that I had never again found the sweetness of the kiss at les Oublis. (B. f. 82r)

I thought then about what anybody else would think who had *seen* [*vu*] me kissing my mother with such a melancholy tenderness earlier . . . (B. f. 79v)

Out of a total of twenty-seven agreements of past participle relating to the feminine "I," a quarter are thus in the masculine. Are these grammatical errors significantly more frequent than in other manuscripts of Proust or in the manuscripts of other masculine authors writing in the feminine? It is difficult to respond to this question, but in Proust's manuscripts, the accumulation of the same error in such a short space seems to be exceptional. It is especially remarkable that they appear almost exclusively in phrases dealing with the relationship with the mother. This is true of the last error, which, contrary to the preceding ones that are corrected in the fair copies, remains through the three proofs (which show no corrections at all) and into the published edition of 1896:[20]

I would be happier if my mother had *seen* [*vu*] me commit other offenses and even that very one . . . (B. f. 79v; C1. f. 109 and C2. f. 132)

These facts of writing betray a certain degree of projection of the author into the skin of his character. Here again Henry's hypothesis seems arguable: "since Proust renounces in his 'La Confession d'une jeune fille' the theme of sexual inversion and replaces the beautiful lesbian with a young girl seduced by a bad man, we see that the amount of autobiography in this second version of the story is infinitesimal" (78–79). This is especially arguable because the lapses occur almost always, as I've noted, in places that bear on the relationship with the mother. This relationship has many points in common with Jean's in *Jean Santeuil* or the narrator's in *À la recherche,* and in fact seems to escape the control of fictional writing. These lapses, which emerge in the narrative moments when autobiographical aspects take the upper hand, are revelatory hints of the link that unites writing to life.

Elsewhere everything is normal, or almost. Almost, because the genetic dossier records other clues as to how the writing performs an act of sharing between the text's virtually autobiographical and explicitly fictional status.

(c) Censured Passages

Aside from an important addition of two paragraphs that deal exclusively with the relationship with the mother (f. 82r), most of the modifications done on the fair copies and on the rough draft itself concern what one may call "style." Yet certain operations have a specific function: to modify the entire text. What they have in common is that they are variants of rereading, brought out solely on the clear copies, and they concern the world of sexuality. In the following excerpts, I give first the phrase in the handwritten version (B) and then the same phrase from one of the two clear copies (C1 or C2):

However, my awakening puberty made me suffer greatly. (B. f. 80r)
During my sixteenth year, I went through a crisis in which I suffered greatly. (C1. f. 95)

My friends slowly persuaded me that all young girls did the same thing and that parents knew very well what was going on but were unaware of the details because it was more convenient . . . (B. f. 80r)
My friends slowly persuaded me that all young girls did the same thing and that parents pretended not to know because it was more convenient . . . (C1. f. 96)

My love ended, but the habit of not resisting the temptation of pleasure had naturally succeeded it. (B. f. 80r)
My love having ended, habit had taken its place. (C2. f. 123)

The lies that I was forced to tell each time colored my imagination with the semblances of prudish silence on the subject of a physiological necessity . . . (B. f. 80r)
The lies that I was constantly forced to tell my imagination soon colored with the semblances of prudish silence on the subject of an inevitable necessity (C1. f. 96)

What seemed to me to be an imperious and inevitable need many times a week I went many months without ~~achieving~~ satisfying. (B. f. 81v)
(*This phrase is completely suppressed in C1.*)

And as for the fateful scene:

Suddenly Jacques T., who was across from me and staring at me, said: "Please come with me and play some pool." (B. f. 81v)
Jacques approached me and said, staring at me: "Please come with me. I would like to show you some verses that I've written." (C1. f. 106)

Luckily he [Jacques] had been quick. Soon they would finish the card game and return . . . (B. f. 79v)
Soon my uncles would finish their card game and return. (C1. f. 107) (*The first phrase is suppressed.*)

All the modifications brought to the text through these variants move in the same direction: at best towards a certain indistinctness, a certain imprecision, at times towards suppression pure and simple—they correspond to a phenomenon of autocensure. Thus "my awakening puberty" is replaced by "a crisis"; "the details" on the subject of which "the parents knew very well what was going on" are suppressed, as is "the temptation of pleasure." More revealing about Proust's point of view during these processes of rewriting is the transformation of "physiological need" into "inevitable need" and the radical suppression of the words that bear on this "imperious and inevitable need many times a week [that] I went many months without satisfying."

It was probably not prudishness that led Proust to modify or suppress these phrases (the concrete notations mentioned earlier remained intact). More likely, they seemed to him—rightly—incompatible with what a young woman of the time, even a liberated one, could allow herself to say about her own sexuality, and therefore they betrayed an obviously masculine point of view. Phrases betraying a conception of sexuality perceived as "imperious and inevitable" and "a physiological need" were certainly not current at the time for a young woman of the milieu described.

The heterogeneity of the points of view is even clearer in the phrases that deal with the final scene. The pretext proposed by Jacques to "play some pool" obviously betrays an exclusively masculine perspective. (Is a pool hall not a masculine place par excellence, a place where men go to be alone and a place charged, as well, with obvious sexual connotations?) It is better to replace this with a more neutral proposition, one that better fits a young girl of a bourgeois milieu: "listen to some poetry." As to the last words cited (which Proust suppressed), "luckily he had been quick," their crudeness is completely incongruous in the mouth of a woman of good society, however libertine she may be.

These phenomena of censure are the mark of a work of rewriting that goes from autobiography to fiction—autobiography being understood here in the widest sense.[21] Even if nothing allows us to affirm that these are "lived experiences," it is certainly the point of view of the writer Marcel Proust that flourishes in these censured passages, and this point of view contradicts the fictional perspective. The modifications Proust made to the fair copies aimed to reduce this narrative doubling, to reinforce the novelistic fiction, and to efface, as he would later say, "the overly vulgar traces of composition."

One Sex from the Other: Toward a Multiple Reading

Even if one brackets the remarks founded on the study of the genetic documents, the story, as it was written and published by Proust, still invites a double—or even multiple—reading.

Indeed, the final text presents a certain number of dissonances that Proust did not deem it wise to remedy. Even if his goal was not to produce a realist work, far from it, they are nonetheless sufficiently striking to merit examination. Woven into these dissonances, precisely, is the ambivalence of the text—as it is delivered to the reader—and of its status, somewhere between autobiography and fiction.

Dissonances

I call "dissonances" certain passages or events that appear unbelievable if, as a reader, one places oneself in the "official" point of view of the female narrator. For example:

- The mother's attitude toward the narrator's admissions. Just after the scene of heterosexual initiation, the narrator feels "a wild need for my mother." Yet the mother proves to be extremely expansive and generous in the face of these admissions. At the very least, this attitude is surprising on the part of a mother toward her adolescent daughter, if only because the risk of pregnancy has theoretically been run. Besides, it contrasts with the violence of the final scene:

I cried for a long time as I told her all the vile things that required the ignorance of my age to tell her and that *she listened to divinely, without understanding them, diminishing their importance* with a goodness which lightened the weight on my conscience. (87)

Later the same scene is repeated: "I felt at first some horrible remorse, and I made some admissions *that were not understood*" (90). What are these admissions? And who is the "I" who is speaking here? These admissions not understood and this incomprehension make no sense in the heterosexual context of the fiction. This incomprehension is in fact an indication that (1) it is Proust speaking here and (2) these admissions deal with homosexuality. These admissions can only be rebuffed. Others do not really understand them and translate them in terms of heterosexual experiences—experiences that for their part are nothing reprehensible on the part of a young man.[22]

- The obsessive theme of the struggle against a lack of willpower, against an "extreme" sensitivity, and an exaggerated need for tenderness that is hardly more convincing when one thinks that it is a young girl's:

To toughen me and to calm my extreme sensitivity, she poured kindness upon me that normally she spared. (86)
What pained my mother was my absolute lack of will. (f. 79r)[23]

The following phrase—of a remarkable lucidity if one reads it from the point of view of Proust—takes on exceptional contours if one remembers that it is applied to a female subject:

What worried us above all else, my mother and me, was the completion of *all my fine work projects,* projects of calm and of reason, because we sensed . . . that it would only be the projected image in my life of the creation by myself and in myself of this will that she had conceived and hatched . . . (89)

How many heroines of novels written by male authors would be likely to hear themselves pronounce such a statement?

- Finally, last but not least, we have the tragic dénouement, which Compagnon describes as "circuslike": the mother dies on the spot, "her head caught between the bars of the balcony," when, through the window, she surprises her daughter kissing her lover.[24] The fatal violence of this reaction is somewhat surprising for a mother who has shown herself to be so tolerant up to this point, especially if one recalls that the young girl is already twenty-six and that the scene that the mother witnesses is in a completely banal heterosexual context. Compared to a "normal" sexual encounter, it is the mother's reaction that is abnormal.

In sum, certain elements supposedly pertaining to a woman and to heterosexuality don't quite "pass." These dissonances manifest the double perspective that runs through the story, the doubling of a subject-author and a subject-narrator that reduces to nearly nothing the distance that separates them.

If one takes the opposite path, however, and suppresses the feminine marks characterizing the narrator from the text, thereby conjoining the two subjects—the uttering subject [*sujet de l'énonciation*] and the subject of the utterance [*sujet de l'énoncé*]—then everything works perfectly, including the marriage episode:

My fiancé was precisely the kind of young man who, with his extreme intelligence, gentleness and energy, could have the happiest influence on me. Besides, he had made his mind up to live with us. So I would not be separated from my mother, which would have been for me the cruelest pain . . . (92)

The retransposition of this passage gives, word for word:

My fiancée was precisely the kind of young woman who, with her extreme intelligence, gentleness and energy, could have the happiest influence on me. Besides, she had made up her mind to live with us. So I would not be separated from my mother, which would have been for me the cruelest pain.

This passage would fit quite well in the most traditional context.

"The Confession of a Young Man" would then have had an entirely different, and obvious, meaning; it is precisely what Proust wanted to avoid.

A last point remains to be examined, the role played by the epigraphs adorning the text. Their number, the fact that Proust took the time to inscribe them on the fair copies himself, and above all their choice make them, beyond the fact that they were in fashionable texts, an important element of Proust's text. The first, taken from Thomas à Kempis's *Imitation of Christ,* opposes sensuality to remorse in the context of Christian mysticism. The second, from Henri de Régnier, alludes to the "sweet melancholic perfume of lilacs"—lilacs that are mentioned twice in the text and are always associated with the idea of purity (perhaps of non-sexuality, or of sexuality not shared?).[25] The first mention occurs during the confession of sexual initiation:

> A divine sweetness emanated from my mother and from my renewed innocence. Soon I sensed an odor just as pure and fresh beneath my nostrils. It was a lilac . . . which, invisible, embalmed . . . (87)

The second is also associated with the idea of purity:

> What virtue does this morning odor of lilacs possess to traverse so many fetid vapors without mixing or weakening in them? (88)

Most of all, however, we are interested in the last two epigraphs, both borrowed from Baudelaire's "condemned pieces"; one is excerpted from "Femmes damnées," the other from "Le Cygne." Now, as Gide reports in his *Journal,* Proust was convinced that Baudelaire was himself homosexual—notably because of his poems on Lesbos.[26] These epigraphs function therefore as a code, suggesting to the attentive (and initiated) reader a hidden reading.[27]

(b) Consonances

After all of this, where are we? And what points does the female narrator—the subject of the utterance [*sujet de l'énoncé*]—have in common with the uttering subject [*sujet énonciateur*], the author Proust?

I call consonances certain elements that characterize the heroine of "La Confession" and which will later be developed at length in *Jean Santeuil* and then in *À la recherche.* They crystallize mainly around the ambivalent relationship with the mother.

- The famous episode of the goodnight kiss (*Recherche* 1: 37) is already in place in "La Confession":

> Each of the two evenings that she spent at les Oublis she came to kiss me good-night in my bed, an old habit that she had lost because I took too much pleasure

and pain in it, and because I never went to sleep since I kept calling her back to kiss me good night again . . . (86)

The episode is followed by other kisses that bear witness to a privileged relationship:

At the moment when we were sitting down to eat, I pulled her face near to me at the window. . . and I kissed it with passion. . . . That night's kiss was as sweet as any other. Or rather, it was exactly the same kiss from les Oublis which, evoked by the attraction of a similar moment, slipped gently from the depth of the past and came to place itself between my mother's rather pale cheeks and my lips. (94)

- The ambivalence of these sentiments—sweetness and tenderness—is answered with the sadness and cruelty of separation. The theme of love is linked (from the start) to that of the presence/absence of the beloved:

No place is more full of my mother, so much did her presence and, even more, her absence, impregnate it with her person. For anyone who loves, is not absence the most certain, the most efficient, the most lively, the most indestructible, and the most faithful of presences? (85)

- The theme of the lack of will returns like a leitmotif, with its paradoxical aspect:

What grieved my mother was my lack of will. (89)

Desiring to have willpower did not suffice. What I needed to do was precisely what I could not do without willpower: to will it. (90)

Moreover, the lack of will plays a decisive role in the heroine's inability to resist guilty pleasures:

he accustomed me to letting myself produce vile thoughts *which I did not have the will to oppose,* the only power capable of sending them back to the infernal shadows from whence they came . . . (90)

- Entering into high society:

To distract and chase away these bad desires, I started to go out into society much more. Its desiccating pleasures taught me to live in perpetual company . . . (90)

- The Baudelairian theme of the undissolvable link between sensuality and culpability, between sensuality and evil:[28]

This little cousin . . . taught me things that made me shiver right away with *remorse and sexual feeling.* (87)

. . . Now it appeared confusedly to me that, *in every sexual and guilty act,* there is as much ferocity on the part of the body which takes pleasure, and in us as many good intentions, as there are pure angels who are martyred and weep. (95)

Let us also mention that a certain number of variations produced by rereading tend to accentuate the culpability of the heroine. The "pleasure of the senses" becomes "guilty pleasure" (B. f. 80r), the "unleashing of my senses" becomes "the criminal secret of my life" (B. f. 80r), "the young man who corrupted me" becomes "the accomplice of my crimes" (B. f. 80v). These variations seem to emerge from an external, social judgment rather than from guilt itself, strictly speaking, which is relatively absent in the first draft.

- Finally, the theme of the defamed mother appears here for the first time in Proust's œuvre.[29] Certainly the matricide is involuntary and nonviolent; the mother *sees* and dies from having *seen.* If one takes this literally, then the unbelievability is shocking. A mother dies of a seizure from seeing her daughter kiss a young man, and the most universally recognized heterosexual activity is qualified as "the greatest of crimes," and, even beyond this, as a "secret crime." The gap between the dramatic intensity—literally terrifying—and the believability of the event obviously calls for some imaginative response. The "secret crime" can hardly refer to a heterosexual behavior, socially considered to be perfectly normal. This episode offers the reader the clearest hint that a second level of interpretation is warranted.

If, as is likely, the event is on the order of the fantastic, then the desire—or the constraint—for the young Proust to hide his homosexual activities from his parents, and the fear that they will discover them, probably has a very real foundation.

The staging, with the window and the mirror, announces the Montjouvain episode (*Recherche* 1: 159ff) where the narrator surprises Mlle Vinteuil and her female friend at the window, defiling the image of the young girl's recently deceased father. We know too that, in "Sentiments filiaux d'un parricide"[30] written in February 1907, Proust took up the defense of Henri van Blarenberghe, assassin of his mother ("I wanted . . . to show that the poor patricide was not a criminal brute"; *Contre Sainte-Beuve* 157). Proust later developed (especially via Charlus) the idea that sons, inverts or not, consummate, in their search for pleasure and "in their very looks," nothing less than "the profanation of their mother."

Functioning both as a novelistic element and as an autobiographical clue, the dénouement of "La Confession" confirms the potential double level of reading offered to the reader. A first, literal level would situate itself in a purely fictional perspective, evoking via certain aspects (the pastiche of Saint Augustine's *Confessions*, for example) the literary exercise such as Proust practiced it in other stories in *Les Plaisirs et les jours*. The second level, in the autobiographical perspective of the veiled confession of personal experience, demands that we decode a double system of transposition. On the one hand, a male turns into a female narrator (a banal procedure in itself), and, on the other, a story with a masculine homosexual context is translated into a heterosexual framework seen in theory from the feminine side.

If Painter and Bardèche deem that the transposition that is the goal of "La Confession" is justified by Proust's desire to hide his homosexual tendencies from his parents[31]—in the way the publication of *Les Plaisirs et les jours* was meant to convince them of his writer's vocation—it is nonetheless true that an autobiographical discourse in the broad sense wells up beneath the fiction, and that the text both offers and hides itself. The whole art of Proust consists in creating this ambiguous space, in imbricating and deliberately making two levels of reading coexist between opacity and transparence.

Because it sheds light on the places where the work of writing is anchored, and through them on the young writer's confrontation with the complex problems of transposition—an art of which he will later become the undisputed master—the genetic trek through the avant-textes of "La Confession" has an exemplary value. The avant-textes bear witness to a work of transformation, or rather of transfiguration, of the subject, in a movement from autobiography to fiction, in an ambivalent space that only writing can create.

In many ways, then, "La Confession d'une jeune fille" prefigures works to come, not only in the themes that are tackled but also in certain formal traits such as the anonymity of the narrator and the circular structure of the text. Above all, it is in the very clear affinities that link inversion—as a lived experience—to the play of transposition, that is, to literary constructions, in the work to come. Proust will later make it clear in the *Recherche* that inverts, forced into social and interior constraints, have in the past been "forced to *hide their life*, to *change the gender of many adjectives* in their vocabulary."[32]

Source: "'La Confession d'une jeune fille': Aveu ou fiction?" *Bulletin d'Informations Proustiennes* 22 (1991): 7–24.

Works Cited

Bardèche, Maurice. *Marcel Proust romancier.* Paris: Les Sept Couleurs, 1971.

Bem, Jeanne. "Le Juif et l'homosexuel dans *À la recherche du temps perdu*: Fonctionnements textuels." *Littérature* 37 (February 1980): 100–112.

Brun, Bernard. "Brouillons et brouillages: Proust et l'antisémitisme." *Littérature* 70 (May 1988): 110–28.

Compagnon, Antoine. "Ce Frémissement d'un coeur à qui on fait mal." In *L'Amour de la haine.* Special issue of *Nouvelle Revue de Psychanalyse* 33 (1986): 117–39.

———. Notes to *Sodome et Gomorrhe: À la recherche du temps perdu.* 3 vols. Pléiade ed. Paris: Gallimard, 1988. 3: 1185–1261.

Foucault, Michel. *La Volonté de savoir: Histoire de la sexualité I.* Paris: Gallimard, 1976. *The History of Sexuality,* vol. 1, *An Introduction.* Trans. Robert Hurley. New York: Pantheon, 1978.

Gide, André. *Journal.* 2 vols. Pléiade ed. Paris: Gallimard, 1966.

Henry, Anne. "*Les Plaisirs et les jours*: Chronologie et métempsychose." *Études proustiennes 1.* Paris: Gallimard, 1973. 69–93.

Lejeune, Philippe. "Autobiographie et homosexualité en France au XIXe siècle." *Romantisme* 56 (1988): 79–100.

———. "Écriture et sexualité." In *Proust II.* Special issue of *Europe* 502–3 (February–March 1971): 113–43.

———. *On Autobiography.* Ed. Paul John Eakin. Trans. Katherine Leary. Minneapolis: University of Minnesota Press, 1989.

———. *Le Pacte autobiographique.* Paris: Seuil, 1975.

———. "Le Pacte autobiographique (bis)." *Poétique* 56 (1983): 416–34.

Michelet, Jules. *La Mer.* Paris: Calmann-Lévy, 1923.

Musset, Alfred de. *La Confession d'un enfant du siècle.* Paris: Garnier, 1968.

Painter, George D. *Marcel Proust.* New York: Random House, 1987.

Proust, Marcel. *À la recherche du temps perdu.* 3 vols. Pléiade ed. Paris: Gallimard, 1954.

———. *Complete Short Stories.* Trans. Joachim Neugroschel. New York: Cooper Square, 2001.

———. *Contre Sainte-Beuve, précédé de Pastiches et mélanges et suivi de Essais et articles.* Pléiade ed. Paris: Gallimard, 1971.

———. *Correspondance.* Ed. Philip Kolb. 2 vols. Paris: Plon, 1970–76.

———. *Jean Santeuil.* Trans. Gerard Hopkins. New York: Simon and Schuster, 1955.

———. *Les Plaisirs et les jours.* 1896. In *Jean Santeuil, précédé de Les Plaisirs et les jours,* ed. Pierre Chirac with Yves Sandre. Pléiade ed. Paris: Gallimard, 1971.

———. *Textes retrouvés.* Ed. Philip Kolb and Larkin B. Price. Urbana: University of Illinois Press, 1968.

Further Works by the Author

Grésillon, Almuth, Jean-Louis Lebrave, and Catherine Viollet. *Proust à la lettre: Les Intermittences de l'écriture.* Tusson: Éditions du Lérot, 1990.

Lejeune, Philippe, and Catherine Viollet, eds. "Autobiographies." Special issue of *Genesis: Manuscrits, Recherche, Invention* 16 (2001).

———. *Genèses du "je": Manuscrits et autobiographie.* Paris: CNRS, 2000.

Viollet, Catherine. "Autobiographie et disparition du 'je': *Kindheitsmuster* de Christa Wolf." In *Leçons d'écriture: Ce que disent les manuscrits. Hommage à Louis Hay.* Paris: Lettres Modernes, 1985. 195–206.

———. "Discourse Strategies—Power and Resistance: A Socio-Enunciative Approach." Trans. Constance Greenbaum in *The Nature of the Right: A Feminist Analysis of Order Patterns,* ed. Gill Seidel. Amsterdam: Benjamins, 1988. 61–79.

———. "*Kindheitsmuster* de Christa Wolf: Problématique de l'identité dans la genèse du roman." *Cahiers de l'Institut d'Études Germaniques de l'Université Paul Valéry de Montpellier* 5 (1988): 110–17.

———. "Petite cosmogonie des écrits autobiographiques: Genèse et écritures de soi." *Genesis* 16 (2001): 37–54.

Viollet, Catherine, and Ruth Vogel. "'Und alles liegt am Wort': Zur Genese von Bachmanns 'Böhmen liegt am Meer.'" *Œuvres et Critiques* 23, 1 (2000): 141–62.

Chapter 11
Auto-Genesis: Genetic Studies of Autobiographical Texts

Philippe Lejeune

Since the mid 1970s, Philippe Lejeune has been a leading voice in the international field of autobiography studies. His reputation, spurred initially by the success of the 1975 book *Le Pacte autobiographique*, has since grown steadily thanks to numerous other publications. *On Autobiography*, an English-language collection of his essays drawn from several of his books, appeared in 1989.

While specifically genetic work is only a part of Lejeune's overall interest in autobiography, it is an especially innovative, groundbreaking part and one that he sees as a growth industry. In 1995 he cofounded with Catherine Viollet a team at the Institut des Textes et Manuscrits Modernes devoted to genetic studies of autobiographical manuscripts. Those two authors recently revealed some of the team's best recent work when they coedited "Autobiographies," the Fall 2001 issue of *Genesis*.

The essay translated here, "Auto-Genesis: Genetic Studies of Autobiographical Texts," is really two essays conjoined—one on autobiographies in general, one on the special case of diaries—and its main thesis is that genetic inquiry does not represent a radically new approach to autobiography. Rather, it affords readers different contexts in which to ask and unfold their favorite questions: what are the key psychological and aesthetic aspects of "self"-construction? How and what do authors of autobiographies choose from their memories and their pasts? How and what do they tell? Since the functional essence of an autobiography is to represent the truth of a self's past, it is revealing to confront a text with its own wild childhood, that is, those raw rough drafts of itself, the avant-textes. And personal journals and diaries—writings that seem by definition "incapable of having avant-textes"—are a kind of ultimate riddle or test case for genetic theory: what kind of pretextual activities even *exist* for single-draft kinds of self-writing and how can we interpret them?

Personally attracted to such questions, Lejeune develops his thesis not by providing close readings of sample texts but by illustrating instead the wide applicability and interest of key genetic concepts and techniques for autobiography. He culls out larger patterns and problems from the case studies he has pursued elsewhere, and his examples—Sartre, Perec, Sarraute, Leiris, Anne Frank, as well as many noncanonical and nameless writers—tend to number among the more self-aware writers of self-texts. They are authors, that is, who keep control over their texts and passions by either following or inventing rules, formal mechanisms, tricks, and narrative strategies.

And so do geneticists of autobiography, we learn, for these singular critics are not so much empirical scientists as engaged, conscientious Sherlock Holmeses. While they usually produce verifiable detective work, their results also tend to take the shape of compelling narratives rather than reports or critiques. True to this attitude and method, and to himself, Lejeune foregrounds his own personal history as a geneticist and shares his enthusiasms and disappointments with various authors and their writings.

This essay ultimately creates the impression that geneticists, readers of autobiographies, and autobiographers are all kissing cousins. They are apt to be united, on the one hand, by the built-in requirement that to do their work properly they be passionately interested in it and, on the other, by their willingness to employ many, if not any, means to learn the secrets of personal and textual self-becoming.

How does one become a "geneticist?" Why didn't I become one earlier? And have I really become one? It is a fact that for nearly five years I have been working on the avant-textes of contemporary autobiographies: Sartre's *Les Mots* (1964), Perec's *W ou le Souvenir d'enfance* (1975), Nathalie Sarraute's *Enfance* (1983), and, more recently, the *Diary* of Anne Frank. I did not begin these studies with any overall plan—it was a series of chance occasions: an invitation to be part of the Sartre team at the Institut des Textes et Manuscrits Modernes, a seminar on Perec, hearing a lecture by Georges Raillard on the manuscrips of *Enfance*, a new edition of the *Diary* (or rather *Diaries*) of Anne Frank. But there's no such thing as chance.

A glance backward reveals that my curiosity has deep roots. My first essay on Proust's "petite madeleine" was part of a comparison of two drafts of that famous episode ("Écriture et sexualité," 1971). Next, I studied the transformations of childhood narrative in Rousseau (*Le Pacte autobiographique*, 1975) and Vallès (*Je est un autre*, 1980). I tried to "undo" some finished products: Victor Hugo's "biography," written by his wife (*Je est un autre*), the film *Sartre par lui-même* (see "Ça s'est fait comme ça,"

1978), the ethnographic narrative of Adélaïde Blasquez, *Gaston Lucas, serrurier* (*Moi aussi,* 1986). I also rummaged through archives for the truth about my great-grandfather's memoir (Xavier-Édouard Lejeune, *Calicot,* 1984).

A glance inward reveals something about my own motivations. First of all, of course, intellectual curiosity: can one fail to think that the history of a text will illuminate its structure? Yet I also felt a detective's curiosity—the desire (as naïve or fruitful as it may be) to see if and how the autobiographical "pact" was respected. Finally, deep down was the curiosity of a fetishist and a lover. These are the books that I love, and I was very pleased to partake of a little more of their intimacy. I had the occasional joy of being treated like a "favorite." Or else the impression of being initiated into a secret, of bearing witness to a sort of "primal scene" of literature. Without strong motivations like this, one cannot overcome the doubts and discouragements of a long, dreary, unrewarding, trivial, and sometimes fruitless task.

I would like to offer here two essays on the activities of geneticists, both of which raise the same problems: Do *generic* specificities exist for the work of literary creation? Is the avant-texte of a fictional work strictly comparable to that of an autobiography or a diary? Or, put slightly differently, do generic specificities exist for the *study* of such a work?

The first essay deals with autobiography. It suggests that there really is something particular to it, even if this something is not everything. Above all, it shows that genetic study deals with a new terrain on which to treat the thorny questions theorists of autobiography ask themselves about the relations between the self and language, art and truth.

The second essay deals with diaries. This is a very special case: diaries, by definition, seem incapable of having avant-textes. Yet they do, and this little study, written as an introduction to the analysis of the *Diaries* of Anne Frank, is something akin to a future research program.[1]

Autobiography

The first thing to notice is that from the *reader's* point of view the autobiographical text has a different relationship to its avant-textes than do texts of fiction, poetry, or thought. Knowing something about a novel's or a poem's avant-textes may be of interest to specialists who think about creative mechanisms, but it changes nothing about how these texts function for a reader. It may even annoy readers if it ruins the pleasure of reading. The opposite is true for an autobiography. Far from being a parasitical element, knowledge of the avant-textes is relevant and relates directly to the central purpose of the text and to the reader's expectation. This is so for two reasons:

- The subject of an autobiographical text is the past history of its author. Yet autobiographical writing is itself part of this history, and in fact is often represented in the text itself. To differing degrees, autobiographies comment on their own genesis: authors may stage their project's origin, keep some sort of writing journal or chronicle, or comment on the techniques they employ or the difficulties they will face. Readers are thus deeply interested when supplementary information surfaces on all these points, for they are put in a position to verify what the text says. All the more so because:
- The object of an autobiographical text is the truth of the past, and its contract implies both the possibility and the legitimacy of verification. Indeed, readers will have different reactions depending on whether the text has the appearance of being truthful or mendacious, a problem that has little meaning for a novel or a poem. One of the possible ways we can go about verifying texts is to confront them with external historical data (documents, testimony, etc.), but for most subjective and private elements this is impractical. Comparing texts with their avant-textes, however, allows for an investigation into precisely these areas. One can see the additions, suppressions, and transformations that are so full of meaning.

In *Enfance*, Nathalie Sarraute recounts her childhood by staging in dialogue form the progress she makes in exploring her own memory and her understanding of the past. Now, Sarraute's real childhood is not available to me. The "childhood" of the text *Enfance* would become accessible, however, if the author were to agree to send me its rough drafts, and indeed she did, giving me the avant-textes for chapter 2. So, suddenly I had the tools to compare the staged genesis in the book's "fictional" dialogue with its real genesis, to see how, and why, through these various versions, the contents of memory are modified.

Of course, the danger would be to believe that avant-textes tell "more truth" than texts when they simply tell something else. Our detective curiosity, which takes the requirements of the autobiographical pact with utmost seriousness, has an undeniable but limited pertinence. It must be used as a means to go beneath the surface, to tear ourselves away from what is obvious and from the univocality of the "final text" and to gain access to the movement that produced the text. Generally, what one discovers in penetrating backstage is so complicated that one is quickly forced to abandon any "regressive" attitude of verification. One must replace that attitude with the more "progressive" task of constructing what Paul Ricoeur calls a "narrative identity."[2] This is not to be understood as a translation, more or less accurate, of a preexisting truth, but as the creation of a self in language. It takes place on two levels, psychological and aesthetic.

Psychology

Avant-textes allow for in-vivo study of the mechanisms of memory and of the evolution of a self-image. This last is something that can change as a function of time or of intended audience. What one observes is not necessarily on the order of the unconscious. Yet it is something that authors either do not see (is it possible to perceive the changes in one's own memory?) or have no interest in showing.

One can therefore see memory in the act of *sifting*. I was able to study, thanks to the avant-textes of *Les Mots*, but also thanks to the early work for *Carnets de la drôle de guerre*, the way Sartre had removed from *Les Mots* not only every memory of his childhood sexuality, but especially every memory of his "literary" youth that did not square with his intended demonstration (a child without contact with reality, an author without a public).

One can see memory in metamorphosis: memories of childhood change in signification or even in content as a function of the ideological evolution of the author. Between 1939 and 1950, Sartre changed certain memories of his childhood religious life from positive to negative. During an intense period of work that must not have exceeded a few weeks, the key phrase of chapter 2 of Sarraute's *Enfance*, which was supposedly branded in memory, changed formulations several times in order to adapt to a varying psychological interpretation.—True or false?—That would be a problem for a biographer seeking to scrutinize the past. For a geneticist, these are simply clues about the transformation of the autobiographer's present project. As early as 1764, Rousseau described this double dimension of "truth" in autobiography: "In abandoning myself both to the memory of received impressions and to my present feeling, I will paint the state of my soul doubly, both the moment when the event occurred to me and the moment when I write it; my style . . . will itself be part of my story."[3] Genetic study permits one to unfold the second dimension.

It sometimes happens that autobiographers themselves decide to take control of this genetic work, thereby becoming "auto-geneticists" of sorts. It is a difficult enterprise and therefore rare. The process of observation may be retrospective—I think of Mary McCarthy's *Memories of a Catholic Girlhood* (1957) or of chapter 8 in Georges Perec's *W ou le Souvenir d'enfance*. It can also be prospective, as in Perec's great unpublished project, *Lieux* (1969–75), which was a system of writing under strict constraints designed to enable him to observe directly the evolution of both his memory and his writing. Perec's "experimental genetics" was supposed to last twelve years. He assigned himself the task of writing, at twelve Parisian locations related to his own life, two texts a year: an objective description of the place, done on site, and an evocation of memories linked to that place. As soon as they were written, the texts were sealed in an envelope that was not to be opened for twelve years. He abandoned the experiment in the sixth year, however, and never opened the "memory" envelopes. I described the whole project in *La Mémoire et l'oblique* (1991). These examples seem to me to *authorize* the genetic study of autobiographies. Far from being a reductive approach, externally imposed, this kind of study might be an extension of the autobiographical act itself.

Aesthetics

One can also look at the author's own search for a seductive and convincing form to express the truth of a self and a history.

For writers, this form owes much to the abilities acquired during work on earlier writing. While studying Rousseau, Leiris, and Sartre, I was struck by the way they reinvested their earlier works—the mythological or dialectical structures for Rousseau and Sartre and the mechanisms of language for Leiris—in their autobiographical writing. Autobiography is often a "second" writing that must be understood in an intertextual space. In this sense there are no grounds for assuming that the avant-textes of autobiographies are anything unique: in my opinion, we should study them in something like an "inter-genetic" space. This could best be done by comparing the work procedures—such things as the distribution of the different stages from the initial project to the definitive text or the techniques of correction—with those of other works. Different writers would probably produce different results. Sartre's manuscripts, for example, show different registers depending upon the genre. There is a long, flowing, theoretical kind of writing, often written while the author was on speed, a style that is the opposite of a "literary" writing (*Les Mots* belongs here), that is, a more meticulous work involving corrections and revisions on separate sheets. Moreover, Sartre himself has many registers of autobiographical writing. The *Carnets de la drôle de guerre*, similar to a letter, excludes "on the spot" as well as a posteriori corrections—a practice of writing totally opposite to that of *Les Mots*. Without having seen other manuscripts of Nathalie Sarraute, I can only assume that the meticulous work on words and phrases in the manuscript of *Enfance* is analogous to her practice in her novels, what she calls "choosing her wool, her colors, and mixing the hues"—weaving the tapestry of text.

As far as overall procedure is concerned, however, Sarraute did in fact change her method. At first, her novels were written entirely in a single go and then reworked several times from start to finish. *Enfance*, by contrast, was written step by step, chapter after chapter, without any primary work on the overall whole. She would not begin a new chapter until the preceding one had reached a quasi-final state. At the same time, her resistance to the classic genre of childhood memories led her to introduce a daring system of exposition, a dialogue between two voices (herself and her double). There, in a totally different context, she made use of the experience in writing dialogue that she had acquired in her works for radio. It is exciting to see her "test out" this system in the avant-textes for chapter 2, varying proportions and connections as she seeks a very delicate balance.

More generally, one might think that the autobiographical situation forces the writer to make some methodological changes. The many practical guides for writers in the United States do not give exactly the same advice, after all, to those who wish to write a novel and to those who attempt an autobiography. Among other things, the inventory of one's memory, the narrative organization, the articulation of a previous as well as a contemporary point of view, the choice of a system of exposition (and an audience) all pose specific problems.

Autobiographers often explain their own method in their preambles or at other crucial points in the narrative. It also happens that they devote a great part of their text to describing their "workshop." Michel Leiris gives us examples of both: the method of writing in *L'Age d'homme* (1939) is later described and evaluated in "De la Littérature considérée comme une tauromachie" (1946). "Tambour-Trompette," the final chapter of *Biffures* (1948; the first volume of *La Règle du jeu*), is devoted to the "constraint" that was used to produce the book (to write a text from an itinerary determined by a pack of index cards). As in the case of Perec, this "auto-genetic" behavior generally legitimizes genetic studies at the same time as it pulls the rug out from underfoot, or at least complicates everything. Leiris gave Catherine Maubon all the index cards that were the basis of *Fourbis* (1955; the second volume of *La Règle du jeu*) and the rough drafts of its first chapter "*Mors*." In her book *Michel Leiris au travail* (1988), Maubon had no choice but to implicate herself in (and then develop and illustrate) the very problem Leiris himself proposed.

Two main things are therefore at stake in genetic studies of autobiography: *generic specificities* (how does autobiographical writing differ from other forms of writing?) and *generic innovations* (how and why is a writer led to innovate?). Current research has a tendency to concern itself with the second of these, as one can see by glancing through the "Examples of Genetic Criticism" section at the end of this essay. Maubon has explored Leiris's "constrained" writing, and Catherine Viollet has compared thirty-three attempted beginnings for the autobiographical novel *Kindheitsmuster* to see how Christa Wolf avoided writing "I." Viollet has also engaged in wider research on the avant-textes of the beginning sections of modern autobiographies or autofictions; she aims to see how writers feel their way into a system of exposition and a contract with those who will read their narrative. I have myself worked on several Perec inventions. As of now, his editing procedures, strategies of self-limitation, and contractual and expository games are probably the most interesting points to pursue—to which one may add, shifting the subject from creation to "manufacture," the genetic study of "autobiographic," collaboratively produced documents. These documents create a transparent effect: "Here we have, straight from the horse's mouth, the life of X." If one has access to all the avant-textes of these documents (tapes, transcriptions), one can better see that above all they express the ideology of whomever has put the narrative together or made the transcription, edition, or presentation.

Difficulties

For autobiographical as well as for other texts, the difficulties are enormous. I will indicate them rapidly, so as not to discourage those who would like to participate in research that for the most part is exciting. The main difficulties deal with the availability of avant-textes and the ways they are used.

It is rather difficult for us to know how classical authors up until the nineteenth century worked because they thought it natural to destroy their rough drafts. Since the manuscripts we do have are often the author's final clear copies, they do not give us much information. For Rousseau's *Confessions,* for example, we possess very little: aside from the two final manuscripts, only a partial copy of one intermediary stage (the Neuchâtel manuscript) and a few loose pages. Hermine de Saussure's study attempts to fill in this enormous gap through meticulous analysis of the correspondence. We also suffer from scarcity in the case of the *Mémoires d'outre-tombe* because Chateaubriand decided to erase the traces of his work (a fact that may seem paradoxical, or else very understandable, because he involves the work in the narrative itself).[4] Yet this erasure was not complete: anyone who is interested should see the fundamental work of Jean-Claude Berchet on the first few books of the *Mémoires.* For Stendhal, the situation is the reverse. The manuscripts of all the autobiographical texts have been preserved, but they were themselves planned according to a very modern and improvisational manuscript aesthetics that renders them exciting, atypical, and virtually impossible to edit. Reading recent essays on the *Vie de Henry Brulard,* for example, one has the impression that only the *happy few* who have actually seen the manuscript know what they are talking about.[5] But the great problem is that no inventory of nineteenth-century autobiographical texts has yet been compiled. This would be the first thing to do and would perhaps allow us to find exciting collections of avant-textual material. All too often, the modern "critical editions" use the available avant-textes as mere "variants" or as documents to confirm or deny the "veracity" of the final text. That is the case in the recent edition of Marie d'Agoult's *Mémoires, souvenirs et journaux*, which uses avant-textes without really attempting any genetic study of that great unfinished autobiography. Yet at the moment when she was writing her *Mémoires* in 1865–66, Marie d'Agoult jotted down in one notebook her ideas, her first sketches, and the problems she had in elaborating them. Sandrine Cotteverte has begun to study and edit this notebook, of much greater interest than the simple genesis of Marie d'Agoult's text. It could serve as the basis of a sort of general grammar of autobiographical "gestures."[6]

The problem is different for contemporary authors. It has become more common to keep rough drafts; authors are interested in the traces of their own work. If they are famous, they are also aware of the market value of autographs. Yet it is problematic for authors to capitalize upon them while still alive. Such a practice puts the author in a kind of space beyond the grave, takes away control of the work, and, when the work is autobiographical, takes away life itself. Sarraute was at first rather hesitant about giving me the rough drafts of a chapter of *Enfance*. Why should she make public something with which she had precisely not been satisfied, something not as good as the final text?

Making real use of avant-textes is itself a long and laborious process. Before being able to analyze the work of a writer, one must establish the text and reconstruct its history with precision. This preliminary task can absorb, and even exhaust, a researcher's strength. Without having established the chronology of the writings under consideration, it is impossible to do genetic study. Yet this is all the more difficult because the genetic documents themselves have tremendous gaps. For chapter 2 of *Enfance*, Sarraute gave me everything she found: ten sheets that she called the "Final manuscript" comprising the corrected fragments of two earlier versions (all of which, incidentally, did not entirely add up to the published text) and twenty-five loose sheets that belonged to about ten early versions, only one of which was (more or less) complete. The rest were the beginnings and middles of a short narrative whose sequence I couldn't use as a compass because it was exactly what Sarraute was trying to vary in as many ways as possible. When, taken by despair, I went to see her for some hints, she looked at the sheets all fanned out and said meditatively: "That's work . . ." The time came when I too was forced to reflect upon this. The Sartre team at ITEM, working on the manuscripts of *Les Mots* acquired by the Bibliothèque Nationale, faces an enormous, but spotty, archive (about a thousand pages). After study, a single typed page, sitting in a pack of unclassified "random pages," revealed the existence of a whole writing (and typing) "campaign" of which it was the only remaining witness. Some of Sartre's papers, scattered under unbelievable conditions, periodically resurface in small lots at public sales. We work in both hope and fear that one of these resurfacings will send us all back to the drawing board.

The work involved in the transcription, decoding, and unfolding of the writer's different operations (additions, suppressions, substitutions, displacements) is long and dry and can produce documents so complicated that they seem illegible to the uninitiated who look at them. One has the impression that only those who have established them can really use them. If I question whether I'm really a geneticist, it is because I have never accomplished, in a systematic manner, such a work. The transcriptions of *Les Mots* were a team effort. Perec's manuscripts have the characteristic of having very few corrections and are very readable. Sarraute's are heavily corrected, but they have a very clear system. Moreover, since she stipulated that I might comment upon them but not edit them, I was not able to perform that task.

Sometimes you hear that textual geneticism is a very costly operation with very little benefit. People wonder why the prefaces and afterwords in serious editions are so critically emaciated. In fact, genetic criticism is plagued by two dangers: excessive professionalism, the entanglement in a necessary but enormous work from which one emerges weak and without the strength to profit from it; and the opposite danger of amateurism, the impatience of hasty critics who see only their own problems and out of a rich genetic archive select only the elements that support their theses or interpretations. Working as a team allows one to avoid these dangers by lightening the tasks and increasing the comparisons and controls.

A solid genetic archive free from every preconceived idea and interpretation must be established. Yet perhaps it does not really reveal its richness until one comes to it with a question. One's question may be theoretical, such as Viollet's about speech acts, or it may deal with the selection and transformation of memories. It may also be a test of a hypothesis. In 1973, I did a study of the narrative sequence in *Les Mots* and put forth hypotheses about its dialectic rather than chronological nature and about the gaps in its construction. Today the manuscripts of *Les Mots* are available. I will be able, once the order of the writing "campaigns" has been established as solidly as possible, to analyze the variations in sequence and dating of Sartre's memories, the ways they are staged, their soldering . . . that is, to surprise Sartre in his tinker's workshop. Above, I exaggerated the difficulties a little. We overcome them when we really wish to resolve a problem. After having reflected upon Sarraute's comment, "That's work," I ended up by more or less understanding the puzzle of those thirty-five pages because I absolutely wanted to know what relation existed between the fictional image of her work that she gives in her book and the real work of which the manuscripts bear the trace. It's a question of passion.

The last problem to solve: how to communicate to others what one has found? First, by telling them about this passion. Insofar as it is possible, one must relate the genesis of one's own search. It is useless to withdraw into impersonality, leaving the reader to face an inert mass of dead, dreary, scientifically described manuscripts. Portraying the movement of my quest, I can offer it as an image analogous to the lost object that we seek in these drafts and erasures: the movement of creation. It is more interesting to visit a digging site with an archeologist than to see shards of pottery arranged in a window. And it is not less scientific. Genetic studies are destined to result in narratives. To end this first essay, I offer one for the genesis of *W ou le Souvenir d'enfance.*

Genesis

In 1969–70, I subscribed to *La Quinzaine Littéraire*, in which Georges Perec published in serial fashion a bizarre adventure novel entitled *W.* I'm hard-pressed to summarize it. A narrator tells how he was put in charge of finding a child lost in a shipwreck near Tierra del Fuego. For various reasons, he himself had taken on the identity of this child. At the end of six chapters, the text splits in two. The original narrator seems to have disappeared. Taking the place of the narrative already underway is an "objective" and methodical description of an olympic colony established on an island of Tierra del Fuego. Apparently euphoric at first, the description turns slowly into a nightmare: beneath the olympianism, the horror of the Nazi camps appears. Then the description stops suddenly: the island is destroyed by a catastrophe, and we learn nothing of the story of the child. In 1975, Perec published a book (announced as early as 1970 but delayed), this time with the title *W ou le Souvenir d'enfance.* It is the same story, but chapters of his own childhood are interspersed among the fictional chapters. At the center of his childhood story is the disappearance of his mother at Auschwitz in 1943. The reader must read alternately the chapters of each story, which seem to know nothing of each other. These painful gymnastics contradict all of our reading habits. Yet the structure creates a tremendous elliptical effect; it is up to the reader to grasp the relation between the two narratives, and above all to sense why it is impossible to express that relation.

How could one resist the desire to know more? Maybe directing one's curiosity to the history of such a book is itself a manner of escaping the horror it designates. Yet at the same time it repeats the story that is told in the book. A narrator goes off to find a lost child. I go off to find a lost narrator. Genetic research takes the baton from "genealogical" research.

It is rare, and impressive, to work on the posthumous manuscripts of a writer who is your contemporary. (I was born two years after Perec, who died in 1982.) In 1987, I was able to access all the documents relating to his work. First, I did historical research to date and categorize the different elements of the story I found, and then I reconstructed something like a "psychological novel" of its creation.

Twice in a row, for the magazine and then for the book, Perec went through the same cycle of hardships. He experienced failure and silence and was unable to escape his despair except by inventing procedures capable of transmitting that very despair to the reader.

Inspired by an adolescent fantasy, the serial novel was at first supposed to have been an exciting science-fiction adventure novel à la Jules Verne, one that would have expressed his childhood indirectly. Yet very rapidly (how could he not have foreseen it?), he was submerged in the horror that he had to put forth, to the point where he lost his voice (the second part of the serial novel is not written in the first person) and was forced to abridge a text that sickened him and that readers of the journal could hardly tolerate. The failure of the serial novel led him to conceive of writing an autobiographical book into which the *W* fiction would be integrated and its meaning made explicit.

A second project and a new beginning full of hope. He conceived of a revolutionary project, a book intermingling the chapters of three different sequences: the *W* fiction, his childhood memories (told in a completely "straight" manner), and a third series that would elucidate the relationship between the first two by telling the story of W's adolescent fantasy, its resurgence in his adulthood, and the very difficulties he had in writing the book. But these difficulties were such that he was also unable to finish the second project. He started to write the second series, the childhood memories, with great difficulty, and then, on account of these difficulties and others that resonated with his own emotional life, he abandoned everything. Four years later, after a psychoanalytic cure, he took up the manuscript again and found a solution: he had to remove the third series and transmit his discomfort to his readers, confronting them brutally with the unexplained link between the first two series. This procedure recalls the one imposed on him by the magazine—to organize in some way the *disappearance of the narrator.*

One can well imagine the interest there is in reconstructing such an adventure by examining scattered documents and critically reading the final text. Yet that is not all. While taking inventory of these manuscripts, I quickly discovered that they were part of a much larger autobiographical project, of which the plans had been sketched in 1969 in a letter to

Maurice Nadeau (printed in the small volume *Je suis né,* 1990). The unfinished *Lieux,* discussed above, is part of that group. As one thing led to another, I came to explore all of Perec's autobiographical projects, first in order to think about their common strategy and then to explore *Lieux* and *Je me souviens* in detail. In 1987, I plunged into these archives for a few months. The trip wound up lasting four years and has resulted in a book, *La Mémoire et l'oblique* (1991). It is unclear whether these travels are really over.

Over the course of this first essay, I've used the various metaphors of detective investigation, archeology, and psychological novel for genetic research. Perhaps I should add alchemy. Sometimes geneticists say they are progressing toward a "science of literature" as if they hoped to change the lead of avant-textes into pure gold and discover the secrets of creation.

Diaries

By its very definition, the genetic study of diaries seems to have no object. A diary, if it is a real diary, has no avant-texte. It is written from day to day; that is why it has value for the person writing it, as well as for the reader, if there ever is a reader. Reading a diary, I like to believe that I am really reading what was written, in those very words on that very day, and not some artifact rewritten or rearranged afterwards. This has nothing to do with sincerity. Let us assume that the diarist made a mistake, or tried to fool himself and us on a given day; at least I am sure that it is his own bad faith on that very day that I have before my eyes. His blindness or his silences. The very words that he used.

From this perspective, we cannot speak of any "genetic" study except by displacing the meaning of the word. Each diary entry constitutes a unique text, but because the succession of entries is controlled by a system of variations, it can be a site of learning and evolution. I can see how the entries' construction strategies (periodicity, length, internal structure) change or do not change. The same thing goes for the phrasing and the style. I cannot compare the text of August 13 to its avant-textes—there are none—but to the texts of August 12, or 11, yes. Diaries allow one a live view of how a given writing engenders itself by repetition (the tendency to auto-imitate is very strong) or by variation. I catch myself dreaming of quantitative studies: diaries on computer, with graphs. Frequency and length of entries, evolution of the subjects broached, types of discourse used. Diaries are already cut into discrete units, explicitly inscribed in the frame of the quantifiable variable of time. They are practically begging to be analyzed for their rhythms. To classify diaries according to criteria of character seems arbitrary. . . . On the other hand a musical typology might make some sense. . . . But I'm wandering. How could we ever hope to distinguish between what, in a given diary's evolution, is on the order of apprenticeship or work (for which the idea of "genesis" could make sense) and what is on the order of narrative being enacted, of the transformation of life itself? I wander especially far when I abusively extend the meaning of the word "genesis" and then refuse to see it where in fact it is.

The image of the diary as "writing on the first try" is somewhat mythological. No matter how rapid and invisible it is, all writing is the product of an elaboration of some kind, most often mental and occasionally oral. Diarists start writing in their diaries throughout the day, while living. Diarists are ruminants. They live as forms awaiting contents. They have their schemes, their sentence structures, their paragraphs—and their attentions, their turned-on obsessions. Certain things and not others are apt to fecundate this apparatus. Gestation is most often unconscious (but not always) and results in an apparently rapid delivery onto paper. In her *Diary,* Virginia Woolf makes amusing observations about the problems that her mental or oral drafts cause her, when the peripherals of everyday life perturb their gestation (see April 18 and May 28, 1918; *Diary* 1: 139–42, 149–52). The weakness of genetic studies is that they must always deduce mental operations from the traces they leave: here there are no traces.

Sometimes, however, glimpses into this hidden backstage area can be had. The idea would be to compare a diary to its referent. Suppose that a diarist notes a conversation with someone and that, without his knowing it, that conversation had been recorded. Such a thing does not happen every day. It is our luck that it did happen to a famous diarist, Paul Léautaud. On September 4, 1950, on his way to record the next of his interviews with Robert Mallet, he met Julien Benda in the studio, who had himself just finished a recording with Pierre Sipriot. They made a little small talk without knowing (was this malice or a mistake?) that the recording continued. These fourteen minutes, which correspond to three pages in Léautaud's *Journal,* are now in the radio archives.[7] We have two ends of the chain. And it is text against text. Dreaming, now: what if Benda had also kept a diary. There is no need to dream: it is in fact the case. I transcribed it and did a short study. Three levels. One "conversational" analysis based on the recorded sound (hilarious and Molièresque in my view). A study of the narrative of the conversation in the diary, obviously very different, and centered more on Benda. A feast for analysts of reported speech, focalization, etc. The real surprise is elsewhere. It turns out that there is a chicken-or-egg problem here: is the diary the source of the conversation or vice versa? One has to ask because, in rereading the diary from the preceding year, I saw that a great number of words spoken by Léautaud to Benda appeared there. They were either original notations or, already, narratives of conversations, or notes taken from his own letters. Diarists are ruminants with several stomachs.

Yes, we are now very far from the idea of genesis, above all because diaries are forms of praxis, not artistic works. A diary cannot be understood as a trajectory governed by a project. Rather, there is a circulation between conversation, correspondence, and diary, a triad that one must supplement with the invisible interior "monologue" in order to obtain a nice spreadsheet with two series of entries (written/unwritten, internal/external dialogue). Of course, in this circulation, each genre has its own constraints, and I suggested above how diaries can themselves engender diaries. The problem is that the circulatory system of autoengenderment requires difficult and delicate observation.

Let us console ourselves by holding fast to the narrow fringe of genesis that one can read from manuscripts. Working on paper, we erase words, change terms, add something forgotten, and make other minimal adjustments according to the logic of the expressive movement itself. (Marie Bashkirtseff, with the back of a cuff or the swipe of a finger, wipes the wet ink away from the beginning of an unwelcome phrase and then writes over it in the same place. Or perhaps two minutes or an hour later one returns to what one has written, but now with a reader's eye—at this point one's work is already guided by the imperatives of communication.) It also happens that, for reasons of practicality (it is impossible to carry the "real" diary everywhere) or of psychology (the need for a time of maturation), diaries are written at two different times—initial, rapid notes made in some kind of medium and then a clear copy or newer development on the (final?) medium. These corrections and doublings make genetic study possible, even if the stakes involved seem small.

Once the night has passed and a new day has dawned, however, the field of study suddenly widens. Diarists may perform all sorts of operations on their diaries: crossing out words or names, ripping out pages, making corrections or additions—all this either on the original manuscripts or as freewheeling new copies of material that may eventually become entirely rewritten. Perhaps they do such things because they are dissatisfied, because they themselves see their diaries as first attempts at expression or as works to be taken up again later. Or else they are thinking of publication: they must acquit themselves well. Or perhaps a diarist (famous or not) is dead. People want to publish the diary. Exciting, sure, but too long. So it is cut, tailored, resewn, and explained. Maybe the diary *has* no avant-texte: but it *becomes* the avant-texte of the presentation or rewriting that is made of it.

From this perspective, any published diary must be considered to belong to a composite genre. If it is an autopublication (generally before death), then the text must *also* be understood as an autobiographical construction (example: Gide's *Journal* in 1939). If it is a hetero-publication (generally posthumous), then as a biographical construction (example: Bashkirtseff's *Journal*; André Theuriet's 1887 edition of it is partial and doctored).

Unlike a diary, such a genesis does leave traces. Even if the work has been erased, its point of departure remains. Editors rarely burn the manuscripts of the diaries they edit. We have only to compare. Certain cases are enough to set one's mind to dreaming: for example, in Québec, the case of Henriette Dessaules's (1860–1946) admirable adolescent diary (1874–80). Of this we possess only a rewritten version she did by herself between 1898 and 1908 without leaving any trace of the original.

This field of study is enormous since it is likely that almost no diary has been published in the form in which it was written. Maybe the diary is by definition unpublishable: there is an incompatibility between it and the "book-form" that is a veritable Procrustean bed. It is like trying to make a sponge fit into a matchbox. To make a book, one must, at the minimum, cut and explain, perhaps also rewrite. In a way the "diary-novel" that appeared in the nineteenth century is a model of the orthopedic apparatus that has since been often applied to real diaries. But I know I'm exaggerating. I'm wrong to speak in absolutes. The book-form and reading habits have evolved. There is today a public, or fractions of a public, capable of, and enthusiastic about, reading thousands of pages of a diary, but not just any diary: fixating on a chosen author gives one extra strength. Yet I exaggerate only a little. The history of editing teems with examples of diaries that have been censured, pruned, and doctored, sometimes by the authors themselves and sometimes by heirs or editors. And diaries now have prefaces, whether autograph or allograph, to disguise or justify these operations (see Jerzy Lis, "Le Journal d'écrivain"). Nudes with affectations, putting on gloves.

The text of a diary does not inspire the respect that people generally have for texts. Who would have the audacity to rewrite personal correspondence? Who would feel authorized to doctor a poem? When it is a diary nobody seems to mind. As soon as the possibility of publication arises, the text of a diary becomes an avant-texte, a rough draft that needs polishing up or a sick person who needs help getting dressed. More than a hundred years after her death (1884), we are still waiting for a true edition of the diary of Marie Bashkirtseff, the manuscripts of which are available at the Bibliothèque Nationale. The edition of Amiel's diary (*Journal intime*) has just barely been finished. Claire Paulhan, who edited several diaries (including Catherine Pozzi's) in the collection "Pour mémoire" under her direction, admits that she herself feels the necessity to exercise what she calls an "aesthetic censure" in the diaries' own interest. I could take even more striking examples from certain truth specialists (ethnologists, sociologists) who have altered their diaries for delivery to the public. Jeanne Favret-Saada, after having published a theoretical study of witchcraft in the Bocage region of France (*Les Mots, la mort, les sorts*, 1977), chose to divulge her "diary of the terrain," but only the first year of it, and not the actual text of the diary. Instead she asked a friend of hers, Josée Contreras, to rewrite it with her. *Corps pour corps* (1981), a book signed by both of them, is in fact a chronicle presented in the form of a diary, written from a diary, but not at all the original diary, which seems to have been partially destroyed during the operation. Rémi Hess, pioneer of the "institutional diary," considered his own diary unpublishable, and submitted it to a series of operations of aesthetic surgery that he described in the preface of his book (*Le Lycée au jour le jour*, 1989).

These operations can be seen as improving the text (such is the prevailing spirit: make the text "readable," interest the readers, and do not try their patience) or as deteriorating it (the authenticity that gives the value to this genre is reduced or destroyed). Here we are right in the middle of the conflict between expressive and communicative functions. In this conflict, two forms of compromise are common today: (1) diarists reconcile themselves ahead of time to the demands of communication (today's writers know very well how to do this); (2) some readers find it pleasant to read something that was not written for them and agree to pay the tax levied in patience. Either way a conflict remains, and one is greatly tempted to think that what would be unacceptable in a book (the page layout, to start with) is precisely what is most intimate in a diary. Certain types of relationship to the self and to time are lost when we bend to the demands of communication.

People who write diary-novels, of course, attempt to preserve elements that are contrary to communication, but in infinitesimal doses. They produce a kind of "diary effect" in the manner of Barthes's "reality effect." On one side, these elements include length, the fact of repetition, a massive number of things left implicit, discontinuity and gaps in information, and a "first draft" character of writing. On the other side we have immodesty (exposing things about oneself that one would presumably have an interest in keeping secret, such as weaknesses, embarrassment, and faults) and indiscretion (every diary compromises other people, whether by revealing things about some people to third parties, or by revealing how one really sees other people without telling them). But I'm wrong to present these two series of elements as if they were equally opposite to communication; the second—weakness of the human soul!—would in fact have the tendency to facilitate it.

I would propose starting from situations of rewriting and performing a sort of "differential" study, with the idea of bringing forth what is specific to, and irreducible about, diary writing.

Would that be a truly "genetic" study? Yes, although the situation is paradoxical: "genesis" implies a study of a creation and a valorization of the point of arrival. Now, since I consider the final work to be a destruction and I valorize the point of departure, it seems that I am taking the opposite point of view. As we have seen, however, my position is more nuanced; I wish to bring to light the conflict between two logics of writing. Moreover, the paradox is only on the surface. The desire to know the genesis of a created literary work is unnatural, or at least once removed. The desire to know the original state of a diary is perfectly natural, for it is precisely what motivated one to begin reading it in the first place.

There is another reason for doubting whether this is really a "genetic" project: often we will be dealing with rewriting done by somebody other than the author. Now, up until today genetic studies have remained closed within the magic circle of the idea of the author. But the only circle that can contain *these* studies is that of the text. The fact that there are two authors is simply a particular modality of textual work. There is no reason to exclude it.

I tried to complete my project starting with a group of contemporary adolescent diaries. Now differential study assumes that one possesses both a beginning *and* an end point, so as to establish a typology of the operations leading from one to the other. For this study, in every case (except one), I had only the starting point *or* the end point. To finish this essay, I am going to recount the instructive (mis)adventures of this research project. Ultimately, they led me to do a genetic study of the *Diaries* of Anne Frank.

As I say, at times I had only the beginning point. Such was the case for my own adolesecent diary, and for the diaries that I was able to consult in the archives of the "Vivre et l'écrire" association in Orléans. I studied one of these diaries, Cécile's, to see how the text of the diary was put together with all the other accompanying documents (written or not). In every case, I had manuscript pages or notebooks in front of me but no books. Books were only dreams at that point, very distant on the horizon. Obviously, a great deal of work must be done to extract books from such manuscripts. Everything is long, repetitive, and mixed. I mean, *would* be long, repetitive, and mixed, *if it were printed.* Yet when I read the manuscript notebooks, none of those adjectives came to mind. I had plenty of time, and the diaries often seemed brief compared to the time of life that they evoked and accompanied. It is true that my own diary is very badly written. I was tempted, I must admit, to flush it down the toilet. I tried to, and then gave up. It wouldn't have solved anything, and it wouldn't have been me anymore. There I am, clumsy and ungrammatical. Yet the experiment was interesting: I was able to see just how strong the urge is to correct a diary that one is recopying. I also daydreamed while reading Cécile's diary. How could one cull from these eight notebooks the narrative of growing up that she herself was thinking about when she bequeathed her diary to "Vivre et l'écrire"?

Sometimes I had only the terminal point. The book was there and the work had been done, but I no longer had access to the beginning. That is the most frequent case. To facilitate comparisons I had chosen a corpus of adolescent diaries, and with the idea that it would be easier to communicate with the teens or their editors, I had chosen contemporaries. That was a mistake. There were two boys and two girls. The first boy was Gabriel Matzneff. He did not answer my letter. I asked him whether the beginning of his published diary was whole or whether he had made certain selections, and how he had done so. The second boy was Wolinski, whose *Le Bécoteur* (1984) I had greatly admired.[8] His response was to return my own letter to me with "yes" answers or other brief comments in the margin, as if it were a corrected assignment. "I cut out a lot, but I didn't add or change anything." He changed proper names. The beginning and the end of the book correspond to those of the diary. He wrote on perforated graph paper in a little brown folder. That's it. This economical answer was hardly an inspiration to push things further. And why, after all, put one's nose in the diaries of others, even if they have themselves published them? By publishing them they had traced the exact limit of their indiscretion. On the girls' side of things, first of all I had Stéphanie, the author of *Des Cornichons au chocolat* (1983), "with the collaboration of Philippe Labro." A brief preface describes the nature of his role:

> The editor decided, at that point, to have me read the text, and I asked to meet Stéphanie. Together, we were going to work towards a new form for the book. This meant that I played the role of journalist, asking for clarification on certain points and suggesting to Stéphanie that she return to such and such a theme or episode, or else that she go further in letting her emotions, moods, laughters and sorrows show. I never touched her writing. On the contrary, it was necessary to preserve the power of her tone and the originality of her style. Simply, in the way the miners of the Klondike gold rush would sift what they gathered in the river to find the nuggets, so too we would work to select our material. Then we would classify and build. We would change, as well, certain people's names and places so as not to embarrass the real actors in this still-living story.

This rewrite, done after the diary had been handled for two years under the "direction" of a professional writer, seems to have been especially significant (and successful: it is a very good book). But "Stéphanie" wished to remain anonymous; it seemed therefore out of the question that one could ever see the original manuscripts. And Philippe Labro, for his part, kept silent when one of my students wrote him to ask about his work. The second girl was Ariane Grimm, the (posthumous) author of *La Flambe*: *Journal intime d'une jeune fille* (1986), a book her mother published two years after her death in a motorcycle accident. This book (also very successful) suggests the possibility of seeing the original notebooks; the first page of each of the four published notebooks is reproduced in facsimile facing the text, which is itself a literal transcription of it. But as for the rest of the diary, perhaps it was changed after all? I was able to see the notebooks, but the recent death of Ariane made a study of this kind inappropriate.

Thus my entire corpus had disappeared. Choosing contemporary diaries had not been a brilliant idea. One girl and one boy remained. The boy was the adolescent Claude Mauriac; the writer Claude Mauriac, seeing my embarrassment, offered his original diary to me so that I could compare it to the use he makes of it in the vertiginous eleven-volume presentation of *Temps immobile* (1974–88). In this way, the possibility of continuing this study opened up, and I thank him warmly. The girl was Anne Frank, whose original *Diaries* were published for the first time in Holland in 1986. This edition reveals a surprise and sweeps away any doubts one could have had about the authenticity of the texts. Anne Frank was herself the first person to rewrite her own *Diaries.* During the last three months of her stay at the Annex, she almost entirely rewrote the diary of the preceding two years, with the intention of publishing it herself as soon as the war was over. Thus, *two* texts of the *Diary* exist, both in Anne's hand. The situation has been complicated by the fact that neither of these two texts is complete. Some of the original diary's notebooks have been lost, and Anne had not finished the rewriting when she was arrested. In order to construct a coherent book, in accordance with Anne's plans, her father had to perform a kind of structural rewrite. The Dutch critical edition gives us all we need to follow the two rewrites: Anne's, then her father's. However, since this exemplary edition itself remains only on the threshold of the genetic reflection that it makes possible, I have begun, in broad strokes, the genetic study that is required.[9] Anne Frank, rewriting her own diary to give it the form of a book, offers us a sort of ideal experimental situation to seize this "difference" between private writing and public writing.

Autobiography, personal diary . . . Even if generic specificities do not account for all of the processes that one can observe, they have the advantage of opening up reflection in areas where one can generalize.

Studies of the whole corpus of a given author are indispensable, that is obvious. Yet if they are pursued exclusively, they run the risk of resulting in airtight studies on a small number of congenial works. Asking about the specific practices of a whole genre permits us to establish transversal links between different authors, but also to ask about works that are perhaps less inventive but which reveal basic generic constraints. It also lets us avoid the trap of individual psychological interpretations and instead map our questions onto the terrain of writing. Thus one can hope to ask the same questions I posed with respect to autobiographies or diaries about numerous other writing practices, such as theatrical texts, automatic writing, short stories, poems with fixed forms, dialogues . . .

Examples of Genetic Criticism

Eighteenth- and Nineteenth-Century Texts

• Chateaubriand, *Mémoires d'outre-tombe*

Berchet, Jean-Claude. "Le Manuscrit autographe du Livre I des *Mémoires de ma vie* de Chateaubriand." *Revue d'Histoire Littéraire de la France* 87 (July–August 1987): 713–32.

Chateaubriand, François-René, vicomte de. *Mémoires de ma vie (manuscrit de 1826)*. Critical edition by J. M. Gautier. Geneva: Droz, 1976. (Introduction, 1–16.)

———. *Mémoires d'outre-tombe.* Centenary edition, complete and critical, partly unpublished, established by Maurice Levaillant, 1948; with a new critical edition, established, introduced, and annotated by Jean-Claude Berchet. Paris: Bordas Classiques Garnier, 1989.

• Rousseau, *Confessions*

Rousseau, Jean-Jacques. *Les Confessions. Reproduction du manuscrit de Neuchâtel.* Lausanne: Bibliothèque Romande, 1973. (Reproduction in facsimile, and a study.)

Saussure, Hermine de. *Rousseau et les manuscrits des Confessions.* Paris: Éditions de Boccard, 1958.

• Stendhal, *Souvenirs d'égotisme* and *Vie de Henry Brulard*

Écritures du romantisme, 1: Stendhal. Saint-Denis: Presses Universitaires de Vincennes, "Manuscrits modernes" series, 1988. (Five studies on Stendhal's autobiographical manuscripts by Jean Bellemin-Noël, Béatrice Didier, Louis Marin, Gérald Rannaud, and Serge Sérodes.)

Neefs, Jacques. "De Main vive: Trois versions de la transmission des textes." *Littérature* 64 (1986): 30–46. (On Chateaubriand, Montaigne, and Stendhal; translated in this volume.)

Sérodes, Serge. *Signe scriptural et création littéraire: Pour une approche sémiotique des manuscrits autobiographiques de Stendhal.* Thèse du Doctorat d'État, Université de Paris X Nanterre, June 1987.

Twentieth-Century Texts

• Anne Frank, *Journaux*

Frank, Anne. *Les Journaux d'Anne Frank.* Critical edition by the Netherlands Institute for War Documentation. Text established by David Barnouw and Gerrold van der Stroom, 1986; French translation by Philippe Noble and Isabelle Rosselin-Bobulesco. Calmann-Lévy, 1989. [*The Diary of Anne Frank: The Critical Edition.* Prepared by the Netherlands State Institute for War Documentation. Introduction by Harry Paape, Gerrold van der Stroom, and David Barnouw. Ed. David Barnouw and Gerrold van der Stroom. Trans. Arnold J. Pomerans and B. M. Mooyaart-Doubleday. New York: Doubleday, 1989.]

Lejeune, Philippe. "Comment Anne Frank a réécrit le *Journal* d'Anne Frank." Presentation at the conference "Le Journal personnel" (Nanterre, May 19, 1990). Published in Lejeune's *Les Brouillons de soi.* Paris: Seuil, 1998. 331–65.

• Michel Leiris, *La Règle du jeu*

Maubon, Catherine. *Michel Leiris au travail: Analyse et transcription d'un fragment manuscrit de Fourbis.* Pisa: Pacine Editore, 1987.

———. "Michel Leiris, le ficheur fiché." In *Penser, classer, écrire, de Pascal à Perec,* ed. Béatrice Didier and Jacques Neefs. Saint-Denis: Presses Universitaires de Vincennes, 1990. 149–70.

• Georges Perec

Lejeune, Philippe. *La Mémoire et l'oblique: Georges Perec autobiographe.* Paris: P.O.L., 1991.

Pawlikowska, Ewa. "Insertion, recomposition dans *W ou le Souvenir d'enfance* de Georges Perec." In *Penser, classer, écrire, de Pascal à Perec,* ed. Béatrice Didier and Jacques Neefs. Saint-Denis: Presses Universitaires de Vincennes, 1990. 171–80.

• Nathalie Sarraute, *Enfance*

Lejeune, Philippe. "Aussi liquide qu'une soupe." In *Autour de Nathalie Sarraute: Actes du colloque international de Cerisy-la-Salle des 9 au 19 juillet 1989,* ed. Valérie Minogue and Sabine Raffy. Paris: Diffusion Les Belles Lettres, 1995. (Study of the avant-textes of chapter 2 of *Enfance.*)

• Jean-Paul Sartre, *Les Mots*

Contat, Michel, ed. *Pourquoi et comment Sartre a écrit "Les Mots": Genèse d'une autobiographie.* Paris: Presses Universitaires de France, 1996. (Essays by Michel Contat, Jacques Deguy, Geneviève Idt, Jacques Lecarme, Philippe Lejeune, Jean-François Louette, Josette Pacaly, and Sandra Teroni.)

Lejeune, Philippe. "Les Enfances de Sartre." *Moi aussi.* Paris: Seuil, 1986. 117–63.

• Christa Wolf, *Trame d'enfance (Kindheitsmuster,* 1976; *A Model Childhood,* 1980)

Viollet, Catherine. "Autobiographie et disparition du 'je': *Kindheitsmuster* de Christa Wolf." In *Leçons d'écriture: Ce que disent les manuscrits. Hommage à Louis Hay.* Paris: Lettres Modernes, 1985. 195–206.

Source: "Auto-genèse: L'Étude génétique des textes autobiographiques." *Genesis* 1 (1992): 73–87. Another form of this essay appeared in Lejeune's *Les Brouillons de soi.* Paris: Seuil, 1998. 143–61.

Works Cited (Not Listed in the "Examples of Genetic Criticism")

Amiel, Henri-Frédéric. *Journal intime.* Ed. Bernard Gagnebin and Philippe M. Monnier. 12 vols. Lausanne: Éditions l'Age d'Homme, 1976–94.

Bashkirtseff, Marie. *Journal.* 2 vols. Paris: G. Charpentier, 1887. *Journal.* Trans. Mary J. Serrano. New York: Cassell, 1889. Trans. A. D. Hall. 2 vols. Chicago: Rand McNally, 1890. Trans. Mathilde Blind. London: Cassell, 1890.

Berchet, Jean-Claude. "Le Manuscrit autographe du Livre I des *Mémoires de ma vie* de Chateaubriand." *Revue d'Histoire Littéraire de la France* 87 (July–August 1987): 713–32.

d'Agoult, Marie. "Le Cahier 1865 de Marie d'Agoult." Ed. Sandrine Cotteverte. *Genesis* 16 (2001): 137–69.

———. *Mémoires, souvenirs et journaux de la comtesse d'Agoult (Daniel Stern).* Ed. Charles F. Dupêchez. Paris: Mercure de France, 1990.

Favret-Saada, Jeanne. *Les Mots, la mort, les sorts: La Sorcellerie dans le Bocage.* Paris: Gallimard, 1977. *Deadly Words: Witchcraft in the Bocage.* Trans. Catherine Cullen. Cambridge: Cambridge University Press, 1980.

Favret-Saada, Jeanne, and Josée Contreras. *Corps pour corps: Enquête sur la sorcellerie dans le Bocage.* Paris: Gallimard, 1981.

Gide, André. *Journal, 1889–1939.* Paris: Éditions de la Nouvelle Revue Française, 1939. *Journals.* Trans. Justin O'Brien. 4 vols. Urbana: University of Illinois Press, 2000.

Grimm, Ariane. *La Flambe: Journal intime d'une jeune fille.* Paris: P. Belfond, 1987.

Hess, Rémi. *Le Lycée au jour le jour: Ethnographie d'un établissement d'éducation.* Paris: Méridiens Klincksieck, 1989.

Léautaud, Paul. "Journal littéraire." *Mercure de France* 18 (1964): 78–81.

Leiris, Michel. *L'Age d'homme, précédé de "De la littérature considérée comme une tauromachie".* Paris: Gallimard, 1946. *Manhood; preceded by "The Autobiographer as Torero".* Trans. Richard Howard. London: Cape, 1968.

———. *La Règle du jeu.* Vol. 1: *Biffures.* Paris: Gallimard, 1948. Vol. 2: *Fourbis.* Paris: Gallimard, 1961. *Rules of the Game.* Vol. 1: *Scratches.* Trans. Lydia Davis. New York: Paragon House, 1991. Vol. 2: *Scraps.* Trans. Lydia Davis. Baltimore: Johns Hopkins University Press, 1997.

Lejeune, Philippe. [See "Further Works by the Author" for the Lejeune works.]

Lejeune, Xavier-Édouard. *Calicot.* Interviewed by Michel and Philippe Lejeune. Paris: Montalba, 1984.

Lis, Jerzy. "Le Journal d'écrivain: Œuvre d'imagination ou témoignage? Sur le discours préfaciel." *Tangence* 45 (1994): 125–31.

Matzneff, Gabriel. *Journal.* 1976. 2nd ed. Paris: La Table Ronde, 1992.

Mauriac, Claude. *Le Temps immobile.* 11 vols. Paris: Bernard Grasset, 1970–88.

McCarthy, Mary. *Memories of a Catholic Girlhood.* New York: Harcourt Brace Jovanovich, 1957.

Perec, Georges. *Je me souviens.* Paris: Hachette, 1978.

———. *Je suis né.* Paris: Seuil, 1990.

———. *W ou le souvenir d'enfance.* Paris: Denoël, 1975. *W, or, The Memory of Childhood.* Trans. David Bellos. Boston: D. R. Godine, 1988.

Pozzi, Catherine. *Journal, 1913–1934.* Ed. Claire Paulhan. Paris: Ramsay, 1987.

———. *Journal de jeunesse: 1893–1906.* Ed. Claire Paulhan, with Inès Lacroix-Pozzi. Lagrasse: Verdier, 1995.

Ricoeur, Paul. *Temps et récit.* Vol. 3. Paris: Seuil, 1985. *Time and Narrative.* Vol. 3. Trans. Kathleen Blamey and David Pellauer. Chicago: University of Chicago Press, 1988.

Rousseau, Jean-Jacques. *Les Confessions, suivies des Rêveries du promeneur solitaire.* Ed. Francis Bouvet. Paris: J.-J. Pauvert, 1961. *The Confessions and Correspondence.* Ed. Christopher Kelly, Roger D. Masters, and Peter G. Stillman. Trans. Christopher Kelly. Hanover, N.H.: University Press of New England, 1995.

Sarraute, Nathalie. *Enfance.* Paris: Gallimard, 1983. *Childhood.* Trans. Barbara Wright, in consultation with the author. New York: G. Braziller, 1984.

Sartre, Jean-Paul. *Les Carnets de la drôle de guerre, novembre 1939-mars 1940.* Paris: Gallimard, 1983. *War Diaries: Notebooks from a Phoney War, November 1939–March 1940.* Trans. Quintin Hoare. London: Verso, 1984.

———. *Les Mots.* Paris: Gallimard, 1964. *The Words.* Trans. Bernard Frechtman. New York: G. Braziller, 1964. Trans. Irene Clephane. London: H. Hamilton, 1964; London: Penguin, 2000.

Stéphanie, with Philippe Labro. *Des Cornichons au chocolat.* Paris: J. C. Lattès, 1983.

Wolf, Christa. *Kindheitsmuster.* Darmstadt: Luchterhand, 1977. *A Model Childhood.* Trans. Ursule Molinaro and Hedwig Rappolt. New York: Farrar, Straus and Giroux, 1980.

Wolinski. *Le Bécoteur: Journal intime d'un lycéen qui ne pensait qu'à ça.* Paris: P. Belfond, 1984.

Woolf, Virginia. *The Diary of Virginia Woolf,* Vol. 1: *1915–1919.* Ed. Anne Olivier Bell. New York: Harcourt Brace Jovanovich, 1977.

Further Works by the Author

Lejeune, Philippe. *L'Auteur et le manuscrit.* Paris: Presses Universitaires de France, 1991.

———. *L'Autobiographie en France.* Paris: Armand Colin, 1971.

———. "Autobiography in the Third Person." Trans. Annette Tomarken and Edward Tomarken. *New Literary History* 9 (1977): 27–50.

———. "Un Brin de causette: Benda, Léautaud." In *La Conversation: Un Art de l'instant,* ed. Gérald Cahen. *Autrement* 182 (1999): 34–57.

———. *Les Brouillons de soi.* Paris: Seuil, 1998.

———. "Ça s'est fait comme ça." *Poétique* 35 (1978): 269–304.

———. *"Cher Cahier . . .": Témoignages sur le journal personnel.* Paris: Gallimard, 1989.

———. "Comment Anne Frank a réécrit le *Journal* d'Anne Frank." Presentation at the conference "Le journal personnel" (Nanterre, May 19, 1990). In Lejeune's *Les Brouillons de soi,* 331–65. A different version is in *Le Journal personnel,* ed. Philippe Lejeune. Nanterre: Publidix, 1993. 163–179.

———. "Écriture et sexualité." *Europe* 502–503 (February–March 1971): 113–43.

———. "The Genetic Study of Autobiographical Texts." *Biography* 14 (1991): 1–11.

———. "L'Histoire vraie du Journal d'Anne Frank." *La Revue des Livres pour Enfants* 153 (Fall 1993): 47–59.

———. "How Do Diaries End?" Trans. Victoria Lodewick. *Biography* 24 (2001): 99–112.

———. *Je est un autre.* Paris: Seuil, 1980. ("Autobiography in the Third Person," "The Ironic Narrative of Childhood: Vallès," and "The Autobiography of Those Who Do Not Write," translations of essays from this book, appear in Lejeune's *On Autobiography.*)

———. "The 'Journal de Jeune Fille' in Nineteenth-Century France." Trans.

Martine Breillac. In *Inscribing the Daily: Critical Essays on Women's Diaries*, ed. Suzanne L. Bunkers and Cynthia A. Huff. Amherst: University of Massachusetts Press, 1996. 107–22.

———. *Lire Leiris.* Paris: Klincksieck, 1975. ("Epilogue," a translation of one section of this book, appears in Lejeune's *On Autobiography.*)

———. *Lucile Desmoulins: Journal: 1788–1793.* Paris: Éditions des Cendres, 1995.

———. *La Mémoire et l'oblique: Georges Perec autobiographe.* Paris: P.O.L., 1991.

———. *Moi aussi.* Paris: Seuil, 1986. ("Looking at a Self-Portrait," "The Autobiographical Pact (bis)," and "Teaching People to Write Their Life Story," translations of essays from this book, appear in Lejeune's *On Autobiography.*)

———. *Le Moi des demoiselles.* Paris: Seuil, 1993.

———. *On Autobiography.* Ed. Paul John Eakin. Trans. Katherine Leary. Minneapolis: University of Minnesota Press, 1989. (Includes essays from *Le Pacte autobiographique, Je est un autre, Moi aussi, Lire Leiris,* and the *Revue de L'Institut de Sociologie.*)

———. *Le Pacte autobiographique.* Paris: Seuil, 1975. Revised and augmented ed. Paris: Seuil, 1996. ("The Autobiographical Pact," "The Order of Narrative in Sartre's *Les Mots,*" and "Autobiography and Literary History," translations of essays from this book, appear in Lejeune's *On Autobiography.*)

———. *Pour l'autobiographie.* Paris: Seuil, 1998.

———. "The Practice of the Private Journal: Chronicle of an Investigation (1986–1998)." Trans. Russell West. In *Marginal Voices, Marginal Forms: Diaries in European Literature and History,* ed. Rachel Langford and Russell West. Amsterdam: Rodopi, 1999. 185–211.

———. "La Voix de son maître: L'Entretien radiophonique." In Lejeune's *Je est un autre,* 103–60.

———. "*W or The Memory of Childhood.*" Trans. David Bellos. *Review of Contemporary Fiction* 13 (1993): 88–97.

———. "Women and Autobiography at Author's Expense." Trans. Katharine Jensen. *New York Literary Forum* 12–13 (1984): 247–60.

Lejeune, Philippe, and Catherine Viollet, eds. *Autobiographies.* Special issue of *Genesis: Manuscrits, Recherche, Invention* 16 (2001).

———. *Genèses du "je": Manuscrits et autobiographie.* Paris: CNRS, 2000.

Chapter 12

Hypertexts—Memories—Writing

Jean-Louis Lebrave

For nearly thirty years now, Jean-Louis Lebrave has been active in genetic studies. Trained in the 1970s as a linguist and a scholar of Heinrich Heine, he became interested in the potential impact, both practical and theoretical, of computers on genetic problems. He currently directs the Institut des Textes et Manuscrits Modernes and continues to explore topics where genetic studies, computer science, and hypertexts overlap.

"Hypertexts—Memories—Writing" counters the image of genetic criticism as slow philology by illustrating its modernity, theoretical ingenuity, and elasticity. First published in 1994 in the journal *Genesis*, the essay represents one of the first and boldest attempts to wrestle with the problem of how changing technologies of artificial memory and information might involve or influence the ways we preserve and interpret avant-textes of all kinds. Lebrave pursues this general question in the specific context of hypertext theory, a still-evolving field that by 1994 had already been greatly innovative in the areas of information processing, nonsequential thought, and nonlinear writing. By adapting these conceptual developments and their associated descriptive terms to specific genetic dossiers, he builds the thesis that advances in writing technology naturally generate new theoretical perspectives, perspectives that can retrospectively illuminate key episodes in the history of writing. If hypertexts signal the end of dominance for certain kinds of linearity in reading, writing, and remembering, then the interpretive consequences and opportunities proper to a postlinear, postbook textual era, Lebrave argues, might help us model the notoriously nonlinear genetics of writing.

The two authors he selects as examples, Pascal and Stendhal, could not be more different. Nor, precisely, could they better illustrate the idea that hypertext theory is expansive and supple enough to offer real analytical power to geneticists.

Lebrave suggests that some basic questions about the nature of Pascal's works have been awaiting the arrival of hypertext to be properly resolved. The links of ideas and language that exist in a virtual way among the fragments of the *Pensées,* for example, can be understood to be those of a 300-year-old hypertext prototype. In fact, admirers would not be driven to make excessive claims about authors' memories in order to preserve the integrity of famous texts if they did not adhere to obsolete ideas of textual integrity and memory in the first place. As Lebrave suggests, when we better understand the nonsequential, nonhierarchical methods of information processing that characterize hypertexts, we will naturally wish to update the critical premises that for a long time have falsely framed, and limited, our genetic accounts and analyses of books like the *Pensées.*

If Pascal's work invites us to draw metaphors from hypertext theory to describe it, then Stendhal's, we learn, was thoroughly hypertextual from start to finish. Lebrave shows how Stendhal's habits of reading, writing, and communicating—through books, journal entries, letters, notes, and other less classifiable texts—constantly exploded the conceptions that ruled writing during the age of the book. The draft histories for the canonical Stendhal works may be very few, but the virtual links among all his texts are infinite.

Hypertext: A New Space of Writing

In the 1960s, Ted Nelson introduced the computer-science concept of "hypertext."[1] Even before that, at the very dawn of the computer age, Vannevar Bush thought of creating a system named "Memex," an interactive library or encyclopedia that would allow the reader to show two texts on a screen and create links between selected passages in them. The system Bush imagined would have stored these links in such a way that they could later be shown or modified on the screen. Yet these early plans remained just plans until the 1980s, when micro-computer technology allowed for the real development of systems abstractly envisioned in the 1960s. Hypertext then developed spectacularly and made important contributions in the humanities, especially in the United States.

From the perspective of computer science, hypertext is

> a system to manage a collection of information that can be accessed nonsequentially. It consists of a network of nodes and logical links between nodes. (Lucarella 81)

The nodes contain information of various kinds: whole texts, paragraphs, sentences, isolated words, and also numbered images and sounds (in which case one uses the term "hypermedia"). In a generic sense, the term "document" is used to designate entities composed in this way. A hypertext is thus a network, a set of dynamically linked documents among which paths may be created and followed.

For its user, a hypertext will appear concretely in the form of a text shown in a window on a computer screen. Certain elements on the screen have a graphic character, a typographic marking or icon, that signals to the reader that another document is attached to that portion of text. By activating the graphic signal (that is, by pressing metaphorically a button with the help of the mouse), one opens a new window in which a second document appears. This window, in turn, can also contain graphic signals and buttons that give access to a third document, which can also . . . There is no limit to this chain of attached documents, and so, as Jay David Bolter writes, the reader moves inside "a space of paragraphs" (*Writing Space* 15) and no longer, as in a standard text, in the one-dimensional space of printed lines.

This simplified presentation is enough to show that hypertext constitutes a new space for written texts and for writing. What are its physical characteristics? How is this new space different from earlier spaces?

A book qua container is an assembly of pages placed in a row in a fixed order, isolated from the surrounding world by a binding that makes it a singular, tangible object with a visible material presence. This full presence of the material object is obviously absent in hypertext, which for its user appears in the fragmentary form of windows on a screen. The contents of the windows correspond to places inside an electronic memory, where they are identified by an "address," to which one gains access through a link that is nothing but an instruction of the type "go to the following designated address." Of course, we find the equivalent of such links in the space of books when, for example, a note refers the reader to another part of the text, in the form of an "instruction" of the type "Cf. p. #." But in books, the referring instruction is secondary with respect to the passage's place in the sequential order of the text. In an electronic document, on the contrary, it is the address that becomes fundamental, the linear sequence being only the result of a particular arrangement of links.

This is to say that the memory zones storing the materials do not constitute a linear, ordered "text." A "text," as a sequence, is defined by the succession of links that allow for the passage from one zone to another. It suffices to modify the order of the links to modify the order of the reading, and thus the order of the text as it is read.

Thanks to this flexibility, hypertext can present not only the electronic equivalent of books—pages are metaphorically turned as successive screens—but also of groups of books, bundles of loose sheets, and notebooks like the ones writers use in preparatory phases of work.

It should be added that the size of neither a zone nor the whole is fixed in advance: one can always introduce a new link referring to another document. Similarly, one can treat a zone globally, as a unique entity, or assume that it constitutes all by itself a network of distinct places that specific links assemble through a series of indicators.

As a final characteristic, hypertext, like all technologies of electronic writing, offers a malleable medium that can be reinscribed at will. This radically distinguishes it from all spaces that make of writing a fixed and definitive product such as a roll of papyrus, a medieval manuscript, or a printed book. In fact, the immaterial mobility of the electronic medium brings it closer to ephemeral writing media, for example, a wax tablet or a messy, overwritten page from a genetic dossier.

The physical characteristics of writing spaces have an impact on the activity of writing itself, its products, and its abstract characteristics. How does this work in hypertext?

No longer stored in a medium in a linear way, hypertext is a "nonsequential writing" (Ted Nelson quoted in Slatin 160) that allows the written material to escape from the necessarily linear order that previous media had imposed upon it. Because of this, reading itself becomes "a discontinuous or non-linear process which, like thinking, is associative in nature, as opposed to the sequential process envisioned by conventional text" (Slatin 158).

Hypertext is both nonlinear and nonhierarchical. It disrupts the classifications that we use for literary and other intellectual works and relativizes the hierarchy that makes us privilege a canonical group of "great texts" at the expense of all other books. Hypertext puts *auctoritas* into question, relativizing the fixed nature of the text and destabilizing the position of the author.[2]

More generally, the conceptual space of hypertext invites us to conceive of documents in a *granular* manner. In this case, any document can be considered on two levels and according to two points of view. As an entity, it constitutes an elementary "grain" or "block" that joins with other grains to form a higher-order entity. Yet one can also understand it to be the result of a composition of smaller blocks. For example, a text can be seen as an assembly of chapters, paragraphs, phrases, or even words.

The first of these viewpoints can be illustrated by two well-known structures in book space. The *library* is the material realization of a higher-order entity whose elementary grains, blocks, or atoms are constituted by each of its books. The user of a direct-access library accomplishes in physical trips through the aisles what the hypertext user accomplishes in paths through the immaterial substance of electronic documents. Indeed, one can push the comparison further: the library is also composed of two spaces of complementary memory. There are the shelves where the books are kept and also the catalogue, which contains the call numbers of the books, that is, their library addresses. The user can journey through the library by directly walking in the aisles, exploring sequentially the physical space of the stacks, or by first consulting the catalogue, whose call numbers "link up" with the placement of the books being sought. Conversely, the *encyclopedia,* whose ambition is to unite in one book all the knowledge dispersed in all books, metaphorically offers to its reader the same navigation through textual space that the library allows physically. Here the articles and their parts constitute the grains of the higher-order entity. It is therefore not surprising that among the first commercial hypertext products were electronic encyclopedias and that Ted Nelson, the father of hypertext, conceived of the Xanadu project, a gigantic project for a universal electronic library.

"Outline processors" offer a very striking illustration of the second viewpoint. As we know, tools have been designed and are available in most word-processing software that allow us to change the order of, and links between, sections of text. By varying the granularity of the textual objects we manipulate, we can write, in sequential manner, a series of textual fragments and then treat them as unitary symbols and modify both their own linkage and the hierarchy that subordinates them to each other. In this way, one can "write with those symbols, just as . . . one writes with words" (Bolter, *Writing Space* 17).

Finally, the grains or blocks that constitute a hypertext are characterizable by their strong *connectivity*; this permits

> linking together discrete *blocks* . . . to form *webs* of information, following different paths through the information webs, and attaching annotations (special types of links) to any block of information. (Yankelovich 61)

Of course—and the etymology of the word *text* is explicit—far from being specific to electronic writing, this weaving of links between meaningful elements is constitutive of all linguistic production. But in a printed work the connectivity is a prisoner of the sequential chain and the hierarchical order. Transversal links generally remain implicit and must be (re)constituted by the reader.[3] By contrast, hypertext allows for the elucidation, multiplication, and diversification of links. As Bolter writes, "the texture of the text becomes thicker" ("Topographic Writing" 111).

One can briefly summarize all the characteristics enumerated above by defining hypertext as a *dynamic network* with the following qualities: nonlinearity, nonhierarchy, granularity, connectivity, and variability.

From Hypertext to Book: Pascal's *Pensées*

With hypertext the whole history of books and writing appears in a new light. Three aspects can be recalled here: the place of writing among different forms of artificial memory, the evolution of reading practices and of relationships between the author, text, and reader, and the affinities between hypertext and the sphere of textual production.

As Bolter points out, hypertext is the point that a long history of artificial memory reaches. Ultimately, in this history, the constraints and new possibilities concomitant with successive writing media caused the techniques of memorization associated with orality to fall into oblivion. By paralleling oral poetry or antique rhetoric with the space of writing—from papyrus to electronic space—Bolter means to illustrate the solidarity between the cultural and social practices of reading, the conceptual systems that articulate these practices, and the technological systems that make everything possible. From this point of view, the practices of artificial memory that hypertext introduces diverge from the standard models offered by the universe of writing in its most advanced form. It is also true that hypertext gives new life to technologies that printing seemed to have relegated to the background: the mnemotechnics inseparable from oral poetry; the techniques of memorization transmitted by the arts of memory; and all the processes at work in the production of text.

The effects of hypertext are particularly clear in the various relations between the *author*, the *text* and the *reader*. In the universe of the book, writing has a tendency

> to magnify the distance between the author and the reader, as the author became a monumental figure, the reader only a visitor in the author's cathedral. (Bolter, *Writing Space* 3)

But, in interactive hypertext "the sharp division between author and reader . . . has begun to blur" (Landow 29), and hypertext constitutes "an open-ended structure of knowledge that readers continually extend and re-organize" (Landow and Delany 33). Reading becomes a dynamic activity in which the reader participates in the process of producing the object. Readers can create their own paths through a hypertext by choosing how to circulate in the network. They can also create an original "hyperobject" inside the hypertext by exploiting the property of granularity and creating their own links. Lastly, they can add new blocks that will immediately form part of the textual base. Thus hypertext considerably facilitates the appropriation of text by its readers, so much so that as a technological apparatus one might say it constitutes something like a concrete instance of the propositions advanced by reception-theorists.[4]

Finally, hypertext brings the specificity of practices proper to written production to the fore. This subject is generally not broached in the literature on hypertext. We will see, however, that the writing practices revealed by genetic documents anticipate the function of hypertexts in such a way that one can discover the full richness of hypertext only when both sides (production and reading) are taken into account.

We know that hypertext technology is contemporary with reflections that in literary theory question the canonical model centered on the author and the work. Structuralist textual theorists attacked such ideas as author, text, work, and writing at exactly the moment when, in a totally independent manner, the information revolution was happening and before anyone knew how to make the machines that would permit the futurist utopias to become reality. Looking for precursors or ancestors, Bolter and George Landow put forward precisely those creators whose work accompanied the European theoretical reflection of the 1960s, for example, Sterne, the German Romantics, Joyce, and Borges. Beyond this, does one not feel, in the conclusion that Gérard Genette gives to his 1982 book, the same wind blowing that inspired Ted Nelson's Xanadu project?

> a Literature in a perpetual state of transfusion, a transtextual perfusion, constantly present to itself in its totality and as a Totality all of whose authors are but one and all its books one vast, one infinite Book. Hypertextuality is only one name for that ceaseless circulation of texts without which literature would not be worth one hour of exertion. (*Palimpsests* 400)

More precisely, the notion of *transtextuality*, by which Genette designates "all that sets the text in a relationship, whether obvious or concealed, with other texts" (1), is very near to the hypertext of computer scientists. Most of the transtextual relationships analyzed by Genette are presented in hypertext, whether as "intertext," which refers to the copresence in two or more texts; as "paratext," which creates with its procession of accompanying texts something like a hypertextual halo around the text; as "metatext," a commentary that unites a text with another text about which it speaks; or as "architext," which for Genette designates the general or transcendental categories in which each individual text belongs. It is worth noting that in the terminological and conceptual paradigm constructed upon the root "text," the notion the furthest from computer-science hypertext and therefore the most misleading is certainly "hypertext," which Genette defines as "any text derived from a previous text either through simple . . . or through indirect transformation, which I shall label imitation" (14). In its computer-science meaning, hypertext covers all the transtextual relationships described by Genette: in particular, hypertext and hypotext in the latter sense constitute only fragments of a computer-scientific hypertext.[5]

To give substance to the preceding analyses, one could not dream of a better example than Pascal's *Pensées*. It is a perfect illustration of (1) the contingency of the gap between "reception" and "production," (2) the fragility of every idea developed from *auctoritas* and symbolized in the universe of the book by the "passed for press" [*bon à tirer*] form signed by the author, and (3) the fruitfulness of a hypertextual approach to texts.

Here is a work, as Victor Cousin said, whose manuscripts are in the Bibliothèque Nationale and whose author everybody knows. The patent gap between these manuscripts and this work continues, however, to feed polemics.[6] The problem is that, when it was time, at Pascal's death, to publish the book that was his greatest work, instead of the expected "perfect book," his relatives found only, in the words of Étienne Périer, bundles grouped "in no particular order" and "with no conclusion," "the first expressions of his thoughts," placed on "the first piece of paper that came his way." "And all this was so imperfect and so badly written, that it took all the effort in the world to decode" (Périer 65–68).

This recognition raises two questions linked to the problem of hypertext. The first deals with the relationship between natural memory and the "technologies" of artificial memory, whether its medium is the brain itself,[7] paper, or, since the information revolution, the various electronic media. To escape from the intense disappointment caused by decoding the *Pensées* manuscript, Périer attempts to convince his reader both of the perfection of the work conceived by Pascal, such as he had it "printed in his mind" (40) thanks to his "excellent and one might even say prodigious" memory, and of the necessary imperfection of the fragments that constitute the manuscript of the *Pensées*. To hear Périer, Pascal's memory was so extraordinary that "he did not fear that the thoughts which had come to him could ever escape, and that is why he so often put off writing them down" (40–41). Thus Périer is able to affirm:

> everything was so engraved in his mind and in his memory, that having neglected to write it down when he could have, he found himself, when he wished to do so, in a state of not being able to work on it at all. (41–42)

In this paradoxical situation in which Pascal is betrayed by his memory,

> when some new thoughts, new views, new ideas came to him, or even some turn of phrase and some expressions that he foresaw one day being of use in his project, as he was not then in a state of being able to apply himself as hard as he had when he was well, nor to print them in his mind and in his memory, he preferred to write something down so as not to forget. (64)

How can we understand the coexistence between this prodigious memory and the memory-relay that writing offers, by substitution, when sickness renders the former weak? The very terms Périer employs—prodigious memory, order, engraving, impression—irresistibly evoke the arts of memory to which Frances Yates devoted her book; and it is tempting to suppose that Pascal's memory was one of these artificially trained memories in the mythic line of memory professionals, this family of minds that runs from Simonides of Ceos, "inventor" of the art of memory, to Saint Thomas Aquinas, passing through Charmadas, Metrodorus, Seneca the Rhetor, to Simplicius, the friend of Saint Augustine, who could recite Vergil backwards (Yates 1–26). Illness, then, and death would therefore have stopped Pascal from transferring to the artificial medium the work that he had printed in his living memory. This would mean that Pascal lost both "the greater part of what he had already conceived of his project" and notably, as Périer emphasizes, the "reasons," the "foundations," and the "order" of his work. The only vestige of the whole edifice, then, is the memory of the report that Pascal was "required" to make in front of "several very important people" and about which, because he had not "written down what he had in mind on the subject," he had "to say something . . . aloud" (Périer 42).

In Yates's presentation, the earliest technology of artificial memory, the art of memory, naturally recalls the newer form of memory technology represented by hypertext. It too has recourse to an immaterial medium since the places and the images that serve as a medium for memorizing content are themselves memorized in the very mind of whomever has stored them. Moreover, it allows one to build a dynamic network associating various "documents" and to put into place a veritable system of *navigation* inside a collection of blocks of information because it suffices to rearrange the places and the images they contain to produce another discourse.

Unfortunately, in the case of *Pensées,* only one portion of the "grains" of the hypertext has been preserved: scattered thoughts stripped of the very links that gave them sequentiality and coherence. These thoughts have been detached from the principle of navigation that would permit them to be read, a principle lost forever along with the mind in which it had been engraved.

This irremediable loss raises a second question: what to do with Pascal's manuscript? "How to name it? Under what title to print it as a work? How to write, or rewrite, it to offer it to be read?" (Marin 11). In his Preface to Pascal's *Pensées,* Périer suggested several ways (42). The first was to print the writings "in the same state that they were found." But in so doing, one would give only fragments of a glimpsed work, which would then become "a confused mass, without order, without development, and which would serve nothing." A farrago of "grains" or "blocks" mixed with "the most perfect thoughts, the most developed, most clear and extended," along with others, "half-digested, and a few nearly unintelligible to anyone except he who had written them." No finished work, therefore, and no author. The second solution consisted of writing the work that Pascal hadn't had the leisure to write and to "supply somehow the work that he had wanted" to produce. Yet Périer remarks right away "that this would not have been producing the work of Mr. Pascal, but an entirely different work." A work, this time, and an author, but not the author Pascal.

Périer then explains that Port-Royal opted for a third solution.[8] They performed a double work upon the fragments. First, they eliminated some of them, retaining only the "clearest and the most finished" thoughts and rejecting those "either too obscure or too imperfect." Because Pascal wrote these last fragments "only for himself," they were at most useful as memory aids to his relatives, for they had "heard them spoken from his mouth." The task therefore was to normalize the written trace as a function of the supposed capacities of an external readership. Those fragments that are only artificial memory images were eliminated because they refer to a memory system other than that of a written document with public diffusion. Only those fragments susceptible of being meaningful in and of themselves were kept, that is, those independent of both the writer who produced them and the people close to him.

Along with selecting the thoughts, Port-Royal "put them in some sort of order, and put the ones dealing with the same subjects under the same headings" (Périer 73–74). The disorder of the manuscripts visibly signals the disappearance of the ordering principle engraved in Pascal's mind; thus this second normalization proceeds like an "idea processor" to efface the traces of this lack and to introduce the coherence of a hierarchical structure that groups the "grains" of information together in common unitary rubrics.

The work is thus hybrid and imperfect, but it exists. The work done by the first readers of Pascal's manuscript aimed to be faithful and therefore insignificant and invisible to readers of the published work. As if to reinforce this autonomy of the *Pensées*, Port-Royal even gave this work an author, whose life is recounted by Pascal's sister Gilberte Périer. When she painted an edifying portrait of her brother, she lifted the veil over the private life of Pascal a little, but she also transmuted it all the more into an example and an object of imitation. Essentially, it was a way of conjuring the writer and his private work space, while making every trace of the process of production itself disappear.

At the end of this double reduction—minimization of the work of production effected by relatives, recovering of the space of private production by the publicity of an edifying biography—the *Pensées* have become one of these Parmenidean "perfect works" of which Gilbert Romeyer-Dherbey speaks, a work that "refers only to itself and forgets its genesis."[9]

Let us summarize. At the heart of the canonical list of "great authors" of French literature, the *Pensées* presents the strangeness of a cultural product and defies description according to classical criteria of reception. For over three centuries, this object has combined the traces of an interrupted production process with the results of a collective manipulation of these traces. On the one hand, there are the manuscripts. These are the imperfect, fragmentary, private traces (as Étienne Périer recalls, "he wrote only for himself"), in which one recognizes the hand of a writer also known as the author of other works. On the other hand, there is the result of a reading, explicitly produced by a process of reception—the speech whose contents are reported by Périer—attributed to the author Pascal, labeled, and offered to posterity as a truthful product.

The contradiction between these two sides will be a source of endless polemics: no matter how punctilious "philological" accuracy may be, it cannot transform the manuscripts into something they are not. The work is forever missing: all publication is necessarily falsification because it fills in gaps, constructs hypotheses, and grafts onto veritable traces the results of another production process in which Pascal himself had no part.

We find ourselves in the presence of a double hypertext. The first is made up of the lost totality of Pascal's "design," the project printed in his mind, and the manuscript fragments of *Pensées.* This private hypertext is inscribed in the space of *production*; it is part and parcel of the man who engraved it in his memory and partially transcribed it on paper. Reduced to fragments, this totality has been stripped of its principle of intelligibility. Grains of hypertext are nothing without the links that unite them, for links alone transform jumbled textual fragments into dynamic, meaningful networks.

The manuscript fragments, together with the various "works" elaborated from them since Pascal's death, form a second hypertext in which concurrent paths are proposed inside each manuscript grain and systems of intelligibility are implied in the links and hierarchies. In contrast to the first, this hypertext is situated entirely in the space of *reception*; its different grains each claim the status of a work and refer to a canonized author in the pantheon of French literature. Confronting the manuscript traces raises insurmountable difficulties for this logic of author and work since in reality the work does not exist any more than the author to whom it is attributed. All we have are the manuscript traces of an unfinished process of production.

All this becomes clearer, however, if these two hypertexts, artificially separated by authorial logic, are united and if we understand production and reception as processes, recognizing legitimacy in each. Indeed, from this perspective, hypertext constitutes a space of writing in the fullest sense of the term: it produces both writings and readings.

From Book to Hypertext: Stendhal and Books

Ever since enunciative space was sharply divided by writing into a system of differing/deferred [*différée*] communication, the spaces of production and reception have been two worlds that communicate only through the depthless interface of the medium itself. While the medieval codex opened its margins to the writing of the reader and to the appropriation of the text by the commentary, with the printed word writing became intangible, a space of traces in which it was forbidden to write. Not surprisingly then, it was in the domain of the reception of works that theorists of hypertext first sought to situate the hypertextual revolution. Theirs was an effort, in particular from a pedagogical perspective, to tear reading from passivity and give back the initiative to the reader. However, the other side of enunciation—production—long relegated by all-powerful print to an unknowable shadow, may furnish an even richer terrain of investigation.

Critics have often insisted upon the radical heterogeneity between the written traces of genetic manuscripts and the works that generally result from them. Whether through the problematic of incompletion, the criticism of the teleological illusion, or the demonstration of the failure of critical editions inspired by pure philology, genetic criticism continues to return to the impossibility of pouring the genetic manuscripts into the rigid mold of linear and hierarchized works. At the heart of these demonstrations we find the direct confrontation with the manuscript itself, its "reading." I have shown that what we designate in this way refers in fact to a process quite different from that which takes place in the reading of a linear text ("Lecture et analyse des brouillons"). Someone who "reads" a genetic manuscript juxtaposes moments of reading in the normal sense of the word with phases of analysis and interpretation of graphic traces. Geneticists' eyes are obliged to deconstruct the space ruled by lines, blank space, and pages. They mourn the familiar linearity, for they are forced to use uncommon gymnastics to put the disjointed textual fragments into some kind of relationship. Yet because the fragmenting activity explodes both in the space of the page and transversally over series of pages, every attempt to give a description trips over some excess or another. This is true of notebooks, which materially reproduce the form of the book-object, but which writer-owners, unaware of the logic of the codex, use and fill up with the disorder of capricious writing. It is also true of loose sheets; since writers use them in every sense and dimension, analysts must indefatigably reshuffle them in the attempt to recreate the trace of multiple, partial, and usually contradictory sequences.

Although writers usually succeed in subordinating the movement of writing to the production of a work, genetic manuscripts are everywhere invested with the fundamental antagonism between the logics of production and print. It would be easy to list examples of these hypertextual practices, from Hugo's notebooks, albums, journals, and daily planners to Benjamin's manuscripts for the *Passagen-Werk*, to the notebooks of *Bouvard et Pécuchet*, to Perec's envelopes for the project of *Lieux*, to Winckelmann's and Valéry's manuscripts. Lacking space, I will limit myself to one case whose very singularity illustrates the fruitfulness of a hypertextual approach to genesis. Geneticists have long known of this case because of the notorious difficulty they have in accounting for it. It is Stendhal, whose manuscripts without erasures present a challenge to genetic criticism.[10]

From the point of view of memory technologies, Stendhal is the antithesis of Pascal: "I have no memory" he writes in his diary on February 4, 1813 (quoted in Jacquelot 37). Contrary to Pascal, Stendhal felt the need to note everything that came to mind and to store it on paper. When he was young, he used little hand-sewn notebooks for this purpose:

> When I need thoughts for a competition at the Institute, a discourse, or a preface, I must look for them in my notebooks. That is where I go shopping. (Jacquelot 16; August 22, 1804)

He then proceeded in two ways, first noting his thoughts "on little bits of paper" (17; August 9, 1803) and then copying the notes into his workbook and developing them. As time went on, this "literary" diary that accumulated thoughts inspired by reading was superseded by the book margins he filled in directly (32). Not surprisingly, when his books were bound, he asked that the "margins be cut as little as possible" (25). Starting in 1813, for example, he used a six-volume *Molière* as a diary in which to note his reflections and commentaries (26, 33). To help him pick up the threads of his own annotations, he devised, on the covers and flyleaves of these books, a kind of personal index to organize any annotated or interesting passages. This list in turn sometimes served as a point of departure for new readings.

Understood as an activity inside the space of the page, the Stendhalian use of marginal annotations renews the practice of medieval copyists, for whom the margins surrounding the text constituted a space of gloss and commentary. In this way Stendhal's practice again put into question the frontiers that print established between written spaces and spaces meant for writing, between the space reserved for passive reading and the space of active writing. The page became a physical space of dialogue once more.

How did Stendhal's "shops" function? The notes were not so much the substitute for a "terrible memory" (quoted in Neefs, "Stendhal, sans fins" 20) as the traces of a process of appropriation destined from the outset to be taken up again and prolonged. In the way he wrote down the circumstances of reading—for example. "Noon, 31 July 1804, [*12 th[ermid]or XII*][11] very sunny, moderate warmth" (Jacquelot 20; July 31, 1804)—Stendhal reconstructed immediately the situation in which the preceding reading had been done: in this way, then, the marginal annotations referred simultaneously to the text read and to the mental state of the reader (Stendhal) at the time of reading. This double marking designated both the physical space of the book and the mental space of the reader:

> The least comment in the margins means that if I ever reread this book, I take up again the thread of my ideas and *continue forward.* If I find no such memories in rereading a book, then all my effort must be done again. (75)

For Stendhal the printed text and the accompanying margins were diversified and easily locatable places in which memory-jogging images could be deposited: everything passed through written traces and the physical spaces of their inscription. Moreover, Stendhal's annotated books became an external projection of the "places" and "images" that served as basic tools for memorization in the technology of the arts of memory.

This means that Stendhal's practice conferred upon writing a function that transcended the simple recoding of an oral message by a system of arbitrary and unmotivated signs. Stendhal's taste for abbreviations and "coded" annotations further attests to this complexification of writing functions. As the text became an image it took on an iconic function, and this graphic enrichment of writing transformed it into an assembly of signals that, as in an electronic hypertext, materialized links and chart paths.

Stendhal's practice of memorization not only subverts the printed space of the page, it also affects the book in its entirety, inasmuch as it is an assemblage of folded sheets joined and sewn together. We know that until the beginning of the nineteenth century books were sold with a cover that was really "a provisional wrapping until the book could be bound" (Toulet 935). Stendhal therefore had his books bound, and he took advantage of this procedure to disrupt the univocal relationship between the work and the physical object that the bound book constituted by linking several works or fragments of works together. For example, in 1808, after having annotated and commented upon Crébillon's *Rhadomiste et Zénobie* and Corneille's *Les Horaces,* Stendhal had them bound with other plays at the end of the eighth volume of the works of Saint-Simon (Jacquelot 26). In the same way, he "stuffed" the volumes of

Montesquieu's *Esprit des Lois* with fragments of the first volume of Rousseau's *Nouvelle Héloïse* (73). The binding was therefore not the material delimitation of a single book. Rather, it enclosed something like a portable library, so that the book-object lost its homogeneity (a book containing the work of an author) to the benefit of a new *granularity* (a book formed by assembling various documents whose grouping is meaningful for a reader).

There is more. Taking advantage of the binding procedure, Stendhal inserted things—one is tempted to say shamelessly, in any case, without respect for the printed book—in the books he was reading. He included some groups of blank pages (to be filled with his personal annotations) but also some documents apparently irrelevant to the work. At the end of the first volume of William Coxe's *History of the House of Austria*, for example, one finds "the original of a letter addressed to Matilde, a text on love, a text on women and a sketch on the regulation of duels" (75). Or again, after having asked his friend Mareste to reread, with pen in hand, his own *Rome, Naples et Florence,* he copied his friend's observations and inserted them at the end of his copy of La Fontaine's *Fables* (95). In short, in the same way that he took over the margins of pages he appropriated the whole of the book, and transformed it into a hybrid object in which textual objects of heterogeneous status, printed traces and manuscript traces, were all mixed. It became an anthology of various texts and memories, the journeys of his own imagination. Indeed, was it anything but a paper hypertext?

The hypertextuality of Stendhal's writing practice is without doubt even more obvious in the use he made of his own works as they were printed. There we see that his heterodoxy with regard to the printed text not only concerned his personal position as reader and writer, but also raised the more general problem of the status of the published work and the relationships between author, work, and readers. Immediately after the publication of *Armance,* Stendhal asked that a copy of the novel be bound "with a blank sheet between each printed sheet." He acquired the habit of making copies of his works in which blank pages were interspersed between printed sheets, giving these copies to his friends so that they might note their remarks and commentaries (97). These copies combined printing and manuscript annotation, work and commentary, and the writing-reading of the writer and a few privileged readers. With this method Stendhal circulated *L'Abbesse de Castro, Vittoria Accoramboni, Les Cenci, Promenades dans Rome, Le Rouge et le noir, Mémoires d'un touriste,* and *La Chartreuse de Parme.*

Thus, the work had hardly seen print before Stendhal stopped it from "leaping about in the world, no longer needing its father" (Romeyer-Dherbey 184)—the normal condition of public objects circulating independently of their authors. Restricting the stock of books in circulation, Stendhal abolished the frontier between the public space of reading and the private space of writing. In a single gesture, Stendhal tried to prepare for a new edition of his work and to establish a network of privileged readers—the "happy few" who were invited to adopt the same productive mode of reading-writing as the author himself.[12]

Thus Stendhal followed the rules of publication and trusted an editor to send his work to the public.[13] Yet at the same time, he was nearly indifferent to the public life of his work—or else he was resigned from the start to the incomprehension of his anonymous, contemporary readers—and he canceled the gesture of anonymous circulation by isolating a few copies for private circulation. In this way, he created a network of collective objects that were all different despite their common origin. This network manifested all the characteristics of a computer-science hypertext. His practice of interspersing blank sheets and encouraging free annotation created a nonlinear and nonhierarchical whole marked by a variable granularity in which each grain manifested a strong connectivity and a permanent variability and instability.[14]

Editing Genetic Documents?

Beginning with electronic memory, this trek through artificial memories has shown that there exists a profound solidarity between the ancient art of memory and certain writing practices but that these activities with common origins diverge sharply from standard uses of writing. There is a great similitude between memorization technologies that work by directly engraving places and images in the medium of the mind and forms of writing in which the written space functions as a projected place for the writer's individual mental activity and the social activity of appropriating the written. In the latter case, writing is much more than a simple medium playing the role of memory's external extension. It is both a trace on a medium *and* a process producing this trace. The examples of Pascal and Stendhal give the full dimension of electronic hypertext in this sense.

In the case of the *Pensées* manuscripts, the projection remains partial because in death Pascal took the essential part of the printed hypertext with him in his mind, leaving only a "confused mass" of scattered grains on paper. As a projection of a collective reading-writing it is also biased since Pascal's first readers managed to produce a work only by investing the remaining space with an impossible reading. The manuscript fragments of the *Pensées* had been stripped of the network that gave them meaning. By contrast, with Stendhal the projection is total and fully achieved. The annotated books and manuscripts became a welcoming space for the author's own mental activity and for the reading-writing of those nearest to him. Surrounded by his books, Stendhal likened himself to the silkworm stuffed with mulberry leaves who had only to "climb up somewhere and make himself a prison of some silk" (Jacquelot 81). In this identification, we perceive the extent to which Stendhal's books and productive imagination formed a singular cocoon inside of which the mind's pathmaking was mixed up with pathmaking in book space. This "externalization" of mental functioning is peaking—provisionally—in electronic hypertext, which more than any other artificial medium corresponds to the functioning of human memory.

Through this projection of the mind into an exterior space, the problem of artificial memory is raising fundamental questions concerning the relationship between media and written works, between the activity of creation and its material trace, and between the functioning of the mind and the technical apparatuses that simulate or bear witness to it.

By separating the message from the here and now of the actual speech situation, the development of writing allowed for the existence of autonomous objects that could then escape from oblivion and enter into multiple circulatory circuits. By physical necessity these discrete and self-contained objects offer themselves to their readers as detached from whomever has produced them, and they appear as homogeneous, coherent, and finished units bearing no direct relation to the mental process in which they originated.

Genetic documents illustrate how little the "natural" functioning of the mind relates to the linear, sequential, and detached mode that characterizes standard writing. All the critical work on the beginnings of texts (*les incipit*; see Boie and Ferrer, *Genèses du roman contemporain*) demonstrates that many writers undergo periods of tension, sometimes extreme, before their "writing" becomes "writing for a work," or before the creative process succeeds in conforming to the logic of qualities classically attributed to texts: uniqueness, stability, cohesion, coherence, and finitude. In symmetrical fashion, the principal difficulty one meets in the study of manuscripts is precisely the teleological model of the work, which constantly obfuscates the analysis of manuscript traces and befogs our understanding of the production process. At the same time, no matter their manuscript, geneticists find themselves more or less in the same situation as those doing research on Pascal since written traces are merely a succession of instants inside of a mental process whose essence quantitatively eludes us.

From its inception, genetic criticism has been confronted with a series of challenges that some deem insuperable: to infer an overall mental functioning based on incomplete traces, to resist the temptation to reduce manuscript traces to mere "writing for a work," and nonetheless to take into account in analysis the existence of this work and the links it maintains with the process that originated it.

The preceding hypertextual journey shows that these difficulties are not insurmountable as long as we admit that the conceptual split that seems natural to us to make inside the space of writing is only the reflection of a given state of the technology of artificial memory, that is, the printed word. Hypertext, by contrast, blocks the written word from ever freezing in its trace. By reintroducing the function of living memory, it allows for a complete renewal of the practices of writing and reading: it brings an appropriate tool to describe, analyze, and visualize the totality generally resulting from the manuscripts and the work done on them. It will therefore lend itself to grasping the state of the *Pensées* manuscript fragments. (The burden will be on whomever uses hypertext to explore the paths that these fragments authorize, to compare them with the editions that have been constructed on their basis since Pascal's death and to attempt to reconstruct Pascal's great aim by enriching the fragmentary apparatus.) Hypertext will welcome just as easily, too, the paper hypertexts invented by Stendhal, the "eternal renewal" and unfinishedness of Maine de Biran, all writers who remain prisoners of the "desire never to finish," and the derision of *Bouvard et Pécuchet*'s unachievable encyclopedism.

Source: "Hypertextes—Mémoires—Écriture." *Genesis* 5 (1994): 9–24.

Works Cited

Boie, Bernhild, and Daniel Ferrer, eds. *Genèses du roman contemporain: Incipit et entrée en écriture.* Paris: CNRS, 1993.

Bolter, Jay David. "Topographic Writing: Hypertext and the Electronic Writing Space." In Delany and Landow, *Hypermedia and Literary Studies,* 105–18.

———. *Writing Space: The Computer, Hypertext, and the History of Writing.* Hillsdale, N.J.: Lawrence Erlbaum, 1991.

Bush, Vannevar. "As We May Think." *Atlantic Monthly* 176 (July 1945): 641–49. In *From Memex to Hypertext: Vannevar Bush and the Mind's Machine,* ed. James M. Nyce and Paul Kahn. San Diego: Academic Press, 1991. 85–110.

Contat, Michel. "Pascal: Pensées ou Discours? Autour d'une nouvelle édition procurée par Emmanuel Martineau." *Genesis* 3 (1993): 135–42.

Delany, Paul, and George P. Landow, eds. *Hypermedia and Literary Studies.* Cambridge, Mass.: MIT Press, 1991.

Genette, Gérard. *Palimpsestes: La Littérature au second degré.* Paris: Seuil, 1982. *Palimpsests: Literature in the Second Degree.* Trans. Channa Newman and Claude Doubinsky. Lincoln: University of Nebraska Press, 1997.

Jacquelot, Hélène de. *Stendhal: Marginalia e scrittura.* Rome: Edizioni di storia e letteratura, 1991.

Landow, George P., and Paul Delany. "Hypertext, Hypermedia and Literary Studies: The State of the Art." In Delany and Landow, *Hypermedia and Literary Studies,* 3–50.

Laufer, Roger, and Dominique Scavetta. *Texte, hypertexte, hypermédia.* Paris: Presses Universitaires de France, 1992.

Lebrave, Jean-Louis. "Lecture et analyse des brouillons." In *Manuscrits-Écriture, production linguistique,* ed. Almuth Grésillon and Jean-Louis Lebrave. Special issue of *Langages* 69 (1983): 11–24.

Lucarella, Dario. "A Model for Hypertext-Based Information Retrieval." In *Hypertext: Concepts, Systems and Applications,* ed. Norbert Streitz, Antoine Rizk, and Jacques André. Cambridge: Cambridge University Press, 1990.

Marin, Louis. "L'Écriture fragmentaire et l'ordre des *Pensées* de Pascal." In *Penser, classer, écrire,* ed. Béatrice Didier and Jacques Neefs. Saint-Denis: Presses de l'Université de Vincennes, 1990.

Neefs, Jacques. "*Lucien Leuwen,* le destinataire des manuscrits." In *Écritures du romantisme I, Stendhal,* ed. Béatrice Didier and Jacques Neefs. Saint-Denis: Presses de l'Université de Vincennes, 1988.

———. "Stendhal, sans fins." *Le Manuscrit inachevé: Écriture, création, communication,* by Louis Hay et al. Paris: CNRS, 1986. 15–44.

Pascal, Blaise. *Discours sur la religion et sur quelques autres sujets.* Ed. Emmanuel Martineau. Paris: Fayard/Armand Colin, 1992.

Périer, Étienne. "Préface." *Pensées de M. Pascal sur la religion et sur quelques autres sujets: L'Edition de Port Royal (1670) et ses compléments (1678–1776).* Ed. Georges Couton and Jean Jehasse. Saint-Étienne: Centre Interuniversitaire d'Éditions et de Rééditions, 1971.

Reid, Martine. *Stendhal en images.* Geneva: Droz, 1991.

Romeyer-Dherbey, Gilbert. "Comment cela s'écrit: Le Livre à venir de Maine de Biran." *Exercices de la patience. Blanchot* 2 (Winter 1981).

Slatin, John. "Reading Hypertext: Order and Coherence in a New Medium." In Delany and Landow, *Hypermedia and Literary Studies,* 153–69.

Snyder, Ilana. *Hypertext: The Electronic Labyrinth.* New York: New York University Press, 1996.

Toulet, Jean. "Livre." *Encyclopaedia Universalis.* Vol. 13. 935.

Yankelovich, Nicole, Norman Meyrowitz, and Andries van Dam. "Reading and Writing the Electronic Book." In Delany and Landow, *Hypermedia and Literary Studies,* 53–79.

Yates, Frances A. *The Art of Memory.* Chicago: University of Chicago Press, 1966.

Further Works by the Author

Cerquiglini, Bernard, and Jean-Louis Lebrave. "*Philectre*: Un Projet de recherche pluridisciplinaire en philologie électronique." *Annali della Scuola Normale Superiore di Pisa: Classe di lettere e filosofia* Ser. 4 Quaderni 5 (1998, Quaderni 1): 233–39.

Grésillon, Almuth, and Jean-Louis Lebrave. "Les Manuscrits comme lieu de conflits discursifs." In *La Genèse du texte: Les Modèles linguistiques,* by Catherine Fuchs et al. Paris: CNRS, 1982. 129–75.

———, ed. *Manuscrits-Écriture, production linguistique.* Special issue of *Langages* 69 (1983).

———. "Manuscrits, linguistique et informatique." In *Avant-texte, texte, après-texte,* ed. Louis Hay and Péter Nagy. Paris: CNRS; Budapest: Akadémiai Kiadó, 1982. 177–89.

Grésillon, Almuth, Jean-Louis Lebrave, and Catherine Viollet. *Proust à la lettre: Les Intermittences de l'écriture.* Tusson: Éditions du Lérot, 1990.

Lebrave, Jean-Louis. "La Critique génétique: Une Discipline nouvelle ou un avatar moderne de la philologie?" *Genesis* 1 (1992): 33–72.

———. "Penser, dicter, écrire: Pour une histoire des pratiques de composition." *Romanic Review* 86 (1995): 437–50.

———. "Rough Drafts: A Challenge to Uniformity in Editing." *Text: Transactions of the Society for Textual Scholarship* 3 (1987): 135–42.

———. "Le Traitement automatique des manuscrits de Heinrich Heine et l'analyse des variantes." *Méthodologie Informatique Philosophie* 1 (June 1985): 77–91.

———. "Vers une édition automatique de manuscrits." In *Die Nachlassedition / La Publication de manuscrits inédits,* ed. Louis Hay and Winfried Woesler. Bern: Peter Lang, 1979. 216–23.

Lebrave, Jean-Louis, and Almuth Grésillon, eds. *Écrire aux XVIIe et XVIIIe siècles: Genèses de textes littéraires et philosophiques.* Paris: CNRS, 2000.

Notes

Chapter 1. Introduction: A Genesis of French Genetic Criticism

1. In a statement that may startle Anglophone readers, Jean Gaudon has said that literary critics "are all, in some measure, disciples of Edgar Allan Poe" (130). Thanks in part to the quality of Baudelaire's translations from the 1850s and 1860s, Poe has enjoyed a higher reputation in France than he has in the English-speaking world. See also Jane Blevins-Le Bigot, "Valéry, Poe and the Question of Genetic Criticism in America" and Daniel Ferrer, "La Critique génétique: 'Philosophy of Composition' ou 'Gold Bug'?"

2. Contemporary genetic critics do not all agree on the question of how much, if at all, the study of manuscripts can improve our understanding of the finished work. Many believe that while manuscripts sometimes point to possibilities that are unperceived or even imperceptible in the final text, they cannot *preclude* any reading. Others maintain, more positivistically, that reading manuscripts can help eliminate erroneous interpretations. For the vast majority of French genetic critics, however, the question of how manuscripts relate to an understanding of the finished work is not the central one.

3. For a balanced assessment of the contributions of those pioneers, see Claudine Gothot-Mersch's lucid article, "Les Études de genèse en France de 1950 à 1960." See also Pierre-Marc de Biasi's essay in this volume and Jean Bellemin-Noël's *Le Texte et l'avant-texte* (1972).

4. Levaillant is a special case. After his 1950s work on the intellectual development of Anatole France, he went on to become an important theoretician and practitioner of genetic criticism in the 1970s and 1980s.

5. Both the collection and the university have since been renamed: The Poetry/Rare Books Collection at the University at Buffalo, State University of New York.

6. Groden, for example, wrote that "Joyce's book was composed in ways so idiosyncratic as to be interesting in themselves" (202) but qualified this claim by adding that "the tasks of interpreting and assessing the complete work necessarily take precedence over any questions about the methods of composition" (200–201).

7. For more on "critica delle varianti," see Maria Teresa Giaveri, "La critique génétique en Italie"; Cesare Segre, "Critique des variantes et critique génétique"; Bernard Cerquiglini, "En écho à Cesare Segre; réflexions d'un cisalpin"; and Paolo Cherchi, "Italian Literature."

8. "Does 'Text' Exist?" appeared in an English translation in *Studies in Bibliography* in 1988, and as a result it is the essay in genetic criticism most familiar to English readers. The French title answers the English version's question: "Le texte n'existe pas."

9. The *nouvelle critique* was a critical movement in France spearheaded by the work of Roland Barthes. It drew upon thematic and formal analysis, psychoanalysis, and social science, and it tended to treat literary texts as systems of codes and messages.

10. It is significant that less than ten years later Louis Aragon bequeathed his manuscripts not to the Bibliothèque Nationale, as Hugo had done in the 1880s to serve as a monument to his genius, but directly to the CNRS, so they could be investigated by geneticists. See Aragon's speech on the occasion of the official ceremony of the gift: "D'un grand art nouveau: La Recherche."

11. Jean Peytard had already argued in 1970 that "one does not correct a text by attending to details or series of details, in the way one removes misprints from the publisher's proofs; rather, it is a global process, a work of deconstruction-construction that results in a different text" (44).

12. To avoid using an awkward and misleading English translation of this term (e.g., "pre-text" or "fore-text") and to retain Jean Bellemin-Noël's useful sense of the avant-texte as the text's Other (164; see p. 32 below), we use "avant-texte" throughout this book.

13. A few years later, in "Reproduire le manuscrit, présenter les brouillons, établir un avant-texte" (1977), Bellemin-Noël made the definition more precise, distinguishing between the manuscript (which can only be reproduced), the draft (which must be deciphered), and the avant-texte (which is the result of a critical construction).

14. Interestingly, Bellemin-Noël, the creator of the concept of the "avant-texte," was also the first to speak of the "unconscious of the text." See the introduction to his essay in this volume.

15. Not surprisingly, since Valéry was an important precursor of genetic criticism, the Valéry team, under the intellectual leadership of Jean Levaillant (see note 4), has contributed abundantly to the theory and practice of the discipline. Since several of its members (Judith Robinson-Valéry, Robert Pickering, Brian Stimpson, Paul Gifford) are Anglophone, part of the team's work is accessible to the English-speaking public.

16. Compagnon also asked a series of questions that bear directly on the substance of genetic criticism: is it really a critical paradigm, a true theory of criticism, or is it just helpful advice? Does it represent a real rupture or breakthrough, and does it involve a new object or methodology? What are the relationships between genetic criticism and critical editing? What can and cannot manuscripts tell us of literary genesis? Finally, what can genetic criticism contribute, if anything, to the present American critical scene? (395–400).

17. Sometime in the late 1980s or early 1990s, Jean Bellemin-Noël abandoned altogether the genetic studies that he had been so instrumental in launching. Several members of the first generation of ITEM are now professionally retired, but most of them are still active in the field. Louis Hay publishes regularly and in 2002 released a book-length collection of his essays, *La Littérature des écrivains: Questions de critique génétique.*

18. For instance, the technicians at ITEM have used laser beams to study writing and radioactive betagraphical sources to study watermarks.

19. See Ginzburg's "Spie: Radici di un paradigma indiziario" (translated into English as "Clues: Roots of an Evidential Paradigm"). See also Daniel Ferrer,

"Le matériel et le virtuel: Du paradigme indiciaire à la logique des mondes possibles."

20. For accounts of these three editing traditions, see G. Thomas Tanselle, "Textual Scholarship"; D. C. Greetham, "Textual Scholarship"; Hans Walter Gabler, George Bornstein, and Gillian Borland Pierce, eds., *Contemporary German Editorial Theory*; Bernard Cerquiglini, *In Praise of the Variant*; and Mary B. Speer, "Old French Literature." Gabler has discussed the lack of contact between Anglo-American and European editing theories and practices in "Unsought Encounters"; see also Geert Lernout's "La Critique textuelle anglo-américaine: une étude de cas."

Also worth mentioning is the Italian tradition of "critica delle varianti," which is less divorced from philology than is French genetic criticism, and the Russian tradition of "textology," which is very rich but almost completely untranslated and little known in the Western world. See note 7 for references to "critica delle varianti," and see also Edward Kasinec and Robert Whittaker, "Russian Literature."

21. It is a significant historical accident that, because the first manuscripts to be studied by a team of genetic critics were Heine's, there were quite a few Germanists among the initial group of French genetic critics.

22. This point is developed further in Daniel Ferrer, "Production, Invention, and Reproduction: Genetic vs. Textual Criticism."

23. See Jacques Derrida, "Psyche: Invention of the Other" 335 and passim.

24. See Michael Groden, "The National Library of Ireland's New Joyce Manuscripts."

25. See Paolo D'Iorio and Daniel Ferrer, eds., *Bibliothèques d'écrivains.*

26. *James Joyce and the Politics of Egoism*, 183, 196. Rabaté has made the case for the "ideal genetic reader" in earlier versions of the chapters of his book: "Back to Beria! Genetic Joyce and Eco's 'Ideal Readers'" and "Pound, Joyce and Eco: Modernism and the 'Ideal Genetic Reader.'"

Chapter 2. Genetic Criticism: Origins and Perspectives

1. Translated from Baudelaire's introductory "Note" to his translation of Poe's "The Philosophy of Composition," which he rendered as "Genèse d'un poème" (*Œuvres complètes* 2: 345). [Trans.]

2. Hay is referring to the works in *Essais de critique génétique* (Paris: Flammarion, 1979). This essay was first published as an afterword to that volume. [Trans.]

3. Translated from Novalis, "Poëticismen," in *Schriften* 2: 537. [Trans.]

4. Goethe's letter to Karl Friedrich Zelter, August 4, 1803. Translated from Goethe, *Sämtliche Werke, Briefe, Tagebücher, und Gespräche*, Sect. 2, vol. 5, 368. [Trans.]

5. The *nouvelle critique* was a critical movement in France spearheaded by the work of Roland Barthes. It drew upon thematic and formal analysis, psychoanalysis, and social science, and it tended to treat literary texts as systems of codes and messages. [Trans.]

6. The phrase "New Criticism" is in English in the original. Like the German movement Werkimmanente Interpretation, Anglo-American New Criticism preferred intrinsic textual analyses to wider social and political critique. [Trans.]

7. See Catherine Fuchs et al., *La Genèse du texte: Les Modèles linguistiques.* [Trans.]

8. Bellemin-Noël's essay appeared in *Essais de critique génétique*, along with the ones by Brun, Debray Genette, and Mitterand mentioned by Hay in the next paragraph. [Trans.]

9. Translated from Novalis, "Freiberger naturwissenschaftliche Studien 1798/99—5: Physicalische Fragmente," in *Schriften* 3: 85. [Trans.]

10. Translated from Friedrich Schlegel, "Lessings Gedanken und Meinungen," (1804) in *Kritische Friedrich-Schlegel-Ausgabe* 3: 60. [Trans.]

11. Duchet published a collection of conference papers, *Sociocritique: Colloque organisé par l'Université de Paris-VIII et New York University*, in 1979. [Trans.]

Chapter 4. Toward a Science of Literature: Manuscript Analysis and the Genesis of the Work

1. Barthes's "Le Texte" appeared in 1973 in "Corpus," the first large section of the *Encyclopedia Universalis* (de Biasi's article is from the 1989 annual *Encyclopedia Universalis* Symposium). An English version of Barthes's article, called "Theory of the Text," appears in *Untying the Text.* [Trans.]

2. The reference is to Bellemin-Noël's seminal essay "Reproduire le manuscrit, présenter les brouillons, établir un avant-texte." See the introduction to Bellemin-Noël's contribution to this volume. [Trans.]

3. "Chain-lines" or "chain-marks" are widely spaced lines made by chain wires in laid paper. When scholars wonder whether specific leaves belong in a manuscript or a printed book, the pattern of chain-lines can help them decide. [Trans.]

4. The example of transcription code that de Biasi discusses is different from the one generally used in this volume. [Trans.]

Chapter 5. Flaubert's "A Simple Heart," or How to Make an Ending: A Study of the Manuscripts

1. It seems to me that the term *excipit* has the merit of naming the inverse of the *incipit* precisely. With a wider point of view in mind, Philippe Hamon speaks of *clausules* in his informative article "Clausules." Time has shown that this term, overly marked by rhetorical tradition, has not taken root. The amiable modesty of the terms *beginning* [*début*] and *ending* [*fin*] inclines me to use them, but they often lead to imprecision. Let us not, at any rate, reopen the old and lengthy quarrel between the generalist and the specialist.

2. This theorem and the following short quotation come from Gérard Genette's "Vraisemblance et motivation" 98 (in English, "Plausibility and Motivation" 184–85). [Trans.]

3. Modern novels seek to escape from every clear form of *excipit.* They often cannot stop themselves, however, from alluding to the models they avoid. Thus the end of Claude Simon's *Géorgiques*—"but once again do you think I have so many years to throw out of the window? . . ." (322) [*et encore une fois croyez-vous que j'aie tant d'années à jeter par les fenêtres?* . . . (477)]—announces the death of the first character (or, better, everyone's end).

4. See "A Simple Heart," *Three Tales*, trans. Robert Baldick, 56. Unless otherwise indicated, this translation will be used. [Trans.]

5. "The example of Flaubert is noticeable for its juxtaposition of the thematics of termination (death of the heroine, 'last breath') with the thematics of opening ('heavens opening,' 'she thought she saw')" (Hamon 517 n. 56).

6. The phrase "good ladies" is from A. J. Kreilsheimer's translation. The rest is Baldick's translation. [Trans.]

7. Translation altered. [Trans.]

8. For the use and justification of this term, I refer to my "Génétique et poétique," especially 23–49, and, of course, to Jean Bellemin-Noël's *Le Texte et l'avant-texte.*

9. My classification had already been completed when it was confirmed by George A. Willenbrink's *The Dossier of Flaubert's "Un Coeur simple"* and by conversations with Giovanni Bonaccorso during a seminar at Messina in March 1982. Bonaccorso has since published (with different transcription marks) a magnificent genetic and documented edition of "A Simple Heart" in his *Corpus Flaubertianum.*

10. On the elements involved in this gestation, see Alison Fairlie's crucial article "La Contradiction créatrice."

11. The trip to Trouville in August 1853 may have been an inspiration in the middle of writing *Madame Bovary.* But why stop writing *Madame Bovary*? In any case, this is one of the possible versions of the "Flemish novel of the young girl who dies old and mystical" (letter to Louis Bouilhet, November 14, 1850), the union of earthly love with nearly unquenchable mystic love. To me it does not seem necessary to link the origin of this outline to any trip to Trouville. The outline does not mention the setting. The love-structure idea is more fundamental and, so to speak, more primitive in Flaubert's thought.

12. Deleted words are crossed-out: ~~deletion~~. Additions are enclosed in pointed brackets: <addition>. [Trans.]

13. Matthew 5: 3, 8. New Revised Standard Version. [Trans.]

14. Here and throughout the author is referring to the sense of hypertextuality developed by Gérard Genette in his 1982 study *Palimpsestes* (translated as *Palimpsests* in 1997): "By hypertextuality I mean any relationship uniting a text B (which I shall call the *hypertext*) to an earlier text A (I shall, of course, call it the *hypotext*) . . . [L]et us posit the notion of a text in the second degree, . . . i.e., a text derived from another preexistent text" (*Palimpsests* 5; Genette's italics). See also Jean-Louis Lebrave's essay in this volume. [Trans.]

15. See *Madame Bovary,* trans. Lowell Bair (New York: Bantam Books, 1989), 184. Unless otherwise indicated, this translation will be used. [Trans.]

16. Very likely the series runs in this order: (1) 2; I to XI; ABCDE; I, II, III. Folio 394 functions as an ending to these last three series; it was used or repeated three times when convenient.

17. These were simple color prints depicting religious, historical, and legendary themes. [Trans.]

18. In an article entitled "Battements d'un simple coeur," Juliette Frølich very rightly and delicately shows that "from that point is presented, at least virtually, the project of thematizing Félicité's last *moments* by evoking the last *movements* of her heart" (31). Yet engaged as Frølich is in her general argument on the stereography and sonorization of the story, she attends only to the manuscript details that support her argument. It seems to me that this *excipit* is built on complex and contradictory networks. At first, Flaubert is not inclined to write a gentle death. The interesting thing might be to show the zig-zags, diverging postulations, and tensions that produce a resolution. One cannot invoke only those moments in the mansucripts "where this material can enrich the argument and give depth to the definitive text" (30 n. 9), for it is there that we perceive that the microstructures of the manuscripts are not those of the final text, although they work to form them. The same goes for the clichés that we will

study. Flaubert is not searching for something that sounds right. What is of more interest is that he inevitably and successively passes through clichés like fixed points and we can perceive the shadow they cast on the final text.

19. See Pierre-Marc de Biasi's study of the stained-glass window as a metasymbolic element.

20. Flaubert used to shout his sentences out loud to judge their sound. He referred to this as "le gueuloir." [Trans.]

21. "Génétique et poétique: Le Cas Flaubert" 40–43.

22. Frølich's commentary on the "gentle" death is particularly pertinent (31). Quite simply, it seems to me that the "images" (comparisons?) and metaphors appear only after considerable organization and outgrowths of different meanings have taken place and that, seen this way, they must be taken as part of a general structuration. Style, in Flaubert, is very much an affair of vision.

23. Flaubert disliked the grandiloquence of these Romantic writers. [Trans.]

24. There is an obvious comparison to be made with Emma's death throes: "and of all the sounds of the earth she heard only the spasmodic lamentations wrung from her poor heart, gentle and indistinct, like the last echoes of a fading symphony" (275) [*et de tous les bruits de la terre Emma n'entendait plus que l'intermittente lamentation de ce pauvre coeur, douce et indistincte, comme le dernier écho d'une symphonie qui s'éloigne* (352)]. The evocation of the beating heart is itself a great and specifically romantic cliché that attracts other clichés. One can accept the echo of a symphony in a lady who plunks a piano and has been to the opera once, but Félicité has never heard a silver string, and there are very few precipices in Normandy. On the other hand, echoes and fountains have been part of our heroine's life.

25. According to Flaubert, "La bêtise c'est de vouloir conclure" [It is foolish to want to conclude]. [Trans.]

Chapter 6. With a Live Hand: Three Versions of Textual Transmission (Chateaubriand, Montaigne, Stendhal)

1. The critical, integral edition includes previously unpublished material: Chateaubriand, *Mémoires d'outre-tombe,* Édition du Centenaire, edited by Maurice Levaillant. See also Levaillant's introduction to the Pléiade edition, 1951. On the history and preservation of the manuscripts, see also Levaillant, *Deux livres des Mémoires d'outre-tombe.* This is a critical edition based on unpublished manuscripts. [Note added by Jacques Neefs for this translation: see also the more recent and accurate edition of *Les Mémoires d'outre-tombe,* edited by Jean-Claude Berchet (Paris: Classiques Garnier, 1989–98).]

2. On this version of "immortality," see Mouchard, "Deux secondes vies."

3. Text of the Combourg archives, published by M. J. Durry, *En Marge des Mémoires d'outre-tombe* 56–57, cited by M. Levaillant, Flammarion edition of the *Mémoires* lxviii.

4. See Blum, "La Peinture du moi et l'écriture inachevée," which describes well the functioning of the aesthetics of addition: "addition is the memory of change." On the chronology of the *Essais* and their postmortem aspirations, see Garavini, "*Les Essais* de 1580, ou 'la mort par publication.'"

5. See Marin, " Le Tombeau de Montaigne."

6. See also Jean-Louis Lebrave's discussion of Stendhal in his essay in this volume. [Trans.]

7. In what follows, I summarize the description that I made of these manuscript-volumes in "Stendhal, sans fins." The manuscripts of *Lucien Leuwen* and *Henry Brulard* are held in the Bibliothèque Municipale in Grenoble.

8. This phrase is in English in the original. [Trans.]

9. The words "For me" and "love" are in English in the original. [Trans.]

10. The words "this novel," "printed," and "fair trial" are in English in the original. [Trans.]

11. "Omar" is Stendhal's anagram for "Roma." He abruptly decided to suppress the projected Rome episode from *Lucien Leuwen*. [Trans.]

12. Pages vii and viii of Stryienski's preface to the 1890 Charpentier edition of *La Vie de Henry Brulard, autobiographie.*

Chapter 7. Genetic Criticism and Cultural History: Zola's *Rougon-Macquart* Dossiers

1. Édition Gallimard, 5: 1669ff. Bibliothèque Nationale, Manuscrits, Nouvelles acquisitions françaises, MS 10345.

2. Mitterand uses the English word "remake" in the original French version of this essay. [Trans.]

Chapter 8. Paragraphs in Expansion (James Joyce)

1. References to *Ulysses* give page numbers (from the 1986 Random House printing) followed by the episode and line number, a system used in both the *Critical and Synoptic Edition* and the 1986 printing. [Trans.]

2. This essay was originally published in *De la lettre au livre: Sémiotique des manuscrits littéraires,* a collection dealing with the semiotic value of all the successive material components of manuscripts. [Trans.]

3. Academic rhetoric willingly prescribes an equivalence between idea and paragraph. But any clever schoolchild quickly notices that one idea per paragraph is both too many and too few: any paragraph built literally upon one single idea would be terribly bare; on the other hand, one real idea per chapter, even per whole work, is more than one ordinarily finds, and in that sense one idea per paragraph would be a wild prodigality.

4. See Faulkner 836–40. This is noted by editors Joseph Blotner and Noel Polk: see "Note on the texts" 1025–26.

5. To such a point that it was neglected by the printer of the original edition, who inserted the title at the beginning of the preceding paragraph.

6. Le Ny 129. See the whole of this article and Henri Mitterand's "Le Paragraphe est-il une unité linguistique" in the same volume. [Trans.]

7. For further readings of the same manuscript, see Ferrer, "The Open Space of the Draft Page: James Joyce and Modern Manuscripts" and "'Practise Preaching': Variantes pragmatiques et prédication suspendue dans un manuscrit des 'Sirènes.'" [Trans.]

8. See Ferrer, "Archéologie du regard dans les avant-textes de Circé." For a discussion of different types of narrative focalization, see Gérard Genette, *Narrative Discourse* 189–94.

9. The list juxtaposes, in the most absurd manner, Hebrew names and names from Central Europe that can be considered Jewish, but also some Irish, Anglo-Saxon, etc., names. . . . As soon as one seems to perceive a logic ("Weiss" leads, in

more ways than one, to "Schwartz"), this logic dissolves immediately and cedes the place to another contradictory logic. What is parodied here, in the mouth of a papal messenger and in the form of a Judeo-Christian genealogy, is no doubt the genealogical delirium of racism that nothing can stop in its infinitely regressive quest.

10. On Joyce's use of sigla in the development of the *Wake* characters, see Roland McHugh, *The Sigla of Finnegans Wake.* On the genetic history of the sigla and their relationship to marginal revision marks, see Finn Fordham, "Sigla in Revision." [Trans.]

11. [A word of warning might be added here after a few years: Joyce's reading of Freud could postdate the writing of this MS page by a few weeks, and the caret could then indeed refer to a missing additional manuscript. However, we still believe in this interpretation's symbolical validity. D. F. and J.-M. R.]

12. Stéphane Mallarmé, "Quant au livre," *Œuvres complètes* 320.

13. See, for example, the typographically beautiful volume of Roland McHugh, *Annotations to "Finnegans Wake".*

Chapter 9. Still *Lost Time*: Already the Text of the *Recherche*

1. I thank Bernard Brun for all his help. He transmitted manuscripts and transcriptions, and he shared information in discussions with me.

2. This type of transcription aims to reproduce the manuscript in its material aspects; it respects the unity of the page, the line, and the placement of substitutions and additions.

3. No doubt this intuition is linked to the fact that even a nonspecialist knows in some confused way about the problem of time in Proust's work. Yet it is not important to locate the origin of this intuition; it is better to scrutinize the implications to which it can lead linguists.

4. My Proustian information comes essentially from three articles: Claudine Quémar ("Autour de trois 'avant-textes'" and "De l'Essai sur Sainte-Beuve") and Bernard Brun ("Le Dormeur éveillé").

5. The work of Bernard de Fallois and Pierre Clarac, editors of a "text" by Proust entitled *Contre Sainte-Beuve*, is thus extremely questionable: Proust left only rough drafts and fragments.

6. I consulted only the manuscripts with a direct relation to my topic. I offer them in chronological order. (The numbering of the Notebooks has nothing to do with chronology.)

7. This morning with Mama will later be transformed in *Le Temps retrouvé* into a morning with the Princesse de Guermantes (see Bernard Brun, "Le Dormeur éveillé").

8. This illness seems entirely erased from the *Recherche.* Although it returns with a vengeance in the drafts for *Le Temps retrouvé*, at this point the text mentions only "the state of illness which would have me confined to a sanatorium."

9. Recall that before the three-part version of the novel in 1913, Proust had planned a novel in two volumes, *Le Temps perdu* and *Le Temps retrouvé.*

10. We know that the first version of the novel was published by Grasset at the author's expense.

11. For this important evidence, I again use a diplomatic transcription. All manuscript changes are in bold. I have added line numbers.

12. After a certain point in the draft process, the respective parts of each series were always linked by the word "yet," a fact that emphasizes that the two processes are semantically contradictory.

13. The order in which I present the occurrences is not that of the genesis in the drafts.

14. Note that this "description" has only the value of a gloss. It refers to an abstract utterer who is not to be confused with the real speaker. The recourse to the verb "to be surprised" can be illustrated effectively by a *well now!* For example: "Well now! it looks as if I'm out of money already [*déjà*] / out of money again [*encore*]."

15. The relation set up in this way between the utterer and the utterance emphasizes the presence of modality as well as aspect (see Fuchs, "De Quelques problèmes" 101).

16. In cases of finished processes + *already*, my analysis differs slightly from Fuchs's, which insists only on the endpoint that is reached. Obviously this implies, a fortiori, that the beginning point has been reached as well. But for the coherence of the descriptions of *already*, I think it useful to insist doubly upon the starting point as well.

17. I am assimilating this occurrence with another, which would follow the same description: *I could still hope* . . .

Chapter 10. Proust's "Confession of a Young Girl": Truth or Fiction?

1. See Lejeune, "Autobiographie et homosexualité en France au XIXe siècle."

2. Two letters explicitly mention the existence of the story, which Proust wished to dedicate to Robert de Montesquiou. There is a letter from Montesquiou to Proust dated 1 October 1894, and a letter from Proust to Montesquiou dated 2 October 1894 (*Correspondance* 1: 339, 341–42).

3. We find the same contrast in the short *tableaux de genre*, of which a few only, such as "Les regrets, rêveries couleur du temps" (*Complete Short Stories* 108–49), discreetly use an "I" as subject.

4. Published in 1893 in *La Revue Blanche*, this story was eliminated by Proust from the 1896 edition of *Les Plaisirs et les jours*. It was printed again in *Textes retrouvés* (ed. Kolb and Price) and in an appendix to the Pléiade edition (167–71).

5. For George Painter, "'La Confession d'une jeune fille' is the only certain case of 'transposition' in Proust's early short stories: it is abundantly clear that the heroine is Proust himself" (176).

6. Notably Fernand Gregh.

7. Proust makes a very brief allusion to this theme, but only in the feminine, in a story that he had also recently published in the *Revue Blanche*, "Mélancolique villégiature de Mme de Breyves," as well as in "Violante ou la mondanité" (*Les Plaisirs et les jours* 67–79, 29–37; "The Melancholy Summer of Madame de Breyves" and "Violante or High Society," *Complete Short Stories* 68–82, 29–38). Proust relies mainly on Janet's studies of psychological automatism and on Binet's studies of fetishism.

8. Nothing suggests, as Painter claims (139), that this friend is also her lover. On the contrary, Leslie takes pains to be unambiguous: "As little as I asked, you have given me that much more and more, in truth, than if sensuality had had some role in our tenderness. . . . I loved you with an affection and sympathetic understanding that was never disrupted by hope of carnal pleasure" (*Les Plaisirs et les jours* 168).

9. Unless otherwise indicated, all italics are Catherine Viollet's. [Trans.]

10. Russian literary influences can be detected in this text: Tolstoy and

especially Dostoyevsky's *Brothers Karamazov.* There is also an adaptation and, in some passages, what seems to be a pastiche of Augustine's *Confessions.*

11. The description of the countryside and the beginning of the dialogue after it (167–68) are strictly identical with the passage that we find, in the form of reported speech, in "La Mort de Baldassare Silvande" (*Les Plaisirs et les jours* 19; "The Death of Baldassare Silvande, Viscount of Sylvania," *Complete Short Stories* 19) except for two words: "the Normandy countryside" is replaced by "the Sylvania countryside," and instead of Françoise, it is the duchess Oliviane. Proust reused this passage a second time in the same text (always in quotation marks) while transposing the verbs into the future tense (23).

12. In a letter that Kolb dates from 25 or 26 September 1894, Proust writes to Suzette Lemaire: "You have been perfectly nice and have done me a world of good. I slept last night and that has not happened in a long time—and whenever I awoke I felt darling little hands, industrious and cool little hands—. . . I was saying before this parenthetical remark that whenever I awoke I felt your dear adroit cool little hands placed on my brow and I assure you that it was not disagreeable. . . . I will return in permitted kisses all the good that they have done me (I have just corrected *permitted,* which was not legible and which seemed to me to be one of the important words in the sentence) . . ." (*Correspondance* 1: 335–37; Proust's italics). Troubling is the similarity of this passage—whose authenticity can hardly be doubted—with, on the one hand, a passage in "Avant la nuit" (published, however, before the letter): "You alone understood how to cool my feverish brow with your maternal and expressive hands" (*Les Plaisirs et les jours* 168), and, on the other hand, a passage strictly identical to the one in the letter in "La Mort de Baldassare Silvande," which Proust was writing at the time of the letter (*Les Plaisirs et les jours* 34; *Complete Short Stories* 19–20). Does this passage not bear witness to the complexity of the relationship between writing and living?

13. As Jeanne Bem emphasizes, one of the effects of meaning that runs through the whole of the *Recherche* is the *negation of difference*—sexual in particular—in such a way that "the gap between the sexes becomes irrelevant, and as a consequence, stops us from separating signs in general into binary paradigms" (109).

14. Painter points out that it was a social mistake to use the full form (Montesquiou Fezensac) of Montesquiou's name (124). [Trans.]

15. This is the first appearance of this name, which probably corresponds to the garden of Auteuil and will be used again in certain fragments of *Jean Santeuil* (on 308, for example) alternating with Et(h)euilles or Etreuilles. "Les Oublis" is a discovery that Proust later abandoned. The term often appears uncapitalized in the manuscript.

16. George Painter wonders whether this story deals with a real life experience, and especially whether this is the event to which the narrator of the *Recherche* alludes when he gives the proprietor of Bloch's brothel Aunt Léonie's sofa "on which I first tasted the pleasures of love with a little girl cousin" (176).

17. This folio is itself an addition.

18. Proust's parents were still alive when he wrote this story.

19. In the following quotations, the French forms of the italicized words imply that the speaker is masculine. [Trans.]

20. Is this a wink from the unconscious? This error is duly rectified in the Pléiade edition (95).

21. By "autobiography" I mean the definition (cited by Lejeune) given by Vapereau in the *Dictionnaire universel des littératures* (1876): "a literary work . . . of which the author had the *open or secret* intention of telling his life, expounding

his thoughts, and painting his feelings" [Viollet's italics]. I also mean the second part of the definition articulated by Lejeune: "What I call autobiography may belong to two different systems: a 'real' referential system (where the autobiographical encounter, even if it passes through books and writing, has the value of an *act*) and a literary system in which writing does not claim transparency but can copy and mobilize perfectly well the beliefs of the first system" ("Le Pacte autobiographique [bis]" 422).

22. I thank N.-C. Mathieu for perspicacious remarks on this passage.

23. Proust attenuated the force of this declaration by crossing out "absolute" in the first copy.

24. The term "dead" appears in the rough draft and was subsequently removed.

25. The smell of lilacs also recalls a passage in Cahier 5 for the *Recherche*, where it is associated with one of the young narrator's experiences of solitary pleasure.

26. The dialogue between the two writers, as it is reported by Gide, has a particular relish to it: Proust "tells me of his conviction that Baudelaire was a uranist: 'The way he [Baudelaire] speaks of Lesbos, and even has the need to do so, is enough to convince me' and when I protest, 'Anyway, if he was a uranist, he almost didn't know it; and you cannot think that he ever practiced it. . . .'—'What now!' He cries out, 'I am convinced of just the opposite; how can you doubt that he practiced it, him, Baudelaire!'" (Gide, *Journal*, May 14 [1921], 1: 691–92).

27. Another hint, paratextual this time, points in the same direction: Proust had decided to dedicate "La Confession" to Robert de Montesquiou, whose acquaintance he had made in the spring of 1893. Ultimately he abstained from doing so.

28. On this point see Antoine Compagnon, "Ce Frémissement d'un coeur à qui on fait mal."

29. As Proust mentions in *Sodome et Gomorrhe*, this is a theme that could have been the subject of an entire chapter. Besides, as Compagnon points out, the themes of inversion and the defamed mother are linked in the first pages of Carnet 1 (1908) ("Notes" 1197).

30. In *Pastiches et Mélanges* [in *Contre Sainte-Beuve*, Pléiade ed., 150–59]. In "Ce Frémissement d'un coeur à qui on fait mal," Compagnon develops at great length the comparison between the dénouement of "La Confession" and of "Sentiments filiaux d'un parricide." It would also be necessary to ask about the role played by the allusions to Michelet's jellyfish in this last text and in "Avant la nuit," especially as the symbol of a painful process of emancipation. "The jellyfish" writes Michelet, "is an emancipated polyp." It is the "first, heart-rending escape of the new soul, still defenseless, beyond the safety of communal life, trying to be itself, to act and suffer on its own behalf . . .—an embryo of liberty" (Michelet, *La Mer*, 162–70).

31. This desire probably explains the absence of "Avant la nuit" from the published *Les Plaisirs et les jours*.

32. *Recherche*, vol. 2, *Sodome et Gomorrhe* 1: 619–20.

Chapter 11. Auto-Genesis: Genetic Studies of Autobiographical Texts

1. Lejeune first presented his work on Anne Frank at a 1990 colloquium on diaries in Nanterre. In 1998 he published a revised version of the essay in *Les Brouillons de soi* (331–65). [Trans.]

2. Ricoeur develops this idea in *Time and Narrative* (3: 244–49). [Trans.]

3. This quotation is from the Neuchâtel manuscript of Rousseau's *Confessions.* It is not normally included in French or English editions of the *Confessions.* [Trans.]

4. In his essay in this volume, "With a Live Hand: Three Versions of Textual Transmission," Jacques Neefs gives a detailed genetic analysis of Chateaubriand and Stendhal. [Trans.]

5. Several of Stendhal's books, including *Le Rouge et le noir* and *La Chartreuse de Parme,* are dedicated in English "to the happy few." [Trans.]

6. Cotteverte has since published this edition as "Le Cahier 1865 de Marie d'Agoult" in *Genesis* 16. [Trans.]

7. I spoke of this recording in "La Voix de son maître: L'entretien radiophonique," 116. See also Paul Léautaud, *Journal littéraire,* entry for September 5, 1950, and my "Un brin de causette: Benda, Léautaud."

8. Wolinski is a cartoonist known only by his surname. [Trans.]

9. See note 1. [Trans.]

Chapter 12. Hypertexts—Memories—Writing

1. For a full history, see Laufer and Scavetta, *Texte, hypertexte, hypermédia* 39–43. [For a history in English, see Snyder, *Hypertext: The Electronic Labyrinth,* Chapter 2. Trans.]

2. For a critical analysis of the literary "canon" and its relation to the fixity of traditional spaces of writing, see Bolter, *Writing Space* 151–53.

3. Nevertheless, footnote references, running headers, legends and figures, indexes, etc. associate the printed text with a group of links.

4. For a discussion, see Bolter, *Writing Space* 153–58 and Slatin, "Reading Hypertext" 159.

5. For Genette, hypertextuality is the relationship between a text B, the hypertext, and an earlier text A, the hypotext, upon which B "is grafted in a manner that is not of commentary" (*Palimpsests* 5). [Trans.]

6. Polemics that are very much alive, as witnessed by the debate over Emmanuel Martineau's edition of Pascal's *Pensées,* called *Discours sur la religion et sur quelques autres sujets.* See Contat, "Pascal: Pensées ou Discours?"

7. I refer here to the whole tradition of "mnemotechnics" and to the arts of memory. See Yates, *The Art of Memory.*

8. "Port-Royal" is the name for a group of seventeenth-century scholars who assembled to live an Augustinian life devoted to the study of theology, logic, and grammar. Pascal, their contemporary, supported them. [Trans.]

9. Romeyer-Dherbey, "Comment cela s'écrit" 184. I thank Gilbert Romeyer-Dherbey for drawing my attention to the writing of Maine de Biran and to the interest that it has for reflections on genesis. [Maine de Biran (1766–1824) was a philosopher and mystic; most of his writings were published after his death. Trans.]

10. See also Jacques Neefs's discussion of Stendhal in his essay in this volume. [Trans.]

11. "Thermidor," was a notation used in the republican calendrical system during postrevolutionary France. [Trans.]

12. Several of Stendhal's books, including *Le Rouge et le noir* and *La Chartreuse de Parme,* are dedicated in English "to the happy few." [Trans.]

13. Incidentally, we possess the genetic documents neither for *Le Rouge et le noir*

nor for *La Chartreuse de Parme.* Jacques Neefs goes so far as to speak of "a pleasure in expunging the abiding, waiting writing from the manuscript (towards the book?)" ("Stendhal, sans fins" 16).

14. These deviations of the printed book would need to be compared with the treatment that Stendhal gives his own "manuscript books." See Jacques Neefs, "Stendhal, sans fins" and "*Lucien Leuwen,* le destinataire des manuscrits." Regarding the *Vie de Henry Brulard,* see Martine Reid, *Stendhal en images.*

Index

À la recherche du temps perdu (Proust) 152–70, 187, 189–90, 246–49
Abbott, Charles D., 4
Agoult, Marie d' (Daniel Stern), 201
Albouy, Pierre, 63
Amiel, Henri-Frédéric, 208
Angremy, Annie, 62
Aquinas, Saint Thomas, 226
Aragon, Louis, 21, 64, 240
Aristotle, 134
Arnheim, Rudolf, 4
Auden, W. H., 4
Augustine, Saint, 172, 176, 190, 226, 248
Autobiography, 9, 11, 13, 171–72, 184, 190, 193–217, 248–50
"Avant la nuit" (Proust), 171, 173–79, 247–49
Avant-texte, defined and described, 8, 29–32, 34, 38, 42–43, 72–73, 240

Bakker, Bard H., 63
Baldick, Robert, 242
Balzac, Honoré de, 48, 62–63, 116, 120–21, 123–24, 126–28
Bardèche, Maurice, 190
Barthes, Roland, 2, 5, 8, 41, 71–72, 209, 240–42
Bashkirtseff, Marie, 207–8
Baudelaire, Charles, 3, 18, 126, 187–88, 239, 241, 249
Becker, Colette 63–64
Beckett, Samuel, 132
Beginnings, 70–72, 152–70. *See also* Endings
Bellemin-Noël, Jean, 7–9, 12, 22, 28–35, 43, 239–40, 242–43
Bem, Jeanne, 248
Benda, Julien, 206–7
Benjamin, Walter, 230
Benn, Gottfried, 19
Benveniste, Émile, 152, 165
Berchet, Jean-Claude, 200, 244
Best-text editing, 10
Biasi, Pierre-Marc de, 12, 36–68, 239, 242, 244
Bibliothèque Historique, Paris, 48
Bibliothèque Nationale, 7, 17, 44–46, 50, 73–74, 119–22, 125, 153–54, 158, 201, 208, 225, 240, 245
Binet, Alfred, 247
Blasquez, Adélaïde, 195
Blevins-Le Bigot, Jane, 239
Blotner, Joseph, 245
Blum, Claude, 244
Boie, Bernhild, 234
Bolter, Jay David, 220, 222–24, 250
Bonaccorso, Giovanni, 61, 78, 92, 243
Bonaparte, Marie, 32
Bonnet, Henry, 62
Borges, Jorge Luis, 224
Bornstein, George, 241
Bossuet, Jacques Benigne, 106
Bourdieu, Pierre, 2
Bradford, Curtis, 4
British Library, 137–38, 148
Brun, Bernard, 23, 62, 242, 246
Bruneau, Jean, 63
Buffalo, University at (SUNY), Poetry/Rare Book Collection, 4, 137, 143, 145, 147, 239
Burke, Kenneth, 4

Bush, Vannevar 219
Butor, Michel, 64

CAM. *See* Centre d'Analyse des Manuscrits
Canetti, Elias, 112
Casanova, Robert, 63
Castex, Pierre-Georges, 62
Cécile (diarist), 210–11
Céline, Louis-Ferdinand, 63
Cellini, Benvenuto, 112
Cento, Alberto, 74
Centre d'Analyse des Manuscrits (CAM), 8, 17, 64
Centre National de la Recherche Scientifique (CNRS), 8–9, 17, 62, 64, 240
Cerquiglini, Bernard, 239, 241
Charmadas, 226
Chateaubriand, François-René, vicomte de, 12, 91, 96–107, 109, 200, 213, 244
Cherchi, Paolo, 239
Citron, Pierre, 63
Clarac, Pierre, 4, 40, 246
Claudel, Paul, 65
CNRS. *See* Centre National de la Recherche Scientifique
"Coeur simple, Un" (Flaubert), 61, 69–95, 242–44
Coleridge, Samuel Taylor, 4, 19
Columbia University conference, 9
Compagnon, Antoine, 9, 175, 186, 240, 249
Comparative manuscriptology, 96
Computerization of manuscript research, 65–66, 233–35
"Confession d'une jeune fille, La" (Proust), 171, 173, 176–90, 247–49
Contat, Michel, 5, 63, 250
Contini, Gianfranco, 5
Contreras, Josée, 209
Copytext editing, 10
Corneille, Pierre, 106, 231
Cotteverte, Sandrine, 201, 250
Cousin, Victor, 225
Coxe, William, 232
Crébillon, Prosper Jolyot de, 231
Critica delle varianti, 5, 241
Critique génétique, 1 and passim
Culioli, Antoine, 165
Cultural genetics, 116

Darwin, Charles, 116, 125
Debray Genette, Raymonde, 8, 12, 23, 69–95, 152, 242–44
Debraye, Henry, 113
Deconstruction, 2
Definitive manuscript, clear copy, fair copy, 39–40, 46, 48, 51–54
Definitive text of a work, 8, 38, 40, 42–43, 46, 49–53, 55, 62, 102, 105, 108
Delany, Paul, 223
del Litto, Victor, 113
Deppman, Jed, 13
Derrida, Jacques, 5, 8, 241
Deschanel, Émile, 123, 129–30
Dessaules, Henriette, 208
Diachronous/synchronous, 5, 41
Diaries, 193–95, 205–13
D'Iorio, Paolo, 241
Diplomatic edition, 61
Dostoyevsky, Fyodor, 176, 248
Drafts (*Yale French Studies*), 5, 96
Duchet, Claude, 8, 24, 76, 242
Duffieux laboratory (Besançon), 65
Dumesnil, René, 54–55
Durry, Marie-Jeanne, 4, 20, 40, 244

Eliot, T. S., 4, 19
Endings 69–95, 152. *See also* Beginnings
Error and variation, 11
Essais (Montaigne), 107–9

Fairlee, Alison, 243
Fallois, Bernard de, 246
Faulkner, William, 138, 245
Favret-Saada, Jeanne, 209
Felman, Shoshana, 77
Ferré, Alain, 4, 40
Ferrer, Daniel, 12, 132–51, 234, 239–41, 245–46
Finnegans Wake (Joyce), 12, 133, 136–39, 141, 147–50
Flaubert, Gustave, 8, 12, 37, 40, 44–61, 63–64, 69–96, 230, 235, 242–44
Fordham, Finn, 246
Foucault, Michel, 176
France, Anatole, 40
Frank, Anne, 194–95, 209, 212, 214, 249
Franklin, Ralph W., 4
Freud, Sigmund, 29, 32, 129, 148–49, 246
Frølich, Juliette, 83, 86, 243–44
Fuchs, Catherine, 165–66, 241, 247

Gabler, Hans Walter, 241
Garavini, Fausta, 244
Gardner, Helen, 4

Gaudon, Jean 63, 239
Gender and sexuality, 2, 12, 171–92
Genesis, biological and textual, 118
Genesis (journal), 193, 237
Genetic editing, 10, 61–64, 233–35
Genette, Gérard, 2, 77, 242–43, 164, 224, 245, 250
Giaveri, Maria Teresa, 239
Gibson, Walker, 4
Gide, André, 187, 208, 249
Gifford, Paul, 240
Ginzburg, Carlo, 9, 240
Giono, Jean, 63
Godard, Henri, 63
Goethe, Johann Wolfgang von, 10, 18, 241
Goethe- und Schiller-Archiv, 7, 20
Goldin, Jeanne, 61
Goncourt, Edmond and Jules de, 40, 116, 126, 124–25, 129
Gothot-Mersch, Claudine, 4, 40, 63, 239
Gracq, Julien, 21
Green, Julien, 21
Greetham, D. C., 241
Greg, W. W., 10
Gregh, Fernand, 247
Grésillon, Almuth, 3, 12, 152–71, 246–47
Grimm, Ariane, 212
Groden, Michael, 4, 141–42, 239, 241
Groethuysen, Bernard, 129
Guyon, Bernard, 4

Hamon, Philippe, 71, 242
Hay, Louis, 1–2, 5, 7–8, 11–12, 17–27, 152, 240–42
Hayman, David, 4
Hegel, Georg Wilhelm Friedrich, 128
Heine, Heinrich, 7, 17, 64–65, 152, 155, 218, 241
Henry, Anne, 175, 182
Herschberg-Pierrot, Anne, 77
Hess, Rémi, 209
Hollier, Denis, 5
Homosexuality 172–92
Hugo, Victor, 7, 40, 63, 96–97, 102, 230, 240
Hypertext, 9, 12–13, 218–37, 250–51

Indexical paradigm, 9
Institut des Textes et Manuscrits Modernes (ITEM), 2, 8–9, 17, 64, 69, 132, 152, 171, 193–94, 201, 218, 240

ITEM. *See* Institut des Textes et Manuscrits Modernes

Jacquelot, Hélène de, 230–32, 234
James Joyce Archive, 137–38, 143, 145, 147–48
Janet, Pierre, 247
Jarry, André 63
Jensen, Wilhelm, 32
Johnson, Samuel, 3
Journet, René 4, 40
Joyce, James, 9, 12, 64, 132–51, 224, 239, 245–46

Kasinec, Edward, 241
Keats, John, 4
Kleist, Heinrich von, 19
Koeppen, Wolfgang, 24
Kolb, Philip, 247–48
Kreilsheimer, A. J., 243
Kristeva, Julia , 129

La Fontaine, Jean de, 232
Labro, Philippe, 211–12
Lacan, Jacques, 8
Lamartine, Alphonse de, 91
Landow, George P., 223–24
Larousse, Pierre, 123
Laufer, Roger, 147, 250
Léautaud, Paul, 206–7, 250
Lebrave, Jean-Louis, 11, 13, 152, 218–37, 243–44, 250–51
"Légende de saint Julien l'Hospitalier, La" (Flaubert), 44–60, 73–74, 77, 89
Leiris, Michel, 194, 198–99, 214
Lejeune, Philippe, 11, 13, 171, 193–217, 247–50
Lejeune, Xavier-Édouard, 195
Leleu, Gabrielle, 4
Le Ny, Jean-François, 245
Léonard, Anne-Marie, 165–66
Lernout, Geert, 241
Letourneau, Charles, 120
Levaillant, Jean, 4, 40, 239–40
Levaillant, Maurice, 98–99, 102–4, 244
Lévy-Bruhl, Lucien, 30
Linguistics, linguistic analysis, 2, 9, 12, 21, 40, 41–42, 152–92
Lis, Jerzy, 208
Little Review, 139
Littré, Émile, 123
Litz, A. Walton, 4

Lubin, Georges, 63
Lucarella, Dario, 219
Lucas, Prosper, 120, 123, 126–28
Lucien Leuwen (Stendhal), 109–13, 251

Maine de Biran, Pierre, 235, 250
Mallarmé, Stéphane, 6, 19, 22, 32, 149, 173, 246
Mallet, Robert, 206
Manuscript analysis, operations involved in, 43–60
Manuscript studies, precedents for genetic criticism, 7, 20, 40
Manuscriptology, 18, 39, 96
Manuscript-volumes, 109–13
Marin, Louis, 226, 244
Marivaux (Pierre Carlet de Chamblain), 70
Martineau, Emmanuel, 250
Martineau, Henri, 113
Marxism, 36, 41
Mathieu, N.-C., 249
Matzneff, Gabriel, 211
Maubon, Catherine, 199
Mauriac, Claude, 212
Mauron, Charles 32
McCarthy, Mary, 197
McHugh, Roland, 246
Mémoires d'outre-tombe (Chateaubriand), 97–107, 200, 213
Memory, 218–19, 223, 225–26, 244
Metrodorus, 226
Michelet, Jules, 63, 123, 249
Milly, Jean, 63
Mitterand, Henri, 8, 12, 23–24, 62, 64, 116–31, 242, 245
Mitty, Jean de, 113
Molière, Jean Baptiste Poquelin, 206, 230
Montaigne, Michel de, 12, 96–97, 107–9, 244
Montesquieu, Charles de Secondat, baron de, 232
Montesquiou, Robert de, 180, 247–49
Moreau de Tours, A., 120, 126, 128
Morgan, Owen, 64
Mouchard, Claude, 244
Musset, Alfred de, 172

Nabokov, Vladimir, 110
Nadal, Octave, 4
Nadeau, Maurice, 205
Narratology, 2, 8, 42, 69–95
National Library of Ireland, 12, 241
Neefs, Jacques, 5, 12, 96–115, 231, 244–45, 250–51
Nelson, Ted, 219, 221, 224
Nerval, Gerard de, 63–65, 173
New Criticism, 20, 241
New Historicism, 2, 5, 36
Nossack, Hans Erich, 24
Nouvelle critique, 7, 20, 24, 240–41
Novalis (Friedrich von Hardenberg), 18, 22, 70, 241–42

Pagès, Alain, 64
Painter, George, 190, 247–48
Paragraphs, 132–51
Pascal, Blaise, 96, 218–19, 222–28, 233–35, 250
Paterson, John, 4
Paulhan, Claire, 208
Pensées (Pascal), 219, 222–28, 233–35, 250
Perec, Georges, 96, 194, 197, 199–200, 202–5, 214, 230
Périer, Étienne, 225–28
Périer, Gilberte, 227
Peytard, Jean, 240
Philology, 2, 118, 228
Pichois, Claude, 63
Pickering, Robert, 240
Pierce, Gillian Borland, 241
Pierrot, Roger, 63
Poe, Edgar Allan, 3–4, 6, 19, 32, 239
Pommier, Jean, 4
Ponge, Francis, 6–7, 21–22, 64, 86
Pope, Alexander, 4
Port-Royal scholars, 227, 250
Poststructuralism, 2, 5
Pound, Ezra, 132
Pozzi, Catherine, 208
Prévost, Jean, 20
Price, Larkin B., 247
Proust, Marcel, 8, 12, 23, 40, 62–64, 76, 152–92, 194, 246–49
Psychoanalysis and psychoanalytic criticism, 2, 12, 28–36, 41–42
Psychobiography, 32
Psychocriticism, 2, 32

Quémar, Claudine, 246

Rabaté, Jean-Michel, 12, 132–51, 241, 245–46
Racine, Jean, 32, 106, 112
Raillard, Georges, 194

Récamier, Madame, 98, 100–101, 104, 106
Régnier, Henri de, 187
Reid, Martine, 251
Ricatte, Robert, 4, 20, 40, 63
Richards, I. A., 4
Ricoeur, Paul, 196, 250
Riffaterre, Michael, 80
Rimbaud, Arthur, 30
Ripoll, Roger, 119–20, 123, 126, 128
Ristat, Jean, 22
Robert, Guy, 4, 20, 40
Robinson-Valéry, Judith, 240
Romains, Jules, 62
Romeyer-Dherbey, Gilbert, 227, 232, 250
Rouen municipal library, 73–74
Rough drafts, 29–30. *See also* Avant-texte
Rougon-Macquart novels (Zola), 116–31
Rousseau, Jean-Jacques, 172, 194, 197–98, 200, 213, 250
Rybalka, Michel, 63

Sagnes, Guy, 63
Sainte-Beuve, Charles Augustin, 32, 157–59, 189, 246
Saint-Simon, Duc de, 231
Salvan, Albert J., 64
Sand, George, 63
Sarraute, Nathalie, 194, 196–98, 201–2, 214
Sartre, Jean-Paul, 9, 63–64, 194, 197–98, 201–2, 214
Saussure, Hermine de, 200
Scavetta, Dominique, 250
Schlegel, Friedrich, 3, 18–19, 23–24, 242
Schmidt, Arno, 150
Seebacher, Jacques, 63
Segre, Cesare, 239
Semiotics, 42, 133–34, 245
Seneca, 226
Serres, Michel, 126
Shakespeare, William, 10, 112
Shapiro, Karl, 4
Simon, Claude, 64, 242
Simonides of Ceos, 226
Simplicius, 226
Sipriot, Pierre, 206
Slatin, John, 221, 250
Snyder, Ilana, 250
Sociocriticism, 2, 8, 24, 42
Speer, Mary B., 241
Spence, Joseph, 2, 4
Spender, Stephen, 4
Staël, Germaine de, 3
Stallworthy, Jon, 4
Stauffer, Donald A., 3–4
Stendhal (Marie Henri Beyle), 12, 70, 96–97, 109–13, 124, 200, 213, 218–19, 229–35, 244–45, 250–51
Stéphanie (diarist), 211–12
Sterne, Laurence, 224
Stimpson, Brian, 240
Structuralism, 2, 5, 7, 41, 224
Stryienski, Casimir, 112–13, 245
Studies in Bibliography, 240
Synchronous/diachronous, 5, 41

Tadié, Jean-Yves, 63
Taine, Hippolyte, 116, 123–24, 126, 129–30
Tanselle, G. Thomas, 241
Teleology, 2, 4, 32, 38, 44, 49–51, 61–62, 234
Text and textuality, 2, 5, 7, 11, 21, 29–32, 37, 41, 220
Textoanalysis, 28
Textology, 241
Textual criticism, distinguished from genetic criticism, 2, 10–11. *See also* Best-text editing; Copytext editing; Genetic editing
Textual genetics, 38–43
Theuriet, André, 208
Thomas à Kempis, 187
Time and temporality, 12, 21, 42, 152–70
Todorov, Tzvetan, 2
Tolstoy, Leo, 176, 247
Toulet, Jean, 231
Tournier, Michel, 64
transition magazine, 138
Transtextuality, 224
Trelat, Ulysses, 120
Triolet, Elsa, 21

Ulysses (Joyce), 12, 133–34, 139–48, 239, 245
Unconscious of the text, 28, 31–32
Urfé, Honoré d', 70

Valéry, Paul, 1, 6, 9, 11, 64, 230, 240
Vallès, Jules, 194
Vapereau, Gustave, 248–49
Variation and error, 11
Verlaine, Paul, 173
Verne, Jules, 204

Vial, André, 4
Vie de Henry Brulard (Stendhal), 109–13, 200, 213, 251
Vigny, Alfred de, 63
Viollet, Catherine, 12, 171–93, 199, 202, 247–49
Visick, Mary, 4
Vivre et l'écrire association, 210–12

Warren, Austin, 2
Wellek, René, 2
Werkimmanente Interpretation, 20, 241
Whittaker, Robert, 241
Willenbrink, George A., 78, 243
Winckelmann, Johann Joachim, 230
Wolf, Christa, 199, 214
Wolinski, 211, 250
Woolf, Virginia, 132, 206

Yankelovich, Nicole, 222
Yates, Frances A., 226

Zola, Émile, 8, 12, 23–24, 63–64, 116–31

Acknowledgments

The editors wish to thank the twelve authors and the original publishers for letting us include translations of these essays in this collection. We appreciate the various kinds of help we received from one of the authors, Almuth Grésillon, in the project's early stages. We are grateful to Olivier Brossard, Chargé du Livre in the Office of French Cultural Services in New York, for a translation grant that helped us complete the book. For help with specific annotations and identifications, we thank Robert Leventhal of the Intelex Corporation, Prof. Hans-Harald Müller of the University of Hamburg, James H. Spohrer, Germanic Collections librarian at the University of California at Berkeley, and Prof. Kathryn Wildgen, University of New Orleans.

We also wish to thank several people at the University of Pennsylvania Press for their support in taking on this complex project and for their help in working with us to prepare the book for publication: Eric Halpern, Director; Alison Anderson, Managing Editor and our project editor; Alison Johnson, copyeditor; George Lang, Production Manager; Debra Liese, Promotions Manager; Chris Jack, Assistant to the Director; and the two anonymous readers of the original manuscript.

We would also like to give individual thanks: Jed Deppman to Hsiu-Chuang Deppman; Daniel Ferrer to Véronique Galimand and Juliette Ferrer; and Michael Groden to Molly Peacock.